BALLISTIC
MISSILE
DEFENSE

ASHTON B. CARTER *and* DAVID N. SCHWARTZ
EDITORS

BALLISTIC MISSILE DEFENSE

*A study jointly sponsored
by the Brookings Institution
and the Massachusetts Institute of Technology*

THE BROOKINGS INSTITUTION
Washington, D.C.

Copyright © 1984 by
THE BROOKINGS INSTITUTION
1775 Massachusetts Avenue, N.W., Washington, D.C. 20036

Library of Congress Cataloging in Publication data:

Main entry under title:
Ballistic missile defense.
    ''A study jointly sponsored by the Brookings Institu-
tion and the Massachusetts Institute of Technology.''
    Includes index.
    1. Ballistic missile defenses—Addresses, essays,
lectures.   2. Ballistic missile defenses—United States
—Addresses, essays, lectures.   3. Ballistic missile
defenses—Soviet Union—Addresses, essays, lectures.
I. Carter, Ashton B.   II. Schwartz, David N., 1956–
III. Brookings Institution.   IV. Massachusetts Institute
of Technology.
UG740.B35   1984   358'.17   83-24064
ISBN 0-8157-1312-6
ISBN 0-8157-1311-8 (pbk.)

2 3 4 5 6 7 8 9

Foreword

THE Anti-Ballistic Missile Treaty of 1972, which severely restricts testing and deployment of ballistic missile defenses by the superpowers, has not foreclosed controversy. Indeed, many of the issues that were contested before ratification of that treaty continue to produce disagreement. Whether defenses against ballistic missiles can be made to work, or whether it is wise even to attempt to build them, are recurring questions as the U.S. defense community seeks options to ensure the survival of land-based missile forces. These questions are now moving to the forefront of national debate on defense policy, particularly since President Ronald Reagan's speech of March 23, 1983, in which he declared comprehensive missile defense an explicit national goal.

This study, jointly sponsored by the Brookings Institution and the Center for International Studies at the Massachusetts Institute of Technology, examines the strategic, technological, and political issues raised by ballistic missile defense. Eight contributors assess developments in their areas of expertise, which include the relationship of missile defense to nuclear strategy, the nature and potential applications of current and future technologies, views on missile defense in the Soviet Union and among the smaller nuclear powers, the meaning of the Anti-Ballistic Missile Treaty for today's technology, and the present role and historical legacy of ballistic missile defense in the context of East-West relations. The volume's editors give a comprehensive introduction to this wide range of subjects and an assessment of future prospects. In the final chapter, nine knowledgeable observers offer their varied personal views on the ballistic missile defense question.

Ashton B. Carter is a research fellow at the Center for International

Studies at MIT. David N. Schwartz was a research associate in the Brookings Foreign Policy Studies program before his appointment as deputy director of the Office of Policy Analysis in the State Department's Bureau of Politico-Military Affairs. The editors thank John Steinbruner, director of Foreign Policy Studies at Brookings, and Jack Ruina and George Rathjens of the Center for International Studies for their advice and guidance. They are also grateful to Nancy Ameen and John Lepingwell for assistance in research, Thomas Somuah for secretarial services, and Jan Liss and Patricia O'Brien for administrative support. Carol Cole Rosen and Venka Macintyre edited the manuscript; Alan G. Hoden and Christine Potts verified its factual content; and Diana Regenthal prepared the index.

Brookings is grateful to the Ford Foundation for financial support for its work in defense studies. The interpretations, conclusions, and recommendations presented here are those of the authors and should not be ascribed to the organizations with which they are affiliated, to the Ford Foundation, or to the trustees, officers, or other staff members of the Brookings Institution.

BRUCE K. MACLAURY
President

December 1983
Washington, D.C.

Contents

Tables

Figures

CHAPTER ONE

Introduction
to the BMD Question

ASHTON B. CARTER

WHY does so natural and seemingly so compelling a goal as national defense against nuclear missile attack provoke controversy? And how does so arcane and technical a subject as ballistic missile defense (BMD)—dealing with radars, interceptor missiles, and the like—become a touchstone for competing strategic, political, and moral ideas about the role of nuclear weapons?

In part the answers to these questions are intrinsic to the subject. Defenses respond to the instinct to work free somehow of the staggering vulnerability to which the societies of both the superpowers, and increasingly even their nuclear forces, are subject. National leaders and military planners would be negligent if they did not consider, and periodically reconsider, defensive measures. At the same time, less-than-perfect defenses can seem fraudulent, a chimerical technical "fix" to the unpleasant reality of the mutual hostage relationship, or at least an invitation to a compensating offensive arms buildup.

Other answers to these questions are circumstantial, having to do with today's situation and with recent history. First, in the present state of technology, intercepting ballistic missiles efficiently remains a challenging engineering task, whereas offensive missiles themselves are abundant and cheap. Experts dispute the promise of future technologies. Thus there is more at stake than deciding whether to "like" BMD or not; it is necessary to decide what is out there to like or dislike. Deciding this technical issue is itself a source of controversy.

Second, the controversy more than a decade ago over deployment of

1

the Sentinel and Safeguard antiballistic missile (ABM, predecessor to today's equivalent acronym BMD) systems occasioned a wide-ranging debate on nuclear policy. When BMD is brought up today, these memories are stimulated and the broad debate rekindled.

Third, the existence of the ABM Treaty reached at the first round of the strategic arms limitation talks (SALT I) in 1972 automatically makes any change in the current state of BMD much more momentous than other nuclear weapons initiatives, such as deploying cruise missiles or choosing an MX basing mode, irrespective of technical or military factors. The action-reaction phenomenon of the superpowers' strategic competition would probably occur in the aftermath of any strategic weapon deployment. But in the case of BMD the treaty adds to the strategic link between the actions on one side and compensating actions on the other a direct and immediate political link. Neither side can pretend that unilateral decisions can be made about BMD deployment; deployment on one side is very likely to result in mutual deployments. In the U.S. domestic arena, the treaty is a symbol of arms control and is therefore a lightning rod for the powerful emotions for and against agreements with the Soviet Union and increased military spending.

BMD is reemerging into prominence after a decade of relative quiescence. It is easy to enumerate the proximate causes for increased awareness of BMD: President Ronald Reagan's celebrated "Star Wars" speech to the nation in March 1983, which made comprehensive missile defense an explicit national goal; claims that new technologies might at last give the defense the upper hand over the offense; attention to defenses against tactical ballistic missiles in Europe, including the U.S. Pershing II and the Soviet SS-20; allegations about Soviet transgressions of the ABM Treaty. But these are mere manifestations, possibly evanescent, of deeper currents sweeping BMD into prominence.

Probably the most fundamental current is the coming of strategic parity between the United States and the USSR, which has had the effect of making U.S. policymakers more attentive to disadvantages and opportunities at the margin of the strategic balance, where even BMD systems with modest technical capabilities are seen by some to make a difference. Another symptom of unease with Soviet interpretations of parity has been the elaboration by some U.S. strategists of more differentiated and detailed views of nuclear war and of the requirements of deterrence, in the so-called warfighting strategies. These strategies identify important roles for less-than-perfect defenses.

A second current bringing BMD to attention has been the long quest for survivable basing modes for the MX intercontinental ballistic missile (ICBM). Defense has always been an alternative or supplement to the many options that have been discussed for basing MX: racetracks, airplane basing, Densepack, and the like. As frustration grew with these basing modes, the defense community began looking longingly at the "forbidden" alternative of BMD. This second current has been building for several years with little public attention. A third current is the widespread disenchantment with traditional arms control, which has prompted questioning of the intellectual and even moral basis of its most conspicuous achievement, the ABM Treaty.

It seems that new controversy and perhaps new BMD deployment proposals could well arise in the next few years, though it is impossible now to predict with confidence which form they might take. While opinion differs over how to greet such proposals, there is a body of basic information on BMD about which there really cannot be informed disagreement. The present book covers this common ground, as well as points of controversy. This introduction tries to encapsulate the areas of broad agreement among experts and the straightforward facts that people coming newly to the subject of BMD need to know first.

This volume aims to provide a comprehensive and unified treatment of the technical, strategic, and political aspects of ballistic missile defense, with an eye to offering the public and policymakers a basis for discussion and analysis. It can serve as a guide or reference to a renewed national discussion of BMD. The book is not intended to promote any particular BMD policy and makes no recommendations.

Since the subject has historically attracted high emotion, this volume strives, to the extent possible, for a more detached and analytical tone. It makes an effort throughout to represent a range of well-informed viewpoints fairly and in their best possible light, but at the same time it does not ignore the task of presenting the interested nonexpert with the information and analyses to make up his or her own mind. An important part of the book is a technical grounding, describing the workings of BMD systems in a way accessible to the nonexpert and assessing in detail what real as opposed to hypothetical BMDs can do. The book also makes an effort to respond to the possibility that the arguments and analyses of the Safeguard debate and SALT I a decade ago might no longer hold in view of subsequent changes in technology or in the strategic context. These arguments should be addressed afresh and either be shown still to hold today or be replaced by new judgments.

Chapter 2, the strategist's perspective, describes how BMD fits into the major contending theories about the proper roles and purposes of strategic nuclear forces. Chapter 3 describes BMD systems and technologies in a way accessible to the reader who is not a scientist or a defense specialist. Chapter 4 continues the technical discussion, presenting analyses of the performance of these systems in various defensive roles and identifying the assumptions and key factors that influence assessments of whether BMD is effective or not. The Soviet BMD program and Soviet attitudes about strategic defenses, always influential factors in U.S. deliberations about BMD, are treated in chapter 5. Chapter 6 describes the provisions of the ABM Treaty reached at SALT I, applying them to important issues of today—the new technologies, the ambiguities and alleged Soviet violations, and the issue of modifying the treaty to relax or stiffen its constraints on BMD activity. The full text of the treaty and accompanying documents is reproduced in the appendix. Chapter 7 discusses the threat that would be posed to the effectiveness of British, French, and Chinese nuclear forces by a Soviet BMD that was expanded beyond the treaty bounds. Chapter 8 explores the international political aspects of BMD, including Soviet and European interpretations of the treaty regime and likely reactions to any U.S. initiatives. After presenting a brief history of BMD, chapter 9 assesses what about BMD has changed since the great ABM debate a decade ago and what remains the same. Chapter 10, a counterpart to this introduction, looks ahead to the future, bringing together the material in the previous chapters in a composite picture of each of the several courses BMD might take in coming years.

The editors are aware of at least one serious omission in this book: an analysis or survey of the domestic political scene, ranging from the views of "elite" or "expert" groups to those of the general public, which is increasingly attentive to nuclear issues. Fortunately, information about this critical aspect of the BMD issue (indeed of the whole nuclear issue) is relatively easy to find in other publications, whereas the technical, strategic, and international political analyses presented here are somewhat less common.

The authors of chapters 2 through 9 were asked to adopt, as far as possible, a relatively neutral perspective, providing information and analysis about their assigned subjects without taking positions on issues that are legitimately matters of judgment. Obviously no one can write an information-laden chapter entirely free of personal views, and the authors of chapters 2 through 9 are no exception. The authors of chapter

11, in contrast, were asked to adopt a different approach, namely, to provide their personal judgments on whatever aspects of the BMD issue they were convinced were most important for the well-informed person to grasp. The earlier chapters provide a factual background to which the authors of chapter 11 have freely referred without having to introduce basic information. In this way the book seeks to expose the reader to the personal attitudes and perspectives of knowledgeable and responsible observers.

All the authors have had some direct experience with the defense, arms control, or intelligence programs of the U.S. government. They probably all take seriously, though not for granted, much of the common wisdom about the contribution of nuclear weapons to national security. In the broader currents of today's questionings about the role of nuclear forces, therefore, this book—being about a rather specialized subject and written by specialists—enters in midstream. Nevertheless the subject of ballistic missile defense, by its nature and by historical circumstance, tends to gather beneath its mantle some of the broadest and deepest questions of the nuclear age.

The newcomer to the issue of ballistic missile defense might be justifiably perplexed by the extent to which commentators seem to be asking or answering two different questions, but rarely at the same time or in the same debate. These questions are: Does BMD work? Is it a good thing? On the one hand, the political, moral, and doctrinal issues are often discussed detached from the technical realities, that is, without answering the first question. There seems little point in discussing the pros and cons of worlds with BMD that we cannot create. Yet a purely technical discussion, especially if it is doubtful about the capabilities of presently achievable defenses, seems to beg the second question. It leaves us wondering what to think *if* more effective technologies emerge. Even technical pessimists cannot dismiss this question as being of purely theoretical interest, since answers to it are essential to shape U.S. research and development (R&D) programs, to measure and interpret Soviet efforts, and to settle whether or why an ABM Treaty, such as the one in force, is good in any fundamental sense.

A second perplexing thing about these two questions is that commentators frequently give the same answer to both. Technological pessimists tend to express doubt about the wisdom of deploying BMD, and advocates of the strategic value of BMD tend to be optimistic about the promise of near-term and future technologies—when pressed. When not pressed, advocates usually prefer to argue the benefits of defense rather than its feasibility, and doubters prefer to find practical flaws rather than problems of principle. Not all commentators fall into these two categories, but many do, suggesting that the two questions are not as independent as they seem. They are in fact linked by the *goal* or *purpose* of the BMD deployment. The proper way to ask the questions is: Will BMD work at achieving a *specified defensive goal?* Is *satisfying that goal* a good thing?

The third question that needs an answer is: What happens next? If a major change in the BMD status quo—initiated by the United States or the USSR—looms in coming years, what directions could it take? What issues should the informed observer be on the lookout for? With a characteristically bold, if unexpected, flourish, President Reagan's Star Wars speech inspired an expectation—actually long in building in expert circles—that something is about to happen, that after a decade of rest the BMD issue is on the move again.

Does BMD Work?

Does BMD work *for a given purpose?* That is the question that should properly be asked. Without a clear statement of the purpose or goal of the defense deployment, it is meaningless to pronounce whether a given BMD system "works" or not. A surprising amount of the disagreement among technical experts derives not from dispute over the detailed performance of the technology, but over the standards against which it is being measured—standards frequently left unstated. Is the defense supposed to protect ICBM silos, other military targets, or cities? Is its purpose to guarantee survival of some specified fraction of the defended targets; to force the attacker to expend many nuclear weapons instead of just one to destroy each target, discouraging attack or making an offensive arms buildup to counter the defense too expensive; merely to sow confusion in the attacker's calculations, eroding confidence in the predictability of the outcome of nuclear strikes; or to provide a truly impenetrable shield over valuable targets?

How well do we know how a BMD would work? At least five factors affect the confidence and assurance with which technical statements can be made about BMD. First, BMD systems are complex and present many technical uncertainties and unknowns. This is particularly true of less-mature technologies, but an important residue of uncertainty would remain about even a fully tested operational system's performance in the unprecedented circumstance of nuclear war.

Second, the defense cannot predict the offense's reactions. Will the offense really deploy decoys or employ subtle tactics to overcome the defense, or will it consider such ploys too risky? With one assumption the system "works," but with the other the system has a fatal Achilles' heel.

Third, the same BMD system will look very different to the defender, aware of all the system's hidden flaws, and to the attacker, prone to give the system the benefit of the doubt when contemplating the prospects for mounting a successful nuclear strike. The offense and defense views of the BMD system's worth could therefore diverge widely.

Fourth, the performance of a BMD is usually described and calculated in analysis as the most likely outcome of a duel between defense and offense. Other outcomes are also possible, though less likely. Thus analysis might predict that the most likely outcome of Soviet attack on the 1000 U.S. Minuteman ICBM silos defended with a hypothetical BMD would be 300 surviving silos, but 50 survivors or 900 survivors might also be possible outcomes. In a nuclear crisis, decisionmakers asking if BMD will work would be just as interested in the range of possibilities as in the most probable outcome, but analysis can rarely provide the relative likelihood of all possibilities (and frequently does not even call attention to them).

Fifth, a BMD system that would perform poorly against a well-organized first strike might do quite well against a poorly coordinated "ragged" retaliation.

The superpowers program their offensive nuclear missiles to attack three categories of targets, and the BMD mission is divided accordingly. These missions differ in how difficult and costly they are to perform and in how controversial they are. ICBM silos, the first target category, would be defended as an alternative to other survivability measures, such as the many basing modes considered over the years for the U.S. MX ICBM. ICBM defense as an abstract BMD goal is relatively uncontroversial: most people agree that vulnerable deterrent forces tend to make both sides more open to the dangerous suggestion that they might be better off striking first rather than second. Defending silos is also the easiest goal technically. Since the defense knows exactly where the offense will aim, several silos can be within reach of a single BMD battery, and survival of only a fraction of the silos is usually considered adequate performance.

Defense of the second target category—other military targets (OMT) and command, control, and communications (C³) targets—is much more controversial than silo defense. Defense of this target set is important in strategies that foresee using nuclear weapons as military tools much like conventional weapons to destroy airfields, bridges, ports, command bunkers, garrison areas, and similar targets. Analysts who recommend these strategies are certainly aware of the profound difference between nuclear and conventional weapons, but they maintain that the threat of punishment through deliberate attack on cities is not an effective deterrent in all foreseeable circumstances: one must be able to use strategic nuclear weapons to stop opposing military forces in their tracks as well as to destroy their society. If the enemy could defend its military forces, deterrence would be weakened in certain circumstances. Others contend that attacking and defending military targets does indeed blur the distinction between nuclear and conventional warfare: BMD of C³/OMT targets contributes to this blurring and should be avoided. Technically, defense of C³/OMT targets is more difficult than silo defense because the targets are spread relatively thinly over wide areas and because a larger fraction of them must survive if the defender's military machine is not, in fact, to be stopped.

Cities—with their people, homes, businesses, and historic areas—are the third target category. One can hardly object in the abstract to defense of human beings, but controversy is intense when it comes to the question of whether less-than-perfect city defenses are worthwhile. Expensive BMDs are clearly a bad investment if the offense can overcome them with inexpensive improvements in attacking forces—a technical question—but argument also centers on the emotional issue of whether even efficient, but imperfect, defenses (if these could be built) would be dangerous, creating false expectations of nuclear safety when their real effect might be to reduce the number of people at risk in a certain scenario from, say, tens of millions to several millions. City defense is technically the hardest BMD mission of all: the offense has the options of concentrating intense attack on a few big cities or attacking where the defense is light or absent; the defense has to protect a large fraction of the targets, unlike with silo defense; and the superpowers value the ultimate threat to one another's existence so highly that they would make a determined effort to overcome any "damage-denying"

BMD by expanding and elaborating their nuclear arsenals. Missile defenses also do nothing directly to thwart the many other means of delivering nuclear weapons to the cities of opposing nations.

The BMD scene today and for the foreseeable future comprises five basic types of technology:

—Traditional BMDs consisting of radars and interceptor missiles.

—So-called simple/novel systems that spread a curtain of projectiles in the path of an attacking warhead during the final few seconds before arrival at the target.

—Dust defense, consisting of nuclear bombs buried near targets that when detonated spew dust and debris up into the paths of attacking warheads.

—Advanced Overlay midcourse intercept systems that use small rocket vehicles with heat-seeking infrared sensors to home in on attacking objects as they fly through space on their intercontinental trajectories.

—Conceptual systems for destroying attacking missiles in their boost phase shortly after launch, sometimes involving lasers or particle beams. These systems can appear singly or in "layered" combinations.

The BMD systems that the United States and USSR know how to build and deploy *today,* and whose performance can be stated with relative assurance, are the traditional, simple/novel, and dust defenses that intercept warheads as they fall toward their targets, carried within conical reentry vehicles (RVs) that protect the nuclear bomb from the stresses of passing through the atmosphere. Any actual proposal in either country to deploy BMD today must necessarily be chosen from this set of systems. Traditional BMDs can force the attacker to expend several—somewhere between two and eight—accurate and reliable RVs, instead of one, to have a good chance of destroying a target. That is, they can force the attacker to "pay" an "attack price" of several RVs for every target. Thus BMD might raise the price to destroy most of the 1000 Minuteman silos to several thousand accurate RVs, from the 2000 required in the undefended case (two-on-one targeting compensates for imperfect accuracy and reliability). The experts disagree within the range of two to eight. Few doubt that a BMD can be made good enough to force the attacker to shoot twice at soft targets; few would claim to extract an attack price of more than eight RVs; and most quibble about the range between three and six. Simple/novel systems can enforce an attack price of two and perhaps three RVs for each target. The technical performance of dust defense is agreed to be very high; its chief liability has to do with the acceptability of planning to detonate nuclear weapons deliberately on U.S. soil.

Views are divided on whether the capabilities of the Overlay and boost-phase systems (perhaps working together or with reentry defenses in a layered architecture) will eventually open up new vistas in attack price or cost effectiveness, or indeed even surpass those of traditional systems. People unfamiliar with complex technical systems sometimes fail to appreciate the difference between a concept and an actual engineering design. For the Overlay and boost-phase systems we have only the former, whereas for the traditional systems we have a twenty-year history of detailed design, development, and testing. Between the Overlay and boost-phase systems there is probably as great a gap in this regard as between traditional systems and the Overlay. Rough concepts gloss over all the difficult design problems and tradeoffs that inevitably limit achievable performance and turn up serious problems; nonetheless, identifying potentially unsolvable problems at this early stage of study does not prove that they will remain insurmountable. Sounder technical assessments can be made of the traditional systems than of the Overlay or boost-phase systems. Naturally, the advantages of the better-understood traditional systems do not seem so dramatic, nor the flaws so clear-cut, as they sometimes seem for the advanced systems. These uncertainties make technical assessment of advanced BMD concepts less a matter of analyzing the capabilities of a well-defined system than of judging the technical risk associated with what is unknown and undefined. This circumstance is very different from the Safeguard debate of over a decade ago, which involved a BMD system that was thoroughly designed and could be subjected to explicit analysis.

Disagreement among experts about the promise of advanced BMDs is by no means confined to technological issues involving the performance of the individual devices that would compose the system—homing vehicles, infrared sensors, lasers, and so forth. Most often the crux of the disagreement is the system as a whole, particularly the question of whether one can fashion from the individual devices a robust, reliable wartime system immune to precursor attack and to offensive penetration tactics—even if all the technological elements work perfectly. Supposing, for instance, that directed-energy weapons can generate lethal intensities and be pointed accurately at targets, can they be based in such a way that they are not themselves vulnerable to precursor attack? Since the 1960s, no one has doubted that traditional radar-and-interceptor systems can intercept RVs successfully; the issue has always been the efficiency and resiliency of the total defensive system. Guessing the chances of a technological breakthrough is thus not as important as seeing how such technologies could fit into a sensible architecture. (In this connection, it might be borne in mind that dramatic new offensive capabilities are possible as well and might even use the same technologies as new defenses.)

Another source of disagreement among experts is their assumption regarding the vigor and confidence with which the offense would employ elaborate and tailored countermeasures to sidestep the defense. Does an elaborate countermeasure theoretically fatal to the defense constitute an Achilles' heel making investment in the system foolish, even though the system performs very well against all other threats? For instance, would the Soviet Union really base its nuclear attack strategy on massive use of decoy RVs to fool a U.S. Overlay?

However inconclusively they can be analyzed, the prospects for the technical future of BMD must necessarily divide into two broad possibilities. Either there will be dramatic new capabilities—virtually impenetrable defenses or very inexpensive defenses—which will open the door to entirely new strategic issues; or there will be significant but less-than-perfect capabilities, which will leave unsettled the issue of whether useful but relatively modest missions—defense of silos or C³/OMT targets—can be found for them. In particular, a conscious decision needs to be made whether the missions that modest BMDs can perform, and the strategic doctrines that attach meaning to these missions, are worth support. If these missions or doctrines are judged to have little importance, the future of BMD will turn entirely on whether dramatic new defensive capabilities come along. But if these other missions are persuasive in gaining support, technical advances might not be as crucial to a decision to deploy BMD as costs, arms control implications, political side effects, and the like.

Two broad conclusions relevant to the question, Does BMD work? appear to enjoy the support of most knowledgeable observers. The first conclusion is that the prospect that BMD will thwart the mutual hostage relationship—if this is taken literally to mean the ability of each superpower to do socially mortal damage to the other with nuclear weapons—is so remote as to be of no practical interest. First, mortal damage in nuclear terms means detonation in selected areas of tens or hundreds of nuclear weapons—between a few tenths of a percent and a few percent of the current Soviet or U.S. ICBM arsenal. There is no extrapolation from present BMD capabilities and costs that could enforce near-perfect, high-confidence protection against a determined opponent willing to expend comparable or even greater ingenuity and money to maintain some penetration. Second, one can reasonably assume that the "assured destruction" mission is the last one that either superpower would be willing to surrender to a defense on the other side. ICBM basing modes might be allowed to frustrate counterforce targeting when the "exchange ratio" between attacking RVs and ICBMs being attacked becomes unfavorable; preferential defenses might prevent confident targeting of other military targets if the offense decides that this mission is no longer worth the cost of penetrating the defense; but neither side would give up the elemental capability of assured destruction without a determined struggle. Third, it is not clear that political leaders could be persuaded that a technical system they understood only superficially was actually an impenetrable shield, behind which they could risk war with impunity. Last, ballistic missile defense by itself will obviously not prevent delivery of nuclear weapons to the homelands by other means. For these reasons mutual assured destruction, seen as a condition of technological life rather than a chosen doctrine, seems unavoidable. Other missions, for less-than-perfect defenses, are technically achievable and might be very useful. And missile-delivered nuclear weapons might indeed be rendered "impotent and obsolete," to use President Reagan's phrase in his speech of March 1983 in the following sense: defenses might someday be possible for which each missile warhead added by the offense could be offset by defensive improvements of comparable or lesser cost. This would make marginal increases in missile forces unattractive to the offense, and ballistic missiles would be "obsolete" as the cheap, effective delivery systems they are today.

A second broad technical conclusion is that no militarily meaningful BMD can be deployed without termination, abrogation, or substantial revision of the ABM Treaty. The drafters of the treaty, whatever their strategic wisdom, did their drafting job well if this was their purpose. Only one exception to this observation has ever been broached: a defense of the Densepack basing mode for the MX missile was studied, which held out the prospect of enhancing Densepack's effectiveness with a defensive arsenal of 100 traditional interceptors—the number permitted by the treaty. This prospect, far from a certainty in the first place, was abandoned when Densepack itself was abandoned. One important corollary of this second conclusion is that a plain-English reading of the treaty, including its vague clause dealing with "new physical principles," does *not* support an interpretation permitting deployment of directed-energy BMDs or any other advanced BMDs. The treaty is comprehensive and restrictive, prohibiting all but token deployments of traditional systems. Another corollary is that the system presently deployed around Moscow, and undergoing substantial and costly improvements, is not a serious strategic barrier to any U.S. targeting goal, even in a retaliatory second strike. More worrisome than the system itself are its implications for Soviet attitudes and plans regarding BMD.

Is BMD a Good Thing?

Good *in what role?* Just as one cannot say BMD works without specifying the mission, so one cannot pronounce it good—ethically, militarily, politically—without specifying the purpose of the deployment in question. Silo defense is usually seen as a stabilizing mission for BMD, since it tends to remove the incentive for the offense to limit damage by destroying the other side's ICBMs preemptively. Defense of C^3/OMT targets is more controversial, since its value is tied to warfighting roles and strategies for nuclear weapons. Assessment of whether deploying a BMD is a good or bad thing to do might also depend on an estimate of the odds for success: objections to population defenses usually have less to do with the mission itself than with the wisdom of trying if the prospects for success are poor.

In assessing the wisdom of BMD deployments, the action-reaction dynamics of offense and defense are particularly important. In the case of offensive weapons systems, which engage relatively inert and un-changing sets of targets, it is easier to ignore the link between deploy-ments on one side and the reactions of the other side. In the case of defense, one cannot even begin to analyze technically the military worth and cost of a deployment without thinking through the reactions of the offense: will they deploy penetration aids, for example, or will they increase the size of their offensive arsenal to keep pace with the defense? Since any BMD deployment would take nearly a decade to complete, its capability must be measured against the *future* and *potential* offensive arsenal. One reason for the controversial nature of strategic defensive proposals, including civil defense and air defense in addition to BMD, is their potential to stimulate the competition in strategic arms. Besides this intrinsic relation between offense and defense, the very existence of the ABM Treaty makes a strong political link between BMD actions on one side and reactions on the other side. If there were no ABM Treaty, it would be possible to think of the Soviet Union, for example, deploying a BMD and the United States deciding not to do so. This is approximately the case with air defenses today. But it is hard to imagine that Soviet withdrawal from the treaty regime would not create strong pressures for BMD deployment in the United States, even if the purely military rationale for doing so was not compelling.

It is therefore important not to fall into the trap of calculating what the immediate benefits to U.S. national security would be if the United States today deployed a BMD to engage the present Soviet arsenal targeted in the present way. Nor is it legitimate to add up the military advantages of a U.S. BMD without assessing the impact of a Soviet deployment on our targeting plans. The relevant assessment for those weighing BMD deployment options in the United States is whether a net, long-term benefit to the United States is likely or not. For instance, is it worth using BMD to defend the MX and Minuteman ICBMs from Soviet attack if the surviving missiles thereby assured cannot threaten Soviet targets because those targets are defended by a Soviet BMD? If a net, long-term benefit is demonstrable, is it large enough to be worth the cost of the defensive deployment—probably well over $10 billion— or would other improvements in strategic or general-purpose forces, not to mention nonmilitary expenditures, offer better return on investment? Last, in looking at the long-term effects, it is impossible to ignore the unpredictable consequences of adding to the strategic calculus a new and complicated component. The capabilities of BMD systems are not easily encapsulated in simple statements or counting rules. Can the nontechnical communities involved in national security planning— national leaders, diplomats, legislators, strategists, and the public— accommodate the new feature in the strategic landscape in the straight-forward way foreseen by its technical purveyors? Or will BMD just add further confusion and disarray to nuclear planning rather than having any well-defined or rational long-term effect?

Very little can be discerned about Soviet BMD activities or predilec-tions that offers a clear guide to U.S. policy for the future. If serious doubts exist in the Soviet leadership about the wisdom of maintaining the ABM Treaty, they are not visible from the West. Two things about Soviet BMD do seem clear, however, and seem to represent a consensus of knowledgeable observers. The first is that the Soviet military, in its activities and planning, takes the whole area of strategic defense—BMD, air defense, civil defense, and even countersilo targeting—as a natural and integrated complement of its overall strategic posture. The views of the Soviet political leadership could well differ from the military view. The strategic communities in the United States, both military and civilian, have tended in contrast to place much less emphasis on strategic defenses and to make a clear separation between offense and defense. Second, the Soviet BMD research and development activities that are observed seem geared toward, or at least are more appropriate to, defense of command and control and other military targets than toward defense of ICBMs or defense of the general population. The U.S. BMD program has tended in the last decade to direct its energies almost exclusively toward ICBM defense. Any change in the current state of BMD that would permit deployments on both sides would have to face immediately these asymmetries in goals and predilections between the two superpowers. These asymmetries are also frequently adduced as reasons to reorient or reemphasize BMD efforts in the United States.

The value one attaches to achievable—and therefore modest—BMDs depends on one's views about the proper role of nuclear weapons, that is, on one's favored strategic doctrine. Chapter 2 identifies four main currents in strategic doctrine:

1. Minimum deterrence doctrines hold that deterring nuclear strike on the United States, and possibly on close allies, through a general or unspecified threat of retaliation should be the only purpose of strategic nuclear forces. Minimum deterrence is sometimes confused with "mutual assured destruction," which in common usage refers to the *circumstance* of the mutual hostage relationship between the superpowers and not to a *preferred* strategic doctrine.

2. Warfighting doctrines are varied, but they share a rather detailed view of deterrence and of nuclear war itself. Nuclear weapons are to be used for a variety of purposes, including deterring certain kinds of conventional conflict. Warfighting doctrines are also concerned with the course of a nuclear war, on the presumption that war is possible and must be fought purposefully and also that giving the other side evidence of such detailed plans is the best deterrent.

3. Countervailing strategy lies somewhere in between minimum deterrence and warfighting. It accepts the value of some warfighting capability, but primarily or solely as a deterrent.

4. Defense emphasis foresees a time when strategic defenses might

have the upper hand over offenses, meaning that, unlike the situation today, targets could not be confidently threatened simply by buying offensive weapons and lobbing them into the other country. This circumstance, should it ever arise from technological change, might usher in its own family of doctrines. At the moment these doctrines are not very well defined, but they are under active study and elaboration by strategists interested in BMD.

The differences among these doctrines reveal the main tensions in strategic doctrine and indeed in popular thinking about the proper purpose of nuclear weapons. Opinion is divided along the following lines:

—a belief in the theoretical benefits of a more detailed and differentiated strategic posture and planning beyond minimum deterrence *versus* fear that these theories and plans spur on the arms race and make nuclear war more "thinkable" and therefore more likely;

—a continuing frustration over the moral and political strictures of the mutual hostage relationship *versus* a sense of futility in seeming to deny an ineluctable technological fact;

—a concern about the political dynamics of the Soviet Union *versus* a concern about the dynamic of the arms competition;

—a desire to defend only the homeland with nuclear weapons *versus* a desire to extend nuclear protection to allies; and

—a willingness to rely on nuclear weapons *versus* a preference for relying on conventional forces for military security.

All of these tensions are present in discussions of whether BMD is a good thing. In particular, warfighting, since it entertains such a detailed view of nuclear war, can find numerous useful roles for defenses of even modest technological performance. Though adherents of minimum deterrence might agree that BMD would be technically successful in these roles, they would disagree that such missions are necessary or even desirable. The relevance of defense emphasis, whatever this phrase turns out to mean, depends on the fruition of yet-unrealized technology.

In assessing the value of BMD, the symbolic value of the ABM Treaty is such as to make it a major factor irrespective of "objective" technical, military, or strategic factors. However much one would like to view an arms control treaty as something that can be changed or jettisoned the moment it no longer serves one's view of national security—and presumably virtually everyone would subscribe to this view in the abstract— the ABM Treaty has taken on a life of its own. It stands for commitment to arms control and for commitment to some form of superpower understanding (for many, détente is the appropriate word) in the United States, in the USSR, and in Europe. It is impossible, as a practical matter, to separate the treaty's intellectual underpinnings—military, strategic, moral—from its symbolic meaning for the process of arms control. To opponents of traditional arms control, this process itself is seen as the worst pitfall, far worse than the terms of the treaties themselves, since these opponents feel the process works against the Western democracies in the long run. For supporters of arms control, on the other hand, the same is probably true: the commitment to control of nuclear weapons implied in the process of negotiation is more important than the concrete "stabilizing" measures that end up in the treaties. Through the treaty the BMD issue gets swept up in the entire issue of strategic arms control and is supported or denigrated accordingly.

Though it is possible to imagine a businesslike agreement between the United States and the USSR to modify the ABM Treaty to mutual satisfaction, far more likely is an abrasive process leading to abandonment of the treaty, its replacement with a virtual dead letter, or a substantial worsening of East-West relations. Raising the subject on either side would naturally call into question the proposer's commitment to the course of arms control since the signing of the treaty. It is also by no means clear that the two sides' desires in amending the ABM Treaty would be similar in magnitude or in kind. Finally, the likely negative reaction of America's European allies would create a separate political issue, accompanied by the usual Soviet temptations to exacerbate frictions within the alliance.

The reaction of the European allies—almost surely negative—to any U.S. proposal to change the BMD status quo would derive from their concerns over its implications both for East-West relations and arms control, and, in the case of Britain and France, over the ability of their own strategic nuclear missiles to penetrate the Soviet BMD that would be almost certain to follow a U.S. deployment. This latter concern need not necessarily be justified, if the Soviet deployment were aimed at defense of military targets rather than cities or if it were prone to selective saturation. In these cases the rather modest but growing arsenals of Britain, France, and also China could probably continue to achieve their deterrent purpose of threatening large-scale damage to Moscow and other major Soviet cities.

What Happens Next?

Probably nothing. As much as editors of books like to predict the increasing relevance of their subject, in the case of BMD it seems quite likely that the current situation—essentially no BMD deployments on either side, and treaty regime intact—will persist for several years to come. The report of the President's Commission on Strategic Forces led by General Brent Scowcroft devoted but a few paragraphs to BMD, and these none too enthusiastic. Among the authors of chapter 11 of this volume are several who are profoundly disturbed with the state of U.S. strategic forces, the course of U.S. and Soviet BMD research and development, and the wisdom of traditional arms control, but only one author (who does not necessarily even share these concerns) recommends an actual deployment, and that is a treaty-constrained simple/novel defense of Minuteman ICBMs. It is true that important elements of the present administration are favorably inclined toward BMD and have long been so. But they are also politically pragmatic. They are surely aware that there is scarcely a broadly based movement in favor of BMD; on the contrary, opposition to a deployment proposal would be swift and strong. On the Soviet side, there is a continued high level of R&D activity and new deployments around Moscow, but no sign that the political leadership has ideas comparable to those President Reagan expressed in his March 1983 speech.

Still, it is unquestionable that the subject of BMD, something of a pariah for the past decade, is undergoing a renaissance of interest. The most obvious signs are those that capture the news headlines, but there are deeper and longer-lasting currents of interest as well. Besides the president's speech, the most apparent signs of interest involve claims about new technologies—rapid and compact data processors, sophisticated infrared sensors, and especially directed-energy devices (particularly those employing explosive power sources)—that offer the promise of enhanced effectiveness. Other factors bringing BMD to attention at this moment are the revelation of work by both the United States and the USSR on antitactical ballistic missile (ATBM) systems in the European theater and the continued improvements in Soviet surface-to-air missile (SAM) air defense systems, raising questions about the technical and legal distinctions between BMDs, ATBMs, and SAMs. Last, recent alleged transgressions of the treaty's bounds by the Soviets raise a broader question of the extent to which the language of the treaty continues to speak clearly to the technical and strategic situation.

Behind these epiphenomena, one can detect some more fundamental factors that guarantee that the subject of BMD will continue to arise in years to come. The first among these is the vulnerability of ICBMs. The Scowcroft Commission put to rest temporarily the anguished quest for survivable basing modes for the MX missiles, defense among them, but the issue of survivability is fundamental and, if not solved for MX, will arise again with the single-warhead "Midgetman" ICBM recommended for development by the commission. In fact, ICBM vulnerability is part of a broader pattern of "offense dominance," where it is theoretically possible to mount attacks against all manner of strategic targets—most notably command, control, communications, and intelligence (C^3I) targets in addition to ICBM silos—with virtually no way for many of these crucial targets to escape destruction. Many see the increasing capability for "surgical" (at least in intention) or "decapitating" attacks as a dangerous trend in the strategic arena.

A second factor likely to persist is the general anxiety about the U.S. strategic posture, which appeared at the close of the 1970s and which was reflected strongly in the 1980 election. The anxiety focuses on the concern that the Soviet Union interprets "parity" as license for politically unacceptable behavior or, worse, as a way-station en route to "superiority." It is commonplace to hear that the current situation is "rough equivalence" *but* that "all the trends are unfavorable." Concern over the strategic balance leads to niggling over numbers, as at SALT and the strategic arms reduction talks (START), and to attention to relatively small details of the strategic calculus. Accompanying this detailed view of the balance, as mentioned previously, is a rather detailed view of nuclear war itself, expressed in various elaborations of strategic doctrine. Associated with these doctrines are phrases such as "countervailing strategy," "warfighting," "limited war," "protracted war," and "strategy beyond mutual assured destruction [meaning beyond minimum deterrence]." These ideas reflect an effort to strengthen deterrence (and frequently to enjoy political benefits in peacetime) through a more vivid military planning for nuclear war. These detailed views both of the balance and of nuclear war create numerous opportunities for BMDs of all sorts and for missions—defense of silos and C^3/OMT targets—that do not require unimaginably advanced technologies. And the perception of an adverse trend in the balance prompts a search for something to redress it. With MX, Trident, B-1, cruise missiles, and improved air defense under way, BMD is virtually the only strategic activity that is not already being pursued.

A third underlying factor tending to prompt discussion of BMD is the uncertainty about the future of traditional arms control. To those thinking that the detriments to national security of the SALT/START process had begun to outweigh its benefits, the ABM Treaty is a natural target. The treaty is the most important standing monument to traditional arms control, and its demise would signal the collapse of the entire SALT regime. Meanwhile, START promises substantial reductions in strategic offensive forces which, if they were actually to come about, could not help but make the job of BMD easier and thus any deployment more plausible technically. Nonetheless, despite a possible connection between START reductions and strategically effective BMD deployments, it is difficult to see the amicable atmosphere of dramatic and successful arms control as the stage for the dismemberment of the ABM Treaty.

A final factor calling attention to BMD today, and also likely to persist in the future, is the apparently steady and purposeful course of Soviet BMD research and development (and new deployments around Moscow), together with the emphasis on strategic defenses in Soviet military doctrine and the continued activity in civil defense and air defense. Besides raising questions about Soviet commitment to the ABM Treaty regime, this Soviet activity has several concrete consequences. It is generally accepted that if either side abrogated the treaty today, the Soviets would be the first in the field with a working BMD deployment. This prompts the question of whether the U.S. research and development programs on BMD (especially system development) and penetration aids have preserved an adequate hedge against "breakout" from the treaty. The United States has long retained the capability to resume atmospheric nuclear testing promptly as a hedge against breakout from the Limited Test Ban Treaty of 1963. Preservation of a strong hedge is usually thought to strengthen the treaty by removing any incentives for one side to steal a march on the other. In addition, Soviet activities at the margin of the treaty's provisions (it is unlikely that there have been outright violations) call to mind issues regarding the technical health and clarity of the treaty. Do its provisions, drafted more than a decade ago, still account satisfactorily for new technologies, deployment of large Soviet radars, SAM systems, and ATBM systems?

Arrayed against the factors tending to make BMD a persistent future issue are several factors that militate against dramatic change, at least against change initiated by the United States. The first is the substantial growth in offensive forces on both sides in the decade since the signing of the treaty, with more to come. Though important technological advances in BMD have taken place since then, it is not obvious that the balance between offensive and defensive capabilities and costs is much more favorable to defense now than it was a decade ago. One of the original arguments for the ABM Treaty was that neither side had a militarily compelling deployment option at hand. The same might be true today.

A second factor is the notable lack of enthusiasm for new BMD initiatives among the great majority of the strategic community. The report of the Scowcroft Commission is an example. Though far from a scientific sampling, it suggests that the group devoted to BMD—as opposed to a sizable uncommitted but largely uninterested group, and a smaller group unalterably opposed—is no larger than it was several years ago, but simply more influential.

Public attitudes toward BMD are harder to fathom. An interesting research effort—unfortunately not represented in this book—would examine likely public reactions to a BMD deployment proposal. The initial reaction would undoubtedly be, "What's BMD?" It is likely, however, that a more informed and reflective second opinion would be negative for at least three reasons. First, the missions most plausible for near-term BMD—defense of ICBMs and C^3/OMT targets—are not widely understood or appreciated outside the "expert" communities. Second, disposing of the ABM Treaty would create a vision of the wholesale abandonment of arms control, a vision that could not be dispelled with any amount of patient explanation of the deployment's supposed beneficial effects. Third, the antinuclear movements in the United States and Europe, growing in power and sophistication and by now fully competent to understand all the arguments, would provide an organized opposition.

Leaving aside the likelihood of the various possibilities, what *could* happen next? There are at least six distinct future courses, all of which are elaborated in chapter 10:

—*Status quo:* No U.S. or Soviet BMD deployments; no major change in the ABM Treaty regime.

—*MX defense:* The United States initiates discussions with the Soviet Union to permit defenses of Minuteman and MX ICBMs, while maintaining restrictions on other types of BMD.

—*Major U.S. initiative:* The United States puts an effective end to the

ABM Treaty, accompanied by the maximum BMD effort that can be justified by strategic utility, cost, and technical feasibility.

—*Soviet initiative:* The Soviet Union initiates talks to amend the ABM Treaty to permit its own defense against France, Britain, or China, defense of its ICBM silos, or a nationwide warfighting defense of other military targets.

—*Soviet breakout:* The Soviet Union abruptly terminates the ABM Treaty and begins deploying the systems it has in development today.

—*New arms control arrangements:* Reductions in offensive deployments, as in START, result in new assessments of BMD capabilities. Or restrictions on BMD are extended to other strategic defenses. Or restrictions are negotiated on qualitative changes in offensive forces (such as testing of penetration aids) to permit unopposed silo defenses.

It is not hard to predict the general arguments that would fuel the public and congressional debates if serious deployment proposals were broached by the United States in the future, though it is a bit harder to predict which would end up playing the crucial role. Moreover, it could well be that strategically peripheral concerns, such as the environmental impact of the deployment or the location of any nuclear-armed interceptors, could be just as important as the issues that enflame specialists.

Leaving aside questions of technical feasibility and specific issues related to the details of the deployments, the following arguments would probably be made by proponents of BMD:

—Strengthening deterrence through defensive deployments responds to a natural urge for self-preservation and is morally preferable to continued offensive deployments.

—U.S. BMD is required to forestall or respond to imminent Soviet efforts, since the Soviet Union is well known to place emphasis on strategic defenses.

—Refusal to consider changes in the ABM Treaty illustrates the "religion of arms control" that supports even restrictions harmful to U.S. security.

—ICBM vulnerability requires BMD.

—Warfighting requires BMD.

The arguments against BMD would include the following:

—BMD makes war more likely because it promotes a false sense of nuclear safety and implies that the route to true security is through technical gadgetry, whereas the only true route is political.

—BMD makes war more likely because defenses intrinsically benefit the first-striker (whose BMD need only face a ragged retaliation) rather than a second-striker.

—BMD deployments encourage compensating offensive arms deployments, fueling the arms race.

—No detailed military/strategic argument should be allowed to prevail over the basic good sense of preserving whatever limits, such as the ABM Treaty, exist to restrain the arms competition.

Any serious intensification of public debate and discussion of the future of BMD, and most certainly the reaction to any concrete proposal by the United States, could well be acrimonious. It would likely be in important respects a replay of the Safeguard debate of a decade ago, featuring many of the same issues and undoubtedly many of the same actors. In fact, it could well be that the tendency of both sides to hark back to the past would obscure the most important topic, which is, What, if anything, is *new* since 1972?

CHAPTER TWO

The Strategist's Perspective

LEON SLOSS

VIEWS about the efficacy of ballistic missile defense vary widely; there are a number of reasons for these differing views. Among the most important are differences over strategy—what the objectives of our defense posture should be and how we should go about achieving these objectives. To understand why some defense experts advocate different approaches to ballistic missile defense and some oppose it altogether, it is necessary to understand the place of BMD in different strategic concepts. Frequently these views of strategy are unstated. The pros and cons of missile defense often appear as technical arguments, but behind these arguments usually lies a set of assumptions about the roles of national defense, military power, and nuclear weapons in our society.

In this chapter BMD is examined in a broad "strategic" framework, and some of these generally implicit assumptions are made more explicit. In the course of this examination, major strategic issues and problems of BMD are outlined and discussed.

Defining Strategy

What is strategy about? What is a "strategic" perspective? Broadly speaking, *strategy* refers to the art of formulating *objectives* and relating these objectives to *means* or resources. A strategic perspective of BMD will indicate how BMD might contribute to the broad objectives of U.S. security policy; how defensive and offensive systems relate and interact in meeting those objectives, and how various defensive measures relate to each other.

Strategy is developed at several levels. National strategy relates

24

overall national objectives and means. For example, at this level strategy would deal with the relative priority of national security and other national objectives, such as improving education or providing social welfare, economic growth, and full employment. It would also deal with combining the various means of promoting national security including, for example, defense, diplomacy, trade, aid, and arms control.

Defense strategy reconciles defense objectives and commitments with available and projected defense resources. At this level, strategy begins with a definition of national objectives and an assessment of the role of military power in meeting those objectives. It also involves priorities and tradeoffs. For example, how much of our total defense effort should be devoted to the defense of the continental United States, to the defense of Europe, Asia, or sea lanes? In addition, defense strategy is concerned with striking a balance between various military instruments: nuclear and nonnuclear forces; strategic and nonstrategic forces; ground, sea, and air forces. Defense strategy must also take into account decisions about the relative importance of developing new types of weapons systems, modernizing existing forces, and ensuring the readiness of currently deployed forces. Defense strategy is also concerned with selecting the best way to achieve a given military objective. For example, strategists have debated for years the capabilities required to deter nuclear attack. An awareness of this debate is essential to an understanding of the differing strategic views of antiballistic missiles.

The following sections discuss some broad strategic concepts such as deterrence, stability, and the role of arms control. The last section presents several major strategic views and focuses on the relationship of BMD to each.

The Roles of Nuclear Forces

Military power plays a vital role in peace as well as in war. The purpose of U.S. military power is:

—to *deter* adversaries from taking actions that are inimical to U.S. interests (such actions can be political as well as military);

—to *assure* friends and allies of protection, thereby cementing alliance ties, and;

—to *defend* the United States or friendly nations if deterrence fails to prevent war.

Deterrence

With respect to deterrence, four major questions concern strategists. What types of threats to U.S. interests should we seek to deter with nuclear power? How far should deterrence extend beyond the continental United States? How is deterrence to be effected? What constitutes stable deterrence?

How much to rely on nuclear weapons is a long-standing issue among strategists. Over the past three decades, the United States has come to depend heavily on nuclear weapons to deter not only nuclear war, but also a range of nonnuclear threats both to itself and to other nations. The United States seeks an ability to deter nonnuclear conflict because nonnuclear conflicts are undesirable in themselves and because they have a potential to "escalate" to nuclear conflict. Deterrence of nonnuclear conflict is an essential aspect of efforts to deter nuclear war.

Increasingly, questions are being raised about the role of nuclear weapons in deterrence. Some strategists contend that nuclear weapons should be used only to deter an adversary's use of nuclear weapons. Others hold that nuclear weapons can and should contribute to the deterrence of nonnuclear aggression, or even the use of military power for political ends—deterrence across the "conflict spectrum." Today the United States relies heavily on nuclear weapons to deter a range of threats, in large measure because at their current levels nonnuclear forces are insufficient to accomplish the job alone. However, the very existence of nuclear weapons inevitably has its impact on *any* conflict or crisis and, thus, has a role in deterrence. The salient question facing strategists today is whether heavy reliance on nuclear weapons can continue to be an effective or politically acceptable means of deterring nonnuclear aggression.

Obviously, the more extensive the reach of deterrence, the more demanding are its requirements. Deterrence does not function uniformly well in all situations. Rather, the quality of deterrence depends on *three* distinct factors: (1) capability, (2) the will to use it, and (3) mutual perceptions of the issues at stake. Thus, a given mix of capability and will could produce a strong deterrent effect if both sides perceived that issues of vital national interest are involved. Conversely, if only marginal issues are involved, that same mix may not sustain deterrence credibility; a threat to use nuclear weapons may not be believed by an adversary. This point was succinctly stated by Klaus Knorr: "In other words, there is no such thing—as is too often assumed—as an absolute ability to deter, fixed in power and constant at all times regardless of changeable circumstances. Rather, the power to deter is the power to deter a particular adversary in a particular situation."[1] Threats of recourse to nuclear warfare that are not credible (that is, believable) to the enemy are unlikely to achieve a deterrent effect.

The extension of deterrence to other nations is the second issue. Since World War II the United States has undertaken to extend deterrence, particularly nuclear deterrence, to other nations in the belief that this would contribute to a more stable world. U.S. nuclear assurances have been a central feature of the alliance system that has been a cornerstone of U.S. foreign policy since the late 1940s. The so-called nuclear umbrella has also been a means of discouraging the proliferation of nuclear capabilities, substituting guarantees of U.S. nuclear protection for possible local nuclear capabilities. Despite these U.S. assurances, however, pressures for national nuclear forces have grown in several countries. The risks to the United States of extending deterrence to others have increased with the growth of Soviet nuclear power. Now some strategists question whether the benefits of our alliances are worth the corresponding costs and risks of extending these nuclear guarantees—particularly in an era of U.S.-Soviet strategic nuclear parity.

The deterrence mechanism, or how deterrence functions, is a third issue. Some maintain that deterrence functions through the threat of punitive retaliation. In this view, a deterrent force should be designed to threaten or "hold at risk" things of value to an adversary, such as cities or industry. Others argue that an effective, credible deterrent must deny an adversary the political and military objectives of aggression. This group would concentrate deterrence on direct, specific means of denying these objectives, rather than on punishment.

Of particular concern to strategists in the West is what will deter the Soviet Union most effectively. One view argues that the Soviet Union, like the United States, is deterred by the punitive threat of massive nuclear retaliation against its cities or industrial facilities. Others argue that because the Soviet Union seems to plan seriously for fighting a nuclear war, an effective U.S. deterrent must be able to deny the Soviet Union any major military advantages in war. As the Soviet ability to

---

1. Klaus Knorr, *On the Uses of Military Power in the Nuclear Age* (Princeton University Press, 1966), p.106.

inflict similar punitive damage on the United States has grown, many strategists have argued that the threat of punitive retaliation is not credible unless the most vital national interests are at stake—unless the United States is directly threatened. Moreover, these strategists maintain that the threat of massive punitive retaliation is a particularly inappropriate means of extending deterrence to other nations.

A fourth issue has to do with strategic stability. Almost all strategists advocate a deterrent that is "stable," but they emphasize different aspects of stability. At least two types concern strategists: "crisis" and "arms race" stability.

Crisis stability is a state of affairs in which pressures and incentives for the use of force in a situation of extreme tension are minimized. For example, the more a strategic force is vulnerable to attack, the more the national leadership controlling that force may be tempted to use it, fearing that it will otherwise be destroyed. The opposing leadership, knowing that the first party is under pressure to use the "vulnerable" forces before they are destroyed, may in turn be tempted to strike first. With Soviet and U.S. development of highly accurate, multiple independently targeted reentry vehicles (warheads)—otherwise known as MIRVs—atop a single missile, anxieties about crisis stability have increased. When both states have reliable, accurate MIRVed missiles in their "inventory" of strategic forces, the side that strikes first is able to use but a fraction of its missiles to destroy a large portion of the opponent's land-based missile force. This ability to destroy enemy nuclear forces is sometimes referred to as a counterforce capability. Fear of surprise attack in a period of crisis could also tend to precipitate a nuclear conflict. Crisis instability also could result from vulnerable command-and-control systems. Degradation of command and control would add confusion to a crisis or an initial nuclear incident. The recent attention that the United States has given to the vulnerability of strategic forces and command-and-control systems stems in large measure from this concern about crisis stability.

A second type of stability, *arms race stability,* has to do with the incentives for arms competition created by force developments. A stable strategic posture should not compel an adversary to compete in an arms buildup in order to compensate for the opposing side's force improvements. In the past, one of the major criticisms of a U.S. BMD was that the Soviet Union would be forced to respond to such a U.S. deployment in order to offset its effect on Soviet strategic capabilities, thus creating greater arms competition. There is, however, considerable debate among strategists as to how closely Soviet or U.S. forces respond to one another's force developments. Although it is likely that the Soviet Union would respond in some way to a U.S. BMD program, Soviet weapons programs have a certain momentum independent of U.S. activity. The precise interaction is complex and not fully understood. Nevertheless, there clearly is some relationship. It is also clear that efforts to reduce arms competition have played a role in U.S. defense planning. For example, the decision in the 1960s to halt the Minuteman missile program at a level of 1000 was based, at least in part, on a desire to curb arms competition.

Soviet Views of Deterrence

U.S. views of deterrence are perhaps less important than Soviet views since it is the Soviet Union that we are trying to deter. Soviet strategists, mostly drawn from the military, appear to have taken quite a different view of nuclear deterrence. While not ignoring it, they reject the contention that deterrence can be manipulated and finessed. In essence, the Soviet attitude toward deterrence is almost fatalistic. When deterrence is not subjected to a severe stress, they believe it will hold easily. When subjected to such stress, deterrence might still fail. Marginal adjustment in nuclear force capabilities will not appreciably alter this situation. To a Soviet strategist, deterrence is most likely to fail in a tense crisis when both sides perceive vital issues to be at stake (because of the profound clash of political interests between capitalism and socialism) and neither is willing to capitulate. Obviously, gross asymmetries in strategic nuclear power could in themselves precipitate conflict. Nevertheless, the Soviet strategists maintain that such asymmetries in the strategic nuclear balance are unlikely to arise. Marginal changes in force capabilities are not held to affect deterrence appreciably.

In the Soviet view, a belief that small increments of additional military power will not necessarily buy a higher-quality deterrent is no prescription for military paralysis. Military power has a function: in peace, to support national objectives; and if deterrence fails, to defend national interests. The objective of the Soviet buildup in strategic forces is to maximize the probability of a favorable war outcome. Although the possibility of "victory" may not be high and awesome destruction would be the result of any nuclear war, in the Soviet view the task of rational decisionmakers is to minimize destruction and enhance the chances of a favorable termination of hostilities. To Soviet strategists the current impossibility of providing a high-confidence war-winning scenario is not a justification for failing to improve the situation as much as possible.

Assurance

A second objective of military power is to assure both domestic constituencies and allies that their security is being protected. One of the central functions of the state (reflected, for example, in the U.S. Constitution) is to promote the common defense, and the public expects its government to raise and maintain military forces sufficient to ensure national security. While public attitudes in the United States toward defense needs fluctuate quite widely, creating corresponding fluctuations in defense budgets and programs, history suggests that any administration that falls short of meeting public expectations for the nation's security will ultimately face criticism.

In addition, having entered into a series of alliances to which the United States has committed military power, we must maintain adequate strength in order to assure those allies that their security is being protected. They must be persuaded that the United States is living up to its alliance commitments. However, these generalizations leave many questions:

—What are the proper roles of the United States and its allies in contributing to our common defense? Many Americans believe the United States has come to shoulder too much of the supposedly shared burden. Some argue that the role of assurance has become an albatross, drawing excessive national resources to the defense of foreign countries.

—What should be the role of nuclear weapons in extending assurances? As noted above, nuclear guarantees are a unique U.S. contribution to most of our allies' defense efforts, which they either cannot or do not wish to furnish themselves. However, the emphasis on nuclear weapons in alliance deterrence policy, and particularly the stationing of nuclear weapons on the territory of overseas allies, has become a lightning rod for political opposition.

According to Michael Howard, the role of nuclear weapons was more critical to assurance than to deterrence at the inception of the North Atlantic Treaty Organization (NATO).[2] In the years immediately follow-

---

2. Michael Howard, "Reassurance and Deterrence: Western Defense in the 1980s," *Foreign Affairs*, vol. 61 (Winter 1982–83), p. 310.

ing World War II Western Europe seemed on the verge of economic and political collapse. The creation of NATO in 1949, accompanied by the permanent stationing of U.S. forces *and* a nuclear guarantee, demonstrated to Europeans that the United States was firmly committed to Western Europe and would not retreat into isolationism. Some strategists argue that the European fear of deliberate Soviet attack in the late 1940s was relatively low and was heightened only briefly by the outbreak of the Korean War in June of 1950.

The twin functions of nuclear weapons—deterrence and assurance—have always complicated defense planning. The success of assurance was, in some respects, an obstacle to deterrence. It is precisely because West Europeans felt reassured by the U.S. nuclear umbrella in the 1950s and 1960s, and therefore ranked the prospects of Soviet aggression as low, that they were unwilling to shoulder the costs involved in creating a substantial nonnuclear ("conventional") force. The same might be said of Japan in later years.

As NATO entered the 1970s, the growing Soviet nuclear arsenal engendered a fear of "decoupling," that is, a fear that the threat of a U.S. nuclear response to massive Soviet nonnuclear aggression would no longer be believable. Some Europeans, most notably President Charles de Gaulle of France, were concerned that a U.S. president might not risk the destruction of U.S. cities to halt Soviet aggression in Europe. Moreover, the erosion of U.S. strategic nuclear superiority by the 1970s exacerbated the decoupling anxiety. The United States, through a variety of means, has sought to convince the Europeans that U.S. nuclear forces remain linked to West European defense, for example, by developing limited nuclear response options for U.S. strategic forces, the use of which would be more credible than massive retaliation. The latest such measure is the planned deployment of intermediate-range nuclear forces (INF), but this has had some perverse effects, generating vocal, organized opposition in some European countries.

During the late 1970s, another concern resurfaced among some segments of European public opinion. It has sometimes been feared that U.S. policy in relation to the USSR might drag our NATO allies into a war that they otherwise might not have become involved in. The stationing of new nuclear weapons in Western Europe has caused this concern to be emphasized once again. No West European government has *officially* taken this position; however, it is espoused by an increasingly vocal minority.

It is essential to grasp that a traditional task of nuclear weapons—to be a source of assurance to U.S. allies—has been severely impeded by the contradictory nature of West European concerns. There appears to be no action that the United States can undertake that would *simultaneously* convince NATO that the United States is not decoupled from Western Europe, does not intend to fight a limited war on European soil, and would not drag its European allies into a conflict with the Soviet Union.

The inherent difficulties of assurance have been reinforced by a recent trend to debate nuclear strategy publicly. The small band of strategic experts on both sides of the Atlantic no longer controls debate on strategic matters. It is extraordinarily difficult to persuade the general public in Western Europe and in the United States to accept contradictions inherent in a dual U.S. policy of nuclear reassurance and deterrence. Henceforth, strategists can ignore the public dimension of nuclear weapons policies only at their peril. All new strategic initiatives, whether they are related to doctrine, arms control, or force modernization, must take this political aspect of deterrence into consideration.

Defense

Finally, military power is designed to defend important national interests if deterrence fails. The first national interest in war is defense of the United States, but U.S. defense interests and commitments extend well beyond our own shores. In the nuclear age, many question whether it would actually be possible to defend the United States if it were attacked by nuclear weapons. This is a central issue affecting BMD, and it is discussed further below.

The global growth of Soviet military power has severely strained the ability of the United States to meet its worldwide commitments. As a result, we have relied heavily on nuclear deterrence rather than conventional defense to ward off various forms of aggression in many areas of the world. We could find such dependence extremely dangerous should deterrence fail or threaten to fail. The danger is twofold. Clearly, overreliance on nuclear weapons could result in massive destruction if war did occur. Less often recognized is the danger that excessive dependence on nuclear weapons could paralyze U.S. decisionmakers from taking any action, leaving the United States and its allies subject to coercion by nations with superior conventional forces or with fewer scruples about their threat to use nuclear weapons.

Moral Issues in Nuclear Strategy

The moral issues of just wars and the appropriate use of force long predate the nuclear era. However, their application to nuclear war and deterrence has raised new and troubling issues for our time. Morality has recently become a more prominent issue in public discussions of nuclear strategy, most notably in the pastoral letter issued by the U.S. Catholic bishops in May 1983.[3] A full discussion of the moral issues of war goes well beyond the scope of this chapter, but it is important to sort out the principal views.

The view of the Catholic bishops in their pastoral letter is that the use or threatened use of nuclear weapons against civilians is morally wrong. Even use against other targets is wrong if it results in unintended death to innocents. The solution, in their view, is nuclear disarmament, but the bishops recognize that this is not an immediately achievable goal. In the meantime, they allow that deterrence requires nuclear weapons and the threat to use them, but sanction only the threat of retaliation. First use is eschewed, and a nuclear freeze is endorsed as a first step to nuclear disarmament. Since use against people is morally wrong, and use against military targets is recognized to involve large-scale destruction of people, the bishops' defense doctrine rests on the *threat* of use against targets that are not defined, except to exclude people.

Critics of the letter stress that it weakens deterrence because it makes virtually any use of nuclear weapons immoral. These critics maintain that it is also immoral for a nation to fail to defend its values.[4] They point out that nuclear weapons cannot be "wished away" and argue that as long as these weapons exist in unfriendly hands their use must be deterred. With some regret, and accepting the proposition that nuclear war would inevitably be highly destructive and entail tens of millions of civilian casualties, they conclude that a credible threat to use nuclear weapons is essential to deterrence. Some make the stronger argument that protecting our values by threatening nuclear retaliation is less of an

3. "The Pastoral Letter on War and Peace, The Challenge of Peace: God's Promise and Our Response," *Origins*, vol. 13 (May 19, 1983), a publication of the National Catholic News Service.

4. See, for example, Michael Novak, "Moral Clarity in the Nuclear Age," *National Review*, April 1, 1983, for commentary and criticism of the first and second drafts of the pastoral letters.

evil than incurring the risk of nuclear war. A failure to maintain a credible threat would subject the nation to unacceptable pressures from the Soviet Union and eventually increase the risk of war, hardly a morally defensible outcome.

There is now a third view emerging that differs from the pastoral letter and most of its critics.[5] In this view, it is indeed morally wrong to threaten innocent civilians. Moreover, this threat makes a poor deterrent, because it is subject to equally potent counterthreats. In this view, a believable, effective, and moral deterrent can be devised. Emerging developments in weapons technology will permit a far more discriminating use of both nuclear and nonnuclear weapons. This group maintains that military targets are the appropriate ones to threaten and to attack if war does occur. Nuclear weapons should threaten military targets, not civilians, and nonnuclear weapons can and should increasingly replace nuclear weapons for many military targets.

Arms Control and Strategy

The focus of arms control efforts since World War II has been on controlling and reducing nuclear arms. At the present time, one can identify three general views about the role of arms control and its relationship to strategy.

One view holds that arms control and disarmament are imperative in the nuclear age. In this view, the arms race itself is a major threat to U.S. security. Thus, arms control and disarmament are generally perceived to have a higher priority than strengthening defenses in order to ensure national security. Indeed, the nation's strategic posture would be shaped by arms control considerations. Particular importance is attached to avoiding technical developments (such as a BMD or MIRV) that could stimulate arms competition. In the past, this view has tended to stress disarmament or major arms reductions rather than arms control. Today, this school of arms control supports the nuclear freeze proposal. Although a number of its advocates acknowledge that the freeze is more an expression of political concern than a serious approach to arms

5. Albert Wohlstetter, "Bishops, Statesmen, and Other Strategists on the Bombing of Innocents," *Commentary*, vol. 75 (June 1983), pp. 15–35.

control, it has gained wide public and political support as a viable arms control alternative.

A second school sees arms control as an integral part of national strategy, but holds that arms control measures must be consistent with the nation's broader strategic objectives. In this view, the emphasis would be placed on arms control measures that enhance crisis stability, rather than arms reductions as such. The present focus of this school is to reduce or eliminate MIRV missile systems, which are seen as particularly destabilizing because of their counterforce capabilities. This group's approach was reflected in the recommendations of the President's Commission on Strategic Forces (Scowcroft Commission) issued in April 1983. The commission's proposals were based on several concepts put forth earlier.[6] Proponents of this approach could generally accept a BMD for the defense of ICBMs, but would oppose BMD for cities because, in their view, it would decrease crisis stability.

Finally, a number of analysts are disillusioned with arms control. Some are former advocates of arms control who have become discouraged with the lack of progress. However, most are skeptical of Soviet arms control objectives. To this latter group, any arms control agreement that the Soviet Union accepts is likely to be contrary to U.S. strategic interests. Thus, they think arms control should play a distinctly subordinate role in U.S. strategy. Proposals for deep reductions in strategic weapons adopted by the Reagan administration are often characterized by critics as an anti–arms control view, because they incorporate measures unlikely to be acceptable to the Soviet Union. The administration argues that these proposals are in the interest of both the United States and the Soviet Union, if the Soviet Union is truly interested in mutual arms control.

Arms control theory has evolved over the years. Before the strategic arms limitation talks (SALT), there was an emphasis on arms control as a means of achieving strategic stability.[7] With SALT the focus shifted to numerical limits and attempts to enshrine the concept of U.S.-Soviet

6. Albert Gore, Jr., "Cold, Hard Facts on the Freeze," *Washington Post*, December 7, 1982; Henry Kissinger, "A New Approach to Arms Control," *Time*, March 21, 1983, pp. 24–26; and Jan M. Lodal, "Finishing START," *Foreign Policy*, no. 48 (Fall 1982), pp. 66–81.

7. Bernard Brodie, *Strategy in the Missile Age* (Princeton University Press, 1959), pp. 302–4; and Thomas C. Schelling, "Reciprocal Measures for Arms Stabilization," in Donald G. Brennan, ed., *Arms Control, Disarmament, and National Security* (Braziller, 1961), pp. 167–86.

strategic nuclear "parity" in specific quantitative measures. Today many strategists have returned to the emphasis on stability rather than on numbers, but the widespread support for the freeze suggests that relatively simple solutions still capture the public imagination.

Strategic Defenses in General

This book concentrates on ballistic missile defense, but a strategist must consider the broader context of strategic defense. Defenses of various types interact and these relationships must be taken into account in an overall analysis. The various types of defense include:

—*Ballistic missile defenses*. These are designed to intercept ICBMs and SLBMs.

—*Air defenses*. These are designed to intercept bombers or other "air-breathing" vehicles such as cruise missiles. These defenses can be airborne (for example, interceptor aircraft) or ground based (for example, surface-to-air missiles). In the future, they might be space based.

—*Passive defenses*. These protect potential targets by such means as warning, mobility, and sheltering, rather than by intercepting an attacking force. When designed to protect the general population, they are called civil defense, but passive defenses can be used to protect military forces and industry as well. For example, hardened silos are a passive defense system for land-based ICBMs, as are the "racetrack" and Densepack basing schemes proposed for MX. Aircraft can escape their bases on warning, and ground forces can disperse from garrison areas. The sandbagging of factory equipment would be a passive defense measure employed to protect industrial assets.

—*Antisubmarine warfare* (ASW). This defense employs various methods of detecting, tracking, and destroying enemy ballistic missile submarines. Detection and tracking equipment can be fixed (as in sonar arrays emplaced on the ocean bed) or mobile (on a ship, submarine, plane, or helicopter). The means of destruction can be delivered by air, surface vessel, or submarine.

Some strategists view counterforce capabilities employed against nuclear delivery systems in the same category as defense because the two have a similar military objective—to negate enemy nuclear capabilities before they can destroy their own intended targets. The term frequently used for this objective, including both various defensive missions and counterforce, is "damage limitation."

Defensive measures interact in mutually reinforcing ways and, thus, if a BMD deployment is to be considered, other defensive measures also need to be taken into account. For example, a missile defense would make it more difficult for ICBMs arriving first in an attack to eliminate air defenses and facilitate the penetration of bombers. The sheltering or dispersal of population will enhance active defense measures, such as BMD or air defense, by facilitating a preferential defense of the target system.

Alternative Strategies and the Role of BMD

In this section, views of missile defense are related to strategy and arms control. Three broad strategic theories and four main strategies are described; how ballistic missile defense does or does not play a role in each is also discussed. One important caveat should be noted: these are constructs or abstractions, and our actual national defense strategy is likely to be a mix of these theories. Furthermore, one could describe other strategic theories. Nevertheless, those presented below are representative of the range of strategic views currently being discussed.

Deterrence-Only Strategies

Under "deterrence-only" theory, the sole objective of strategic nuclear forces is to deter. Deterrence-only theorists differ over what is to be deterred and how this is to be done, but all agree that nuclear weapons cannot be used to fight a controlled or limited war. In the deterrence-only view, strategic forces can and should extend deterrence of nuclear attack to allies insofar as it is possible. Differences of view exist over the role of nuclear weapons in deterring nonnuclear attacks, however. The principal deterrence mechanism is the threat of retaliation; but there are differences among those who hold a deterrence-only view regarding how this threat is to be directed.

One group holds that an adequate way to deter nuclear attack is to maintain the capability to threaten retaliation against targets of value such as cities or industries. This has come to be known as the "minimum deterrence" view. Advocates of this view are particularly concerned that more complex strategies weaken deterrence by opening the possibility that a nuclear war could be fought to some rational conclusion—a prospect they deny.

A second view of deterrence is that in order to deter, U.S. nuclear forces must be able to pose "not incredible" threats to the military forces and leadership of the Soviet Union, in addition to threats against cities and industry. This view, best explained by then-Secretary of Defense Harold Brown in a speech before the Naval War College in 1980, came to be known as the "countervailing strategy." Like minimum deterrence, the countervailing strategy emphasizes deterrence, but differs in the emphasis placed on the targets to be attacked or threatened.

MINIMUM DETERRENCE. In a minimum deterrence strategy, strategic forces are planned primarily to threaten urban industrial targets. A driving assumption of minimum deterrence is that the threat of massive damage to population and industry should deter the Soviet Union as much as it deters us. Another underlying idea is that escalation is certain once nuclear weapons are used. Some advocates of minimum deterrence believe it is important to place budgetary constraints on strategic forces so as to permit funds to be spent on nonnuclear forces and for other purposes.

Minimum deterrence theory is strongly driven by the desire to avoid arms competition and the hope, though not necessarily the confidence, that if the United States shows restraint the Soviet Union will as well. Arms control plays a central role in minimum deterrence theory, one objective being to proscribe weapons that would support alternative strategies.

Strategic offensive forces and related command, control, communications, and intelligence (C^3I) targets require only sufficient survivability to permit a small number of preplanned retaliatory strikes. Flexibility to retarget forces is not required because planning is based on striking a relatively limited number of fixed targets in a single massive strike. In a stereotypical minimum deterrence force posture, a counterforce capability is undesirable because of its destabilizing first-strike character.

Under a minimum deterrence theory, BMD is considered destabilizing and should be avoided. More important, by far, is the maintenance of the ABM Treaty of 1972 inviolate, as this helps to curb competition in offensive arms. Proponents of this strategy argue that a meaningful defense is not feasible; at the same time they worry that a deployment of defenses would force an adversary to respond (on the assumption the defense might work) with increased arms deployments. Arguments have also been made to the effect that strategic defenses in general might lead national leaders to feel more secure about a "favorable war outcome" and thus somewhat more inclined to use nuclear weapons or threaten war. Air and civil defense are also considered destabilizing.

There is one striking paradox apparent in many arguments of the minimum deterrence school. Although this strategy implies a much greater reliance on nonnuclear capabilities to deter and cope with nonnuclear threats because it postulates a very limited role for nuclear weapons, many (but not all) advocates of a minimum deterrence strategy are indifferent or opposed to improved nonnuclear forces. Instead, they place strong reliance on arms control measures to contain external security threats.

COUNTERVAILING STRATEGY. The principal objective of this strategy, like that of minimum deterrence, is to deter nuclear attack on the United States and its allies. It differs from minimum deterrence in that it seeks to assign nuclear weapons a broader deterrent role. The countervailing approach aims to reinforce the deterrence of both nonnuclear attacks and the use of military power for political coercion. Advocates of this strategy are concerned that minimum deterrence is insufficient to extend credible deterrence to our allies.

The principal method of deterrence is to foster within the Soviet leadership serious uncertainties regarding their ability to achieve, by the use or threat of force, any political or military objective that jeopardizes important U.S. interests. This requires a U.S. capability to inflict substantial damage not only on Soviet cities, but also on Soviet military forces, C^3I targets, and defense industries in an initial retaliatory attack. In addition, a capacity must exist to hold a reserve force of significant size for negotiating a termination of hostilities with the Soviet Union and protecting the United States from coercion during and after the war.

A credible capability to defeat Soviet forces (as opposed to destroying a set portion of its national population and industry) and to threaten the domestic control of the Communist party leadership is believed to be necessary to extend deterrence across the conflict spectrum and to U.S. allies. Nevertheless, the threat to urban-industrial targets remains the ultimate deterrent, held in reserve to deter attacks on U.S. cities. It is generally recognized by advocates of this view that budgetary constraints and pressures against overreliance on nuclear weapons will constrain actual warfighting capabilities. In addition, proponents recognize the tension between their desire to strengthen deterrence and their fear that movement toward a warfighting posture could be destabilizing.

Arms control is viewed as an important element of this strategy, and particular emphasis is given to reinforcing stability. A relatively high importance, therefore, is given to concluding the strategic arms reduction talks (START) and INF negotiations under way in Geneva.

In the countervailing strategy, U.S. offensive forces must be sufficiently survivable to ensure a deliberate retaliatory strike against a wide array of preplanned targets, many of which will be hardened military facilities. Targeting "flexibility" must allow the execution of a broad range of attack options. There must be a capability to update these strategic attack plans fairly rapidly in peacetime because many of the important military targets of this strategy often change location. A small secure reserve force and its supporting C^3I and logistics must have the ability to endure a nuclear conflict of at least several months in order to prevent coercion of the United States and provide it with bargaining leverage in negotiating a favorable end to hostilities. This force would be mixed, but primarily sea based.

The countervailing approach places great importance on the survival of U.S. C^3I capabilities. It is important to be confident of an ability to execute a deliberate and selective response to a nuclear attack in order to foster a Soviet perception that the deterrent could be employed. U.S. C^3I facilities also must have some endurance as insurance against the contingency of a protracted war. This strategy demands some survivable counterforce capability as well in order to make a counterforce response credible, but the precise requirement for counterforce has been debated for years. The need for a prompt counterforce (such as ICBMs) is usually justified in terms of the perceptions of equality or bargaining leverage for reducing Soviet ICBMs that would result rather than in terms of precise, quantifiable military objectives.

BMD might play a role in the countervailing strategy, protecting ICBMs and critical C^3I nodes. Some strategists holding this view would advocate some expansion of air defense, so that the BMD system could not be easily circumvented by enemy bombers or cruise missiles. However, the countervailing strategy is dominated by offensive forces; defenses would be deployed, if at all, primarily to strengthen the survivability of the deterrent force and its related C^3I facilities. Urban defense is unlikely to be part of this strategy. Even the defense of some forces and C^3I assets would be opposed by some adherents of this view as being destabilizing, too costly, and likely to divert funds from more important programs.

Warfighting Strategies

In these strategies, a capability to fight a war in which nuclear weapons are used for a whole range of military purposes is considered essential to deterrence. These strategies presuppose that nuclear war could occur; therefore, plans must be made for the most effective military use of nuclear weapons, for defending against them, and for terminating conflict on favorable terms. Fighting such a war implies the ability to employ nuclear weapons discriminately (that is, with minimum damage to targets not intended for destruction, most notably population) and to defend military and civil assets. These strategies seek to deter not just nuclear attack, but also nonnuclear conflict and military coercion by an adversary.

The deterrent mechanism of warfighting strategies is a credible capacity to deny an adversary the attainment of his political or military objectives of war. Some strategists in this school speak of a U.S. requirement to have a relatively high confidence of prevailing ("winning") in any conflict, even if nuclear weapons are used and even if the conflict is protracted. However, the concept of prevailing, and indeed the theory of how a nuclear war might end, has not been clearly described. Nevertheless, the goal of favorable conflict termination is considered important in this class of strategies, rather than futile.

The warfighting class of strategies has several variants. In the first two years of his tenure at the Pentagon Secretary Robert McNamara advocated a damage-limiting strategy, which was perhaps a precursor of today's more demanding "warfighting" approach. The secretary sought a strategic posture that would be capable of limiting damage to the United States by a combination of counterforce strikes against enemy nuclear forces and defenses that could mitigate the consequences of an enemy nuclear attack. In his now famous Ann Arbor address of June 1962, McNamara argued for targeting enemy forces rather than populations—the so-called no cities doctrine. During this period, the Defense Department sponsored extensive research and development of highly accurate ballistic missiles, as well as serious efforts to improve civil defense.

However, by late 1963 McNamara had become convinced that damage limitation was not feasible at any reasonable cost and that U.S. efforts to achieve this objective would result in no net increase in U.S. national security.[8] Therefore, damage limitation was largely abandoned as declaratory policy in the latter half of the 1960s, as was McNamara's support for a continued expansion of U.S. counterforce capability. Damage limitation was replaced by "assured destruction," a type of "minimum deterrent" strategic theory incorporating an ability to inflict a predetermined level of destruction on Soviet society. For example, McNamara noted a U.S. potential to destroy 20–30 percent of Soviet population and 50–75 percent of Soviet industrial capacity in a single retaliatory strike as being sufficient to ensure strategic nuclear deterrence.[9] However, U.S. strategic targeting plans continued to incorporate counterforce concepts; Soviet strategic forces would be attacked in the event of nuclear war.

In the late 1960s, the fledgling Sentinel ABM system, which had been designed for a light area defense, was renamed Safeguard and redirected toward the defense of ballistic missiles. Efforts initiated in the early 1960s to develop a civil defense program languished as the concept of damage limitation lost official backing. Although U.S. strategic posture continued to incorporate certain warfighting capabilities (for example, counterforce targeting), official policy pronouncements clearly deemphasized the warfighting approach as the concept of mutual assured destruction was embraced.

The more recent version of the warfighting approach is quite different in its thrust. This view has long been espoused by certain nuclear experts and reached its zenith during the Reagan administration's first months. According to proponents of this version, the United States must have a capability, if deterrence fails, to fight and win a nuclear war, even if such a war lasts for many months. Not only are such plans held to be good from a *defense* point of view, but they are also thought to be the best way to *deter* and probably to *assure* as well. This view, particularly in the terms initially set forth by the Reagan administration, has been criticized as being both provocative and impractical. The administration has retreated, at least in public statements, from more extreme forms of warfighting and even from use of the term. More recent public formulations of the doctrine, including disclaimers as to the ability to "win" a

8. Department of Defense News Release 1486-63, November 18, 1963.
9. Jerome H. Kahan, *Security in the Nuclear Age: Developing U.S. Strategic Arms Policy* (Brookings Institution, 1975), pp. 94–96.

nuclear war, suggest that current nuclear strategy is very much closer to the Carter administration's countervailing strategy. Nevertheless, a number of strategists continue to insist that in order to deter less than all-out attacks and extend alliance guarantees, the United States must have the capability to fight and win a nuclear conflict. They argue that there is no *real* difference between deterrence and warfighting, and that efforts to make such distinctions are basically exercises in self-delusion.

The more recent warfighting strategies require a capability to destroy hard and movable military targets with confidence (high "damage expectancy"), as well as defense industries. A substantial reserve force with endurance and a flexible replanning capability sufficient to be able to operate for a period of several months is also required.

A range of potential arms control environments exists that would be consistent with warfighting strategies. However, most advocates of this school do not place a high priority on the conclusion of arms control agreements, as do deterrence-only advocates. In the warfighting strategy, arms control is seen primarily as an adjunct to defense strategy. Its potential consequences are viewed as ranging from marginally useful to disruptive of necessary progress in military modernization and technological advancements.

The character of defenses in such a strategy should permit the United States to emerge from a nuclear conflict in a relatively favorable power position, particularly in relation to the Soviet Union, but also in relation to third powers. In logic, this strategy would contemplate not only strategic defenses for offensive forces and C^3I facilities, but also an area defense to protect population, industry, and other resources of the society. This strategic theory implies a major expansion of all strategic defenses: civil, air, and BMD. And many proponents do support this approach.

Although defenses might be a logical element of warfighting theory, not all advocates of the strategy are strong believers in defense. Some share the view that an effective defense, as desirable as it might be, is not feasible. Others fear that defenses will divert resources from needed offensive systems.

Defense Emphasis

A fourth strategic concept has recently been given increased emphasis by the Reagan administration. This concept has been termed "defense emphasis.''[10] Because this strategy has not been as fully developed as the other three it is more difficult to describe precisely. It still is evolving. Nevertheless, the ultimate objective of this strategy is to make both current deterrence concepts and nuclear offensive forces obsolete by limiting strategic offensive systems and expanding and improving strategic defense. With strategic forces on both sides emphasizing defense, delivering nuclear strikes with high confidence and with well-defined military objectives will be impossible.

The would-be attacker will be discouraged from attacking by the prospect of a militarily poor or uncertain outcome, rather than by the threat of retaliation. In the extreme case, even attacks on cities as well as militarily motivated attacks would be frustrated by highly capable BMDs and limited offenses. An important motive for studying this strategy is the belief that in the long run moral, political, and technological pressures will impel the United States and the Soviet Union to place far greater emphasis on defense then they do today.

Clearly this is a very long-range goal, and many questions remain regarding both the technical feasibility of achieving such a goal and the potential for dangerous strategic instabilities during the transition from our current "offense dominance" to the age of "defense emphasis."

Skeptics of defense emphasis, and there are many, doubt that technological developments will permit a "leakproof" defense. They argue that a defense that permits even a few nuclear weapons to reach their targets will result in unacceptable casualties. At the same time, many of the same critics fear that the still-imperfect defense will increase the prospects of war and nuclear escalation. Many seem to be uncomfortable with the prospect that some future U.S. president might not be deterred from taking actions to defend U.S. interests that could lead to war because of his or her faith in U.S. strategic defenses.

Supporters of defense emphasis argue that the technology of defense has not yet been fully explored because of budgetary limits. They maintain that we cannot be sure what capabilities might result in the future from an intensive research and development (R&D) effort. Defenses combined with limits on offense could, in time, create a new and safer form of deterrence based on the knowledge that nuclear attacks will largely fail to achieve their intended damage objectives. Should this

10. For an earlier exposition on BMD, see D. G. Brennan, "The Case for Missile Defense," *Foreign Affairs*, vol. 47 (April 1969), pp. 433–48.

come to pass, it would eliminate deterrence as we have come to know it. It is acknowledged that this process will take time and that the results are uncertain, but supporters of defense emphasis argue that this goal is worth the effort. Furthermore, supporters argue that strategic defense need not be perfect to have a deterrent utility and they disagree with arguments that a U.S. or Soviet leader would be more eager to start a war if faced with the prospect of a few million casualties from nuclear weapons rather than tens of millions.

Probably the most difficult problem for both the supporters of defense emphasis and the skeptics is to think through the process of getting from where we are now to the new environment without encountering a period of some strategic instability along the way. Serious questions must be answered. For example, in terms of arms race stability, will either of the superpowers accept limits on offensive forces while defenses are built up, in effect permitting the capabilities of their offensive deterrent to deteriorate in the process? This appears to assume a degree of mutual confidence and cooperation that is currently lacking. If such a process could be started, what temptations and possibilities would exist for evasion of any offensive agreement? How would this affect stability? As defenses are built up, but not perfected, would the temptation to use nuclear weapons increase? Would a new emphasis on strategic defense favor the Soviet Union, which has invested far more in air and civil defense as well as in BMD R&D than the United States has since the ABM Treaty was signed in 1972? These issues require further examination.

Meanwhile, if the United States should move toward a defense emphasis strategy, it will do so over a period of some years. There could be periods along the way when strategic defense has objectives short of altering or revolutionizing the state of deterrence.

One interim goal might be to develop a stronger strategic defense capability that would reinforce overall deterrence by increasing an attacker's uncertainty about the precise results of an attack. Another, more ambitious, goal would seek to limit damage significantly (for example, so as to be capable of protecting 50 percent of the population) in the event deterrence failed. In the short run, deterrence would still be based on offensive threats, but the existence of strategic defenses would complicate attack planning and thus reinforce deterrence. In the much longer run the objective would be to thwart a nuclear attack with strategic defense systems that could overwhelm offensive forces. The role of remaining offensive forces is uncertain. They might serve as insurance against unanticipated defense vulnerabilities or a clandestine offensive buildup by the other side.

Arms control appears essential to the achievement of the ultimate goals of such a strategy. Offensive forces will have to be reduced and limited. Arms control agreements would permit defenses to grow to include area defense, while offenses would be progressively reduced. As already noted, such a regime will require a major change in the attitudes and relations of the major nuclear powers.

The defense emphasis strategy contemplates a progressively improved nationwide BMD nuclear defense effort. It seems likely that such a strategy will require the development of midcourse or boost-phase missile intercept systems. It would also be necessary to strengthen air defenses significantly in order to prevent a shift by the offense to air-breathing forces as ballistic missile defenses are strengthened. Civil defense efforts would also be important. It is likely as well that nonnuclear forces would have to be strengthened to compensate for the reduced reliance on nuclear weapons.

Summary

The preceding discussion illustrates how the role of BMD would differ depending on the defense strategy selected. In the minimum deterrent strategy BMD is considered destabilizing for at least three reasons. First, deployment of a BMD would stimulate compensating actions by the other side—probably defensive as well as offensive. It is argued that this would fuel arms competition and upset arms race stability. Second, any substantial BMD deployment would stimulate radical modification or abrogation of the ABM Treaty. This would tend to undercut the arms control process, which has a high priority in this strategy. Third, some fear that a defense would result in a situation in which national decision-makers are more likely to use nuclear weapons. Critics of minimum deterrent strategies contend that this form of deterrence is increasingly incredible and, as a result, opens the United States and its allies to nuclear blackmail in the absence of much strengthened conventional forces. They argue that the adoption of a minimum deterrent strategy by the United States would result in catastrophe if deterrence failed or even threatened to fail.

The countervailing strategy emphasizes counterforce and counter-C³I targeting. It provides for a possible modest role for BMD in the defense of ICBMs and some critical command and control facilities. This strategy (albeit absent defense) has been the major trend of U.S. strategic thinking in the 1970s and early 1980s and was conceived as a response to the perceived weaknesses of minimum deterrence. The countervailing strategy has been criticized from both right and left. Some believe such a strategy—in contrast to minimum deterrence—is provocative to the Soviet Union, disturbing to our allies, subversive of arms control, and too costly to be fulfilled. They perceive it to be a warfighting strategy. Critics on the right point to its ambivalence and construe it as little more than minimum deterrence. While stressing the need for credible counterforce to deter, many advocates of the countervailing strategy also go to some lengths to point out the risks of escalation and the difficulties of escalation control, thereby vitiating, in the view of the critics, much of the deterrent effect of the strategy.

A warfighting strategy demands a major role for BMD and other defense measures, including air and civil defense. In this view, there is some serious prospect that nuclear war could occur. Thus, the United States must plan for it, and every reasonable effort should be made to defend the country and defeat the adversary. Advocates of this strategy contend that taking the prospect of nuclear war seriously and thinking through ways to prosecute such a war as best we can are essential to deterrence. In this strategy defense becomes an important element. However, offensive forces continue to dominate strategy. Critics contend that a major defense program initiated with warfighting in mind would be costly, destabilizing, and ineffective. It would, in their view, increase the risk of nuclear war without significantly reducing its consequences; be a cause for concern to allies as much as or more than to the Soviet Union; and severely damage, if not destroy, the prospects for arms control.

The defense emphasis strategy would give BMD and other defensive measures the central role. It would also appear to have a major role for arms control. Movement to a defense-dominant strategy would probably ultimately require agreed measures to limit offensive forces. Because this strategy is relatively new, even its advocates often appear to have conflicting views. Some see defenses as strengthening deterrence; others see strong defenses as ultimately supplanting deterrence, at least as we have known it during the past four decades. Critics voice all of the arguments noted above with respect to arms race and crisis stability and the effects on the arms control process. Many believe that technology cannot support a defense-dominant strategy in the foreseeable future. Others cite the enormous cost of prospective defense. At this point, much of the commentary is speculation and guesswork, for the issues of defense are only beginning to receive detailed and serious examination.

These views of strategy are likely to remain under debate for years to come and thus BMD will continue to be a focus of strategic controversy. However, it seems likely that the role of defenses is now going to receive more serious consideration in this debate than it has for almost two decades.

CHAPTER THREE

Systems and Technology

STEPHEN WEINER

THIS CHAPTER describes the major technical aspects of various ballistic missile defense (BMD) systems and components.[1] Such systems include "traditional" systems using ground-based radars and nuclear-armed interceptors operating within the atmosphere or exoatmospherically; area defense systems using infrared (IR) sensors and nonnuclear interceptors operating in space; so-called simple/novel terminal defense systems; nuclear-explosive-generated dust cloud defense; and boost-phase systems using either directed-energy weapons or interceptor missiles.

The approach here is to identify the functions that the system must perform and to determine the corresponding requirements for the components. Here and there sample calculations of component performance are made to indicate what factors influence a defense system designer. Finally, the attacker's options to degrade the system's performance are discussed, the emphasis being on the critically important point that BMD is a "game" played against a hostile opponent rather than an optimization problem in a benign natural environment.

This chapter concentrates on the workings of individual defense components and batteries. Chapter 4 will discuss the deployment of these individual batteries to perform various BMD missions and the

1. The reader interested in pursuing this topic further should refer to James Constant, *Introduction to Defense Radar Systems Engineering* (Spartan Books, 1972); Samuel Glasstone, ed., *The Effects of Nuclear Weapons,* U.S. Atomic Energy Commission (Government Printing Office, 1962); Richard D. Hudson, Jr., *Infrared System Engineering* (Wiley-Interscience, 1969); John C. Toomay, *Radar Principles for the Non-Specialist* (Belmont, Calif.: Lifetime Learning Publications, 1982); and Ashton Carter, "Background Paper on Directed-Energy BMD" (being prepared for the U.S. Office of Technology Assessment).

level of effectiveness that can be expected of them. An attempt is made here to compare and contrast BMD technical problems with similar problems occurring in other fields, particularly air defense and space missions.

Several premises underlie the discussion throughout this chapter. The first, alluded to above, is that the attacker will use components and tactics to make the defender's job as difficult as possible. The defense must thus be designed to handle this "worst case" attack. A second premise is that, in predicting the outcome of any attack, both the attacker and the defender must consider a number of uncertainties and unpredictable occurrences. These include equipment failures and inaccuracies, uncertainties about nuclear weapons effects, and uncertainties about the tactics and equipment of the opponent. If both attacker and defender make conservative assumptions about the random events and uncertainties, they may come to different conclusions regarding the outcome of the attack. Thus, the attacker must design to handle a worst-case defense and the defender to handle a worst-case attack. Differences in the attacker's view and the defender's view are responsible for much of the controversy regarding BMD effectiveness. The final premise of this chapter is that most BMD designs represent compromises among performance, cost, and risk. For example, better system performance at greater cost can be achieved by using either higher-performance components or a greater number of lower-performance components. Equal or better system performance at lower cost but higher risk can be achieved either by using more advanced technology or by assuming the attack is constrained in size or tactics.

The next section contains a summary of the characteristics of the intercontinental ballistic missiles (ICBMs) and submarine-launched ballistic missiles (SLBMs) that BMD systems must handle and the environment in which they must operate. This summary is followed by a discussion of the functions generic to all BMD systems, the choice of components to perform these functions, and potential countermeasures to these functions. The remainder of the chapter deals with specific BMD concepts and their major technical issues.

Ballistic Missile Characteristics

To appreciate the differences between BMD systems, it is necessary to look briefly at the nature of ICBM and SLBM trajectories. Figure 3-1

Figure 3-1. *Trajectory Phases*

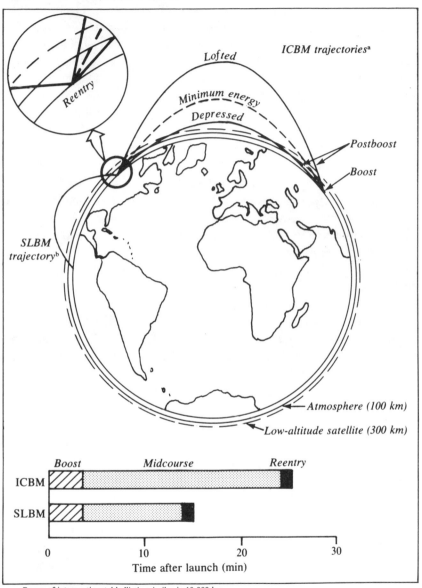

a. Range of intercontinental ballistic missiles is 10,000 km.
b. Range of submarine-launched ballistic missiles is 5000 km.

illustrates the four major phases of some sample trajectories: boost, postboost, midcourse, and reentry. The boost phase typically lasts several hundred seconds, during which the missile starts at rest and accelerates to about 7 km/sec by the time it reaches an altitude of about 200 km. Typically an ICBM is a three-stage rocket, each stage of which contributes more than 2 km/sec to the missile velocity. During the boost phase, the missile is easily visible to space-based sensors and relatively vulnerable. However, the boost phase does not last very long and occurs far from the defender's territory. BMD systems that operate against missiles in their boost phase are discussed in a later section.

In sophisticated missile systems, a postboost or deployment phase follows boost. This phase may last another several hundred seconds. During this phase, a postboost vehicle (PBV) or "bus" maneuvers to achieve a variety of very precise trajectories and then deploys individual reentry vehicles (RVs) on each trajectory. The RV consists of a nuclear warhead with sufficient structure and heatshield to survive reentry and a fusing system to detonate it at the appropriate time. The bus can also be used to deploy decoys or other penetration aids. The bus carries a very accurate inertial guidance system to determine its position and velocity. It maneuvers to correct any trajectory errors produced during the boost phase and to place individual RVs on slightly different trajectories to attack different targets. This type of system is called a multiple independently targetable reentry vehicle (MIRV) system and enables one missile to threaten several enemy targets. The bus uses much lower thrust levels than does the booster, and consequently its rocket exhaust is less visible to BMD sensors.

After the reentry vehicles are deployed, they follow ballistic, that is, freefall, trajectories for approximately 1000 sec, climbing above 1000 km and then falling toward earth and eventually reentering the atmosphere. BMD operation against missiles in this midcourse phase can take advantage of the long time available and the predictibility of freefall RV trajectories in the vacuum of space. Disadvantages for BMD operation in this phase include the difficulty of distinguishing RVs from decoys and other lightweight penetration aids in the absence of atmospheric interaction and the need for sensors and data processing to track thousands of objects including spent booster motors, buses, and deployment hardware, as well as RVs and decoys. Furthermore, the SLBM and depressed trajectory ICBM shown in figure 3-1 cause serious problems in midcourse for BMD systems because the RVs spend less time at high altitudes. BMD systems operating in midcourse are discussed in more detail later.

The final phase of the missile trajectory is reentry, which starts when the RVs and other objects are at altitudes of around 100 km and begin to interact with the atmosphere. Reentry typically lasts from 30 to 100 sec, depending on the specific trajectory and the drag characteristics of the RV. During reentry, atmospheric drag causes reentry vehicles to slow down with peak deceleration on the order of 50–100 times the acceleration of gravity. This drag also causes RVs to heat up to incandescence. Lightweight objects do not survive reentry, and RVs must be carefully designed and manufactured to survive reentry and maintain their accuracy. This underlies a major advantage of reentry BMD systems: the atmosphere acts to filter out booster, bus, and other debris, as well as many decoys and other penetration aids. Other advantages include the relatively modest ranges at which the sensors and interceptors must operate. The primary disadvantage of reentry operation is the very short time available to perform defense functions. This allows only limited defense coverage and very little margin for error. The lofted trajectory ICBM shown in figure 3-1 presents more problems for reentry systems than do the other trajectories, because of its faster reentry. Reentry BMD systems are also discussed later.

The final event on a missile trajectory is detonation of the missile's nuclear warhead; this is the primary purpose for which the booster, bus, and reentry vehicle have been designed. The characteristics of nuclear weapon detonations and their effect on different defended targets influence the requirements on BMD systems and components and the environment in which they must operate.

Nuclear weapon detonations in the atmosphere produce blast waves, thermal radiation, and nuclear radiation, all of which can damage or destroy defended targets. Thermal radiation is attenuated by clouds or shielding, and nuclear radiation is attenuated by the atmosphere or shielding, so damage criteria are generally based on the blast wave overpressure. The overpressure measured in pounds per square inch (psi) is a function of the weapon yield measured in megatons (MT) and the range from the burst (see figure 3-2). At small ranges, the blast is extremely strong and attenuates with distance much more rapidly than would a sound wave, which weakens primarily by geometric spreading.

Various targets that might be defended by a BMD system have different hardness levels. An idea of the "keepout" distance for "point"

Figure 3-2. *Relationship of Overpressure to Distance from Explosions of Different Yields*

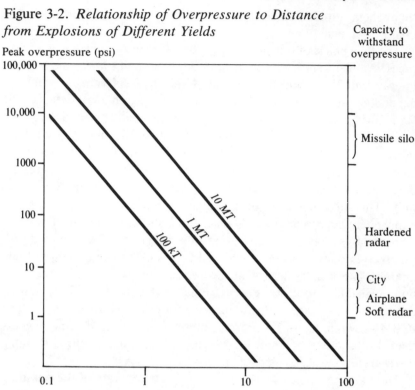

targets such as missile silos or radars can be obtained from figure 3-2. The BMD system must destroy attacking RVs before they can penetrate this keepout distance and explode. For "extended" or "area" targets such as cities or airbases, the keepout zone extends laterally beyond all portions of the defended target (see figure 3-2 for the distance and altitude). By selecting a specific keepout volume and designing components to achieve this capability, the defense is implicitly stating that nuclear detonations just outside this keepout volume will not destroy the target or make the defense ineffective.

BMD Functions

All BMD systems must perform the same sequence of functions; they differ primarily in how and where each of these functions is carried out.

Figure 3-3. *Sample Timelines*

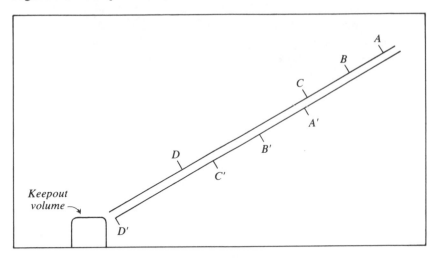

Note: Events on the timelines are as follows:

	Earliest	Latest
Start of search	A	A'
Start of track	B	B'
Interceptor commit	C	C'
Intercept	D	D'

The major stages of BMD operation are target acquisition, tracking, discrimination, interceptor control, and target kill; these stages must occur for each attacking object. *Acquisition* is the process of searching for and detecting any potentially threatening object. *Tracking* involves taking a sequence of sensor measurements of the target's position and determining its future trajectory. *Discrimination* is the process of deciding whether or not a particular object is an RV that should be intercepted or a nonlethal booster fragment or decoy. *Interceptor control* and *target kill* ensure that the interceptor gets close enough to the object to kill it. If any of these functions is unsuccessful, the defense will fail and the target will "leak" through the system. To ensure that the overall system performs acceptably, the permitted leakage must be "budgeted" among the individual BMD functions.

The sequencing of functions can be readily illustrated by a "timeline" of events along an RV trajectory. Two such timelines can be drawn for the reentry defense of a point target, one representing the earliest intercept and the other representing the latest intercept (see figure 3-3). The earliest intercept timeline is obtained by working forward in time. If the maximum detection range (or altitude) occurs at point A, the time from A to B represents the minimum time required to search for the target. Following detection, the target must be tracked and discriminated until the earliest point, C, at which a decision can be made to commit an interceptor. If an interceptor is launched when the RV is at point C, it will get to point D at the same time as the RV. Thus point D represents the earliest intercept.

The latest intercept timeline is obtained by working backward in time. The latest intercept is at point D' just outside the target keepout volume. Since the interceptor takes a certain time to fly to point D', by backing up the trajectory this amount of time, the RV is located at the point C' at which time the interceptor is launched. If tracking, discrimination, and search require minimum time intervals, then the start of track and search must occur by points B' and A', respectively.

The timeline is often divided into a "precommit" and a "postcommit" period. For the particular timelines in figure 3-3, the precommit phase is "redundant" in that, if an RV is not detected or discriminated between A and C, the defense has another opportunity to perform these functions between A' and C'. However, the postcommit phase is not redundant since there would be insufficient time to launch another interceptor if an interceptor failed at point D. For other timelines, the precommit phase could be nonredundant or the postcommit phase could be redundant. If the postcommit phase is redundant, the defense is said to have defensive "shoot-look-shoot" capability.

The region between the earliest intercept, D, and the latest intercept, D', (called the "battlespace") represents the flexibility that the defense has in planning its intercepts. This flexibility is particularly important if many reentry vehicles are attacking the defended point almost simultaneously because it enables intercepts to be spaced so that one interceptor does not destroy another interceptor when it detonates, an occurrence called "defense fratricide."

The requirements for the acquisition or search function are determined by considering all potentially threatening trajectories attacking the defended region and calculating the points along these trajectories where the RVs must be detected. This exercise yields a "search volume" that must be examined by the acquisition sensor in less time than it would take an RV to pass through this volume. The acquisition sensor must have sufficient sensitivity to detect an RV in the search volume and sufficient resolution to isolate the RV from nearby objects.

Viewed from the defended target, the search volume has a certain extent in range, azimuth (angle with respect to north), and elevation (angle above the horizon). The extent in range can be determined from the timeline, as indicated above. The extent in azimuth depends on the location of potential launch sites of missiles threatening the defended target. This in turn depends on the BMD mission. For example, in the defense of U.S. ICBMs, the principal threat is Soviet ICBMs because they are numerous and highly accurate. Since these must be launched from Soviet territory, the azimuth extent of the search volume is limited to within about 30° east or west of north. The principal threat to U.S. strategic bomber bases is short-range SLBMs because of their short time of flight. (They might arrive before the bombers have had time to escape the base.) Since these SLBMs could be launched from waters surrounding the United States, the azimuth extent of the search volume would be selected accordingly.

The elevation extent of the search volume is determined by the minimum and maximum reentry angles that can be used to attack the defended target. A given booster delivers a given payload to its greatest range on the so-called minimum energy trajectory, with a reentry angle of 20°–25° for ICBMs. A missile system with a given maximum range and payload can be flown either on a lofted or a depressed trajectory to a shorter range; or it can be flown with a lighter payload. There are theoretical and practical limits to these changes in reentry angle. On depressed trajectories (low reentry angles) the RV heats up more during reentry and its accuracy is reduced. Lofted trajectories (high reentry angles) result in greater RV deceleration at reentry and increased time of flight since the flight path is longer and the RV is slower at the top of its trajectory. Excursions of about 10° in either direction about minimum energy represent a practical limit (for ICBMs), although greater excursions are physically possible and may be effective—particularly if they could approach from the south, as with a fractional orbit bombardment system (FOBS).

The requirements for a surveillance sensor to cover a given search volume depend on its location relative to the volume. A nominal case corresponds to locating the sensor near the defended target. If the sensor is moved uprange (toward the search volume), the required sensor range is decreased but its field of view (the fraction of the sky covered by the search volume) must increase. Conversely, if the sensor is moved downrange, the required field of view is decreased, but the maximum range must increase. For both radar and infrared sensors, the difficulty of the sensor's job increases with increased range and increased field of view.

Radar sensors transmit microwave signals in a narrow beam into a portion of the search volume. If a target is located in the direction of this beam, it will scatter the microwave energy in all directions, including back to the radar. The signals are transmitted until the entire search volume has been illuminated. By measuring the time delay between transmission and reception, the radar can determine the range to the target (since radar signals propagate at the speed of light, 3×10^5 km/ sec). When the frequency shift of the radar signal (Doppler shift— analogous to the red shift in astronomy) is measured, the velocity of the target along the radar line-of-sight can be determined. The elevation and azimuth of the target are obtained from the direction of the received signal. Most radars measure range more accurately than they measure angle. Radar operation is discussed in more detail later in the chapter.

Infrared sensors detect the thermal radiation emitted by the target itself. The intensity and wavelength spectrum of this radiation depend on the size and temperature of the target. The target can be detected if its temperature is different (usually higher) from that of its background. In the boost phase, the hot rocket exhaust can be detected against the background of the warm earth. In midcourse, the warm RVs can be detected against the background of cold space. Infrared sensors operate much like television cameras in that they use a system of lenses or mirrors to focus the incident radiation onto detectors that convert this radiation into electrical signals. Infrared sensors can measure a target's angular position very accurately but cannot measure its range at all. More will be said about these topics later.

The offense can try to degrade the BMD system search performance in several ways. For example, it can use either super-lofted or super-depressed trajectories so as to avoid the search volume, but such tactics are relatively easily countered by expanding the sensor search volume. A more effective way of countering the search function is to reduce the observables of the RV; this process is known as "stealth." The radar observables of an RV are characterized by its radar cross section (RCS), which gives the fraction of the incident radar energy that is reflected back to the radar. The target RCS can be reduced by shaping the RV so that most of the incident energy is scattered away from the radar rather than toward it. Because the streamlining required for high-speed reentry also serves to reduce the RCS of the RV, BMD radars have traditionally been designed to detect targets with low observability.

The observability of targets being tracked by infrared sensors can be degraded either by reducing the signal originating from the target or by increasing the competing signal coming from the background. In the boost phase, the signal comes from the booster exhaust, which is virtually impossible to hide. In midcourse, the signal derives primarily from the RV's thermal radiation in the infrared portion of the spectrum. The infrared signal can be reduced by cooling the target or by making it reflective, but this is unlikely to prevent detection. Detection can be postponed more effectively by using a depressed trajectory to increase the chance that the RV will be viewed against a warm earth background rather than against cold space. During reentry most RVs heat up to well over 1000°K and radiate many kilowatts of thermal energy. However, an infrared search sensor operating in reentry is ineffective on a cloudy day.

Several other techniques have been considered for countering the search function of a BMD system. For example, the sensor can be prevented from detecting the target by setting off nuclear weapons between the target and sensor; this technique is called "blackout" for a radar (a similar technique is called "redout" for an infrared sensor). Blackout is explained in more detail in the next section. Another way to counter the search function is to increase the noise level of a radar by electronic jamming to the point where the target signal cannot be detected. These techniques impose constraints on both the attacker and the defender; any BMD system must take into account the threat of these countermeasures in both its component design and operating tactics.

Once a target has been detected, it is tracked to determine where it is going. The accuracy of this prediction depends on the accuracy of the sensor measurement, the length of time the target has been in track, and the length of time for which prediction must be done. Trajectory prediction is used principally to determine the target impact point and to select potential intercept points. The impact point prediction must be sufficiently accurate to determine whether or not the attacking object is a threat to a defended target. The intercept point prediction must be sufficiently accurate to permit an interceptor to maneuver to within a kill radius of the object.

For most BMD systems, tracking and trajectory prediction do not impose particularly stressing requirements. (An exception is some of the simple/novel systems discussed later in the chapter.) If a sensor is sensitive enough to perform search, it is generally capable of tracking any objects that have been detected. (The detection thresholds must not be too low, however, or too many spurious detections will overwhelm the capability of the tracking data processor.) For reentry systems, a few seconds of track usually suffice to achieve the needed prediction accuracy for nuclear intercept. For exoatmospheric systems using radar, a few tens of seconds of track are needed. Midcourse systems using infrared sensors generally require track time of 100 sec or more because passive sensors cannot measure range, but only angular position of a target; as a result they require long track time to infer range information from the change in angular position.

Since tracking is relatively easy for a BMD system, it is not particularly vulnerable to countermeasures. The most serious threat to tracking is a maneuvering RV that could make a strike far from its predicted impact point. This tactic is effective if the defense is trying to save some subset of the targets being attacked and wants to intercept only RVs heading for these targets.

After tracking the target, the BMD system must carry out its next function, discrimination, to determine which targets should be intercepted. This area has been the focus of major disagreements regarding BMD effectiveness. Reentry vehicles must be large and heavy enough to carry a nuclear warhead; decoys, to be useful, should be much lighter and take up less room on the booster. If the offense decides to use decoys, it must remove one or more RVs from the booster and replace them with a larger number of decoys. These decoys help the remaining RVs penetrate the BMD system in two related ways: (1) "leakage" can occur if the defense mistakes an RV for a decoy and fails to shoot at it; and (2) a decoy may be mistaken for an RV and an interceptor wasted on it, with the result that not enough interceptors will be available for the remaining RVs. Discrimination performance always involves a tradeoff between these two types of errors.

Discrimination is a remote sensing process in which the target signature—such as radar cross section or infrared radiance—is measured as a function of time. The measurements are then analyzed by computers to determine whether the target is an RV or a decoy. In a benign environment, remote sensing can be extremely effective. Virtually all of the findings of astronomy and astrophysics derive from remote measurements. Remote sensing of the earth from satellites can be used to identify crops and even to evaluate the health of the crops. Countermeasures to remote sensing (or spying) have also had a long history. Techniques such as signature suppression, camouflage, and masking have been used in activities ranging from conventional warfare to the concealment of illegal crops.

The types of discrimination measurements and potential decoys needed differ considerably according to the defense operating region. Discrimination is a strong point of boost-phase BMD systems, since it would be very difficult to design an inexpensive decoy to match the signature and trajectory of a burning booster, whereas it may be the weakest point of midcourse BMD systems since lightweight decoys can have radar or infrared signatures comparable (in magnitude) to the RV signatures. Only by looking at the fine-grain details of these measurements can the defense hope to discriminate. Since exoatmospheric decoys need not survive reentry, they can be physically as large as an RV despite their light weight. Many exoatmospheric radar or infrared decoys are inflatable objects.

Since the defense's objective is to identify the fine detail of the signature, anything the attacker can do to make the signature noisier will degrade discrimination. For example, radar chaff or infrared aerosols can be added in the vicinity of both RVs and decoys to obscure the details of the signatures. Chaff consists of many thin wires (equal in length to half the radar wavelength) that are efficient radar scatterers. Aerosols consist of millions of microscopic particles that can reflect the earth's thermal radiation toward an IR sensor. If these random targets are used in great quantity, not only can they hide the details of the target signatures, they can even hide the target altogether since the defense may not be able to tell whether a chaff or aerosol cloud contains a target or not. This method of defeating discrimination is known as masking.

Confidence in discrimination is much higher for reentry BMD systems than for midcourse systems. Lightweight masking objects are stripped off by the atmosphere: generally aerosols first, then balloons, and finally chaff. An effective reentry decoy must match both the trajectory and the signature of an RV. A physically large lightweight decoy will have greater deceleration because of drag than will a heavier RV of the same size; thus a lightweight reentry decoy must be smaller than the heavier RV it is to match. The signature of a reentry target includes that of the target itself and of the hot ionized wake behind it. The lower the discrimination altitude, the more difficult it is to build a decoy to match an RV trajectory and body and wake signatures. Electronic jamming can also be used to degrade the discrimination function and may be effective in conjunction with decoys. However, in this case, the attacker is depending on two types of penetration aids, both of which must work.

One final point to keep in mind about discrimination is that the attacker and defender may have some information regarding each other's systems. The attacker's decoys, maskers, and so on represent hardware that must be flight-tested and probably can be observed by the defender's intelligence-gathering systems. Although the defense sensors may be known to the attacker, their performance and especially their discrimination algorithms and the performance of these algorithms are not observable.

The next function of a BMD system is target interception. This function was the subject of the original BMD debate in the late 1950s, which focused on the question, Can a bullet hit a bullet? Experience with air defense systems has shown that an interceptor missile needs a substantial advantage in terms of speed to be able to hit an airplane. In the BMD case, however, the RV often is traveling twice as fast as the interceptor. The reason that BMD intercepts can nonetheless be made rather easily is that the target RV is on a predictable ballistic trajectory. Thus the defense interceptor does not have to chase the RV; rather, once the guidance sensor determines the RV's future trajectory, the interceptor's "mission" is to reach the intercept point when the RV gets there. In this sense, a BMD intercept is closer to a space satellite rendezvous than to an air defense intercept where the airplane is actively avoiding the interceptor.

The final BMD function is target kill, which in traditional BMD systems is accomplished by detonating a nuclear warhead on the interceptor at its point of closest approach to the target. Within the atmosphere, the RV is destroyed by blast or neutrons (or both). The blast wave can destroy the structure of the RV while the neutrons can penetrate this structure and destroy the nuclear warhead within. Outside the atmosphere, X rays are used for kill. When these are absorbed in thin layers of the RV heatshield they cause vaporization within the layers, which destroys the RV structure in much the same way that an explosion would.

The nontraditional BMD systems employ a variety of kill mechanisms. One is nonnuclear kill (NNK), which refers to direct collision with the interceptor or detonation of a fragmentation warhead in the path of the RV, either in reentry or exoatmospherically. Most simple/novel BMD systems use projectiles to impact on the RV in reentry. Dust defense relies on buried nuclear weapons to raise dust clouds to a high altitude in the path of incoming RVs. When an RV flies through such a dust cloud, its heatshield becomes eroded and it cannot survive reentry.

Boost-phase BMD systems can use either interceptor missiles with warheads or directed-energy weapons to kill the booster before it has deployed its RVs. The requirements for these nontraditional kill mechanisms are discussed later. It should be noted that the above list does not include all kill mechanisms or the trajectory regions in which they might be used.

The intercept and kill functions can be countered in two ways: by hardening the RV so it will survive a near miss and by increasing the miss-distance. Hardening offers little hope against nuclear-armed interceptors, although some nuclear hardening will prevent "multiple kill" and force the defense to use an interceptor for each RV. Hardening could be effective, however, against many of the NNK or directed-energy systems. A maneuvering RV can be used to increase the miss-distance, but this type of RV uses preprogrammed maneuvers rather than the responsive type of maneuver that a pilot makes to evade air defense interceptors. Unlike a pilot who detects that an interceptor is about to attack and maneuvers the aircraft in response to the interceptor, a maneuvering RV does not sense the interceptor. Rather it maneuvers at a preprogrammed time in the hope that the interceptor will not be able to respond to these maneuvers. This situation is more like trying to catch a fly ball on a very windy day than trying to catch a rabbit. Maneuvering RVs that use aerodynamic controls might be effective in reentry but are ineffective outside the atmosphere.

Traditional Terminal Defense

Terminal defense systems using ground-based radars and nuclear-armed interceptors operating against RVs in reentry have been under study and development in the United States for more than two decades.

In the 1960s these systems were designed primarily for the defense of cities; since then the emphasis in research and development (R&D) has shifted to the defense of the ICBM force. Recently, the Soviet Union developed similar components (see chapter 5). Despite the changes both in the application and sophistication of offense and defense technology, the basic concepts, the radar and interceptor requirements, and their performance relative to the threat have remained much the same.

This section covers some of the technical issues related to overall systems operations, including defense suppression attacks, blackout attacks, timelines, and coverage footprints. Radar and interceptor design is also discussed and some comparisons made between terminal BMD and defense against aircraft and tactical ballistic missiles.

If the offense is able to destroy the defense radar or interceptors, it can then attack its targets (cities or silos) as if they were undefended. From the keepout volumes and the goals of the attacker and defender in each situation, it is evident that the defense battery is a prime target in silo defense but not in city defense. A defense battery can only defend one city, and the defense goal is to prevent any RVs from penetrating the keepout volume for that city. If the defense components are more resistant to nuclear effects than the city itself, then destruction of the defense implies that the city keepout volume has been penetrated.

For silo defense, on the other hand, a single defense battery can defend many silos. The defense goal here is usually to save some small fraction of the silos, typically 10–50 percent. If the silos are attacked directly, they can be defended preferentially; that is, some silos can be defended heavily while others are not defended at all. If the attacker does not know the order of preference he must attack all silos as if they were defended heavily; thus the cost of the attack is raised significantly since RVs are wasted in overkilling undefended silos. However, if the attacker shoots at the defense battery, it must be defended. This requires "subtractive defense," in which every RV is intercepted (city defense is by its very nature subtractive). If the offense exhausts the defense stockpile of interceptors, it can then shoot at the now-undefended silos without having to worry about preferential defense. Since the defense radars are in general fewer in number, higher in cost, and lower in hardness than the silos they are defending, they are particularly vulnerable to defense suppression attacks.

Much of the effort in ICBM defense has been devoted to making a

Figure 3-4. *Options for Radar Blackout Attack*

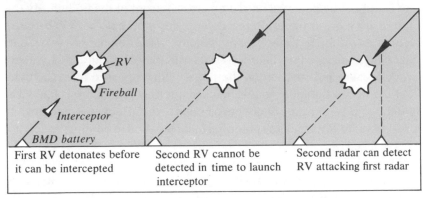

| First RV detonates before it can be intercepted | Second RV cannot be detected in time to launch interceptor | Second radar can detect RV attacking first radar |

defense suppression attack more costly to the attacker, principally by means of radar proliferation and deceptive basing. Proliferation means that four or five radars, say, will be deployed to do the job of two, and a randomly selected pair will be preferentially defended. Since the offense does not know which radars are being defended, it must attack all of them heavily. (If the offense is willing to adopt the risky tactic of launching two attack waves, using the first to discover which targets are defended and the second to concentrate fire on the defended targets—"offensive shoot-look-shoot"—preferential defense is degraded.) Deceptive basing is analogous to the multiple protective shelter (MPS) approach that has been considered for the MX missile. In the BMD case, the radar would be moved periodically among a number of hardened shelters and the attacker would not know the location at the time of launching an attack. Proliferation and deceptive basing can also be employed to protect defense interceptors. It should be noted that, while technically attractive, deceptive basing of BMD components would violate the terms of the ABM Treaty of 1972.

Radar proliferation and deceptive basing are also useful against a radar blackout attack. When a nuclear burst detonates in the atmosphere, the intense heat ionizes the air within a kilometer or two of the burst. This ionization around the fireball persists for tens of seconds and is opaque to radar signals. A radar blackout attack exploits this phenomenon (see figure 3-4). It is particularly effective against a single fixed radar. In this type of attack, an RV (called a precursor) is detonated outside the maximum intercept capability of the defense; a subsequent

RV is targeted at the radar on a trajectory passing through the fireball, but it will not be detected until it emerges in front of the fireball. By this time it may be too late for the defense to intercept the RV before it detonates within the radar keepout volume. If the defense has two radars that can cooperate (see figure 3-4), this simple blackout attack will not work because information on the targets can be passed from the radar that can see to the radar that is blacked out (this procedure is known as "netting"). With deceptively based radars, the attacker would have to use precursor RVs for each potential radar location to be sure the defense was blacked out.

Deceptive basing is near one end of the spectrum of radar mobility. At the other end are the BMD systems deployed to date—the U.S. Safeguard system and the Soviet Moscow system—which use large fixed radars that take years to deploy and involve much on-site assembly. The forms of mobility or transportability have important consequences for arms race stability and arms control verification, as well as for defense system effectiveness. Recently there has been a trend toward more rapidly deployable radars such as the U.S. Site Defense radar for which much of the radar hardware was factory assembled and carried in several trailers that could be rapidly interconnected in the field. The U.S. Sentry radar currently being developed would be completely factory built and assembled. The Soviet Union is also working on more rapidly deployable BMD radars.

To avoid defense suppression or blackout attacks, the radar must be capable of moving to another location in the time it takes the offense to locate the radar and retarget its RVs. A rapidly deployable BMD that would represent a potential treaty-breakout possibility might be moved from factories or warehouses into the field in a year or less. From the standpoint of radar design, mobile or deceptive radar is more constrained than a rapidly deployable radar, which in turn is more constrained than a built-in-place radar.

The way that a reentry BMD system operates can be seen from figure 3-5, which shows schematic timelines for city defense and missile silo defense for a simplified case of a single defense battery (located at point A) containing a radar and colocated interceptors. An analysis of these timelines indicates how defense coverage footprints are obtained. The defense radar may be limited in its detection range by its sensitivity and in its detection altitude by the need to wait for lightweight decoys to burn

Figure 3-5. *Terminal Defense Timelines for City and Silo Defenses*

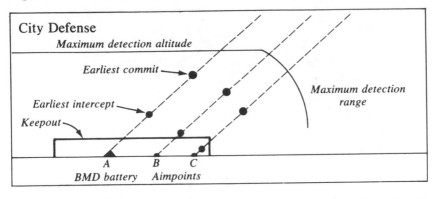

City Defense

Maximum detection altitude

Earliest commit

Earliest intercept

Keepout

Maximum detection range

A   B   C

BMD battery   Aimpoints

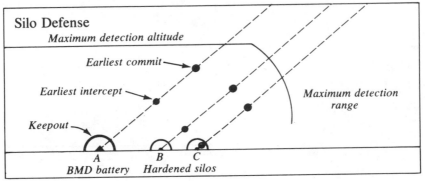

Silo Defense

Maximum detection altitude

Earliest commit

Earliest intercept

Keepout

Maximum detection range

A   B   C

BMD battery   Hardened silos

up or slow down. A family of trajectories attacking the defended targets is considered in this example. Each trajectory is marked with a point corresponding to the earliest interceptor commit. The earliest intercept point for an interceptor launched when the RV is at the commit point is also indicated on each trajectory. The earliest intercept may occur outside or inside the keepout volume (or even after the RV has impacted). The defense coverage footprint is defined as the locus of target points for which it is possible to intercept RVs (on any threatening trajectory) outside the keepout volume. For example, points A and B in figure 3-5 are within the defense footprint but point C is not. For points on the edge of the footprint, the battlespace (see figure 3-3) is zero and the defense has no margin for error. Within the footprint, the battlespace is increased and the defense becomes more confident. The size of the footprint is determined by the radar performance (range, altitude, track time, and

Figure 3-6. *Phased-Array Operation*

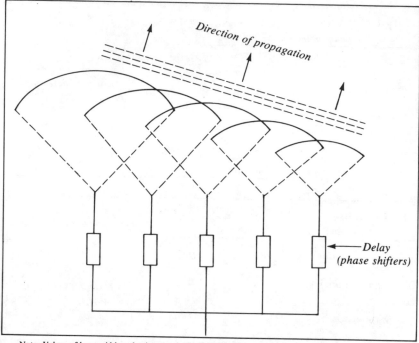

Note: Values of beamwidth and gain are calculated as follows:

$$\text{Beamwidth} \sim \frac{\lambda}{D} \sim \frac{2}{\sqrt{N}}$$

$$\text{Gain} \sim 4\pi \frac{D^2}{\lambda^2} \sim \pi N$$

where D = Antenna diameter
       N = Number of elements (in two dimensions)
       λ = Wavelength.

so on) and the interceptor performance (velocity, acceleration, and so on).

Terminal defense BMD radars are almost always phased arrays for two main reasons: they are resistant to nuclear effects, and they are able to track and handle a number of targets simultaneously. A phased array points its beam in different directions electronically (see figure 3-6) rather than by moving the antenna mechanically. The radar antenna is a plane face composed of thousands of smaller fixed antennas called elements. The signal to each element is delayed electronically by a given time interval relative to the adjacent element. These delays cause the combined signal from all the elements to add up (to be in phase) only in the desired direction.[2]

This technique for phasing multiple antennas has been used in communication, radio astronomy, and radar for many years, but the new development of the last twenty years has been electronic beam steering, which can be computer controlled in a very small fraction of a second and which makes it possible for one radar to conduct the entire BMD engagement. It can simultaneously cover the search volume at a given rate, perform tracking and discrimination on all targets that are detected, and guide interceptors to objects identified as threatening RVs. This capability is particularly important in reentry, where the entire engagement may take ten seconds or less. Mechanically steered dish antennas could not do all these tasks at the same time.

A typical phased array has its elements spaced by half the radar wavelength and can point its beam anywhere within about 60° of the perpendicular to the radar face. With this type of antenna, three or four faces are required to cover all possible directions. The signals from all the antenna elements will be in phase only over a limited span of angles, called the "beamwidth." The radar energy is concentrated into the beamwidth, which is given by the ratio of the radar wavelength and the antenna diameter. The larger the antenna, the smaller the span of angles in which the elements will be in phase. (Figure 3-6 indicates the relations among several antenna parameters.)

It is also of interest to see how the radar search and track performance is related to other radar parameters through the "radar equation." A radar works by transmitting energy into the search volume where it is reflected off the target. Some of the energy is reflected back to the radar and collected by the antenna. If the collected energy is sufficiently greater than the noise energy, the target will be detected.

The "size" of radar required to perform a given search job is measured by its power-aperture product (PA). This represents the product of the average radar power and the area of the antenna aperture. This product is limited by the ABM Treaty to 3 Mw-m^2 for the smaller radars. For search, the PA required is proportional to the fourth power of the maximum search range and the angular extent of the search volume. It

2. In practice, since the radar signal is almost periodic, the time delay needed at each element can be taken as the appropriate fraction (or phase) of a radar cycle.

is inversely proportional to the time permitted to conduct search and the radar cross section of the target to be detected.[3] In practice, the time allowed for search is proportional to the range, so that PA actually varies as the cube of the maximum search range. Thus doubling the radar detection range necessitates an eightfold increase in radar power aperture.

For search, the radar performance is not dependent on radar frequency. The tracking performance, however, improves as the wavelength gets smaller since the radar does not have to spread its energy all over the search volume but can concentrate it into a narrow beamwidth.[4]

The various forms of the radar equation lead to the general conclusion that long wavelength (or low frequency) radars generally require fewer antenna elements, are less costly, are less accurate, and are more suited to the search function. Short wavelength (or high frequency) radars have the opposite characteristics and are more suited to the track function. Wavelength selection depends on the specific requirements of the search and track job as well as other considerations such as discrimination performance, susceptibility to blackout and jamming, and the need for mobility. (Jamming resistance, blackout resistance, and mobility favor

---

3. If a radar with average power, P, scans a field of view, Ω, in a time, t, at a range, R, the energy density on the target will be $Pt/\Omega R^2$. The field of view or solid angle, Ω, is proportional to the elevation and azimuth extent of the search volume. For a radar that must search in all directions and from horizon to zenith, $\Omega = 2\pi$. The fraction of this incident energy density reflected by the target back toward the radar is characterized by the radar cross section, σ, and is $\sigma/4\pi R^2$. The total energy collected by an antenna of aperture or area, A, is thus $(Pt/\Omega R^2)$ $(\sigma/4\pi R^2)$ (A). This received signal is reduced by a loss factor, L, and compared with the radar noise, kT, where k is Boltzmann's constant $(1.38 \times 10^{-23}$ J/°K) and T is the effective noise temperature of the radar. Since the returned signal is very weak, it is only the fact that the radar noise level is so low (owing to the smallness of Boltzmann's constant) that makes radar feasible. The resulting signal-to-noise ratio is

$$S/N = PAt\sigma/4\pi R^4\Omega kTL;$$

this must be above a minimum threshold, typically 30, for confident detection. This equation can be rewritten as

$$PA/kTL = 4\pi R^4\Omega(S/N)/t\sigma.$$

In this form, the left-hand side contains radar parameters, while the right-hand side contains BMD system parameters.

4. In this case, the term Ω/t can be replaced by $(prf \cdot \lambda^2/A)$, where prf (pulse repetition frequency) is the number of radar pulses per second and λ is the radar wavelength. The resulting tracking radar equation is

$$PA^2/kTL\lambda^2 = 4\pi R^4 prf(S/N)/\sigma.$$

Figure 3-7. *Terminal BMD Interceptor Flyout, by Burnout Velocity and Acceleration*

Flyout distance (km)

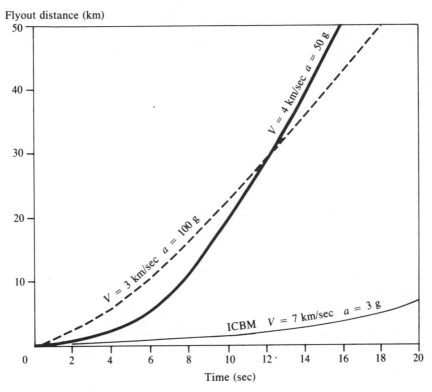

Note: Variables are defined as follows:
V = Burnout velocity
a = Acceleration (g = acceleration of gravity = 10 m/sec²).

short wavelengths; discrimination performance could go either way.) There is no optimum wavelength for all missions, and terminal BMD radars used in the past have ranged over a factor of ten in wavelength.

Another major factor affecting the defense coverage besides radar performance is the interceptor "flyout" capability. Whether or not a target point can be defended depends on whether the interceptor can fly to the intercept point before the RV flies from the commit point to the keepout volume. The interceptor flyout capability is determined primarily by its boost acceleration and its burnout velocity. From the flyout of the two hypothetical interceptors in figure 3-7 it is evident that the higher-acceleration, lower-velocity interceptor is faster for short-range inter-

Figure 3-8. *Terminal Defense Footprints*

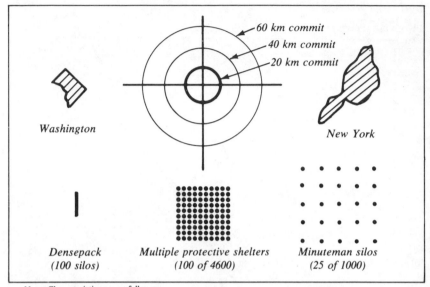

Note: Characteristics are as follows:
—Interceptor: 3 km/sec; 100 g
—RV: 30° reentry
—Keepout altitude: 5 km

cepts while the higher-velocity, lower-acceleration interceptor is faster for long-range intercepts. The ICBM flyout shown for purposes of comparison is obviously inappropriate for reentry intercept.

Because of its fuel requirement, an interceptor with high burnout velocity will be much heavier than one with the same payload but low burnout velocity. In addition, it must be designed to handle greater heating caused by atmospheric drag. An interceptor with high acceleration must have a stronger structure and components than one with low acceleration. It must also use high-burn-rate propellants. A reentry interceptor is essentially a controlled explosion. It weighs as much as a large pickup truck and at 100 g of acceleration can go from 0 to 60 mph in about 30 msec (0.03 sec). The interceptor must be ready to launch on only a few seconds' notice.

Given the radar and interceptor characteristics, it is possible to determine the defense footprint. This is done in figure 3-8 for a high-acceleration interceptor and a moderately lofted RV trajectory with commit altitude as a parameter. Also shown to the same scale are various targets that might be defended. It should be noted that the keepout altitude can be lower for hard targets than for cities, so the footprints for silo defense would be slightly larger than shown. The three commit altitudes parameterizing the footprints may be regarded as low, moderate, and high risk in terms of being able to perform detection and discrimination by the time the RV reaches the commit altitude.

As can be seen in figure 3-8, for the closely spaced silo deployments (multiple protective shelters and Densepack), one defense battery can cover many silos. For the current Minuteman silos, a battery located at one silo may just barely cover an adjacent silo. A small city can be covered by a single battery but a large city will probably require multiple batteries; in no case can a battery in one city defend a nearby city with operation in reentry.

An underlying assumption in the calculation of defense footprints is that if an interceptor can get to an RV, it can kill the RV. For interceptors with nuclear warheads, this is generally the case; the ground-based radar tells the interceptor where to go, guiding it during flight to its intercept point with an error that is small compared with the warhead kill radius. The recent interest in nonnuclear kill (NNK) interceptors carrying fragmentation warheads has led to the resurrection of the question, Can a bullet (or a hand grenade) hit a bullet? Ground radars probably have insufficient accuracy to guide the in-flight NNK interceptor, and most approaches to NNK use homing sensors on board the interceptor as supplements to ground radars to reduce the miss-distance. Considerable work has been done on exoatmospheric NNK, and recently the level of effort on NNK in reentry has increased. NNK offers significant advantages in terms of warhead availability, no requirement for complex nuclear release procedures, public acceptability, and the potential for realistic testing. However, significant technological developments must take place before these advantages can be realized. Consequently any near-term deployment of BMD would use nuclear warheads.

One final topic to be mentioned in connection with terminal defense systems is that of surface-to-air missile (SAM) upgrades or antitactical ballistic missile (ATBM) systems used against strategic missiles. Both SAMs and ATBMs are permitted by the ABM Treaty but neither may be used or even tested against strategic missiles (ICBMs and SLBMs). Figure 3-9 illustrates representative trajectories for ICBMs, SLBMs, TBMs, and aircraft and typical velocity-versus-altitude curves for these objects. Since a long-range TBM trajectory is virtually identical to a short-range SLBM trajectory, an ATBM system would, almost by necessity, be capable of countering SLBMs.

A comparison of anti-aircraft and antimissile requirements is consid-

Figure 3-9. *Typical Trajectories and Velocity-versus-Altitude Curves for Selected Missiles and Aircraft*

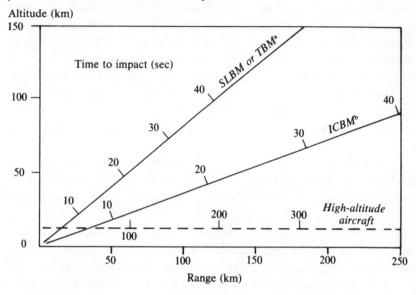

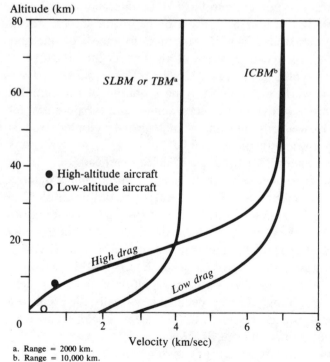

a. Range = 2000 km.
b. Range = 10,000 km.

erably more complicated. Figure 3-9 indicates that a SAM capable of intercepting high-altitude high-speed aircraft should be able to intercept a high-drag (blunt) ICBM; this possibility was a major concern during the first round of the strategic arms limitation talks, when the U.S. missile inventory included large numbers of high-drag RVs. For more modern low-drag (streamlined) RVs, the SAM capability must be evaluated on a case-by-case basis. SAM systems cover a broad spectrum from shoulder-launched heat-seeking missiles to long-range radar-controlled interceptors carrying nuclear warheads and operating in an automated mode. The former have essentially no BMD capability whereas the latter could have significant effectiveness in the appropriate circumstances. The SAM problem is easier than BMD because of the slower speed and greater vulnerability of aircraft but harder than BMD because aircraft try to evade the interceptors and must be detected at treetop level.

As yet, no one has developed an unambiguous scheme for defining an effective SAM system without a BMD capability. The problem becomes particularly difficult when air-launched ballistic missiles like the short-range attack missile (SRAM) on U.S. B-52 bombers are included within the scope of SAM applications.

Traditional Exoatmospheric Defense

Exoatmospheric BMD systems have a history almost as long as terminal defense systems. The Sentinel system recommended for deployment in 1967 was primarily an area defense system designed to protect the entire United States against a light attack from the People's Republic of China. The system that was actually deployed (Safeguard) used many of the same components but for a different purpose, defense of our Minuteman ICBMs. Both of these systems used large ground-based radars (the PAR) and long-range nuclear-armed interceptors (the Spartan). The Soviet Moscow system operates in a similar manner, using long-range Galosh interceptors.

There are two reasons for using exoatmospheric defense instead of (or in addition to) reentry defense. The first is to cover a large area with a single defense battery. As noted earlier, a terminal defense battery can cover at most a single large city; to cover the entire country would require thousands of such batteries. The second reason is to augment a

Figure 3-10. *Area Defense Timeline*

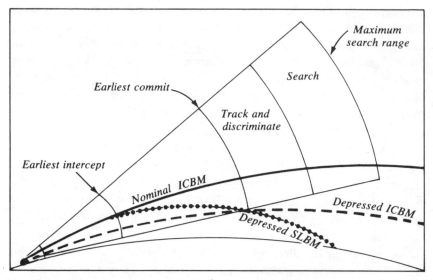

terminal defense system with an extra level of defense for high-value targets. For example, if the exoatmospheric and reentry layers of the BMD system independently have a 90 percent chance of intercepting a single RV, then the RV only has a 1 percent chance of penetrating both layers. (Chapter 4 explains how the survival probability of multiple targets suffering attack by multiple RVs works out with layered defense.)

From the timeline for an exoatmospheric radar system depicted in figure 3-10 it is apparent that depressed trajectories and SLBMs are detected later than lofted trajectories, and consequently, the interceptor coverage is less in these cases. An idea of the numbers that should go in the timeline can be obtained from figure 3-11, which illustrates sample flyouts for exoatmospheric intercepts. Here velocity is more important than acceleration, and the effects of gravity on the interceptor trajectory must be included. Several hundred seconds of interceptor flight are obviously required to achieve significant area coverage (although less time is needed for point defense). Combining this flyout time with the fact that intercepts are made typically 50 sec before impact gives a required commit range of 2000 km or greater. Adding 50–100 sec for radar search, track, and discrimination gives a maximum detection range close to 3000 km. To obtain larger defense coverage, even greater detection ranges are required. Even if radars were sensitive enough to

Figure 3-11. *Exoatmospheric Interceptor Flyout*

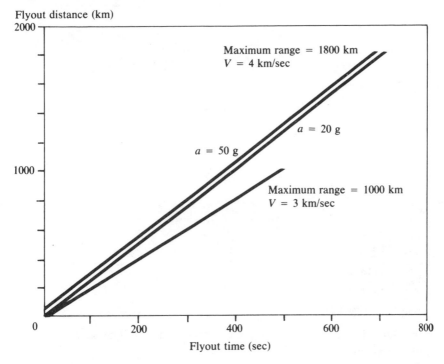

Flyout distance (km)

Maximum range = 1800 km
V = 4 km/sec

a = 20 g

a = 50 g

Maximum range = 1000 km
V = 3 km/sec

Flyout time (sec)

detect attacking objects at these ranges, such coverage may not be achievable against SLBMs or depressed ICBMs because of horizon limitations.

As noted earlier, the size of a search radar (measured by its power-aperture product) varies as the third power of the detection range. Thus an area defense radar with a detection range of 3000 km must have 1000 times the power aperture of a terminal defense radar that detects at a range of 300 km. Examples of such radars are the U.S. PAR or the Soviet Hen House and Dog House. Such radars are too large to be mobile and too expensive to be deployed in large numbers. Consequently, they become very attractive targets to either destroy, black out, or jam. In addition, lightweight exoatmospheric objects such as chaff or balloon decoys can pose severe discrimination problems for such radars.

Against a limited attack not using penetration aids or defense suppression tactics, an exoatmospheric defense system can provide significant area coverage. Figure 3-12 presents the footprint of such a system for a nominal and a depressed ICBM trajectory. The footprint is elongated

Figure 3-12. *Area Defense Coverage Footprints*

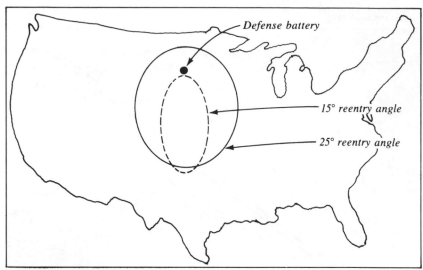

Note: Characteristics are as follows:
—Radar range = 3000 km
—Search and track time = 50 sec
—Interceptor velocity = 4 km/sec
—Interceptor acceleration = 20 g

behind the defense battery since RVs impacting there can be intercepted almost overhead.

In the absence of area BMD, any country possessing several ICBMs can destroy several major cities. To achieve this capability against a thin area defense, it would be necessary to build many more missiles to exhaust or leak through the defense, to develop penetration aids to defeat the defense sensors, or to achieve the precise coordination between missiles required for a blackout attack. However, once such an effort was made, an exoatmospheric BMD using large fixed radars would be quite vulnerable.

Advanced Exoatmospheric Defense

Recently the United States has tended to favor the use of passive infrared sensors and interceptors carrying homing sensors and nonnuclear warheads for exoatmospheric BMD. Although these systems have been applied primarily to Minuteman or MX defense, they could also be used for defense of cities.

Figure 3-13. *Overlay Defense*

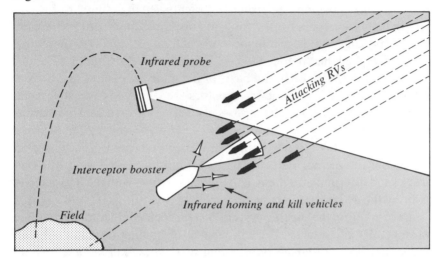

Infrared sensors offer a number of potential advantages. They are small enough to be carried in aircraft or missiles, do not give away their location because they are passive (that is, they only collect radiation and do not emit any), and their "size" requirements vary as R^2 rather than R^3. However, there is considerable uncertainty regarding their ability to perform discrimination. Lightweight objects such as balloons or aerosol particles may be very effective decoys or maskers.

Figure 3-13 illustrates a typical system configuration. (The reader should note that numerous variations have been studied.) The target acquisition function involves scanning a large field of view at a long range with a fairly large sensor that is too expensive to carry on each interceptor. Consequently, most exoatmospheric BMD systems postulate a small number of acquisition sensors carried on aircraft or missiles. The aircraft can remain on station for hours, while a missile can stay aloft for only a few tens of minutes before it must be replaced. The choice between aircraft and missile platforms depends on the expected duration of the attack and the sensor requirements. A satellite platform is less attractive since a high-altitude satellite would view targets against an earth background and too many low altitude satellites would be required to ensure favorable viewing geometry.

Generally the sensors operate by scanning the field of view at a fixed rate and recording all detections in a "track-while-scan" mode. Objects are not tracked individually; rather, measurements are recorded whenever the sensor happens to be looking at the object. Measurements of target angular position and radiance (brightness) in a number of wavelength bands are taken for tracking and discrimination. After about 100 sec of tracking and discrimination on each target, the system control program (called the "battle manager") decides whether or not the target should be intercepted. On the basis of the attack geometry and timing, numbers of exoatmospheric interceptors are launched toward nominal intercept points. These interceptors also carry infrared sensors (generally smaller than the acquisition sensors) that scan small regions of space looking for the RVs to which they have been assigned. The sensor on board the interceptor detects targets within its limited field of view, tracks and discriminates them, and associates them with the RVs handed over by the acquisition sensor.

Depending on the specific system design, each interceptor carries one or several "kill vehicles," each capable of homing on and killing an individual RV. (Although any testing of multiple-kill vehicles would violate the ABM Treaty, the technology can be developed using single-kill vehicle tests.) Each kill vehicle is separated from the interceptor and fires its own small rocket motor to divert it toward a nominal intercept point with the RV to which it is assigned. The kill vehicle also carries a small infrared sensor to acquire its intended RV and a computer that commands maneuvers to home on the RV. The kill vehicle either physically hits the RV or deploys a nonnuclear fragmentation warhead when it gets close enough. The RV is destroyed by hypervelocity impact of the fragments. The kinetic energy of impact is very large even for small fragments since the relative velocity is on the order of 10 km/sec. An RV struck by a fragment would probably suffer enough damage not to reenter at high velocity, so that a terminal defense layer (if used) would not waste an interceptor on it.

Exoatmospheric infrared systems vary greatly depending on the sensor platforms, type of battle management, type of kill vehicles, and number carried per interceptor. However, it should be kept in mind that, whereas large ground-based radar systems have been fully tested and even deployed, infrared systems are still in the research and development stage. Flight tests of discrimination, tracking, and homing have been conducted, but these have been experimental rather than prototype tests of weapons systems. Considerable work would have to be done before such systems could be deployed.

Some of the design issues in exoatmospheric infrared (also known as "optical") systems are reflected in the technical requirements of sensor and interceptor operation. Infrared sensors operate on the thermal radiation emitted by any object that is above absolute zero in temperature. For a perfectly absorbing (black) body, this radiation is emitted in the form of photons (particles of electromagnetic radiation), the number and wavelength of which are given by the Planck radiation formula.[5] Examples of thermal radiation are plotted in figure 3-14, which shows that a target at room temperature (300°K or 27°C) emits most of its photons at a wavelength of 10 μm. This peak wavelength is inversely proportional to the temperature; for example, the sun's surface, where $T = 6000°K$, has its peak in the visible region at $\lambda = 0.5$ μm. The earth, and RVs launched from the earth, have temperatures around 300°K. A black target with 1-m^2 surface area at 300°K emits about 2×10^{21} photons/sec in a 1 μm band centered at 10 μm (a reflective target will emit fewer). Since the energy of each photon is 2×10^{-20} J, the total energy radiated in this wavelength band is only about 40 w.[6] These photons are emitted in all directions; less than 1 out of every 10^{15}, or 10^6 photons/sec, will be incident on a 10-cm diameter telescope aperture at a range of 1000 km. The fraction collected varies with $(D/R)^2$ so that a 20-cm telescope would collect the same number of photons in the same time at a range of 2000 km. The sensitivity of an infrared sensor depends not only on the number of incident photons from the target, but also on how long the sensor can look at the target and the intensity of the unwanted photons from the background. In this respect, infrared detectors are analogous to cameras. The photons incident on the telescope aperture are focused on the focal plane of the sensor just as in a camera. However, instead of containing film, the focal plane contains thousands of detectors, which are solid state devices that convert photons into electrical signals.

The minimum effective beamwidth of an optical sensor is on the order

5. The equation for these curves is

$$N = \frac{2\pi c}{\lambda^4} \frac{1}{\exp(ch/\lambda kT) - 1},$$

where N is the number of photons in a 1 micrometer (μm) band centered at wavelength λ, emitted per second per square centimeter of surface area of a target at absolute temperature T. In this equation c is the velocity of light (3×10^{10} cm/sec), h is Planck's constant (6.6×10^{-34} J/sec), and k is Boltzmann's constant used in the radar equation. The energy of a single photon is hc/λ.

6. The fact that h is so small and individual photons can be detected makes long-range infrared sensors possible (although by no means simple).

Figure 3-14. *Thermal Radiation from Targets*

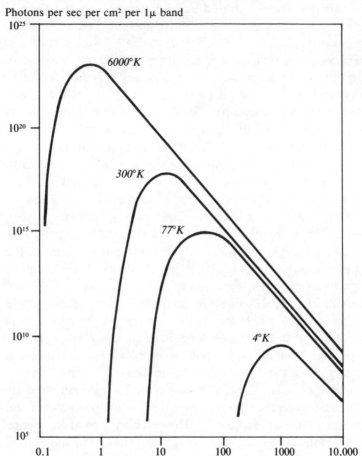

Photons per sec per cm² per 1μ band

Wavelength (μm)

of λ/D, just as for a radar, but since λ is so small the beamwidths are much narrower. For a 10-cm telescope at 10-μm wavelength, the beamwidth is about 100 μradians or 0.006 degrees. The beamwidth is a measure of the field of view that is focused onto a single detector. The 100-μradian case corresponds to the field of view seen by looking through a soda straw 50 m long.

The total field of view that the acquisition sensor must cover is given by the search volume and is on the order of 30° in elevation by 90° in azimuth. This volume contains almost 10^8 individual 100-μradian beam positions. Since it is not practical to put that many detectors on the focal plane, some means of scanning the focal plane (or the entire sensor) across the field of view must be used. If 5000 detectors are placed in a line on the focal plane to cover the elevation extent of the focal plane and scanned in azimuth over 90° every 10 sec, then it will take about ⅔ msec for a detector to scan across the target. During this time, about 600 photons (with wavelengths between 9.5 and 10.5 μm) from the target will strike the detector. Whether or not this is sufficient for detection depends on the efficiency of the detector and the competing background radiation.

The detector itself will emit thermal radiation appropriate to its temperature. The smallest that a detector can be is approximately one wavelength by one wavelength, although in practice they are much larger. Such a small detector would emit about 5×10^{10} photons (9.5 to 10.5 μm) per second if at room temperature, 5×10^4 photons per second if at liquid nitrogen temperature (77°K), and approximately 10^{-143} photons per second if at liquid helium temperature (4°K). Thus the detectors must be supercooled to avoid having their own thermal radiation swamp the desired signal.

Sensors looking toward space see very low levels of background radiation around the targets since the equivalent temperature of empty sky is only 3°K. However this background is supplemented by the stars, the earth, and the sun. With a narrow beamwidth, the sensor is almost never looking directly at one of these sources, but the effective background level will be determined by the ability to keep the radiation from these objects from entering the sensor obliquely. A sensor will also operate against very high background levels if it is looking near a nuclear burst.

Sensors carried on aircraft have to cope with a more serious background problem arising from the natural infrared radiance of the atmosphere. The number of background photons might be much larger than the number of target photons, but the fact that the background is nearly constant might still permit target detection. However, an aircraft-borne sensor is less sensitive than a missile-borne sensor and must be larger to achieve equivalent performance.

Exoatmospheric discrimination is based on spectra similar to those in figure 3-14 for the various attacking objects. By measuring the photon flux or radiance from a target in different wavelength bands, it is possible to fit a Planck curve (shown in figure 3-14) to these data with a given value of T, the "effective" temperature. Changes in the radiance and temperature with time can give information on the shape and motion of the target and its thermal properties. Departures from the ideal "Planck curve" spectra can give information on the surface properties of the target.

The infrared signature of a target is a combination of the "thermal" or "emitted" signature calculated from the target size and temperature and the "reflected" signature that arises primarily from infrared radiation from the earth (called "earthshine"), which is reflected from the target and collected by the sensor. This combined signature is a complicated function (of the sensor viewing geometry, the time of day and season, and the characteristics of the earth beneath the target) that makes it very difficult to assess the performance of either decoys or discrimination techniques with any confidence.

The most significant feature of the kill vehicles carried on the interceptor booster is their ability to perform homing and nonnuclear kill. The kill vehicle must divert from the trajectory it is put on by the interceptor booster to a trajectory that will carry it to the general vicinity of the target. This divert takes a certain amount of time that must be accommodated in the system timeline. The time can be shortened by increasing the kill vehicle's divert velocity (which requires more propellant) or by reducing the divert distance (which may allow fewer kill vehicles per interceptor).

After divert, the kill vehicle sensor acquires the target and carries out homing. Although the RV velocity may be much greater than the kill vehicle velocity, the use of proportional navigation makes the homing function fairly straightforward. Figure 3-15 shows how proportional navigation works. If the target and kill vehicle are on a collision course, the sensor line-of-sight from the kill vehicle to the target will be line AA'. At a later time the kill vehicle will have moved to point B and the target to point B'. Since BB' is parallel to AA', the line-of-sight direction will remain constant. Should the line-of-sight direction change, the kill vehicle will maneuver to an extent proportional to this change, to reduce the change to zero. Proportional navigation works very well for constant velocity targets even if they are faster than the interceptor, as indicated. For intercepting maneuvering targets such as aircraft, the assumptions of proportional navigation are not valid and the interceptor generally needs greater velocity.

Figure 3-15. *Proportional Navigation*

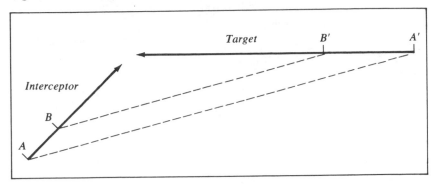

This section has concentrated on several technical points related to infrared sensors and homing interceptors. Added to these hardware concerns are the complexities of the data-processing requirements for these systems. Since many problems can arise because of the very large number of targets and the need to operate in a nuclear environment, these systems cannot be fully and realistically tested. This is not the case for the systems discussed in the next section.

Simple/Novel Systems

In recent years there has been significant interest in so-called simple/novel systems for defense of Minuteman silos. The hoped-for virtues of these systems are that they would use existing (or easily developed) hardware, would be inexpensive, and could be deployed very rapidly. Examples of such existing hardware include anti-aircraft machine guns ("Gatling guns") or missiles. Examples of easily developed hardware include multiple unguided rocket launchers (Swarmjets), large fragmentation warheads (Porcupines), and small short-range radars. Most simple/novel systems have a number of common characteristics: they are intended for the defense of individual missile silos rather than cities; they use nonnuclear kill techniques; they use relatively small and inexpensive radars; and they tend to substitute firepower for sophisticated interceptor guidance. These systems do not claim to hold off a massive attack with high confidence; rather they attempt to raise the number of RVs that must be used to attack a silo and to increase the uncertainty regarding the success of the attack.

These systems differ primarily in the nature of the weapons used to kill attacking RVs, which could be projectiles fired from guns, projectiles launched explosively, multiple unguided rockets, or guided rockets. The final category of guided rockets has more in common with traditional terminal defense using nonnuclear kill interceptors and will not be considered further here.

These systems may all be thought of as "point-in-space" systems rather than guided interceptor systems similar to those described earlier, in which the tracking radar continues to give radio guidance to the interceptor as it flies toward the target. Point-in-space systems work by tracking the RVs and selecting nominal intercept points outside the defended keepout region. This predicted intercept point has an associated uncertainty volume because of sensor measurement errors and uncertainty in the future trajectory of the RV. A sufficient number of projectiles or rockets are then fired to cover this entire uncertainty volume in a pattern dense enough to ensure hitting the RV.

The requirements for these systems can be obtained either by working backward from intercept or forward from target acquisition; here the backward method is used. As an example, consider a salvo of unguided rockets (Swarmjets). Essentially the same analysis applies to machine gun bullets or explosively launched fragments. To kill an RV takes a certain number of projectiles having a given mass and velocity; these are elements of what is known as a "lethality criterion." The lethality criterion is sensitive to a number of target and engagement geometry parameters. The details of the lethality criterion for RVs are only partly understood at present; however, it is known that the effectiveness of many simple/novel systems depends on these details. If it is granted that a "lethal" projectile can be defined, the next job is to put as many of these as practicable into a pattern in the path of the RV and to ensure that the spatial density of projectiles in this pattern is high enough for the RV to hit at least one of them. The number of projectiles that can be fired depends on how they are launched, on the rate of fire of a launcher, and on the number of launchers deployed. The size of the pattern is determined by the accuracy of the projectile launch.

Given the size of the pattern that can be achieved and the time it takes the projectiles to fly to the intercept point, the commit point is determined, as is the accuracy with which the intercept point must be known at the time of commit. This prediction accuracy varies with the radar measurement accuracy, the length of track, and the length of prediction as follows:

$$\text{Prediction error} \sim \text{Measurement error} \times \left(\frac{\text{Predict time}}{\text{Track time}}\right).$$

The quality of the radar track depends on the accuracy of a single radar measurement and the length of time the target has been in track. With only a very short track, the radar can tell where the target is but not where it is going. Once the projectiles are launched, they cannot make use of additional radar measurements (this is characteristic of point-in-space systems). At projectile commit, the estimate of the intercept point is based on extrapolation of the radar-tracking data. The longer into the future this extrapolation must be made, the less accurate it will be.

A number of factors drive these systems toward defense of hard targets with fast projectiles. The prediction time is essentially the projectile flyout time given by dividing the keepout radius by the projectile velocity. The commit range is given by backing up the RV trajectory by the flyout time. As the commit range increases, both the radar measurement error and the prediction time tend to increase and many more projectiles are required to cover the intercept point uncertainty.

One important consideration for these systems is that the properties of the projectile cloud are statistical rather than deterministic. Even if the projectile pattern is very dense and the RV prediction very accurate, there is some chance that enough projectiles will not hit the RV. Conversely, even with a sparse pattern and poor prediction, there is a chance that the RV will be killed. Figure 3-16 shows, for example, the probability of hitting the RV with at least one projectile if 100 projectiles are fired as a function of the ratio of the prediction error to the vulnerable radius of the RV. The prediction error is characterized by the CEP, the circle containing the RV 50 percent of the time. In each case, the projectile pattern size has been selected to maximize the hit probability and the individual projectiles are assumed to be randomly located within the pattern.

For the defense of a missile silo, the keepout radius is a little less than 1 km, the projectile flyout time is 1–2 sec, the prediction error and pattern radius are a few meters (implying a projectile aiming accuracy of a few milliradians). In the absence of any countermeasures, it is likely

Figure 3-16. *Effectiveness of a System of 100 Projectiles*

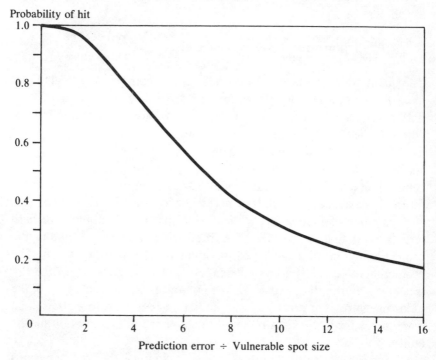

Probability of hit

Prediction error ÷ Vulnerable spot size

that these requirements can be met and such a system could hit an RV. If the defense thinks it can achieve a reasonable hit probability (on the order of 0.7 or 0.8), the attacker, making more conservative estimates of defense firepower and sensor accuracy, and needing a high probability of penetration, might credit the system with greater capability.

As a result, the attacker would probably not be satisfied just to shoot at the silos and hope to penetrate by leakage. A more attractive alternative is to take active steps to degrade the system's effectiveness. One approach is to attack the radars and projectile launchers. These would be much softer than the missile silos and require keepout ranges on the order of 5–10 km (corresponding to 10–50 psi). For these longer ranges, the flight time (and prediction time) is a factor of 5–10 higher and, for the same pattern size, both the sensor accuracy and the projectile aiming accuracy must be much better. With a longer projectile flyout time, the commit range and thus the radar detection range must be much greater, requiring a much larger radar. When all these factors are combined, it seems very unlikely, even from the attacker's view, that any simple/

novel system could prevent an attack on its own defense components. By devoting one or two RVs to suppressing each defense battery, the attacker could then attack the silos as if they were undefended. A potential counter to this attack is to use "pop-up" defense wherein replacement radars and projectile launchers are stored in hardened silos until the original defense components are destroyed. The replacement components are then "popped up" in time to handle the next wave of attacking RVs. The required hardness and pop-up time depend on the specific attack scenario.

A second approach to penetrating simple/novel systems is to use a hostile nuclear environment to degrade the projectile's aiming accuracy. Nuclear bursts produce wind velocities of tens and even hundreds of meters per second that last for tens of seconds. Since the projectiles are not guided after launch, these winds can displace the projectile pattern by many times the diameter of the projectile pattern, reducing the hit probability essentially to zero. The wind environment is very complex even for a single nuclear burst and the attacker could never be sure that every projectile pattern would be moved away from the target. However, by setting off a number of RVs throughout the missile field and then firing two or three RVs at each silo, the attacker can be reasonably confident of penetrating the defense and destroying most of the silos.

Thus for either type of attack, the price of destroying most of the ICBM silos with confidence is roughly doubled by the addition of a simple/novel BMD. This conclusion does not take into account the particular type of simple/novel system used. Whether or not this factor of two is significant depends on how many RVs the attacker is willing to spend to destroy the ICBM force.

Dust Defense

The simple/novel BMD systems are often called "unambiguous" defenses since both sides will see them as potential silo defense systems but not city defense systems. The dust defense system (sometimes euphemistically called "environmental defense") described in this section is the most unambiguous BMD of all.

In a dust defense system, a number of high-yield nuclear weapons are buried north of the silo fields they are to defend. After positive identification of an attack on these silo fields, the weapons are detonated about

5 or 10 min. before the first predicted RV impact. These detonations excavate large quantities of dust and raise it to high altitudes in the path of attacking RVs. (The quantity of dust is approximately one-third of a million tons of mass for every megaton of yield.) This dust will be displaced by wind but will stay aloft in significant density for an hour or more.

At such high altitudes, the RV has not slowed down and runs into the dust particles at 7 km/sec. These impacts can be compared to micrometeors hitting a satellite, and they act to remove small pieces of the RV's heatshield. If the dust is sufficiently dense, the entire heatshield will be eroded and the RV will have to pass through reentry without its protection. It is likely that the RV will heat up and be destroyed or at least its accuracy will be severely degraded. Whether or not the dust cloud is sufficiently dense to do this depends on the thickness of the RV's heatshield and the total yield of weapons used to generate the dust cloud. Despite the uncertainty regarding the effects of dust erosion, there is general agreement that a dust defense could be made effective at relatively low cost.

Dust defense has a number of significant advantages for silo defense. It provides a "shield" that can destroy all attacking RVs rather than just intercept some fraction of them one at a time. This protection lasts for a significant time—certainly long enough to permit a retaliatory strike. (If longer times are needed, a second or third round of dust-producing weapons can be deployed.) The system would be inexpensive and could be put in the field in a very short time. These advantages have to be weighed against one major disadvantage, the requirement for positive identification of an attack or, conversely, the danger of a false alarm. Because of this concern, it is interesting to compare dust defense with a launch-on-warning system.

Both dust defense and launch-on-warning systems respond to identification of an attack on Minuteman by detonating nuclear weapons, but dust defense detonates them in the United States and launch-on-warning systems detonate them in the Soviet Union. Because of this difference, the Soviet Union might try to spoof a dust defense system but not a launch-on-warning system. The consequences of a false alarm are extremely serious for both systems. If the dust defense were used, tens or hundreds of megatons would be detonated in the United States and significant fallout would be produced; however, the weapons could be specially designed to produce less fallout than ordinary nuclear bombs.

This outcome is far preferable to letting the attack penetrate, in which case thousands of megatons would detonate and no attempt could be made to minimize fallout. A false alarm for a launch-on-warning system could result in massive Soviet retaliation in response to U.S. missile launches or detonation.

Dust defense would obviously not be suitable for city defense, even if the false-alarm problem could be completely solved. Several other factors make dust defense less effective for cities. For one thing, although degrading the accuracy of an attacking RV can help with silo defense, it is of no help at all for cities that can be attacked with very inaccurate RVs. The second point is that a city must last much longer than the dust cloud does. If the first wave of RVs is destroyed, the attacker can fire wave after wave, forcing more defense detonations to produce more dust clouds.

Boost-Phase Defense

Boost-phase BMD systems have a number of attractive theoretical features. Since boosters can carry multiple RVs (up to ten or more), destroying one booster is equivalent to destroying many RVs. This destruction occurs over the attacker's territory, and even the residual booster and RV debris will never reach the target. The booster is a large, visible, and relatively vulnerable target that would be extremely difficult to decoy.

Arrayed against these advantages is one major disadvantage and a number of technological risks. The disadvantage is that although the booster is vulnerable for about 200 sec, only a space-based BMD could attack it during this time. Either a large number of satellites or very long-range weapons are required to have a defense weapon in position at all times to attack boosters launched from enemy territory. The tradeoff between number of satellites and weapon coverage is discussed below. Two types of weapons considered are homing interceptors carried aboard satellites and directed-energy (for example, high-power laser) ''battle stations.'' For each, the effective weapon range will be related to other system parameters.

The tradeoff between number of satellites and weapon range is illustrated in figure 3-17. The upper part of the figure shows how several rings of several satellites each would be required to provide coverage of

Figure 3-17. *Requirements for Global Coverage by Satellite*

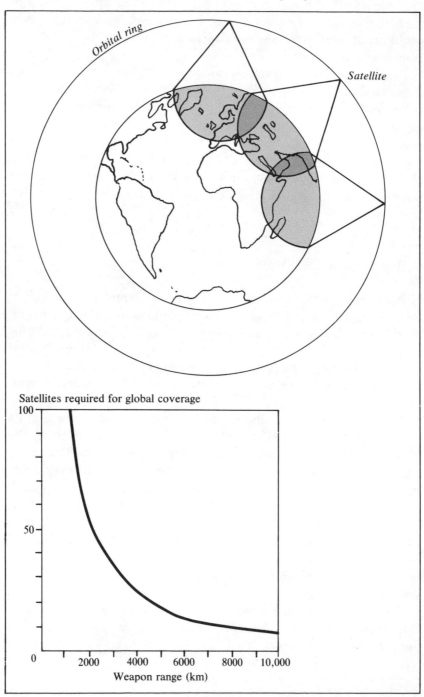

Figure 3-18. *Interception by Satellite during the Boost Phase*

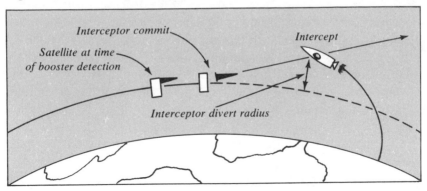

the entire earth at any one time. The coverage of a single satellite is determined by the maximum lethal range of the weapon it carries. Essentially the same number of satellites is needed to provide continuous coverage of any one point (for example, a Soviet ICBM field) on the earth. The satellites must move at least 8 km/sec to remain in orbit. Since the earth turns underneath them, after a relatively short time, a given satellite can no longer cover the enemy launch point, and another satellite must be available to take its place. The lower part of figure 3-17 shows how the number of satellites required for continuous coverage varies with the weapon range. This curve represents the best selection of orbital rings and satellites per ring to give full earth coverage. However, it does not attempt to avoid operation in the Van Allen radiation belt, which presents a hostile environment for electronic components. The number of satellites required to cover just the Soviet ICBM fields continuously is not much less than the number required for continuous worldwide coverage, so a space-based defense against ICBMs automatically has some capability against SLBMs.

Figure 3-17 clearly illustrates the advantage of having long weapon ranges. In the limit of synchronous (stationary) altitude satellites with weapon ranges of about 45,000 km, only three satellites are needed to cover the entire earth and only one to cover the entire Soviet Union. However, it is difficult to achieve long weapon range with lasers and impossible to do so with interceptor rockets carried aboard large satellites. The timeline shown in figure 3-18 illustrates the problem for an interceptor system. The time between interceptor commit and intercept must be 200 sec or less, since this is the total time the ICBM is in its boost phase. Unless the interceptor is a multistage missile like the ICBM that it is to intercept, its divert velocity will be less than 5 km/sec, and its maximum divert distance 1000 km. This means that if the booster does not come within 1000 km of the satellite, it cannot be intercepted. Figure 3-17 shows that, with this weapon range, at least 200 satellites are required to provide continuous coverage. Furthermore, since a hundred or so boosters might be launched simultaneously from the coverage region of a single satellite, each satellite (or group of satellites placed together in the same orbit) needs to carry about 100 interceptors for a total interceptor inventory of more than 20,000. Therefore, even if the intercepts can be made successfully, the system will be quite expensive.

For directed-energy weapons, the coverage is not limited by the interceptor flight time, but rather by the available weapon power and the extent to which it can be focused into a narrow beam and propagated over long distances. Here an initial analysis is done for laser weapons.

To indicate how the laser requirements vary with range, it is easiest to work backward from booster kill. Lasers kill by delivering a sufficient dose of energy density (over a short period of time) to the target booster to burn through or melt its skin. This lethal dose level is a function of the target reflectivity (since a mirrored surface will not absorb much laser light) and any thermal protection (for example, a heatshield) that the target carries. Hence, the numerical value of the required energy density is subject to considerable uncertainty. To show how the rest of the system depends on this dose level, it will be treated parametrically and called F. Consider a laser with average power P, and wavelength λ, which is focused by a mirror of diameter D, on a target at range R. If the laser and the mirror are "ideal" (that is, as perfect as the laws of physics allow), most of the power will be contained in a beam of angular extent λ/D and will form a spot of diameter $\lambda R/D$. If this spot illuminates the target for a time t, the energy density delivered to the target will be

$$PD^2t/\lambda^2R^2 = Bt/R^2.$$

The term $B = PD^2/\lambda^2$ is the "brightness" of the laser, a measure of how bright it would appear to the target when it shines in the target's direction.

If the target is to be destroyed, the quantity Bt/R^2 must exceed F, the lethal level. For a fixed lethal level, a brighter laser needs less time to destroy each target. To get an idea of some of the numerical values, without implying that they are exact, assume $P = 1$ Mw, $D = 1$ m, $t = 1$ sec, $\lambda = 1$ μm (μm = micron = 10^{-6}m), and $R = 1000$ km. In this case the energy density delivered over the 1-sec illumination time will be 100 J/cm², and the spot size will be 1 m in diameter. The power density within the laser spot is about ten times that of an electric iron but less than one-tenth that of a welding torch. The pointing accuracy required to put this spot on the target corresponds to hitting a period (.) of this text at a distance of 200 m. Figure 3-17 shows that to obviate the need for a large number of satellites, the weapon range should be significantly larger than the 1000 km in this example.

Note that the factor PD^2 in the laser brightness corresponds to the effective power-aperture product of the laser. The required power aperture varies as R^2, so increasing the laser range from 1000 to 5000 km would require an increase in PD^2 by a factor of 25. To take advantage of an increase in mirror diameter, which makes the beam narrower, it is necessary to improve the pointing accuracy by the same factor.

To achieve the same laser brightness requires less power aperture at a short wavelength than at a long wavelength. Potential lasers being considered for boost-phase BMD include chemical lasers with $\lambda = 3$ μm and visible lasers with $\lambda = 0.5$ μm. There is a difference between these two lasers of a factor of 36 favoring the visible laser in power-aperture requirement. However, this advantage might be somewhat less when power availability, efficiency, and mirror tolerance requirements are considered.

The technical difficulties of operating such a BMD system can be illustrated with a few simple calculations. To achieve the beamwidth and pointing accuracy required, the surface of the mirror must be machined until it is within a fraction of a wavelength of its ideal shape over its entire surface. The mirrors needed are over a million wavelengths across and must maintain this precision shape while swiveling from target to target in a second or less. Since the laser energy propagates at the speed of light, it takes about 15 msec to go 5000 km to the target. During this time, the target moves about 90 m so the laser must "lead" the target by this much (90 times the spot size). It takes another 15 msec for the return trip before the laser can find out whether or not the energy has hit the target. It is theoretically possible to achieve this type of aiming and pointing accuracy, since the booster is on a relatively predictable trajectory, but it has not yet been achieved in practice.

If it is assumed that boost-phase laser BMD can be achieved, there are a number of ways an attacker could counter the system. One is to harden its boosters against laser radiation. If the booster surface could be made highly reflective, only a small fraction of the incident energy would go into heating the booster. Another approach is to cover the booster with a heatshield similar to that used on reentry vehicles. Such a heatshield could increase the lethal energy level by more than an order of magnitude.

Another way to penetrate a boost-phase BMD is to attack the satellites. If one satellite is destroyed, a hole is opened in the coverage; the offense can calculate when this hole will be over its missile fields and can launch its attack through the coverage "window." Numerous techniques have been suggested for destroying satellites, including nuclear or nonnuclear interceptors, space mines (which are placed in orbit near the satellite to be attacked), and even ground-based laser antisatellite weapons. If a space-based laser can destroy ICBMs, it might also be able to destroy antisatellite missiles if it recognizes them as such. However, it might have more difficulty defending itself against space mines (unless it destroyed them as soon as they were deployed in peacetime), and it would have little capability to defend itself against a ground-based laser.

Boost-phase BMD could also make use of charged or neutral particle beams, but none of these techniques is as advanced in development as the optical or infrared laser weapons.

Intense beams of high-energy subatomic particles can be generated in particle accelerators (sometimes called "atom smashers"). These beams cause severe damage by overheating the target, detonating high explosives in the target, melting nuclear materials, or injuring electronics. The major unsolved problem for BMD applications is how to get these beams from their source to their target. Charged particle beams can be generated and steered by electric or magnetic fields on the weapons platform. Unfortunately, they are also deflected by the earth's magnetic field between the weapon and the target. Neutral particle beams would not be pushed off course by the earth's magnetic field, but the ability to generate and steer these beams on the weapon platform is at present quite limited.

A directed-energy weapon must be able to generate energy, direct it at the target, propagate it through air or space to the target, and induce some lethal effect in the target. Charged particle beams are probably the best at generating, directing, and killing but are clearly the worst at propagating. Neutral particle beams can propagate and kill but cannot yet be generated with sufficient intensities. Lasers are very good at directing and propagating, since light reflects from mirrors, can be pointed like a spotlight, and after leaving the weapon propagates in straight lines.

From this brief review of boost-phase BMD, it appears that each approach offers certain theoretical advantages and other disadvantages. However, further research and development must take place before any of the concepts discussed in this section could be considered for deployment. A combination of an efficient but less-than-perfect boost-phase system with a midcourse or terminal system forming a "layered" defense might in the end be the most practical system.

Summary

A number of points emerge from this discussion of technical issues for BMD systems:

—Ballistic missile defense must operate against a hostile opponent. The attacker will seek out any weak points and try to exploit them.

—The attacker and defender both make conservative assumptions regarding system performance parameters and can come to significantly different conclusions regarding the outcome of an attack.

—The job of defending redundant hard targets such as missile silos is much easier than defending cities.

—All BMD systems must perform the functions of search, track, discrimination, and intercept; different systems operate against targets in different stages of flight with different sensors and interceptors.

—Given the current state of technology, reentry BMD systems have the lowest technical risk, while boost-phase systems have the highest technical risk; the potential payoff is in the reverse order.

CHAPTER FOUR

BMD Applications: Performance and Limitations

ASHTON B. CARTER

EVEN among advocates of ballistic missile defense, there seems to be no consensus on what the goal of a BMD system should be—defense of strategic forces, defense of other military targets, or defense of cities. And despite the diversity of ballistic missile defense concepts that have been suggested, there are no specific proposals for deployment (as distinct from research) in either the United States or the USSR to focus debate and analysis.

This chapter presents the general principles of BMD technical analysis, applying them to a variety of systems and goals. The many examples of BMD applications presented here were chosen because they illustrate particular principles well or because they have received public attention, not necessarily because they are technically optimal or even plausible. If a proposal to deploy missile defenses is made in the United States or the USSR in coming years, one of the examples in this chapter, together with its accompanying discussion, should provide a guide to analyzing it.[1]

Ideally, an actual BMD deployment in the United States would be preceded by three stages of analysis: a study of the underlying technology, an assessment of the technology's effectiveness when embodied in a specific system assigned a specific defensive goal, and a judgment of the desirability or need for the defense. Not all of the BMDs discussed

1. Parts of this chapter draw upon the author's previous analyses in Office of Technology Assessment, *MX Missile Basing,* OTA-ISC-140 (Government Printing Office, 1981), pp. 111–43.

in this chapter have passed the first hurdle, much less the second or third. For the sake of discussion, however, this chapter takes for granted that the individual technological devices within the BMD system would actually work more or less as advertised: the sensor sees, the interceptor flies, and the kill mechanism kills. These technological issues were the subject of the last chapter. This chapter continues with an assessment of the effectiveness of the final system architecture and of its utility in various strategic missions. This, the second hurdle, is usually more difficult for the BMD to surmount than the first.

In some cases, notably schemes that operate in or from space, the systems (and sometimes even the devices within them) exist only as rough ideas. Before these concepts can be assessed reliably, they must be translated into specific wartime systems—if this turns out to be possible. By contrast, less advanced systems are better understood, but even with these systems there is plenty of room for technical uncertainty. The ultimate assessment of any ballistic missile defense must be tentative because, fortunately, no one has ever tested a BMD or an ICBM in a nuclear war—much less a statistically meaningful ensemble of wars. Still, the analysis presented here is probably the best available guide to the likely technical performance of BMD systems in a nuclear war. It is the kind of analysis the government and the public will need to apply as proposed concepts of ballistic missile defense mature and become more specific.

Prerequisites for BMD Analysis

Any defense known or foreseen can in principle be overcome at some price to the attacker, whether in weapons, cost, time, or risk. The question is not whether a defense "works," but *how much* protection it offers. Therefore one needs to establish at the outset a sense of magnitudes—of targets, of offensive arsenals, and eventually of defense performance. Fortunately, the important judgments about BMD will rarely depend on differences as small as 5 or 10 percent in any calculated numbers. Indeed, a rough estimate, reliable to a factor of two or so in either direction, often tells the whole story. Since observers will disagree about what constitutes adequate protection and what is worth the price of investment in BMD, a technical assessment of whether a BMD is "effective" should begin with a clear and firm statement of the goals

Table 4-1. *Approximate Superpower Arsenals, 1982*

Type of weapon	USSR	United States
ICBMS	1400	1000
ICBM RVs	4500	2100
Hard-target ICBM RVs	3000	1000
SLBMs	1000	600
SLBM RVs	1300	5500
Hard-target SLBM RVs	0	0
Long-range bomber weapons	300	2000
Long-range cruise missiles	0	Hundreds and increasing

Source: Author's estimates based on International Institute for Strategic Studies, *Military Balance, 1982–1983* (London: IISS, 1982), pp. 3–6, 11–14.

sought in deploying it and of the level of performance that constitutes "effectiveness." In playing out the game of providing obstacles to each other, the offense and defense have a variety of tactics, all of which need to be considered before a final assessment is made.

Arsenals and Targets

Table 4-1 shows, in rough magnitude, the present U.S. and Soviet arsenals. Two things are immediately apparent: first, the great size of present missile arsenals, and second, the lack of variety, all missiles carrying simple ballistic reentry vehicles (RVs). The former exists despite the absence of substantial BMDs on either side. The latter exists because in the absence of BMD there is no need to make use of the many available technologies for elaborating the offense: both sides are now accustomed to threatening to damage the other simply by lobbing warheads.

BMD would have a substantial job to do to offer meaningful protection against the present arsenals of the United States and the USSR, representing as they do decades of investment. But since any BMD designed now will not be fully deployed for years, it is the *future* and *potential* arsenals against which the capabilities of BMD must be measured. With intercontinental ballistic missile (ICBM) and submarine-launched ballistic missile (SLBM) programs active at this time in both countries, the number of missiles and warheads could conceivably grow substantially in the next decade.

The number of accurate RVs of small-to-moderate yield available to the Soviet Union for attack on U.S. ICBMs must be at least 2000 today, since the 1000 Minuteman silos are already said to be vulnerable to two-on-one targeting. The Carter administration foresaw deploying by the late 1980s a multiple protective shelter (MPS), or "racetrack," system of 4600 shelters. The shelter number was chosen to ensure that half of the 200 MX missiles hidden among them would survive Soviet attack provided the Soviet Union adhered to the limits of SALT II, meaning that another 2300 or so reliable warheads were expected to be available to the Soviet Union to attack MX. The Office of Technology Assessment estimated that with a level of Soviet effort on their ICBM force in the 1980s comparable to their efforts in the 1970s, and with no other constraints, this number could grow to 6000 or 7000 by 1990 and 11,000 or 12,000 by 1995.[2] These assessments, made without reference to BMD, indicate that a BMD system conceived in the United States today must plan to face on the order of 10,000 Soviet ICBM RVs and potentially more.

Counting targets is not as easy as counting weapons, since the offense must make judgments about whether a given installation is worthy of attack, whether all or just some of a given class must be destroyed, and whether a target is worth the price of penetrating a BMD. In BMD analyses, the value of a defense can be artificially enhanced by ascribing a heavy damage goal to the attacker or by proliferating would-be targets so that each is attacked less heavily by a given arsenal and hence defended more easily. Countersilo targeting is relatively unambiguous, but for the other classes of strategic targets these questions of judgment loom large.

Silos and other basing modes for ICBMs are the targets most often discussed as candidates for defense. A second category comprises the instruments of centralized control over military forces and continuity of government. These targets range from underground command bunkers and airborne command post alert bases to antennas, satellite dishes, data-processing facilities, and warning sensors. For the Soviet Union, this target structure is often taken to include more numerous party, government, and military leadership installations and to incorporate passive defenses.[3]

A third category, called "other military targets" (OMT), is divided into those that contribute to the nation's capability to function as a nuclear power and those that constitute its capability to support conven-

---

2. Ibid., p. 43.
3. U.S. Department of Defense, *Soviet Military Power*, 2d ed. (GPO, 1983), pp. 17, 30.

tional military operations. The former class includes ICBM launch control facilities, bomber alert and dispersal bases, submarine bases, storage and fabrication sites for nuclear weapons, air defenses, potential BMDs, long-range theater nuclear forces, and so forth. The latter includes airfields, army bases, ports, rail centers, bridges, communications and intelligence facilities, air defenses, fuel storage sites, and the like. Civilian facilities and industries capable of directly supporting an ongoing war effort might also be included in OMT.

The fourth category—"economic value" or "recovery"—constitutes the society's capability to function after the war in a manner recognizable to prewar eyes and to rebuild itself as an organized industrial society. It includes industry of all kinds; power, transportation, and communications infrastructure; and raw materials processing, food distribution, and other facilities. Observers differ about the extent to which certain of these targets capable of contributing rather directly to warfighting should be grouped with more narrowly "military" targets. Greater controversy arises over whether seeming to class any of these targets as "military" invites the impression that attack on them represents something less than a threat to the population and to society as a whole. Last, there is dispute over how much damage to this target set constitutes the ultimate sanction of "assured destruction."

The final target category is the population itself, together with the houses, places of worship, museums, schools, libraries, and so on that make up the human value of society. Probably neither superpower actually targets human beings as such. Faced with a defense claiming to reduce civilian fatalities to "acceptable" levels, however, the offense could conceivably adopt an explicit goal of maximizing population loss. Table 4-2 compares the rough numbers of targets in the United States and the USSR.

Approaches to Defense

Often controversy over whether a BMD is adequate derives as much from disagreement over the goals of the defense as over the system's technical performance. One of four goals is usually emphasized by proponents or critics of a system, each having distinct implications for the BMD analysis.

1. Enforce a given probability of survival or number of surviving targets. In general, as we will see, the attacker suffers a law of diminishing

Table 4-2. *Approximate Number of Targets in the United States and the USSR*

Type of target	USSR	United States
ICBM silos	1400	1000
Command and control and other military targets		
Command and control, leadership	100–?	100–200
Nuclear force targets other than silos	200–400	Same
Conventional forces and direct war support	Hundreds	Same
Cities		
Economic value/recovery	Thousands	Same
10 percent of population	Roughly 10 urban areas	Same
33 percent of population	Roughly 200 urban areas	Same

Source: Author's estimates; silo figures based on IISS, *Military Balance, 1982–1983*, pp. 4, 13.

returns as the attack intensity is increased, meaning that the first 50 percent probability of damage comes much more cheaply than the last. For the defense this means that high survivability goals are much harder than low goals to enforce against growth in the offense or against poor performance of the defense.

2. Raise the attack price. This goal concedes that the attacker can overwhelm the defense and destroy the targets, but implies that the offense's expenditure to do so can be made so large that it will find the target unattractive, or that the defense should be well satisfied with forcing the offense to make the effort. The precise meaning of attack price will be made clear later, but in principle it includes cost, deployment time, and technical risk as well as number of offensive weapons. The *cost-exchange ratio*, obtained by dividing the cost (total or marginal) of the defense by the cost of the offense needed to overwhelm it, suggests which side should find competition less attractive.

3. Complicate the attack and create uncertainty for the attacker. This goal usually concedes both low survivability and modest price, but only as an analyst's on-paper assessment. The complex tactics or exotic penetration technologies required to defeat the defense cause the attacker to weigh the odds that the outcome of attack will not be the analyst's "expected value," but a less favorable fluctuation.

4. Deny damage. This is the most difficult goal of all, usually discussed in the context of population defense.

To achieve its chosen goal, the defense can select from an assortment of tactics found also in air defense, naval defense, and other missions. Each of these will be discussed in detail in later examples.

Preferential defense is a tactic for enhancing the value of a defense that is too expensive to make intercepting each attacking RV worthwhile, by forcing the offense to attack with several times as many RVs as the defense has interceptors. The defense is designed to concentrate its capabilities on any subset of the targets, but it keeps secret which targets it intends to defend or makes its decision when the attack is already under way. The offense cannot concentrate its attack on the defended targets and is instead forced to attack all the targets as if they were equally defended, wasting multiple RVs on undefended targets. For this scheme to succeed, the defense must have a way of determining which attacking RVs or missiles are heading for which targets at the time critical decisions about committing interceptors must be made. This "impact point prediction" can fail if the targets are closely spaced, if the RVs can maneuver, or if the defense intercepts ICBMs in their boost phase before they have deployed individual RVs. Since a preferential defense only seeks to protect a portion of the targets, allowing (indeed inviting) many RVs to arrive and explode, it is not appropriate to city defense.

Layered defense means arranging to have two (or even more) shots at an RV, by providing two hurdles for the offense. This advantage is purchased at the price of two defenses. The first BMD to engage the attack is called the overlay and the second the underlay. It is often said that the "leakages" of the overlay and underlay—that is, the propensity of BMD to miss an RV and allow it to penetrate the defenses—are multiplicative. Thus, this argument goes, if each allows 20 percent of the RVs to "leak" through, the overall leakage is 4 percent ($0.2 \times 0.2 = 0.04$). This simple arithmetic approach generally does not reflect accurately the number of targets preserved by a layered defense. For one thing, the performances of the layers are not independent and should not be expressed with independent leakage fractions. For example, if the underlay is susceptible to "structured" attacks calling for timed arrival of a number of RVs at given detonation points, and if a small disruption of this structure greatly enhances the underlay's performance, adding even a leaky overlay can be disproportionately effective, breaking up the attack structure with a small number of random intercepts. Another problem with the leakage arithmetic is that the fraction of leaking RVs does not necessarily indicate the fraction of targets destroyed because of complications introduced by preferential offense and defense tactics. Last, the fraction of RVs leaking through can (and usually does) itself depend on the attack size and structure, and so is not a property of the BMD system only.

It is also often said that layered defense requires designing a single type of decoy capable of fooling both layers, but this is rarely true because the two layers usually do not correlate their observations of attacking objects.[4]

In *threshold defense* it is conceded that the target can be destroyed at a price that is not prohibitive, but the presence of defense is thought to require the offense to mount a relatively large and complex attack. The scale of the attack is imagined to exceed some threshold the attacker would be unwilling to cross, either because it would provoke a massive retaliation or because it would provide the victim an assured tactical warning that would mitigate the effect of the attack.

Approaches to Offense

A root of much of the disagreement among BMD assessments is the emphasis given to the wide variety of offensive tactics and hardware available to the attacker. These approaches to offense, described below, need to be reconsidered in the context of each specific BMD deployment example.

MORE ICBMS, MORE RVS. Though it is relatively inexpensive to add silo-based ICBMs and even cheaper to fractionate the payload of existing missiles (that is, to substitute for the current loading a larger number of smaller warheads), adding *survivable* RVs to the arsenal is not so easy. This means that competing against a defense is much easier if preemption is contemplated than if penetration must be achieved with surviving retaliatory forces.

OTHER WEAPONS. Ballistic missile defenses optimized for ICBM defense sometimes have little or no capability to intercept submarine-launched RVs. The unpredictability of the SLBM launch point, together with the short timeline and different trajectory of SLBMs, means that SLBM and ICBM defenses are rather different problems for BMD.

---

4. An underlay-only decoy is passed over by the overlay (otherwise it would be a good overlay decoy, too) and goes on to fool the underlay. An overlay-only decoy has done its job by the time the underlay recognizes the fraud. Only in the hypothetical case where overlay and underlay sensors *both* view the approaching attack object-by-object and share their judgments about each object would a single decoy have to fool both types of sensors.

Bombers and cruise missiles are also obvious alternatives to ballistic missiles for targets whose destruction can wait until several hours into the war. The offense might even be able to introduce nuclear weapons into large cities in commercial packing crates, commercial airplanes, or diplomatic pouches.

ATTACK ON THE DEFENSE. The quest for a survivable basing mode for the MX missile in the United States has driven home the difficulties of protecting strategic targets from destruction by hardening, moving, hiding, and proliferating them. A BMD deployment is itself a prime target, and the system is clearly useless if it can easily be destroyed. The BMD need not be absolutely survivable, but the offense must pay a high enough price to destroy the defense that such a tactic is unattractive. The defense can of course defend itself, but attack on the defense remains for most deployment schemes the most effective tactic for the offense and hence the weakest link in the defense. SLBMs can be a key factor in defense suppression, since they could arrive before the ICBMs and the defense might have little capability to defend itself against them.

ATTACK ON THE DEFENSE'S COMMAND, CONTROL, AND COMMUNICATIONS SYSTEM. BMDs depend on timely warning of attack in order to prepare themselves—turning on radars, bringing electronics up from dormancy, launching space probes, and the like. Nuclear BMD systems require "nuclear release" from a high command level. Once the attack is known to be under way, coordinated working of the defense still requires that key sensors and data processors continue to function and are able to communicate with one another. The offense might try to disrupt command, control, and communication (C^3) in a variety of ways: by disrupting radio wave propagation; by stimulating electromagnetic pulse (EMP); by jamming radio waves; by initiating an antisatellite attack; and by directly attacking ground-based C^3 facilities.[5] This area of BMD vulnerability has received comparatively little attention.

TACTICS WITH ORDINARY BALLISTIC RVS. Lofted trajectories, discussed in the previous chapter, can stress the defense by speeding reentry. Depressed trajectories shorten timelines and can offer bad viewing angles to space-based sensors. Various "laydowns"—patterns of bomb arrival in space and time—can be used to stress the defense. "Spike" attacks, for example, time all RVs to arrive at the target at once, posing

5. OTA, *MX Missile Basing*, pp. 147–64, 277–99, contains a technical discussion of communication links, sensors, and command posts for nuclear command and control, together with the problems of ensuring their adequate performance in wartime.

traffic-handling problems for the defense. Laydowns usually have to be analyzed individually in the context of a particular defense.

NUCLEAR EFFECTS. Heat and radiation from a nuclear detonation cause ionization in the surrounding air. This ionization in turn causes attenuation, reflection, and other propagation disruptions for radar signals, phenomena collectively called blackout.[6] For infrared sensors operating in space a similar effect, dubbed redout, is also produced by high-altitude bursts.[7] The offense may plan to use these effects to limit the defense's ability to track incoming RVs.

SPECIAL HARDWARE. ICBM boosters can deliver a wide variety of other devices besides ballistic RVs to stress the defense. The attractiveness of these devices—called penetration aids or "penaids"—would presumably be weighed, in the offense's planning, against the number of boosters taken to lift them, their cost, the time taken to design and deploy them, and the risk that they would fail to work as predicted. The most important penetration aids are decoys, chaff, and aerosols;[8] maneuvering reentry

6. For bursts at or above 60–80 km (200,000–250,000 ft.), radiation is the primary ionizing mechanism; a single burst can produce a region of ionization tens of kilometers or wider in extent, and disruption can persist for minutes at moderate frequencies. A BMD relying on ground-based search and acquisition radars to view targets at or above this altitude range and in critical attack corridors could therefore be affected. Even if blackout is not complete, propagation disturbances interfere with discrimination and tracking. At low altitudes, the region affected by the burst is smaller, becoming coterminous with the fireball (about 1 km for 1 MT) at sea level. The ionizing mechanism here is heat. The fireball at low altitudes appears as a sharp-edged, perfectly reflecting bubble to the radar, and it rises rapidly.

7. Radiation from a high-altitude burst causes fluorescence—emission of light—from air molecules. The emitted light lies within the long-wave infrared part of the spectrum, so the atmosphere below appears to the sensor to glow more brightly than usual. Since the sensor might be trying to view attacking RVs near or against the edge of the atmosphere, or might need to know the intensity of reflected skyshine to discriminate RVs from decoys, the attacker would be tempted to make defense harder by deliberately detonating a few "precursor" warheads before they could be intercepted.

8. "Precision" decoys seek to fool the defense into intercepting them, while "traffic" decoys merely aim to fool the defense long enough to consume precious data-processing time or disrupt efficient allocation of interceptors. The decoy designer's job is to produce RV-decoy pairs whose "signatures" to the defensive sensors are identical, to deploy them from the bus so that their flight characteristics and position relative to other RVs and to the bus resemble those of true RVs, and to package them so that they are lightweight and fit under the shroud on the ICBM. Discrimination can be further confused by introducing random variations into the signatures of RVs and decoys, a technique called "antisimulation." If all RVs were identical and all decoys were identical, the defense could focus more easily on small differences between the two populations; if the populations are themselves diverse, this focused discrimination is made more

vehicles (MaRVs);[9] jammers;[10] and antiradiation homing (ARH) vehicles.[11] If a defense can be penetrated by one of these tactics, it is not necessarily a failure: forcing the offense to the new tactic and investment is sometimes regarded as adequate return on investment in the defense.

---

difficult. A last general technique to frustrate discrimination is to use "stealth" techniques to reduce the signal the defensive sensor has to work with.

Decoys for endoatmospheric operation are harder to design than exoatmospheric decoys because they must not only look like RVs but must fly through the atmosphere like them as well. In space, by contrast, trajectories are independent of object weight and size because there is no atmospheric drag. Objects reentering the atmosphere also produce a wake of ionized air, which must be matched by a decoy. To make matters worse, the interaction of the RV with the atmosphere changes in a complicated way as the heatshield burns off. Exoatmospheric decoys avoid all these complications.

A technique for fooling exoatmospheric discrimination called "masking" involves spreading clouds of chaff (for radars) and aerosols (for optical sensors) around attacking objects, either hiding RVs among them or using the extra interference to complicate discrimination. Chaff consists of thousands of fine wires that reflect radar signals strongly. Aerosols consist of tiny beads that reflect infrared light from the atmosphere and earth below. Masking does not work in the atmosphere because drag slows the aerosols and chaff, exposing the faster-falling RVs.

Providing a signature similar to the infrared plume of an ICBM booster motor would be difficult because the motor emits hundreds of kilowatts of short-wave infrared energy over a period of minutes. Decoy tactics against boost-phase BMDs are probably not worthwhile.

9. MaRVs are warheads that deploy little fins or other aerodynamic surfaces when they enter the atmosphere, allowing them to turn and dodge rather than fall ballistically. They have no ability to maneuver in space. MaRVs could attempt to defeat a defense in four ways: by "dogfighting" with the pursuing interceptor; by approaching the target from an angle that the defense did not plan for; by overloading a sensor trying to keep track of several dodging objects simultaneously; and by keeping its aimpoint uncertain until the last minute, thwarting preferential defense. The MaRV's maneuverability is limited, and since the defense picks where it is going to intercept, the MaRV's programmer needs to be concerned that the defense will intercept the MaRV before or after its maneuvers. Terminal defenses might be able to wait until the MaRV has descended to such low altitudes that the targets it can swerve to attack have been narrowed down to just a few. Deploying MaRVs, therefore, does not guarantee a total defeat for an endoatmospheric defense. Since MaRVs would in general be heavier and more expensive than ballistic RVs, the offense would have to weigh the benefits of the MaRV attack against the simpler expedient of attacking with the "equivalent" number of ordinary RVs, perhaps two or so RVs for every MaRV.

10. Jammers are radio transmitters accompanying attacking RVs and tuned to broadcast at the same frequency as a defensive radar. These broadcasts add "noise" to the signals reflected from the RVs and received by the radar. Susceptibility to jamming generally decreases with increasing radar frequency, with decreasing altitude, and with increasing radar power.

11. In deployments where the radars are mobile or hidden, a precursor wave of homing MaRVs with radio receivers can, when illuminated by a radar, locate the source radar, and veer to attack it. A follow-on attack on the defended target seconds later finds the defense blinded.

SHOOT-LOOK-SHOOT. Shoot-look-shoot is a tactic for defeating preferential defense or deceptive basing of the defense components. In a first wave, the defense makes intercepts over targets it has chosen to defend preferentially. This wave destroys all the undefended targets and reveals which targets the defense has chosen for survival. Follow-on attack can concentrate on the remaining targets. In this way the offense avoids wasting RVs in heavy attacks on undefended targets and can save the bulk of its arsenal to overwhelm the defense. In a variation of this tactic, the attacker uses a precursor wave to force the radar or other hidden defense components to expose themselves. Follow-on attack is then mounted on the known defense locations and finally on the (now undefended) targets.

There are two obvious drawbacks to shoot-look-shoot. If the defended targets are ICBMs, the defense could well use the period between attack waves to launch in retaliation rather than await the outcome of a subtle stratagem. Second, the methods and sensors used to locate the defended targets or the defensive components could be susceptible to disruption or destruction by the defense. In the absence of such disruption, though, the possibility of shoot-look-shoot means that the defense does not provide *enduring survivability* to the defended targets.

OTHER REACTIVE THREATS. The list above exhausts the complement of generic countermeasures to traditional varieties of BMDs. New BMD ideas will be accompanied by new threats, and it is important that analysis of countermeasures proceed apace with development of new BMD ideas.

Fundamentals of BMD Analysis

The most useful way to encapsulate the overall performance of a BMD is its "drawdown curve" and the associated notion of "attack price." This section derives the drawdown curve for a simple example, a traditional endoatmospheric defense of silos, as a prelude to the many more complex examples that follow. This example is also an occasion to reflect on the many complications that enter the analysis of even so straightforward a defense system. With the language of attack price in mind, we shall be able as well to survey quantitatively what is known about the performance of all the BMD systems described in chapter 3.

Drawdown Curve and Attack Price: A Silo Defense Example

Consider a traditional endoatmospheric system, consisting of numerous small ground-based radars and short-range, high-acceleration nuclear interceptors, deployed in defense of widely spaced silos. Because the target is a hardened silo, everything of importance happens within several kilometers of the aimpoint. Because the spacing is wide, there is no interaction between events at neighboring sites: what happens at a given silo can be calculated without reference to what happens around it.[12]

The first thing one needs to know is the probability that a single, isolated RV attacking this silo would be intercepted successfully. Chapter 3 indicated that this probability can be made rather high—over 80 percent at least. There are a number of reasons why the probability of a successful first intercept is not exactly 100 percent. First, it is not certain that the defense, which has been sitting idly for years, will actually bring itself up from dormancy, emerge from its peacetime basing to assume its defensive position, and find all subsystems in working order. Second, there is a chance that the defense will not receive warning of attack and authority for nuclear release in the half-hour flight time of attacking ICBMs. Third, the performance of each step in the interception process—search, tracking, discrimination, and interception—is not perfect.

What if a second RV attacks? Simple probability theory might suggest that the chance that the target survives two RVs would be the square of the probability of withstanding the first, 72 percent. (That is, 85 percent of the time the silo survives the first attack, and in 85 percent of *those* cases it survives the second attack as well, or $0.85 \times 0.85 = 0.72$.) But in general the second intercept is not as easy as the first, so its probability is less than 85 percent. There could be many reasons for this: the nuclear effects of the first intercept could destroy the second interceptor, blow it off course, or obscure the radar's view of the second RV. Indeed, the offense could time the RVs to cause maximum disruption. Clearly, then, the probability of making a second intercept is less than or equal to the probability of making the first.

The probability of intercepting a third RV after two successful intercepts is smaller still. If each penetrating RV has sufficient accuracy and yield to be sure of destroying the silo, the *product* of these probabil-

---

12. Ignoring possible radar traffic-handling complications.

Figure 4-1. *Drawdown Curve and Attack Price of a BMD System*

Probability of target survival (percent)

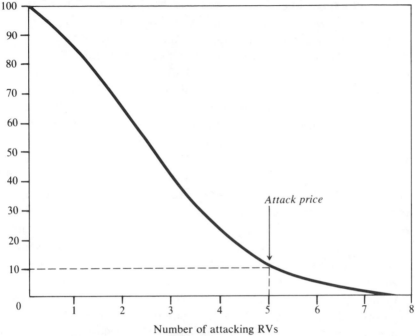

Number of attacking RVs

ities of making successive intercepts measures the chances that the
defended silo will survive attack. A plot of this survival probability on
the vertical axis versus the number of attacking RVs on the horizontal
axis is called a drawdown curve. Figure 4-1 shows what the drawdown
curve might look like for a rather good endoatmospheric defense. In this
example the first intercept probability is 85 percent; the second, 75
percent; the third, 65 percent; and so on. Therefore, the probability of
surviving a one-on-one attack is 85 percent; a two-on-one attack, 64
percent ($0.85 \times 0.75 = 0.64$); and a three-on-one attack, 41 percent ($0.85
\times 0.75 \times 0.65 = 0.41$).

At a certain point, the number of attacking RVs will result in a
cumulative survival probability so small that the defended target is
almost certain to be destroyed. If the offense has this number of RVs
and is willing to dedicate them to this target—if the offense is willing to
pay this "price"—it can destroy the silo. Defining "almost certainly
destroyed" as a 10 percent probability of survival, figure 4-1 gives a
price of five RVs.

These two concepts—drawdown curve and attack price—can be derived for any BMD system and deployment, and they are the most important expression of its capability. The drawdown curve in figure 4-1 was derived for a single aimpoint defended by a BMD battery. If there are many silos, each attacked and defended in this way, the probability of survival of a single silo would give the percentage of all the silos that survived. Thus figure 4-1 predicts that if 1000 silos are attacked by 5000 RVs, 100 silos will survive. For a more general target structure and BMD deployment, the silo drawdown curve in figure 4-1 generalizes to an overall system drawdown curve measuring the percentage of the value of the target set that survives attacks of increasing intensity, with intensity measured in RVs or offensive boosters.

For traditional endoatmospheric defenses of the type in this example, almost all of the disagreement in the technical community lies in the range of attack price between two and eight RVs. Few analysts claim a price of more than eight for these traditional defenses, and many analysts view claims of more than five with skepticism. Virtually everyone concedes that BMDs can be made that would force the attacker to double up—a price of two—to destroy a defended target even if the attacking RVs were perfectly accurate and reliable. Within the two to eight range, of course, there is lively debate. The outcomes of analyses within this range are sensitive to specific details of the BMD deployment and threat. Though one can enumerate these sensitivities in a general way—blackout geometry, interceptor hardness, and so forth—the specifics should be treated case by case.

Complications

So far our discussion of the drawdown curve has been simple, but even this rather straightforward example immediately suggests complications. It is useful to consider eight of these complications before turning in succeeding sections to more complex defense systems.

1. Price was defined in this example as the attack intensity needed to produce 10 percent or less chance of survival. The numerical value of the price for a given defense will obviously change depending on the stipulated damage level—5 percent, 10 percent, or 25 percent. The choice of attack price should reflect the offense's probable damage goals. Although attack price is a useful single number with which to compare BMDs, it can be deceptive. Figure 4-2 shows, alongside the previous

Figure 4-2. *Performance of Two BMD Systems with the Same Attack Price*

Targets surviving (percent)

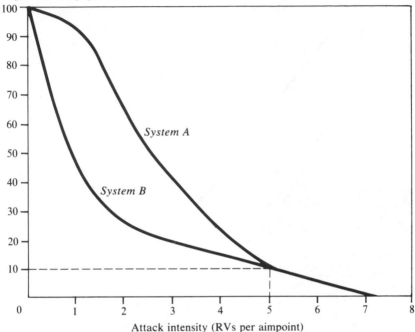

Attack intensity (RVs per aimpoint)

example, a much poorer defense that also claims a nominal price of five RVs.

2. So far in this example the offense has only been allowed the simple tactic of lobbing in RVs one after another. To calculate the drawdown curve correctly requires study of all the possible penetration strategies and reactive threats. One way to decide how large a price to associate with exotic attack hardware is to determine how many ordinary RVs need to be removed from an ICBM booster in order to accommodate the fancy vehicle. For instance, instead of loading four ballistic RVs on an ICBM and targeting them against the silo, the offense might be able to substitute two MaRVs, or two ballistic RVs plus fifteen decoys, or six smaller-yield RVs.

To define the drawdown curve properly, then, one converts each exotic attack into its equivalent in ordinary RVs off-loaded from the booster and calculates which tactic does best against the defense. The probability of surviving this "best" attack determines the point on the

Figure 4-3. *Effect of Offensive Reactions on the Drawdown Curve*

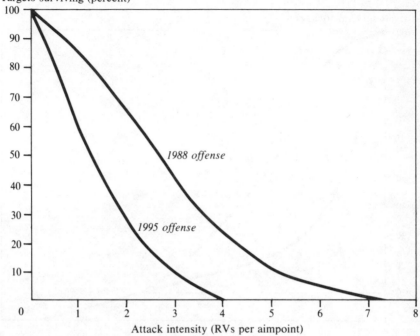

Targets surviving (percent)

Attack intensity (RVs per aimpoint)

drawdown curve corresponding to the given attack intensity. One problem with this mathematical process is that it fails to capture the subjective effect on the offense's confidence of resorting to complicated and exotic attacks, as well as the cost and delay involved in deploying the new offensive hardware in reaction to the BMD. As new penetration aids enter the opposing inventory, the drawdown curve can begin to sag (figure 4-3).

3. Smooth drawdown curves reflect faith that the BMD has no Achilles' heels that would lead to catastrophic collapse of the defense (figure 4-4). In reality this faith may not be justified, particularly for advanced technologies or new ideas that have not yet been scrutinized in a complete system design.

4. In a matter as serious as nuclear planning, both offense and defense are likely to be conservative. Thus the offense, lacking the complete knowledge of the BMD that would be needed to tailor the perfect attack, will have a tendency to exaggerate the system's capabilities and to shrink from the idea of basing its nuclear posture on some subtle tactic or exotic

Figure 4-4. *Catastrophic Failure of the Defense Because of an Achilles' Heel*

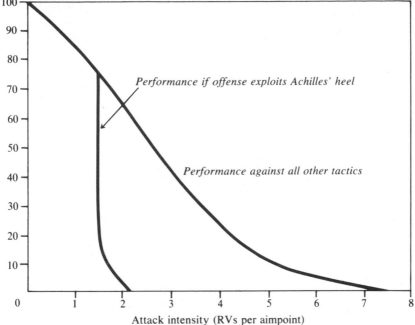

Targets surviving (percent)

Performance if offense exploits Achilles' heel

Performance against all other tactics

Attack intensity (RVs per aimpoint)

hardware. The defense, for its part, will be painfully aware of all the system's hidden flaws. When they calculate the survival probabilities, the two sides are likely to come up with very different answers, as shown in figure 4-5.

Though the curve from the defense's view is defined objectively by the technical characteristics of the defense, the view the offense will take is harder to predict. Presumably it results both from an exaggerated view of the performance of each BMD component and from ruling out altogether attack tactics or hardware that seem too risky.

5. The probabilities of survival calculated by analysts are expected values. They record the fact that in a given engagement of defense and offense the *most likely* outcome is, say, 30 percent of the ICBMs surviving. Other outcomes are not impossible, but merely less likely. It is difficult to specify the relative likelihood of all the possible outcomes, but it is important not to lose sight of the fact that the shape of the probability distribution is as important as its peak value. This is illustrated

Figure 4-5. *Offense and Defense Views of BMD Performance*

Targets surviving (percent)

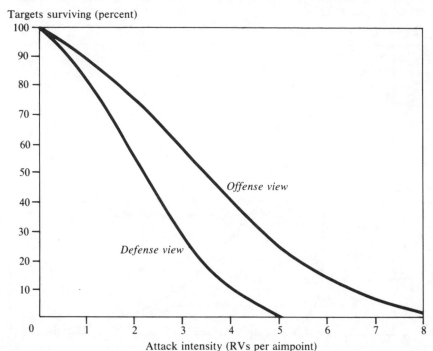

Attack intensity (RVs per aimpoint)

in figure 4-6. The uncertainties that determine the shape of the distribution result both from imperfect understanding of all technical factors and from inherent statistical variability (for example, in certain nuclear effects).

6. Some points on the drawdown curve might be associated with structured attacks of the sort that could only be executed by an undamaged ICBM force. In a retaliatory strike by surviving forces, however, key RVs in a structured laydown might be missing, timing could be affected, or precursor damage to the defense could be incomplete, among other effects. This technical fact underlies the oft-expressed fear that BMD ends up being a better investment for the side that attacks first: the first strike is relatively unimpeded, but the "ragged" retaliation is much less effective. This feature is illustrated in figure 4-7.

7. Nothing has been said so far about the cost of defense. It is usually possible to bolster the system's drawdown curve somewhat with higher-cost improvements to the defense. The value of adding each increment of performance must be weighed against the additional price to the

Figure 4-6. *Relative Probabilities of Various Possible Outcomes of a Defensive Engagement, Plotted for Two Different BMD Systems A and B*

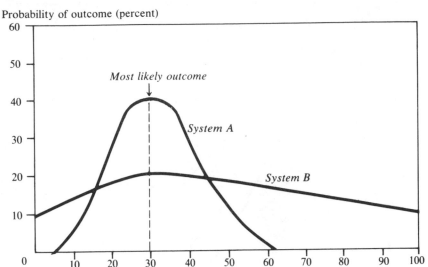

Probability of outcome (percent)

Most likely outcome

System A

System B

Targets surviving (percent)

offense of offsetting the extra performance with improvements in its attacking forces. Beyond a certain point further improvements are not worthwhile.

In many cases, the number of interceptors procured is *not* the critical factor in these tradeoffs. If preferential defense is being used, more interceptors will allow coverage of more targets or even allow two interceptors to be directed at each attacking RV. But it could well be that these extra investments do not increase the attack price because the price is limited by defense suppression, blackout effects, or some other factor that has nothing to do with interceptor number. The number of radars can be critical, not so much because of any extra performance achieved by adding more, but because the price of defense suppression is increased through proliferation. This is obviously an expensive way to compete with the offense.

Fundamental constraints, defined not by cost tradeoffs or the amount of hardware deployed but by basic physical phenomena, ultimately limit the effectiveness of most defenses. For the endoatmospheric system of this example, the attacker can theoretically always get an RV through to the target with the "ladder down" tactic. In essence ladder down involves

Figure 4-7. *Performance of a BMD System against First Strike and "Ragged" Retaliation*

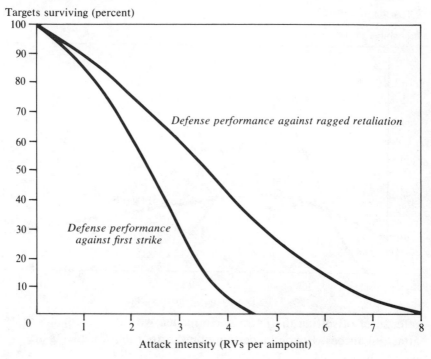

Targets surviving (percent)

Defense performance against ragged retaliation

Defense performance against first strike

Attack intensity (RVs per aimpoint)

scheduling a number of RVs to approach the target in rapid succession. The first RV is detonated just outside the range of the defense; the fireball produced by this first detonation masks the approach of the second RV, which in turn detonates a bit lower. This detonation masks the approach of a third RV to a point a bit lower, and so on. Eventually the target is reached. Other fundamental limitations include, for example, the resilience of radars to nuclear effects and their ability to compete with jammers. The defense performance could not be increased indefinitely with any amount of additional expenditure.

A key factor in any decision to deploy a BMD is the cost-exchange ratio, which measures the outcome of competition between the defense to improve its performance and the offense to maintain penetrability. Computing this ratio is subject to a host of uncertainties—in the cost of hardware (particularly in the Soviet case), in subjective factors like technical risk, and so forth—but the most important factor driving these calculations is usually where in the deployment cycle the counting begins. One might calculate and compare the cost of the new defense and the cost of a new offense needed to counter it. But if the United States were considering deployment of BMD by, say, 1990, the cost-exchange issue might be stated a second way: "Between today and 1990, the Soviet Union could make a certain investment in its offenses in order to preserve its present level of penetration. How would that investment compare with the proposed U.S. investment in defense?" In this calculation, the Soviet investment in their large *existing* offensive forces, already bought and paid for, is neglected.

Yet a third computation would begin in 1990, when the deployment was complete, and would ask, "How would improvements in the offense, and countervailing improvements in the defense, compare in cost?" This third calculation (the marginal cost exchange) is sometimes subject to the fallacy that the Soviet Union would stand still until the U.S. defense is deployed and *then* begin the competition.

8. A system that only aims to make the offense pay a price of two RVs does not need to be very capable. In fact, if the defense only succeeds in making its single intercept more often than it fails, the offense will conclude that it makes better use of its RVs by targeting two RVs at a lesser number of defended aimpoints than by targeting one RV at each of a larger number. The attacker's conclusion is not the result of conservative offensive perceptions (though these too could be important even for a poor defense), but of sober calculation.

To take an explicit, if oversimplified, example, suppose an attacker has 1000 perfectly reliable and accurate RVs with which to aim at 1000 targets, each of which is defended by a BMD whose goal is a single intercept. Suppose also that the defense performs so poorly that it succeeds in making an intercept only 51 percent of the time, fails 49 percent of the time, and has no capability to make successive intercepts over the same target. The attacker has the choice of targeting all 1000 aimpoints with one RV (case 1) or 500 aimpoints with two RVs each (case 2). In case 1, the attack destroys 490 aimpoints because the defense fails to make its intercept this many times. In case 2, all 500 aimpoints targeted two-on-one are destroyed. Thus the offense concludes that it does better by "doubling up" on a smaller number of aimpoints (case 2). But this is exactly what the defense seeks to force it to conclude.

Therefore, if the odds that a single-shot defense actually makes its intercept are greater than 50 percent, the defense achieves its goal of forcing the attacker to target one more RV at each aimpoint. Whether the odds are 51 percent or 99 percent is immaterial, since the offense does not have the option of allocating fractions of an RV, but only one *or* two. And since the price is so low, complex tactics for sidestepping the defense are rarely preferable to the simpler expedient of targeting another ballistic RV.

Overall Assessments of BMD Technologies

Using the language of attack price and keeping in mind the many complications in BMD analysis, the following paragraphs compare the overall performance of various BMD technologies. The remainder of this chapter will explore whether useful strategic missions can be found for these systems.

TRADITIONAL SYSTEMS. These systems consist of ground-based nuclear (or nonnuclear) interceptor missiles, ground-based radars, and perhaps a long-range sensor for target acquisition as well. Years of study have led to fairly general agreement in the technical community that these systems can probably exact no more than eight, but should be able with relative ease to exact two, RVs for each isolated, defended aimpoint in the defense view.

SIMPLE/NOVEL SYSTEMS. These systems include radar-guided missiles with conventional fragment warheads (of which sophisticated versions could be classed with the traditional systems), missiles with homing seekers, swarms of unguided projectiles, and anti-aircraft guns. In general, these systems are designed to enforce a price of only two RVs and cannot claim a higher price without elaborations that carry them into the category of traditional systems.

LAYERED DEFENSE WITH ADVANCED EXOATMOSPHERIC OVERLAY AND TRA-DITIONAL UNDERLAY. The new element here is the infrared homing Overlay, which intercepts individual RVs in midcourse before reentry. Since better-understood and simpler traditional systems exist for modest defense jobs requiring a price of a few RVs for each target, the more complex and expensive layered defense is of interest only if it can exact a high price—say, at least five RVs for each aimpoint. The issue is therefore not whether the layered defense works (meaning whether the devices within it work), but whether it can enforce a higher price than traditional systems. The layered defense is thus logically held to a higher standard of performance than traditional systems.

The Overlay concept differs substantially from traditional systems in the lower level of detail to which it has been designed, tested, and subjected to hypothetical threats. Its performance is correspondingly less certain. The complexity and fragility of the system as a whole is a greater source of technical risk for the Overlay than is the maturity of the technological devices themselves—homing vehicles, infrared sensors, and so on. Of particular concern is the resilience of the complex defense system to disruption and destruction and the susceptibility of its space-borne sensors to being fooled by decoys or other penetration aids.

BOOST-PHASE AND DIRECTED-ENERGY SYSTEMS. These schemes involve interceptors or lasers (X-ray or optical) that would intercept ICBM second stages or postboost vehicles ("buses") before individual RVs are dispensed. (Some directed-energy schemes even attack RVs.) The systems could stand alone or be deployed with other systems in a layered defense. The lasers can be on satellite battle stations or launched into space on high-acceleration missiles upon warning of an attack. These systems present issues of technical risk and uncertainty to an extent much greater than the RV-intercepting Overlay scheme. The price these systems could ultimately exact, and their cost relative to offsetting offensive improvements, are completely unknown. More than for the Overlay, issues remain regarding both the underlying technology and, even more to the point, the possibility of fashioning from this advanced technology a robust, reliable wartime system immune to penetration tactics. Boost-phase systems are incapable of preferential defense, since it is not possible to predict during boost the destination of the missile's payload.

DUST DEFENSE. Buried bombs of sufficient yield and proper placement detonated at the right time can charge an infinite price, since no ordinary RVs can penetrate the dust cloud or debris shield unscathed. (Erosion hardening of RVs might result in a finite, but still high, price in the case of the dust cloud variety.) Like other BMDs, dust defense needs timely and reliable warning of missile attack, but the consequences of mistaken warning are obviously more severe than for defenses that use warning only to turn on radars and other electronic equipment. The other limitations of dust defense are that the protected region is limited and that the cloud needs to be replenished with periodic bursts if protection is to be prolonged beyond a half hour or so. While temporary protection might be adequate for silo defenses, where the missiles could be launched in retaliation while the dust held off further attack, dust defense is not suited to defense of immovable targets of enduring value, such as industrial areas and cities, which are still there when the dust settles.

Defense of ICBMs

ICBM defense is by far the most-discussed BMD mission. The strategic goal of survivable ICBMs is widely shared, albeit with varying levels of urgency. Proposals to defend ICBMs evoke less controversy than defense of other targets: denying the opponent a disarming first strike is universally recognized as stabilizing, whereas attempting to deprive the opponent of the ultimate sanction of destructive retaliation, as in city defense, is often challenged as chimerical or destabilizing. ICBM defense is also regarded technically as the most promising application of BMD, since compared with defense of cities, it is a relatively modest goal and the targets are well defined and subject to the defender's control.

Land-basing schemes for ICBMs include ordinary silos, multiple protective shelters (MPS), Densepack (or closely spaced basing), and various mobile schemes. This section presents a number of examples of ICBM defense for each of these basing schemes. In comparing these examples to one another and to other basing modes offering survivability for ICBMs, it is useful to bear in mind the characteristics that the United States, at least, has sought in ICBM survivability: a significant number of survivors *or* a large attack price; endurance (not always provided by BMD); independence from warning (not provided by BMD); moderate-to-high defense confidence; reliable command, control, and communications; moderate acquisition cost and low operation cost; and acceptable environmental impact. Few proposals for survivable ICBM basing have met all these criteria.[13]

Traditional Defense of Silos

The first example explores in general terms the characteristics and performance of a hypothetical defense of Minuteman by a traditional endoatmospheric BMD. The example could easily be extended to Soviet

13. OTA, *MX Missile Basing*.

SS-18 or SS-19 ICBMs, to the U.S. MX, and to other arrays of isolated, hardened aimpoints.

The ICBM deployment in this example consists of 1000 silos organized into six wings with an 8–10 km (4–5 mi.) spacing between silos and about 20,000 km² (8000 sq. mi.) a wing. Of these 1000 silos, 550 contain Minuteman III missiles with three RVs each, and 450 contain Minuteman II missiles with one RV each, for a total of 2100 RVs. The Soviet Union is likely to attack, and the United States to defend, Minuteman III more heavily than Minuteman II, but for simplicity of discussion consider an "averaged" deployment of 1000 missiles, each "worth" two RVs.

A Minuteman defense begun today would take five to ten years—until the late 1980s, at least—to complete. By that time the Soviet Union will undoubtedly have firmly established, if it has not already, 600-ft. accuracy or better (circular error probable, CEP). Together with megaton-range yields and Minuteman silos hardened to nominal overpressures of a few thousand pounds per square inch (psi), this accuracy means that the probability of destroying an undefended silo is 90 percent or higher. At the very least, yield increases (to, say, 2 MT) accompanied even by 600–700 ft. CEPs would offer essentially certain destruction (greater than 99 percent). Likewise the reliability of Soviet RVs—defined as the probability that an RV assigned to a target will be delivered successfully and will detonate with its full explosive yield—will probably be in the range of 90 percent.

If attack price is defined as the number of RVs needed to furnish 90 percent or greater probability of damage, then the price of each undefended Minuteman silo is (just barely) one Soviet RV of moderate yield. If the product of reliability and probability of kill falls below 0.9, or if extra insurance is desired, another warhead can be added (and customarily is in this type of analysis).

If the United States deployed a traditional BMD with a price of two to eight RVs for each silo, the overall price for attacking Minuteman would be 2000 to 8000 RVs instead of 1000 to 2000 in the undefended case. If the proposed defense were in fact only capable of a two to three RV price, it would presumably not win approval for deployment unless it were inexpensive or unless the Soviet Union were somehow severely hampered in reacting with quantitative or qualitative improvements to its arsenal (conceivably through some radical arms control regime). In the four to eight RV price range, the defense could still be overwhelmed by a straightforward increase in the size of the Soviet RV inventory, yet the exchange ratio—4000 to 8000 RVs to destroy 2000 RVs—would make Minuteman a relatively less attractive target, at least in this arithmetic sense.

Let us examine some of the considerations that arise in designing a generic endoatmospheric defense of Minuteman capable of exacting a total attack price of 5000 RVs. To achieve this price one could deploy 5000 interceptors and design for 10 percent probability of survival in a five-on-one attack, or one could deploy 2500 interceptors, defend half the silos preferentially, and design for 20 percent survival probability against a five-on-one attack. The result in each case would be 100 surviving silos. Preferential defense requires an interceptor with a 10-km or so radius of operation and accurate impact point prediction at the time the interceptor is committed to an approaching object. The interceptors need to be distributed about the silo fields because, if they are aggregated so that one RV can destroy several interceptors, they become attractive targets for a precursor attack. We might want to group the 2500 interceptors into 250 clusters of ten, each cluster forming a single target, in order to economize on communications connections, construction costs, land acquisition, rights-of-way, and so on. Suppose now the attacker uses 2000 RVs in an eight-on-one attack on the 250 clusters. Even though the clusters can defend one another, eight RVs on each means almost certain destruction of all the interceptors. Another 2000 RVs next destroy all the silos, now undefended. The offense has paid a price of only 4000 RVs for Minuteman! Since the design goal is a 5000 RV price, the defense must group interceptors in more than 250 clusters, say, 500. A large number of interceptors, together with appropriate (if expensive) basing, can make a precursor attack on them unattractive.

The radars are a different matter. Assume the simplest radar configuration for this hypothetical BMD: a single transportable radar capable of search, track, and fire control. These fairly sophisticated radars are expensive. Suppose the defense buys 120 of them—twenty for each of six Minuteman wings—and estimates that at least 25 percent of them—five for each wing—need to survive a precursor attack in order to guarantee acceptable defense performance.

If the radars are based so that each presents the Soviet Union with a single, fixed target, 1000 RVs (about eight-on-one) should easily result in less than 25 percent survival, thus virtually eliminating the BMD system. If each radar is mounted on a truck and allowed to roam freely throughout the Minuteman wing and its immediate vicinity, the attack price on the radar is increased. For a wing 200 km from north to south and 100 km from east to west and a radar that can defend from anywhere within 50 km of the easternmost and westernmost silos and 100 km of the northernmost, the total effective "roaming area" is 60,000 km² for each wing. If the radar trucks are destroyed by a 1-MT blast closer than 8 km, then less than 2000 RVs will sweep all six wings clean of radars (unless they defend themselves efficiently).

Another option would be to base the radars deceptively, hiding them in, say, 1000 shelters like a shell game. This implies undertaking construction of a shelter complex comparable in scale to the Minuteman deployment itself, with accompanying cost, land acquisition, environmental impact, and other problems of such a large project. When construction on this scale is contemplated, one is tempted to construct new shelters for the offensive missiles as well, which is called MPS basing. MPS basing will be discussed later.

Even though it is not an easy matter to construct a traditional endoatmospheric defense of Minuteman that claims a price of five RVs a silo and that can defend that claim against fairly straightforward precursor attacks, let us suppose this can be accomplished. We then ask what technical factors besides defense suppression ultimately limit the price the defense can impose. That is, supposing the defense has an infinite number of interceptors and radars based so that they cannot be destroyed, why can't the price be increased indefinitely?

If the offense simply lobs in RVs one after another so that each intercept is independent, the goal of five RVs is easily achieved, since even a 63 percent probability of intercept preserves 10 percent of the silos against a five-on-one attack [$(0.63)^5 = 0.1$]. Obviously the attacker need not simply lob in RVs but can adopt any of the array of offensive tactics discussed earlier, such as blackout, decoys, maneuverable reentry vehicles, jamming, and shoot-look-shoot strategies.

Consider, for example, the threat posed by blackout. The defense designed in this example is not a last-ditch defense: it has been given enough reach to defend widely separated silos preferentially. It therefore examines and commits interceptors to attacking objects judged to be RVs before these objects reach 100,000–150,000 ft. in altitude. The region affected by blackout from a 1-MT burst at 150,000 ft. is about 10 km in radius, so seventy such bursts could produce propagation disruptions at this altitude over the entire approach to a Minuteman wing. These disruptions would persist for at least a few seconds, preventing tracking of RVs, interfering with discrimination, or increasing the defense's susceptibility to jamming. The defense could in principle try to intercept blackout-producing RVs before they detonated, if the interceptor had a long enough range. But the defense is preferential and does not wish to intercept all approaching RVs, yet it is unable to tell which RVs are fused to detonate at high altitudes and which at the silos. The limitations imposed by blackout are therefore unavoidable.

Simple/Novel Defense of Minuteman

A simple/novel defense capable of shooting down the first one or two RVs approaching a silo would obviously be of limited value, since it could only force the Soviet Union to increase its allocation of RVs to Minuteman by 1000 or 2000. Since forcing an attacker to "double up" is an easy defensive task, such a defense would probably not excite technical controversy. But unless the defense were very cheap, the small attack price enforced would not clearly be worth the trouble of deployment.

But it is instructive to examine this defense from the attacker's point of view. This exercise is particularly interesting in the case where the silo kill probability of the RVs is low, meaning that even if a warhead arrives at the target with predicted guidance errors and detonates with full explosive yield, the probability of destroying the silo is significantly less than 100 percent. In this case, the offensive planner needs to ensure that *two* RVs arrive and detonate on target to have a high probability of damage. If the kill probability, K, for a single RV is 70 percent and its reliability, R, is 90 percent, the damage expectancy, DE, is $K \times R = 63$ percent. If two RVs arrive, each one detonating with full destructive power, the probability the silo survives the first RV (37 percent) times the probability it survives the second (also 37 percent) leads to a survival probability of 14 percent ($0.37 \times 0.37 = 0.14$), that is, a compound DE of 86 percent. However, if the first detonation interferes with the second—fratricide—then the DE is only 70 percent, since in this case one cannot compound the kill probabilities. In order to avoid fratricide, the relative timing of the two RVs might have to be adjusted. Too short an interval between arrival of the two RVs, and radiation and blast threaten the later arriver; too long, and dust and debris from the earlier burst or from bursts at nearby silos *might* prevent detonation of the follow-on RV, depending on the height of burst, on the geometry of surrounding silos, and on poorly understood nuclear effects.

Table 4-3. *Effect of a Hypothetical Simple/Novel Defense on the Percentage of Minuteman Silos Destroyed by Soviet Attack*

Single-shot probability of silo destruction	$K = 0.7$[a]	$K = 1.0$
No defense		
1-on-1	63	90
2-on-1 (no fratricide)	86	99
Hypothetical simple/novel defense		
2-on-1	57	81
3-on-1 (no fratricide)	71	81
3-on-1 (fratricide)	57	81
4-on-1 (no fratricide)	94	95
4-on-1 (fratricide)	67	95

Source: Author's estimates.

a. K = probability that detonation destroys the silo if the RV arrives with the predicted guidance errors and detonates with full explosive yield.

In the case of the simple/novel BMD, the offense faces the task of structuring an attack under the dual constraints of penetrating the simple/novel defense at low price and exploding *two* warheads successfully. A simple example shows how even a relatively poor defense complicates the attack planner's job.

Consider a hypothetical simple/novel defense subject to the following rules: (1) If a precursor RV detonates just outside the range of the interceptor and a second RV follows a few seconds later, the defense has no chance of intercepting the second. (2) If either RV detonates near the target, it destroys the defense unit. (3) In all other circumstances the defense is *perfect,* having a 100 percent intercept probability. This view of the defense would correspond to that of an offensive planner confident in the effects of precursors in destroying the soft defense unit but unwilling to plan on simple leakage. Table 4-3 shows the damage expectancies in the undefended case for one and two RVs with Ks of 0.7 and 1.0. With simple/novel BMD, the offense considers five attacks:

—*Two-on-one:* The first RV is burst as a precursor, the second as a silo-killer. The precursor actually arrives 90 percent of the time, and in those events the silo-killer succeeds with probability *DE.* (The offense can consider a "salvage fuse" option for its RVs, where the RV is designed so that impact with a defensive projectile causes the bomb to detonate. In this case, disruptive nuclear effects result even from successful intercepts.)

—*Three-on-one, no fratricide:* The offensive sequence is precursor, silo-killer, silo-killer. All three RVs arrive 73 percent of the time [$(0.9)^3$].

The precursor fails and the other two RVs either do not arrive or are intercepted 10 percent of the time; the precursor works, the second RV does not arrive, and the third either does not arrive or is intercepted 9 percent of the time; and the first two arrive and the third fails to arrive 8 percent of the time.

—*Three-on-one, fratricide:* If both silo-killers arrive, the first to detonate destroys the second (fratricide is certain). The precursor is assumed to cause no fratricide (perhaps because it is burst at high altitude).

—*Four-on-one, no fratricide:* The sequence is precursor, silo-killer, precursor, silo-killer. All four RVs arrive only 66 percent of the time. A variety of other possible outcomes also lead to destruction of the silo.

—*Four-on-one, fratricide:* The same outcomes are possible as without fratricide, but certain fratricide means that there is no compounding of damage in those cases when both silo-killers succeed in arriving at the silo.

Table 4-3 shows that even this simple/novel defense would give an offensive planner problems satisfying a requirement to do near-certain damage to ICBM silos, especially if the planner was concerned about accuracy or about fratricide for the attack sequences used to penetrate the defense.

Layered Defense of Silos

This example involves a substantial defensive investment, amounting to two separate BMD systems, in pursuit of high attack price.[14] Such a large investment probably would have to be able to claim eight or more RVs for each defended silo—8000 or more total for Minuteman—to be considered at all. If a lower price were thought to suffice, there would be no need to consider advanced systems incorporating substantial technical risk; traditional BMDs would do. The layered defense discussed here consists of a traditional terminal (or simple/novel) underlay and the advanced exoatmospheric Overlay using infrared sensing and homing-and-impact kill (see chapter 3).

This section presents calculations about the theoretical effectiveness of a layered defense of silos.[15] But the methods used in making such

14. This section draws in part on the author's previous work in OTA, *MX Missile Basing*, pp. 129–39.
15. These calculations would actually apply to any exoatmospheric BMD that intercepts individual RVs in midcourse; some directed-energy proposals have this characteristic.

calculations, and their outcomes, are *not* the crux of technical disagreement about whether this defense is worth the investment. Nor is the disagreement confined to whether the individual Overlay technologies—infrared sensors, compact data processors, miniature homing vehicles, and so on—are mature enough to entrust to a near-term deployment decision. Rather the crux of the controversy is whether the system architecture that results when all of the parts are assembled is too susceptible to simple penetration tactics, too fragile to withstand precursor attack, or so complex that the defense collapses if a few components do not perform perfectly. Since this system aims to enforce a high attack price, it must stand up to much more persistent attempts at disruption than the traditional or simple/novel systems discussed so far. Probability calculations do not lend themselves to faithful presentation of the many Achilles' heel issues for this layered defense. These potential Achilles' heels include:

1. Cumulative or synergistic effects of small failures in a complex, highly coordinated defensive engagement.

2. Susceptibility of remote sensing in space—probably with infrared sensors—to being fooled by lightweight decoys and other penetration aids.

3. Dependence on a possibly fragile warning system to give notice that attack is under way.

4. Possibly fragile internal communications as the system attempts to coordinate a complex defensive response.

5. Destruction or disruption of the defense by SLBMs or ICBMs minutes before the main attack arrives. It is likely that the Overlay has little capability to intercept SLBM RVs launched from near U.S. coasts. SLBM attack or concentrated ICBM attack cannot be allowed to put the defense system out of commission before it has a chance to defend the silos.

6. Adoption of shoot-look-shoot tactics by the offense. This technique frustrates preferential defense, the main source of the Overlay's effectiveness.

Without a precise system design, it is impossible to assess these problems, but they, rather than dispute over some specific device or theoretical parameter, underlie technical doubts about the Overlay. By contrast, the years of experience accumulated with traditional defenses, making difficult tradeoffs between cost and performance and between solving one problem and causing another, narrow the range of doubt about their performance.

To see how the analysis of a theoretical layered defense works, consider again the Minuteman deployment of 1000 ICBM silos and assume for the moment that the Soviet Union deploys *no penetration aids* or that discrimination is perfect. There is a certain probability that the Overlay will succeed in destroying an RV if it detects, tracks, and allocates a homing vehicle to it. Call this probability the efficiency of the Overlay. It will be necessary further to assume that the probabilities that individual intercepts succeed are statistically independent; this would not be precisely true if, for example, the homing-and-kill vehicles were boosted into space on the same rocket or were dependent on the same acquisition sensor. A very good value for the efficiency would be 85 percent, considering that the much simpler ICBM-booster-plus-RV combination is usually only considered about 90 percent reliable in analogous calculations. A more modest value for the efficiency would be 70 percent, and 50 percent would be disappointing indeed. We shall see that the usefulness of the layered defense depends strongly on Overlay efficiency.

The underlay must also be specified. Many choices are possible, ranging from a sophisticated traditional defense to a single-shot simple/ novel system. Assume that the underlay will make a successful first intercept 70 percent of the time, will make a second intercept of a follow-on RV 50 percent of the time, and has no capability to make a third intercept. This is not a sophisticated underlay, but it is substantial and fairly costly. For preferential defense to work, all silos must be covered even though only some of them will actually be defended.

For the Soviet arsenal, assume initially 8000 RVs, each perfectly reliable and lethal to a Minuteman silo. If the Soviet Union has no reason to target particular silos preferentially, it can direct eight RVs at each silo.

If the Overlay efficiency is 85 percent, then the probability that *all eight* RVs aimed at a *defended* silo are intercepted by the Overlay is 27 percent $[(0.85)^8]$. The probability that one RV penetrates is the probability that seven RVs are intercepted $[(0.85)^7]$ times the probability that one penetrates (0.15) times the number (8) that have a chance to penetrate, for a total probability of 38 percent. The probability that two RVs penetrate is $(0.85)^6$ times $(0.15)^2$, times the number of distinct pairs of RVs (28) that could be the pair of leaking warheads, for a total of 24 percent.

Thus, 27 percent of the time the silo is safe because all eight RVs are destroyed in space. One gets through 38 percent of the time, but the underlay intercepts this leaker 70 percent of the time. Two RVs get through 24 percent of the time, but the first of these is intercepted 70 percent of the time and the second 50 percent of the time. Thus the overall probability that the silo survives is 62 percent [(0.27) + (0.38)(0.7) + (0.24)(0.7)(0.5) = (0.62)].

How many silos are actually defended at all depends on the number of interceptors the United States deploys. If the United States deploys 400 large ICBM-sized Overlay intercept boosters with ten homing-and-kill vehicles each, 500 silos can be defended against the 8000-RV Soviet attack. Then 62 percent of the defended silos survive, for a total of 310 silos or 620 RVs in this averaged Minuteman deployment where each ICBM carries two RVs. The Soviet Union expends 8000 RVs to destroy 1380 U.S. RVs, and over 4000 unintercepted RVs detonate on U.S. soil. If the Overlay efficiency is low, the defense achieves better results by routinely dispatching two homing vehicles against each RV, even though only half as many RVs can be intercepted with a given defensive arsenal.

Figures 4-8 through 4-12 display *theoretical* calculations of the outcomes of perfectly coordinated defensive engagements using this layered BMD against 1000 silos of equal value. Soviet RVs are assumed to be 100 percent lethal to the silos if they arrive, but their reliability is taken as 90 percent. No decoys or other penetration aids are assumed to be deployed by the Soviet Union; alternatively, discrimination is assumed perfect. "Battle management" is assumed to be perfect: each homing vehicle is allocated in the best possible way on the basis of totally accurate, detailed information about the size and structure of the approaching attack (this is called adaptive preferential defense). Included in the information available to the battle management computer is an accurate prediction of the impact point of each attacking RV.

Figure 4-8 shows the ideal performance of the layered defense with Overlay efficiency of 85 percent—probably the most optimistic value. The flat tail of the drawdown curve means that after the Soviet Union has destroyed the first 75 percent or so of the silos, it must pay a higher and higher price for each additional silo destroyed. If the attack price is defined at the 10 percent survival level, then the theoretical layered defense charges a price of more than twelve RVs for each silo.

The defense deployment of figure 4-8 consists of 4000 homing vehicles. If as many as ten homing vehicles can share the same ICBM-sized booster—an optimistic assumption—the defensive deployment consists

Figure 4-8. *Ideal Performance of Layered Defense*

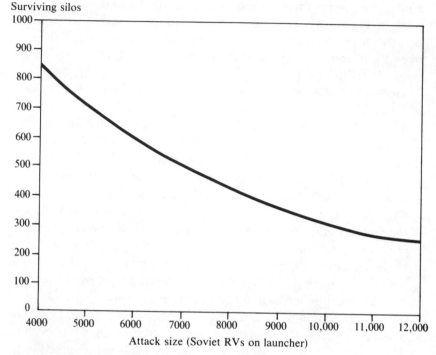

Surviving silos

Attack size (Soviet RVs on launcher)

Note: Characteristics of the system are as follows:
—Overlay efficiency = 0.85
—Perfect discrimination
—Perfect battle management
—Perfect impact point prediction
—Defensive arsenal = 4000 homing vehicles
—Soviet ICBM reliability = 0.9
—Underlay characteristics:
  70 percent intercept probability on first shot
  50 percent intercept probability on second shot
   0 percent third and subsequent shots
—All silos attacked with equal intensity.

of 400 defensive missiles defending 1000 offensive missiles. A problem
immediately arises about how to base the defensive missiles so they
cannot be attacked and put out of commission minutes before attack on
the silos. The Overlay interceptors can, of course, defend themselves,
and for a 400-interceptor deployment with 85 percent efficiency, defense
suppression is not a much better tactic for the offense than the frontal
assault shown in figure 4-8. For smaller defensive deployments or poorer
Overlay efficiency, however, defense suppression might be an effective
way to sidestep the high performance shown in figure 4-8.

Figures 4-9 and 4-10 show the effects of a slip in Overlay efficiency

Figure 4-9. *Effect of Overlay Efficiency on Size of Defensive Arsenal Needed to Ensure 500 Surviving Silos*

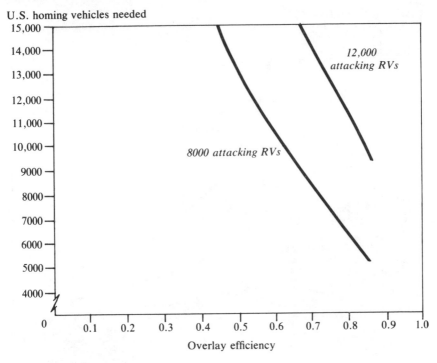

U.S. homing vehicles needed

Overlay efficiency

Note: Characteristics of the system are as follows:
—Perfect discrimination
—Perfect battle management
—Perfect impact point prediction
—Soviet ICBM reliability = 0.9
—Underlay characteristics:
  70 percent intercept probability on first shot
  50 percent intercept probability on second shot
  0 percent third and subsequent shots
—All silos attacked with equal intensity.

from the practical maximum of about 85 percent to lower values. Figure 4-9 shows how many Overlay interceptors the United States would need to deploy to preserve 500 silos. In this idealized Minuteman deployment of 1000 silos with an average MIRV loading of two RVs for each silo, 500 silos contain 1000 RVs. Survival of 1000 RVs was the goal against which the Carter administration's racetrack MPS system was designed. Figure 4-9 shows that practical Overlay deployments stand no chance of preserving this number of Minuteman RVs. Even for an Overlay with 85 percent efficiency, the required defense deployments are large, and preserving the same level of survival against growth in the Soviet attack

Figure 4-10. *Effect of Overlay Efficiency on Size of Defensive Arsenal Needed to Ensure 100 Surviving Silos*

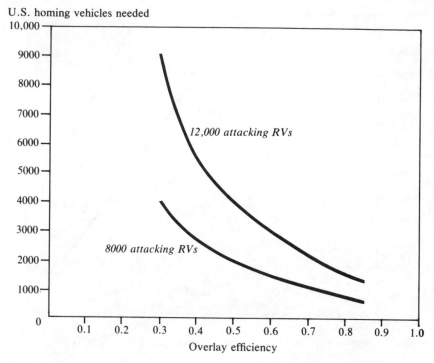

U.S. homing vehicles needed

Note: Characteristics of the system are the same as those in figure 4-9.

requires deploying more than one homing vehicle for every RV deployed by the Soviet Union—surely a losing cost exchange. If the United States is content with 100 surviving silos—200 surviving RVs—the task is easier, as shown in figure 4-10: the Overlay deployments remain below 4000 homing vehicles even when the Overlay efficiency slips well below 85 percent. This behavior reflects the long flat tail on the drawdown curve, where the defense is charging the attacker a high price to destroy the last 25 percent of the silos.

Consider now the impact of penetration aids on the Overlay. The principles of infrared sensing and discrimination in space were described in chapter 3. Consider first a deployment of one perfect decoy along with each true RV. Making room for these decoys would probably require negligible off-loading of RVs from Soviet missiles, meaning little penalty to the Soviet Union if the decoys failed. But the impact on the Overlay performance could be dramatic. If one kill vehicle were allocated to each

Figure 4-11. *Effect of Underlays on Ideal Layered Defense Performance*

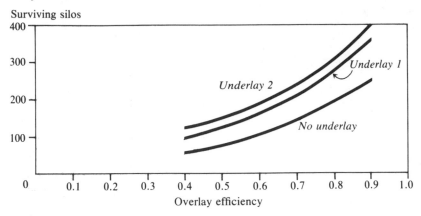

Surviving silos

Note: Characteristics are as follows:
—10,000 RV attack, 10 RVs on each silo
—Defensive arsenal = 4000 homing vehicles
—Perfect discrimination
—Perfect battle management
—Perfect impact point prediction
—Soviet ICBM reliability = 0.9
—Underlay 1:
  70 percent intercept probability on first shot
  50 percent intercept probability on second shot
  0 percent third and subsequent shots
—Underlay 2:
  85 percent first shot
  70 percent second shot
  50 percent third shot
  0 percent fourth and subsequent shots.

RV-decoy *pair,* the effective efficiency would be cut in half, since the intercepted object has only a 50 percent chance of being a true RV. This halving of the efficiency would clearly be catastrophic for leakage of the defense. If the defense directed a kill vehicle at each object, decoy and RV, the same number of silos would survive as in the no-decoy case, but an arsenal of Overlay boosters *twice as numerous* as in figures 4-9 and 4-10 would be needed.

In practice, no decoy is perfect, although the offense could deploy many more than one decoy with each RV. The defense would have to make a tradeoff between leakage (intercepting the object judged most likely to be an RV and allowing an RV to penetrate if the guess is wrong) and wastage (intercepting everything). The need to keep Overlay leakage low means that the best solution for the defense is usually to accept high wastage. An offensive decoy deployment could therefore drive the defense to a costly increase in arsenal.

The decoy problem for infrared-sensing ballistic missile defenses is

Figure 4-12. *Effect of Attack Size on Ideal Layered Defense Performance*

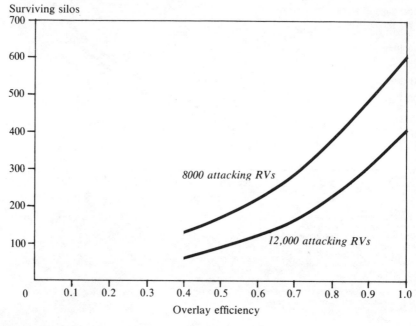

Surviving silos

8000 attacking RVs

12,000 attacking RVs

Overlay efficiency

Note: Characteristics are as follows:
—Perfect discrimination
—Perfect battle management
—Perfect impact point prediction
—Defensive arsenal = 4000 homing vehicles
—Soviet ICBM reliability = 0.9
—Underlay characteristics:
   70 percent intercept probability on first shot
   50 percent intercept probability on second shot
    0 percent third and subsequent shots
—All silos attacked with equal intensity.

fundamental, since it is based on straightforward and inescapable physical principles. The physics of reentry discrimination, by contrast, is much more complex. An RV covered with layers of space blanket insulation with a reflecting coating—an "RV-in-a-thermos"—and an empty reflective balloon are a perfect pair. Deployment mechanisms and in-flight motions are the only complications in principle to designing perfect lightweight exoatmospheric decoys.[16] No general claim that a

16. The defense can in principle make ever more sensitive measurements and perform detailed analyses of the signature data, trying to seize on some small flaw in the matching of exoatmospheric decoys and RVs. But this procedure soon runs into problems. For one thing, discrimination must be done before interceptors are committed, while attacking

long-wave-infrared-sensing exoatmospheric system can discriminate perfectly or that good exoatmospheric decoys must be heavy can ever be substantiated technically.

The answer to the Achilles' heel of discrimination for the advanced exoatmospheric Overlay will not be found in better sensors or discrimination algorithms. It must be found elsewhere, if at all. Three possibilities are: (1) that the defense's components can somehow be made cheaply enough and in large enough numbers to afford wasting them on decoys; (2) that the Soviet Union would not have confidence in its penetration aids and would ignore them in its strategic calculations (and that the United States would then also ignore decoys in its calculations); and (3) that Soviet testing of its decoys would reveal some flaw that the Soviet Union would not detect and correct and that the U.S. BMD could focus on.

Defense of Multiple Protective Shelters

Multiple protective shelter basing is a way of countering the perceived dangers of ICBMs with multiple independently targetable reentry vehicles (MIRVs) by providing several aimpoints, instead of one silo, for each missile. If the number of shelters for each missile equals the number of MIRVed warheads on each booster in the opposing arsenal, it "costs" the offense one missile to destroy a missile. In the Carter administration's proposed racetrack MPS deployment, for instance, 200 MX missiles and 4400 decoys were to be hidden in the Great Basin desert area of Nevada and Utah. The ratio of shelters to missiles in this case was 23:1, larger than the number of MIRVs either side has mounted on a single ICBM.[17]

Suppose that a defense unit—radar and interceptor—is associated with each missile in the shelter deployment and programmed to defend the shelter where the missile is hiding. The offense would then have to pay the attack price—a few RVs—to attack the shelter successfully. But since the offense would not know which of the multiple shelters contained the missiles, it would have to pay the attack price at each shelter. The

objects are still quite distant. Second, interpreting very detailed infrared measurements requires knowledge of the season, weather, and time of day on the portions of the earth overflown by the attacking objects, since some of the radiation from the objects is in fact reflected earthshine. Third, the offense can increase the background noise by redout or by using depressed trajectories.

17. OTA, *MX Missile Basing*, pp. 33–107.

U.S. Army's Low-Altitude Defense System (LoADS), a terminal endoatmospheric system proposed with the modest goal of forcing the Soviet Union to double up, therefore promised to raise the price of destroying all the MX missiles in the racetrack from 4600 RVs to 9200.[18]

SHELTER NUMBER AND ATTACK PRICE. Since the overall price in defended MPS is the attack price times the number of shelters, one has the choice of designing for high attack price and small numbers of shelters or vice versa. For example, a 1000-shelter system was also suggested for MX. To claim a price as high as the racetrack-plus-LoADS deployment, this system would need a defense with a price of nine RVs for each aimpoint. Such a high price is probably not realizable with traditional defenses.

The relationship between the attack price and shelter spacing is important for MPS defense. Widely spaced shelters can each be treated independently, like the silos in the previous examples. As the shelter spacing gets closer, events at adjacent aimpoints begin to affect the BMD's chances of defending the missile. Only a shelter containing a missile gets defended; offensive warheads are allowed to detonate freely at nearby shelters. The defense must survive and operate in this severe nuclear-effects environment. As the shelters—hence adjacent bursts—get closer, the price the defense can claim with assurance goes down (see the representative curve of figure 4-13).

A BMD addition to MPS would become attractive when the number of shelters required to keep ahead of the Soviet RV arsenal grew so large that cost and land acquisition became prohibitive. The Carter administration's MPS system covered substantial portions of the states of Nevada and Utah (though the actual area occupied by the shelters was quite small), a factor that definitely contributed to public opposition. If deployment area is the practical limitation to system scale, a close shelter spacing is to be preferred to wide spacing, even though price per aimpoint increases with wider spacing (see figure 4-14).

DEFENSE DESIGN. Terminal endoatmospheric BMDs are the obvious choice for MPS. First, only a modest attack price for each aimpoint is required, so there is no need to incur the risk and cost associated with more elaborate systems. Second, leverage is obtained by preferential defense; this presupposes the defense can tell, at the time it must commit an interceptor, whether a given RV is heading toward the missile-containing shelter or toward one of the nearby empty shelters. This

18. Ibid, pp. 118–26.

Figure 4-13. *Effect of Shelter Spacing on the Attack Price per Shelter in a Multiple Protective Shelter Deployment*

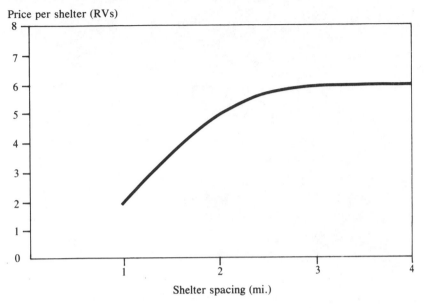

Figure 4-14. *Effect of Shelter Spacing on the Attack Price per Deployment Area in a Multiple Protective Shelter Deployment*

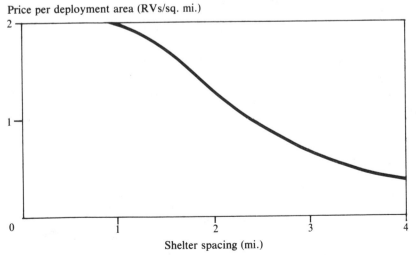

Figure 4-15. *Low-Altitude Defense Unit after Breakout from Racetrack Multiple Protective Shelter*

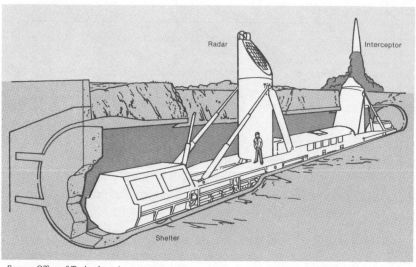

Source: Office of Technology Assessment.

accurate impact point prediction is more difficult to provide for high-altitude defenses. Third, blackout is a real problem for MPS given the density of targets, and a terminal system operating in dense air where fireballs are relatively small fares better.

At close shelter spacing, a mobile defense roaming the deployment area could not be made hard enough to withstand the expected density of bursts. Therefore the defense itself must have the protection of hardened structures. These structures must be numerous or the offense could attack the defense sites, overwhelm the BMD, and then turn to the undefended shelters. This problem is the same as that described for the traditional defense of Minuteman in the first example. In the MPS case one is spared the trouble of building an entire separate set of defensive shelters if use can be made of the missile shelters to house both offensive missiles and defense units (DUs). When attack is on the way, the DUs expose themselves and prepare to defend, using the walls of the shelters for protection. This was the choice made for the proposed addition of LoADS to the racetrack MPS (see figure 4-15).

EFFECTIVENESS ISSUES. The designer of MPS defense must consider the usual spectrum of offensive tactics and hardware, as well as some problems unique to the MPS case. Four issues that arise in planning an effective MPS defense will be discussed here.

1. *Deception.* Addition of the DU to the MPS system complicates deception. In the undefended case, a decoy must match all of the "signatures"—electromagnetic, thermal, optical, acoustic, seismic, chemical, and nuclear—of the presence or motion of the missile. This is a complex engineering task, even though the decoy designer has no other goal than to eliminate all hints of discrimination between the two types of object. The DU, by contrast, cannot be changed freely to match the missile, and in fact brings to the game its own distinctive signatures that the missile and decoy must in turn match. Furthermore, the DU might have to be placed in a shelter near the missile in order to do its job, because in an attack the number of bursts in the shelter field is so great that a DU would have a hard time defending a missile separated by miles of severely disturbed environment. Failure to hide the DU in this case would not only expose the defense to suppression but expose the missile's location as well. Finally, if the offense chose to adopt a shoot-look-shoot strategy, the effectiveness of a deceptively based BMD would be greatly reduced.

2. *Nuclear effects and self-defense.* The goal of defending MPS is to force the attacker to waste many weapons on empty shelters. The resulting high density of offensive bursts in the shelter field compels the defense to survive and operate in a severe physical environment. The offense could contrive a variety of laydowns to intensify the defense's problems.

Hardening a complex and relatively exposed unit to withstand many megaton-range detonations just a few kilometers away introduces some considerations not seen in other nuclear hardening problems. Ordinary silos have to face airblast and ground motion. Communications equipment such as that which carries presidential launch orders in nuclear war must deal with longer-range effects, including ordinary electromagnetic pulse and ionospheric disruption. But the exposed defense units in MPS must handle "close-in" weapons effects like prompt radiation, thermal flash, and "source-region" EMP (involving huge currents of electrons thrust out from the burst point). Hardening against these effects would pose unprecedented problems and would have to be accomplished without adding excessively to the cost of each shelter and within the design constraints placed on the DU by the need to match the missiles and decoys.

The hardness of the exposed DU defines a "keepout zone" around it: RVs approaching this zone must be intercepted if they arrive before the DU has completed its job of defending the missile at the required price. Self-defense is therefore crucial, since with every attack wave on the missile shelter the DU shelter comes under attack as well. The probability that the missile survives two attack waves is thus the probability that the defense makes two successive intercepts over the missile shelter *times* the probability that the DU survives the first wave to make a second attempt at interception. If the defense is too soft and the keepout zone too large, too many intercepts must be made just to keep the DU alive and working.

Operation in the nuclear environment is also a problem. Between the DU and the shelter it defends could be many bursts, through which the radar must see and the interceptor must fly. Since the fireball radius at sea level for a 1-MT blast is about 1 km, comparable to the shelter spacing, a first wave of RVs detonated over the undefended shelters virtually covers the deployment region with opaque fireballs. Though these fireballs rise and cool quickly, they could obstruct the radar's view for the few seconds needed to make an intercept. The offense can control blackout by judicious choice of laydown. Dust swept up by rising fireballs can also interfere with radar propagation.

3. *MaRVs*. Besides dogfighting with the interceptor or attacking from unusual angles, MaRVs threaten to frustrate preferential defense in the MPS defense. The defensive radar is unable to tell whether an approaching MaRV will attack the missile shelter, the DU shelter, or an empty shelter. The defense has to intercept all potentially threatening objects or accept the possibility that the MaRVs will take a free ride to the missile shelters. If the defense only seeks a price of two RVs, encouraging MaRV attack is virtually equivalent to forcing the offense to pay the price, since MaRVs are heavier and more costly than ordinary RVs. But for BMDs seeking a higher price MaRVs are a worry.

4. *Jamming*. The density of targets in the MPS field makes jamming a relatively attractive offensive tactic, since a few jammers can affect radars in the entire deployment area. Coupled with blackout and a high traffic rate, jamming could be a serious limitation on attack price.

Defense of Densepack

The idea for the Densepack basing mode arose from the observation that if the aimpoints are brought ever closer, the offense cannot treat attack on each aimpoint independently. Since Densepack's closely spaced silos are in theory made spectacularly resistant to nuclear blast, they must be attacked one-on-one with high-yield weapons. But as soon as the first RV detonates, nuclear effects begin to engulf nearby aimpoints and, it is hoped, interfere with the RVs attacking them. This fratricide effect of one RV on another is supposed to save a portion of the silos from destruction.

Densepack appeared in 1981 and received considerable attention in the U.S. government during 1982, where it was called Closely Spaced Basing (CSB) and proposed as the basing mode for the new MX missile. Its future is unclear. The quest for MX basing has passed it by, perhaps forever. It is apparent that fratricide cannot by itself foreclose all conceivable attack avenues that a determined future opponent could pursue. A BMD add-on would be designed to handle these gaps in Densepack's self-defense.

UNDEFENDED DENSEPACK. Unlike most other basing modes considered by the United States for ICBMs, Densepack does not aim to provide unrestricted survivability and endurance. Its goal is only to preserve a portion of the silos through the first 10 or 20 min. of a war—long enough for the MX missiles to be launched in retaliation. This goal is to be achieved as follows. Fratricide is supposed to prevent the offense from destroying all of the silos in one uninterrupted attack wave. A first attack wave, though only partially effective, creates a dust cloud over the Densepack field that prevents further RVs from attacking for a half hour or so. During the respite before the offense recommences attack, the missiles are launched from their silos in retaliation. Densepack therefore offers survivability through delayed launch under attack.

A book on BMD is not the place to address the question of whether Densepack basing would offer protection against all the attack tactics that the offense could mount with ordinary ballistic RVs such as those in the Soviet arsenal today. Any argument supporting Densepack's claims about silo hardness and fratricide must invoke specific nuclear weapons effects, many of which probably could not be predicted completely in the absence of atmospheric nuclear testing. Whether in the end these uncertainties would weigh most heavily on the owner of Densepack or on the opposing offensive planner, and whether they would contribute to or detract from crisis stability, would remain the key issue unless and until clear technical judgments or new data emerged.

For stylized threats that the Soviet Union could incorporate into its future arsenal, the situation is clearer. For instance, one approach to defeating Densepack is immediately apparent: detonate all RVs so closely in time that even the nuclear radiation does not have time to pass from one silo to another before detonation of all the RVs is complete. A second approach to attacking Densepack would be to fortify RVs against dust erosion so that a slow, but still uninterrupted, attack could proceed from one end of the Densepack field to the other. A third tactic would involve "earth-penetrating" RVs that burrowed into the ground before detonating. The soil would stop radiation from passing from one RV to another, but the ground shock would destroy the silos.

A tactic called pindown involves exploding offensive weapons— ICBMs or SLBMs—in the flyout corridor above the Densepack field, destroying missiles as they tried to escape from attack. Pindown could be used against Densepack in three ways: (1) SLBM pindown in the period between launch and arrival of ICBMs could keep the missiles in their silos, preventing ordinary launch under attack (this tactic is possible for Densepack but not for Minuteman because the Minuteman flyout corridor is so large that too many detonations would be needed); (2) pindown during the attack could keep all missiles in their silos until the attack on each is finished; (3) pindown at high altitude could keep missiles from being launched during the respite between attack waves when the dust cloud is supposed to be preventing further attack.

TRADITIONAL BMD SYSTEMS WITH DENSEPACK. The role of defense of Densepack would be to defeat the attack strategies that Densepack by itself could not handle. Consider, for example, the so-called spike attack in which all of the RVs arrive and detonate within a microsecond of one another, encountering no fratricide. A traditional defense would have a good chance of destroying many of these RVs since interception would not be complicated by nuclear effects. In fact, since the RVs would be close together as they approached the silo field, just a few nuclear interceptors detonated in space might be able to destroy them all. If a few interceptors could hold off a whole wave, 100 interceptors—the number allowed within the ABM Treaty reached at SALT I—might be able to handle several waves.

Consider next an attack by earth-penetrating warheads. Since high yield is needed in theory to destroy a Densepack silo and since the earth-penetrating armor is heavy, each of these vehicles is worth a price of perhaps five ordinary RVs. If the defense can charge a price of four earth penetrators, the total price for 100 Densepack silos in this model is 2000 RVs, a modest amount by MPS standards but very good for only 100 aimpoints.

Another application for the BMD would be to intercept pindown weapons. This would be worthwhile *if* the defense were prepared to take advantage of it by arranging for missiles to escape while the pindown was interrupted.

Ideas of this sort abound for Densepack defense. Just as many difficult issues arise. Does Densepack really force the attacker to use exotic attacks, or are there gaps in the fratricide argument or shortcomings in the hardening possible for the silos? Second, how is the defense itself to survive? If the defense is going to try to exert such leverage over the offense, it must plan to face a determined effort to disrupt its functioning. Preferential defense, such as that needed to make use of a small arsenal of interceptors, requires impact point prediction capable of distinguishing RVs attacking neighboring silos only a kilometer apart. Such a strategy is clearly susceptible to MaRVs. Soviet deployment of exotic hardware tailored for attack on Densepack would be an unambiguous indication that the Soviet Union sought a capability to mount disarming first strikes. This development would itself presumably have consequences for the United States, perhaps including a disinclination to remain within the numerical limits of the ABM Treaty.

Assessment of the performance of defended Densepack is therefore dominated by uncertainties. Even more important than the uncertainties in the defense are the uncertainties in Densepack itself. If fratricide and silo hardness turned out to limit the types of effective attack to a well-defined and narrow range of the entire spectrum of attack types, defense could probably disrupt the stylized attacks and increase the overall attack price. If the range of effective attacks is *very* narrow, 100 interceptors might offer a significant barrier to attack. But if Densepack's failings are more pervasive, traditional BMD probably will not be able to rescue it.

DUST DEFENSE OF DENSEPACK. Dust defense could be used with all land basing modes for ICBMs, but its application to Densepack is particularly pertinent for two reasons. The small deployment area means that relatively few buried bombs need to be detonated to provide adequate coverage. Second, dust created by Soviet weapons is the basis for presuming that Densepack would be able to make a delayed launch under attack. It might therefore be easier for proponents to explain the U.S. dust defense as being based on the same principle as Densepack yet causing far less residual radioactivity.

Two different methods of defense by buried bombs could be used. In the first, small-fission-fraction, neutron-shielded bombs would be buried a short disance north of the Densepack field in an arc covering all possible directions of attack by Soviet ICBMs. The bombs would be detonated seconds before the arrival of Soviet RVs, throwing up a dense curtain of debris into their path. The dust cloud that would form a little later at high altitudes would provide additional protection for a longer period than the debris curtain, which would fall to the ground in a short time.

In the second scheme, a number of large weapons would be exploded several minutes before arrival of the attack, forming a high-altitude dust cloud. This would be the same type of cloud that attack on undefended Densepack is supposed to produce, only unquestionably denser. It is important to note the difference between this mechanism of dust cloud creation and Densepack's. Densepack's cloud results from surface bursts or airbursts, lofting a much smaller (and more uncertain) amount of dust to high altitude in the wake of the rising fireball. The buried bombs are sure to inject much more material into the atmosphere. Of course, the United States would always have, at least in principle, an (inefficient) dust defense even if it did not wish to build a special system: the missile warheads in the northernmost silos in the Densepack field (or nuclear BMD interceptors deployed to the north) merely have to be exploded in their silos.

Defense of Mobile Missiles and Bombers

Mobile basing schemes for nuclear forces—ICBMs, intermediate-range ballistic missiles (IRBMs), cruise missiles, and bombers—exhibit great variety, and each offers a distinct set of advantages and disadvantages in relation to fixed land basing.[19] All share the feature of presenting the attacker with a large "uncertainty area" within which the precise location of the missile-carrying vehicles cannot be specified and hence targeted. This area must be large enough that the offense cannot barrage or pattern-bomb it with nuclear weapons, sweeping it clean of all vehicles. The size of the uncertainty area is by no means the principal shortcoming of most mobile basing schemes: operating costs, concern about safety and public reaction to moving nuclear weapons around routinely, and susceptibility of vehicles carrying nuclear weapons to attack by nonnuclear means are often cited as reasons to disqualify mobile missiles. In

19. Ibid., pp. 217–32, 257–65.

the case of MX, the missile size itself precludes several mobile basing schemes. But insofar as the size of the uncertainty area becomes the main impediment to deployment or to continued confidence in mobile nuclear forces, BMD can in the right circumstances act to increase the effective uncertainty area.

A variety of vehicles have been proposed for mobile basing of nuclear weapons—trucks, planes, ships, hovercraft, seaplanes, even balloons—but there are two generic types. In the first "untrackable" variety, the offense is presumed unable to locate or track the vehicles and must have recourse to barrage of the entire deployment region. For instance, it is usually agreed that a hypothetical deployment of many small single-warhead ICBMs roaming U.S. highways in disguised (or even undisguised) trucks would be virtually impossible for the Soviet Union continually to locate and attack individually.

In the second variety of mobile basing, "escape from aimpoint," the vehicles are based at a fixed site, or the offense is credited with being able to track them as they move around. In the former case, the vehicles must dash from their bases on warning of attack. In the latter case, the vehicles move randomly away from the point where they were last sighted during the time it takes the offense to transmit their locations from its tracking sites to its missile field, target the location, and deliver a warhead. (This is called the intelligence cycle time.) In either case, the vehicles have moved to anywhere within a large uncertainty area by the time the attacking warheads arrive. Examples of escape-from-aimpoint basing are U.S. B-52 and B-1 bombers and cruise missile carriers, Pershing and ground-launched cruise missiles (GLCMs) slated for European deployment, the Soviet SS-20 IRBMs, and the air-mobile basing proposal for the MX ICBM.

If the uncertainty area of an untrackable mobile scheme is so small that it would be relatively easy to barrage, the defense can increase the size of the deployment area or the hardness of the vehicle. If the offense can barrage much, but not all, of the deployment area, the defense can also increase the number of survivors (though not the fraction of the total) simply by increasing the overall number of vehicles. An escape-from-aimpoint system can be improved by increasing vehicle hardness or speed. In a deployment decision, BMD would have to compete with these methods of enhancing survivability.

How can BMD help increase the effective uncertainty area? If the defense knows the location of each vehicle at the time the barraging RVs arrive, it can shoot down the RV approaching the actual vehicle location. A single-shot defense forces the offense to double the intensity of the barrage, halving the area that can be barraged with a given arsenal. For untrackable systems the itinerary of each vehicle at all times would have to be made available to the defense, unless the defense accompanied the vehicles themselves. For escape-from-aimpoint systems, the BMD would need to know each vehicle's escape plan or to accompany the vehicle. Otherwise the BMD could only pick out a random set of barraging RVs to intercept, a tactic that would only enhance vehicle survival if the BMD had enough interceptors to shoot at a substantial fraction of the RVs.

For example, consider a convoy of Pershing II missiles leaving its base in West Germany. Since the flight time of an attacking Soviet missile is short (say, 10–15 min.), a convoy trying to escape from the base at 50 mi. per hour along four exit routes on the basis of instantaneous warning of Soviet launch would only present an uncertainty length of 10 mi. of highway in any direction. If the vehicles were about 5 psi hard, five 1-MT weapons would be sure to destroy all the missiles (see figure 4-16). A BMD installed at the base could increase the attack price to several times the undefended price.

Suppose that the convoy leaves its base when hostilities become imminent, but a Soviet agent follows it and regularly reports its location to Moscow. Suppose further that the intelligence cycle time from agent sighting to attack arrival is 1 hr. and that the average convoy speed is 40 mph. The convoy could thus have moved 40 mi. in any direction since the agent's last report. An RV would be needed for about each 10 mi. of road barraged, and a BMD accompanying the convoy could again multiply this by the defense price.

Consider next a hypothetical road-mobile deployment of new single-warhead missiles in the United States. If the missiles roamed the highways at random and were untrackable, they would need no BMD because the available road length is so large. But if they were based at military reservations, escaping only on warning, or if they were somehow tracked continuously by the Soviet Union, a BMD accompanying each convoy could increase the attack price just as it did for Pershing. Against thousands of RVs in the Soviet arsenal, the BMD may not provide absolute survivability, but the exchange ratio of Soviet RVs expended for each U.S. RV destroyed could be quite large. For instance, suppose a convoy of 5-psi vehicles carrying eight single-warhead ICBMs can

Figure 4-16. *Plan for an Attack on a Hypothetical Pershing II Ballistic Missile Base in West Germany*

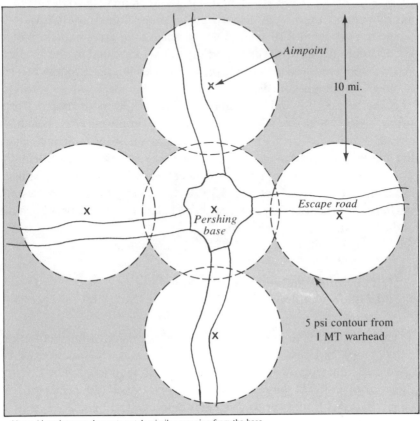

Note: Aimpoints are chosen to catch missiles escaping from the base.

escape from its base by one of four roads at 40 mph. on warning of Soviet ICBM launch. The uncertainty length at the end of the half-hour ICBM flight time is then 80 mi., requiring eight 1-MT RVs to barrage, an exchange ratio of one. This is comparable to MPS with ten shelters per MX missile. A BMD accompanying the convoy and capable of a price of three could triple the exchange ratio.

Last, consider the defense of U.S. bomber bases. Unlike the trucks, aircraft cannot move quickly the moment they receive warning. The crews must get in the cockpit (if they are not already), bring engines up to speed, taxi down the runway, and gather airspeed. Once airborne and traveling at hundreds of miles per hour, though, aircraft generate uncertainty area quickly. SLBMs launched from Soviet submarines near U.S. coasts pose the principal threat to bombers. Though few in number, these RVs could arrive 10–15 min. after launch and try to destroy the aircraft before they were airborne. The more numerous ICBM RVs would not arrive until 10–15 min. later, when their great number would not compensate for the large uncertainty area generated by the aircraft. A BMD deployed at each base and capable of handling SLBM trajectories could give bombers added confidence in their escape.

Nonetheless, it is unlikely that the U.S. would incur the cost of a whole BMD system if bomber protection were its only purpose. Bombers already have a high probability of escape if given proper warning, since the number of dispersal bases is fairly large and their flyout sufficiently fast.[20] Nor would bomber protection necessarily be a natural subsidiary mission of a large BMD optimized for ICBM interception. Such a system might not be adaptable to interception on behalf of the bombers because of the SLBM's different trajectory.

Defense of Command and Control and Other Military Targets

The category of command, control, and communications and other military targets constitutes the nation's capability to function as an organized military power, both nuclear and conventional. The general category of C³/OMT targets comprises four rather different kinds of target: national leadership and nuclear command and control systems; nuclear forces other than ICBMs; conventional military forces and support; and secondary war support. Defense of these targets is less often discussed and arouses much more controversy than defense of ICBMs, chiefly because the significance of this type of BMD is usually associated with the so-called warfighting roles of nuclear weapons. Proposals for U.S. deployment of C³/OMT defense are relatively uncommon. Rather, it is usually seen (at least in Western eyes) as a Soviet predilection, or at least an opportunity for the Soviet Union to make good use of its overall strategic posture with the type of technology it could field in the near term. This section will therefore emphasize the alleged Soviet view and a hypothetical Soviet deployment, by no means

20. Ibid, pp. 217–22.

intending to imply thereby that this view is an accurate reflection of actual Soviet inclinations.

Both the target set itself, and a reasonable defensive goal, are much less clearly defined for defense of C^3/OMT than for defense of ICBM silos. Assessments of the effectiveness of BMD for C^3/OMT targets tend to depend more on these factors than on the technical performance of the BMD. Is it worth defending an army base in nuclear war, especially if cities remain unprotected? If so, how much more worthwhile to defend a command post? How many targets of various kinds must survive to make the enterprise worth its cost and trouble? Does the BMD offer much better protection against ragged retaliation than against a first strike?

C^3/OMT targets differ from silos in that they are distributed nationwide, many of them are soft, and some of them are large in area. The softness means that any kind of weapon—bombers, cruise missiles, SLBMs, as well as ICBMs—can threaten them effectively without pinpoint accuracy, although the large area of some C^3/OMT targets may require more than one detonation to destroy them. Unlike silos, most C^3/OMT targets are not "time-urgent," meaning their destruction could be left to the arrival of bombers and cruise missiles, against which BMD is irrelevant. The relative value of very different types of targets is harder to define than the relative value of silos. To complicate things further, one type of C^3/OMT target depends on another: there is no point to preserving an antenna without a command post or an ammunition supply without a rail delivery system.

A Soviet Nationwide Defense

This example illustrates a type of BMD frequently suggested as the aim of a Soviet "breakout" from the ABM Treaty, as the immediate Soviet response to a near-term U.S. decision to terminate or amend the treaty, or as a Soviet option if they deployed relocatable BMD units ostensibly in defense of silos. Proponents of this suggestion derive it from a certain set of propositions about Soviet inclinations and capabilities. In essence, these propositions are: (1) the Soviet Union has less interest than the United States in ICBM defense; (2) Soviet warfighting doctrine attaches a high value to the kind of protection promised by this BMD; and (3) the Soviet Union has positioned itself, within the treaty, to field such a system in just a few years. These propositions are controversial among U.S. observers and are only stated here because they are needed to understand the purpose of the defense. The rationale for defense of silos (on either side), by contrast, is more widely accepted and understood.

PURPOSE OF THE DEFENSE. Consider a nationwide Soviet deployment of, say, 1000 traditional high-altitude endoatmospheric nuclear interceptors and 200 or so radars. Suppose the interceptors have enough range to intercept RVs heading toward targets within a region about 50 km in radius containing the interceptor battery. Suppose also that the radar can operate autonomously or accept data from early warning radars at the Soviet periphery. Last, suppose the radars and interceptors are mobile, or at least transportable. The job of this BMD is to defend key C^3/OMT targets preferentially, including national leadership and conventional forces. Each interceptor can be used to defend any target within its 50-km radius of action. (Despite the term "radius of action," the interceptor can defend targets farther to its south than to its north.)

It is important to realize that no one would disagree that this defense is extremely limited technically and highly susceptible to many attack tactics described in this chapter. It could nonetheless be useful to the Soviet Union if one attributes to the Soviet Union certain attitudes. The attitudes are, roughly, (1) that even in the midst of the unwanted cataclysm of nuclear conflict, Soviet war objectives to dominate Europe or end up less crippled than the United States and NATO retain their meaning; (2) that an important factor deterring U.S. recourse to nuclear weapons would be a perception that the Soviet Union could proceed to prosecute these aims despite vast damage to its society; and (3) that preserving an effective core or residue of military targets is therefore a significant strategic goal. Coupled to these general attitudes are four other predilections: (1) that survival of the instruments of political control is crucial; (2) that BMD's protection can be augmented with other strategic defenses, including air defense and civil defense; (3) that silo defense is less important because the Soviet Union perceives no threat or plans for mobile basing or for launch under attack; and (4) that the Soviet Union can and should preempt when a U.S. first strike is imminent.

IMPACT OF THE DEFENSE. Let us suppose that with its high-altitude endoatmospheric nuclear BMD the Soviet Union can charge a price of three RVs per defended aimpoint against an organized attack, but a price of five RVs against a ragged retaliation. Suppose also that each of the 1000 most important C^3/OMT targets is located within the coverage of at least one battery. Among these targets there will be substantial variations in value. Some of this variation will be apparent to U.S. planners because it is inherent in the target—a major national command post is more important than a rail bridge. But in other cases the Soviet Union could prepare to make use of, and defend, one airbase or leadership bunker in preference to another. These variations in value would be hidden from U.S. planners. For simplicity, assume that a single detonation (one RV) will suffice to eliminate any target as a functioning installation.

In a first strike the U.S. could attack with the 3000 RVs necessary to achieve 90 percent or greater probability of damage. Even if only 2000 RVs were made available for these targets (others going to silo attack, city attack, or a reserve force), the United States could have a high probability of destroying any 600–700 targets it chose. Alternatively, with 2000 RVs it could direct two RVs at each target and achieve a lower probability of damage against the entire set of targets. Either way, it would appear that attack on this scale would likely bring effective, large-scale, coordinated war efforts to a halt in the Soviet Union. This result probably holds with all reasonable changes in the assumptions, including a bit larger or more capable BMD and passive defense measures.

If the United States faces a nationwide BMD with only its *survivable* arsenal after suffering a first strike, however, the situation is more complex. Suppose the United States had, through some survivable basing mode, preserved 1000 ICBM RVs, after absorbing a Soviet attack. Suppose also that U.S. retaliation is, for a variety of reasons, less well organized for defense suppression, and the attack price against this ragged retaliation is five RVs per aimpoint. The United States can now only be sure of destroying the 200 most important Soviet installations with five-on-one targeting. Alternatively, it could target 500 targets two-on-one and "play the leakage," or adopt other strategies. The outcomes of all these strategies can be deduced from the drawdown curve for the Soviet BMD. The United States can be sure of destroying whichever 200 targets it selects, but the Soviet Union can with reasonable assurance preserve hundreds of military targets, though no single target can be known in advance to be among the survivors. The Soviet Union can limit damage further by dispersing Soviet forces from target areas, to the extent possible; by hardening facilities against the effects of nondirect hits, making it possible for one part of an installation to survive even if another part is targeted; and by playing a shell game with key command elements, aircraft, and other military assets, dispersing them throughout thousands of target areas. Those who worry about this particular scenario maintain that in this way the Soviet war machine would survive and go on to military victory. Whether survival of 800 second-class C³/OMT targets among widespread destruction would really permit "victory," figure prominently in Soviet calculations, or make the cost of this defense worthwhile are all points subject to dispute.

OPTIONS FOR THE UNITED STATES. If the United States became seriously concerned about the Soviet defense, it could take any of the following measures.

1. The United States could build more ICBM RVs. The Soviet BMD is obviously subject to saturation at the cost of a few thousand U.S. RVs. Though these are easy to add to the undamaged U.S. arsenal, adding thousands of *survivable* RVs for retaliatory strike is another matter.

2. The United States could use other nuclear delivery systems to attack the defended targets. A clear way to sidestep the defense is to use bombers, cruise missiles, and SLBMs against the C³/OMT targets which as a rule (but with some important exceptions) are soft and do not need to be hit in the first half hour (as opposed to several hours) of the war. The exceptions are command posts hardened to withstand tens or even hundreds (but never thousands) of pounds of overpressure per square inch, and bases from which forces could be dispersed quickly. The high-altitude endoatmospheric BMD described in this section could well have poor performance against SLBMs approaching from many directions. Air defense could obviously be provided, at cost, for the targets.

3. A U.S. response requiring no new hardware would be acceptance of the capability to destroy "only" Soviet cities and the principal 100–200 Soviet military facilities, arguing that nothing more was needed to deter a sane opponent or that the Soviet war machine could not function effectively after such a strike despite survival of a large number of installations. In this view, 75 percent or so of the 1000 "targets" identified initially are not really essential. If the discussion had begun with only 200 "targets," the Soviet BMD would have looked futile.

4. Finally, the United States could turn to the usual panoply of penetration tactics. Without a more precise definition of the technical characteristics of the BMD, the best tactic cannot be specified. But U.S. analysts of a real nationwide Soviet BMD would have adequate technical

information to exploit coverage gaps, limitations in target handling
ability, and other detailed failings of the system, especially if it grew out
of the well-studied upgrades to the Moscow system. The system hypothesized here probably would commit interceptors to objects while they
were still at a high altitude, meaning the usual susceptibility to decoys,
perhaps chaff, blackout, and MaRVs. Last, if the word "transportable"
applied to the BMD components meant that they could be moved, but
not easily or quickly, defense units could be located by the United States
and targeted.

A U.S. Threshold Defense of Key Targets

The "threshold" rationale is sometimes given for a defense of certain
key targets in the U.S. warning and command and control systems. This
idea seems to have arisen from the observation that the sole deployment
site permitted to the United States by the ABM Treaty is also the location
of the Perimeter Acquisition Radar Characterization System (PARCS),
one of a number of elements in the U.S. missile warning system. The
defense makes no claim to secure the survival of any of the targets, but
merely forces the attacker to shoot a handful of warheads at each target
instead of one or two. The extra intensity of the attack is imagined to
breach some threshold, making the attack a more "serious" act and
making early detection of the attack easier. Thus the threshold defense
would remove any hope of surprise or at least would create uncertainty
in the mind of the attacker about a "surgical" nuclear strike.

Although there is plainly no technical impediment to such a defense,
its rationale can be questioned on several grounds. The military utility
of the attacks the defense aims to prevent is unclear. Under what
circumstances would the Soviet Union wish to destroy warning radars,
satellite early warning ground stations, major command posts, and
communications antennas only, leaving silos, submarine ports, and
bomber bases untouched? Quite apart from the risk that the United
States would respond in kind or more massively, such an attack would
not, in fact, eliminate the ability of the U.S. leadership to survive, receive
warning of follow-on attacks, and communicate strike orders to U.S.
forces. These capabilities for survivable C^3 are improving briskly and
will be more secure against attack in important respects by the time any
BMD could be fielded. Second, do warning systems really operate
technically in such a way that a small attack is hard to detect but an

attack a few times larger is significantly easier? And last, does increasing the price of these targets to a handful of RVs really spell the difference between a "serious" nuclear attack on the United States and a surgical strike? It would seem that the threshold rationale, while perhaps satisfied by a BMD deployed for other purposes, could not by itself justify investment in a BMD system.

Defense of Cities

Despite its universal emotional and moral appeal, city defense remains the most controversial BMD mission. For one thing, the defense technologies that could be built and deployed in the near future are widely agreed to be unequal to the task of city defense. Discussion necessarily shifts to more exotic hypothetical systems about which there is more room for informed disagreement. Beyond these technical questions lies a concern that less-than-perfect defenses might inspire an exaggerated perception of security or invulnerability to nuclear attack and thereby make nuclear war more probable. Defining an effective comprehensive defense of people, homes, and places of business also raises disquieting questions about the level of damage and fatalities judged to be "acceptable" and about what constitutes "assured" destruction or survival.

In its technical requirements, city defense is more demanding than defense of ICBMs or military targets. (It follows that an effective city defense system would be more than adequate for these other goals.) The first difficulty is that economic and human value is very unevenly distributed, with a large fraction of the population and industry concentrated around a very small number of aimpoints. The second difficulty is that the focus of city defense is on very low or near-zero leakage because of the great destructive power of nuclear weapons: recall that in Minuteman defense it was not an easy matter to defend 1000 aimpoints, of identical or similar value, to a mere 10 percent survival level. A third challenge for the defense is that it has little or no control over the target structure of cities. Missiles can be based in a number of ways to enhance defense effectiveness, but New York City obviously cannot be hardened, moved, or broken up into a number of pieces and dispersed. Civil defense shelters and crisis relocation plans can reduce the vulnerability of the urban population but cannot reduce damage to homes and businesses. A fourth and crucial difficulty of city BMD is the obvious fact that missile defense by itself can never eliminate the Soviet Union's threat to large numbers of cities, since other means of delivering nuclear weapons are also available.

Defensive and Offensive Objectives

As in the cases of ICBM and C³/OMT defense, an assessment of the effectiveness of city defense requires a clear statement of the defense's goals and criteria of success. Disagreement over the effectiveness of city defense is frequently at base a disagreement over the objectives both of the defense and of the offense. Many of the same disagreements arise in discussions of civil defense.

The relevant target set is commonly divided into two parts, distinguishable in principle but not always in practice. The first, constituting the nation's "economic value" and ability to "recover" from nuclear attack, comprises factories, refineries, transportation facilities, power plants, and so forth. The second set, the nation's "human value," consists of the population, together with homes, places of worship, museums, libraries, schools, hospitals, and the like.

The economic value/recovery targets are distinguished, albeit imperfectly, from the "war support" category of OMT: rather than contributing in an immediate way to military operations, the economic value targets contribute in the longer term to the nation's ability to prosecute a war effort and to remain a potent adversary after the war. While C³/OMT targets tend to be widely dispersed, economic value targets often are not, meaning that a relatively small number of penetrating warheads would destroy a large fraction of the important industries. Moreover, if the attacker's purpose is to eliminate the defender as a potent enemy, it is not clear that a large fraction of the industrial facilities need be destroyed. The military value of attack on silos, antennas, and airfields is easier to quantify.

Obviously, human value is largely colocated with economic value, and tens of millions or more human fatalities would result from attacks whose nominal aimpoints were economic value/recovery installations. Though human beings are not, strictly speaking, an explicit object of attack in the war plans of the superpowers today, human fatalities are often used as the measure of the effectiveness of a proposed city BMD. If deployment of such a BMD would have no effect on present targeting objectives, this method of analysis presents no problem: one merely adds up casualties from attacks intended to maximize economic destruction (or damage to military and C^3 targets), comparing the pre-BMD and post-BMD cases (taking into account, in the usual way, changes in the offense's targeting and tactics to continue to maximize damage to the targets, but not to people, in the face of BMD). Confronted with a BMD claiming to be able to reduce the defense's fatalities significantly, however, the offense could presumably retarget its forces, making the infliction of human casualties an explicit objective.

One goal cited for city BMD (and for civil defense[21])—saving people's lives—is purely humanitarian and seeks no meaningful military or strategic advantage from the BMD deployment. If this goal is clear to the Soviet Union, and if the defense does not interfere too much with Soviet military targeting objectives (enough to make it worthwhile for the Soviet Union to try to overcome it), the United States could expect some reductions in fatalities to result from even a modest defense.

Another goal could be to reduce fatalities and damage in order to enhance U.S. "flexibility" in a crisis, to allow the United States to "coerce" the Soviet Union from a position of reduced vulnerability, or to enhance U.S. ability to persist in its war effort despite receiving a massive Soviet nuclear strike. (Alternatively, the U.S. defense might be needed to prevent a Soviet monopoly on flexibility, coercion, or nuclear warfighting.) The net result of the BMD deployment, according to this objective, is supposed to be that the U.S. president, in dealing with the

---

21. The literature on civil defense reflects the tension between the "strategic" and "humanitarian" objectives of population defense.

The *Annual Defense Department Reports, FY 1976 and FY 197T* argued that the United States should plan to have the same crisis relocation options as the USSR for two reasons: (1) "to be able to respond in kind if the Soviet Union attempts to intimidate us in a time of crisis by evacuating the population from its cities"; and (2) "to reduce fatalities if an attack on our cities appears imminent;" see p. II-24.

At about the same time, three physicists argued, "A nation's civil defense preparedness may determine the balance of power in some future nuclear crisis. . . . In our opinion, we must strive for an approximately equal casualty rate." The authors cited reducing U.S. deaths in a massive attack from 45 percent to 11 percent of the population as an example of the desired civil defense performance. Arthur A. Broyles, Eugene P. Wigner, and Sidney D. Drell, "Civil Defense in Limited War—A Debate," *Physics Today,* vol. 29 (April 1976), pp. 45, 46, 56.

More recently, a study urging strengthened U.S. strategic defenses stated: "The protection of our citizens must be prime, but civil defense . . . would reduce the possibility that the U.S. could be coerced in a time of crisis." Daniel O. Graham, *The Non-Nuclear Defense of Cities: The High Frontier Space-Based Defense Against ICBM Attack* (Abt Books, 1983), p. 122.

Soviet leadership, would be willing to accept or would appear to be willing to accept a higher probability that a crisis would escalate to nuclear war because the consequences to the United States are presumed smaller.

Unlike the humanitarian objective, this second objective would seem likely to stimulate a Soviet effort to put the same number of American lives at risk regardless of the defense. In this way, the Soviet Union could retain the strategic advantages that (by hypothesis) the BMD deprives them of. The effectiveness of the defense should be assessed in this case in relation to a possible change in Soviet targeting objectives to enhance U.S. fatalities. The issue then becomes the cost-exchange ratio measuring the price to the Soviet Union of retaining its "advantage" relative to the price of the U.S. defense. In practice, of course, the distinction between a humanitarian and a strategically meaningful defense would probably not be plain to either side.

At the limit of hypothetical BMD technologies offering near-total protection, one encounters the ultimate defense objective of thwarting assured destruction, attaining assured survival, or, in the words of President Reagan, making nuclear weapons (at least as delivered by missiles) "impotent and obsolete."[22] Even a small number of nuclear weapons penetrating a defense to certain selected U.S. aimpoints would do extraordinary damage to homes, businesses, cultural institutions, and, unless they had been evacuated, people. This demographic fact raises questions about the definition of "unacceptable damage" and about the defense performance needed from a BMD system to reduce the "seriousness" of nuclear attack on the United States. Observers will differ in these judgments and thus in their assessment of BMD effectiveness. The offensive objective of assured destruction is presumably the last one either superpower would be willing to surrender to a defense on the other side. Although today there is no need for either side to seek to maximize population losses, this goal could be adopted in the face of a near-perfect BMD promising virtual invulnerability to the nation deploying it. The effectiveness of such a hypothetical BMD needs to be measured against this ultimate offensive goal. It is therefore incorrect to take an attack from *today's* Soviet war plan (as well as this can be surmised), engage the near-perfect defense, and add up the resulting fatalities and damage.

22. "The President's Speech," *New York Times*, March 24, 1983.

Two other objectives for city defense can be considered. The first is to prevent attack from smaller nuclear powers. A Soviet BMD might attempt to prevent the British, French, or Chinese nuclear forces from threatening the USSR with unacceptable damage. This objective is discussed in chapter 7. The U.S. Sentinel system was justified in the 1960s as an anti-Chinese defense, but there seems to be little appetite in the United States to revive this objective. A second BMD goal would be to defend against accidental or unauthorized launches. This objective would seem insufficient by itself to justify a large investment in nation-wide BMD, but might be met by a defense deployed for a broader purpose.

Effects of Nuclear Attack on Cities

Studies of the effects of nuclear strikes on cities and population[23] are surprisingly scarce in comparison to the volume of detailed studies on the destruction of hardened military structures and the characteristics of weapon systems. In part this results from the uncertainties and imponderables in such estimates, making precise quantitative analysis infeasible. In part also it results from the fact that the number of Americans put at risk even in less-than-maximum nuclear strikes is today so large that there is little interest in resolving imprecisions in the estimates, even if the range of uncertainty amounts to millions of lives. However, the prospect (or even discussion) of reducing the threat to society by a "strategically meaningful" amount, or to "acceptable" levels, immediately focuses attention on such estimates. This has been true for discussions of civil defense in the United States and would probably be true for any proposal to deploy city BMD.

Prompt human fatalities are generally calculated on the basis of semiempirical relationships between the probability of survival for a person residing in an urban sector and the overpressure to which that sector is subjected. (Damage to industrial sectors is computed similarly.)

23. See U.S. Arms Control and Disarmament Agency, *An Analysis of Civil Defense in Nuclear War* (ACDA, 1978); OTA, *The Effects of Nuclear War* (GPO, 1979); ACDA, *The Effects of Nuclear War* (ACDA, 1979); "Economic and Social Consequences of Nuclear Attacks on the United States," prepared for the Joint Committee on Defense Production, 96 Cong. 1 sess., 1979; J. Carson Mark, "Global Consequences of Nuclear Weaponry," *Annual Review of Nuclear Science,* vol. 26 (1976), pp. 51–87; National Research Council, *Long-Term Worldwide Effects of Multiple Nuclear-Weapons Detonations* (National Academy of Sciences, 1975).

The calculation then amounts to counting the people within a set of concentric circles about each detonation point. The density of people in an urban area, and hence the computed fatalities, changes with time as they commute between home and work or leave for holiday weekends. In general the canonical circle of destruction produced by a single detonation in these calculations does not entirely cover an urban area, so that more than one weapon may be considered necessary to destroy a city completely (figure 4-17).

Burns from thermal radiation or from fires ignited by it, as well as exposure to nuclear radiation from the detonation itself and (for ground-bursts) from relatively large radioactive particles that settle out of the mushroom stem in the immediate vicinity of ground zero, should also, in principle, be included among the sources of prompt fatalities. In practice, these effects are analyzed by widening the circles of destruction a little depending on yields and heights of burst. Casualties from downwind fallout can be estimated if the population is assigned a specific degree of radiation protection and the wherewithal (food, water, and other supplies) to remain protected until local ambient radiation levels permit returning to outdoor or above-ground activities. These calculations are also sensitive to wind, weather, and burst heights. Fallout casualty estimates are usually attempted only for massive attacks, where national averages smooth out large variations in local conditions.

Calculations of fatalities on the basis of blast circles and fallout patterns overlaid on the population distribution, whatever relationship they might bear to actual wartime fatalities and injuries, obviously do not capture other effects that might enter into an attacker's judgment of the seriousness of the damage resulting from nuclear warheads exploding on a city. These include the destruction of homes, downtown areas, historical and cultural monuments, and other elements of value to society besides factories and human lives themselves. Calculations also do not capture the effects of the destruction of a major city on the rest of the country; nor do they measure the dependence of the attacked city on the outside world to help prevent the injured from becoming fatalities, to feed the survivors, and to rebuild. Large-scale attacks would bring with them widespread and long-term effects that are presently difficult to quantify. These include the effects of fallout on exposed crops and livestock and the action of oxides of nitrogen (formed in nuclear bursts) on atmospheric temperature and ozone concentration.

Physically, the target structures presented by the population and

Figure 4-17. *Plan for an Attack on Leningrad with Ten 40-kT Airburst Warheads*

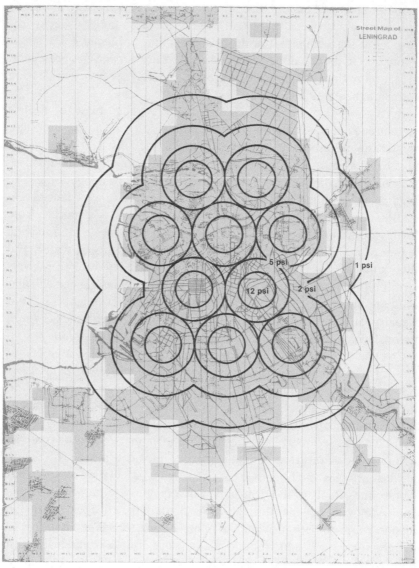

Source: U.S. Congress, Office of Technology Assessment, *The Effects of Nuclear War* (Government Printing Office, 1979).

Figure 4-18. *Distribution of U.S. and Soviet Urban Population According to Land Area*

Percent of urban population

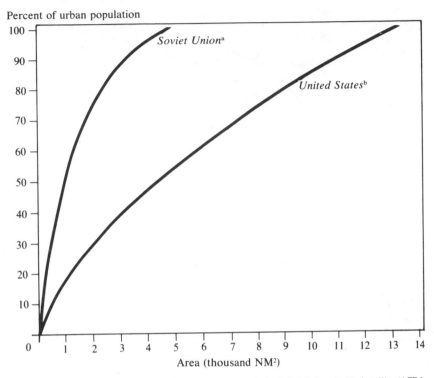

Area (thousand NM²)

Source: U.S. Arms Control and Disarmament Agency, *An Analysis of Civil Defense in Nuclear War* (ACDA, 1978), p. 3.
a. Soviet urban population estimated at 126 million, or 49 percent of total population.
b U.S. urban population estimated at 131 million, or 61 percent of total population.

industry in the United States and in the USSR are similar. More than half of the 250 million American and 280 million Soviet citizens are concentrated within urban areas of 25,000 or more people. Figures 4-18 to 4-20 show the national distributions. The Soviet Union has slightly greater urban population density, comparable industrial concentration, and greater colocation of population and industry. In both countries, the ten largest cities contain about a tenth of the national population and a fourth of the industry. The 200 largest cities contain about a third of the population and some three-fourths of the industry. A typical city has an effective area of some 100 sq. mi., meaning that four or five 1-MT bombs or their equivalent would blanket it with overpressures greater than 10 psi, virtually flattening it. A few very large cities like Moscow have an

Figure 4-19. *Distribution of U.S. and Soviet Rural Population According to Land Area*

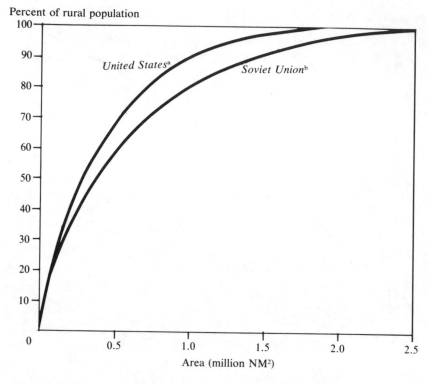

Percent of rural population

United States[a]

Soviet Union[b]

Area (million NM²)

Source: Arms Control and Disarmament Agency, *An Analysis of Civil Defense in Nuclear War*, p. 4.
a. U.S. rural population estimated at 86 million, or 39 percent of total population.
b. Soviet rural population estimated at 129 million, or 51 percent of total population.

effective area of some 350 sq. mi. About 80 percent of the Soviet urban population, or 40 percent of the total, lives within 2900 sq. mi., which could be flattened by just over 100 MT equivalents.

Table 4-4 presents fatality estimates made by the U.S. government for attacks on the United States and the USSR today, without significant BMD on either side. (The number of people injured is not reflected in these figures.) The estimates are made for three cases: strikes on ICBM silos only; strikes on silos plus submarine bases, bomber airfields, and other nuclear force sites; and massive strikes on nuclear forces, C^3/OMT, and economic value/recovery targets. In the third case, the USSR is assumed to strike first and the United States to retaliate with its surviving deterrent forces. The results depend on whether the attacks are preceded by a period of tension during which the sides change from

Figure 4-20. *Comparative Colocation of U.S. and Soviet Industrial Installations*

Percent of industrial installations located within circles

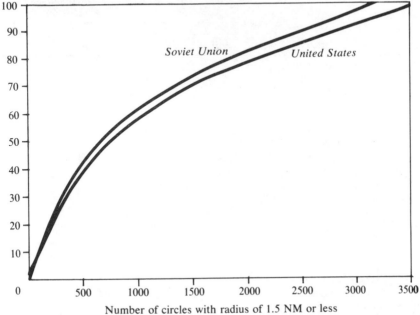

Number of circles with radius of 1.5 NM or less

Source: Arms Control and Disarmament Agency, *An Analysis of Civil Defense in Nuclear War*, p. 5.

normal peacetime ("nongenerated") alert to increased ("generated") alert, sending in-port submarines to sea and taking steps to ensure safe bomber takeoff.

Table 4-4 shows that by retargeting dispersed population and ground-bursting, the United States could virtually restore Soviet fatalities to what they would have been without civil defense measures. However many lives evacuation might save, it obviously cannot spare the population its dwellings, industries, and services, which remain behind in the target area.[24]

Effects of Adding BMD

Unlike civil defense, which removes people from regions of attack, BMD reduces the actual number of detonations. Only the fraction of the

24. If only silos were attacked, fallout protection could clearly be very effective; the value of civil defense for this type of attack should be assessed separately from the case of total attack.

Table 4-4. *Fatality Estimates*

Millions, unless otherwise noted

Type of attack	U.S. fatalities by alert status of Soviet forces		Soviet fatalities by alert status of U.S. forces	
	Generated[a]	Non-generated[b]	Generated[a]	Non-generated[b]
Massive attacks on military, command and control, and economic value targets[c]				
No civil defense	. . .	105–131	. . .	81–94
With urban sheltering[d]	107–126	76–85	80–88	60–64
With urban sheltering[d] plus evacuation[e]	69–91	. . .	23–34	. . .
With urban sheltering[d] plus evacuation[e] plus deliberate attack on evacuees[f]	87–109	. . .	54–65	. . .
With urban sheltering[d] plus evacuation[e] plus deliberate attack on evacuees[f] plus groundburst of all weapons to enhance fallout	. . .	. . .	70–85	. . .
With urban sheltering[d] plus evacuation[e] plus groundburst of all weapons to enhance fallout	. . .	. . .	40–45	. . .
Damage to key production capacity (percent)	. . .	. . .	85–90	65–70

	U.S. fatalities	Soviet fatalities
ICBM silos only	1–10	1–5
All strategic nuclear forces	2–20	2–10

Source: For ICBM silos and strategic nuclear forces: U.S. Congress, Office of Technology Assessment, *The Effects of Nuclear War* (Government Printing Office, 1979); for massive attacks: U.S. Arms Control and Disarmament Agency, "An Analysis of Civil Defense in Nuclear War" (GPO, 1978).

a. Normal peacetime alert.
b. Increased alert.
c. Assuming Soviet first strike and U.S. retaliation.
d. Assuming urban population uses existing shelters.
e. Assuming relocation of 80 percent of the urban population to rural areas.
f. Assuming the possibility of retargeting U.S. forces to attack relocated population.

attacking force of RVs that leaks through the defense arrives to explode over cities. However, the level of damage does not decrease linearly in proportion to the leakage factor. A few weapons can do so much damage that even a defense permitting just a few tenths of a percent of leakage (a few warheads out of each thousand in today's arsenals) could not stave off historically unprecedented damage. If the offense's response to the BMD were to try deliberately to inflict human casualties by choosing aimpoints in populated areas, fewer arriving warheads might still inflict the same number of casualties.

Nonetheless, a U.S. defense that intercepted a substantial fraction of attacking RVs—70 to 90 percent, say—before they detonated on U.S. soil could greatly mitigate long-term consequences. First, fallout would be reduced in proportion to the number of RVs intercepted, meaning that the people who would otherwise be exposed to lethal doses of radiation would instead suffer exposures below the threshold for immediate sickness or death. (Even a nuclear BMD reduces fallout substantially for two reasons: the interceptor warhead is likely to have a lower yield than the warhead it destroys; and it bursts high in the air, whereas the intercepted RV might be fused to groundburst.) Second, long-term effects such as ozone depletion might be reduced, in physical magnitude and in ecological effect. Third, with BMD, effective protection can be provided by simpler fallout shelters, and evacuated urban populations do not have to be dispersed over such large areas to avoid harm. Last, even areas that come under attack despite the BMD would fare better in the long run if surrounding areas were undamaged and thus available to offer help. Unfortunately, the attacker can overturn many of these mitigating effects by adopting alternative targeting plans and countermeasures, whereas the defense's principal problem—the concentration and fragility of people and industry—would not be easy to correct.

Figure 4-21 shows how U.S. urban fatalities would increase with the number of penetrating warheads if the aimpoints were chosen to maximize human fatalities. The first few hundred aimpoints in figure 4-21 account for a large fraction of the urban population. Key industry is even more heavily concentrated. It is these aimpoints that the Soviet Union would presumably choose to target heavily if the United States deployed a BMD claiming to deny heavy urban damage. In the case of successful and massive crisis relocation and fallout sheltering, the curve in figure 4-21 should be taken to represent the number of people whose homes and businesses would be destroyed. One should take into account as

Figure 4-21. *Effect of Attack Size on the Extent of Prompt Fatalities in U.S. Urban Areas*

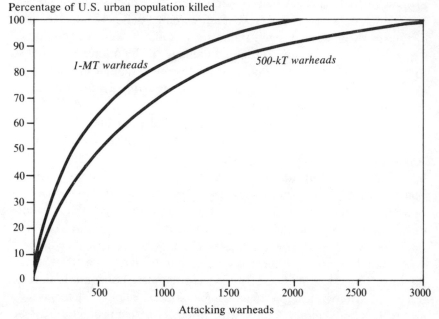

Percentage of U.S. urban population killed

Attacking warheads

Source: Arms Control and Disarmament Agency, *U.S. Urban Population Vulnerability* (ACDA, 1979), quoted in Arthur M. Katz, *Life after Nuclear War: The Economic and Social Impacts of Nuclear Attacks on the U.S.* (Ballinger, 1982).

Note: Aimpoints chosen to maximize prompt human fatalities. U.S. urban population is estimated to be 131 million, as in the 1970 census.

well damage to the homes and businesses of people assumed to be injured (and thus not shown in the figure).

The few hundred megatons that do the lion's share of damage in figure 4-21 represent just a few percent of the Soviet ICBM megatonnage. Table 4-5 shows the effects of less than a thousandth of that arsenal exploded over the ten largest U.S. cities. For each city the aimpoint for the 500-kT bomb is chosen to maximize human fatalities.

To assess a defense aiming to reduce damage below the level of assured destruction, one needs to decide where to set these levels. There can be no question of an analytical solution to this dilemma. In the 1960s, Secretary of Defense Robert McNamara prescribed 20–25 percent prompt fatalities and 50–65 percent industrial damage as the threat to the Soviet Union that would constitute assured destruction. In today's Soviet population this fatality fraction corresponds to between 55 million and 70 million lives.

Table 4-5. *Effects of a Single 0.5-MT Weapon (Airburst)*
on the Ten Largest U.S. Urban Areas
Millions

Metropolitan area	Population in 1970[a]	Fatalities[b]	Casualties
New York	16.3	1.2	3.3
Los Angeles	8.7	0.4	1.1
Chicago	6.7	0.9	1.9
Philadelphia	4.6	0.4	1.4
Detroit	3.9	0.5	1.3
San Francisco	3.6	0.5	0.8
Boston	2.9	0.5	1.1
Washington	2.6	0.4	1.1
Miami	2.3	0.3	0.7
Dallas	2.1	0.2	0.5
Total	53.7	5.3	13.2

Source: U.S. Arms Control and Disarmament Agency, *U.S. Urban Population Vulnerability* (GPO, 1979), quoted in Arthur M. Katz, *Life after Nuclear War: The Economic and Social Impacts of Nuclear Attacks on the U.S.* (Ballinger, 1982), pp. 377–408.
a. Population of entire metropolitan area.
b. Assuming attack is designed to maximize human fatalities; fatalities are prompt only, using usual overpressure-casualty relationships; residents are in their homes at the time of attack.

Table 4-6. *U.S. and Soviet Strategic Arsenals in the Mid-1980s*

Type of weapon	United States			USSR		
	Warheads	Megatons	EMT	Warheads	Megatons	EMT
ICBMs	2100	1200	1200	6600	7100	6900
SLBMs	6600	500	1100	1500	800	900
Bombers, cruise missiles	5200	1700	2300	100–600	2300	1000
Total	13,900	3300	4600	8000–8500	8000–10,000	9000

Source: U.S. Congress, Office of Technology Assessment, *The Effects of Nuclear War,* appendix B, pp. 122–23. All data are approximate.

McNamara's criteria of assured destruction of the Soviet Union were reckoned to be satisfied (with no Soviet BMD) by a force of between 200 and 400 MT equivalents.[25] By comparison, the Allied strategic bombing of World War II totaled less than 3 MT. Table 4-6 shows, in rough numbers, the superpower arsenals as they are expected in the mid-1980s.

25. Equivalent megatonnage (EMT) is a measure of the yield of a nuclear weapon; it takes into account the fact that the blast damage of nuclear weapons does not increase directly with their yields, small warheads being disproportionately effective at destroying urban areas. Thus a 1-MT warhead blankets about 26 sq. mi. with overpressures in excess of 10 psi, but two ½-MT weapons cover 33 sq. mi. The smaller weapons are each assigned more than half the equivalent megatonnage of the larger weapon.

These numbers reflect the arsenal available to each side if it strikes first. Assuming a Soviet first strike and a U.S. defense operating against ICBMs only (and ignoring for the moment SLBMs, bombers, and cruise missiles), the threat against which a city defense needs to be assessed is some 6500 warheads of 1-MT average yield. This force represents thirty or so times as much equivalent megatonnage as prescribed by Mc-Namara's criteria. One part in ten of this arsenal saturates the urban fatalities curve in figure 4-21, and the damage total in table 4-5 represents the effects of less than a tenth of a percent.

Faced with a U.S. BMD claiming to reduce city destruction by a meaningful amount, the Soviets would presumably adjust their arsenal to avoid, as much as possible, a blunting of their attack. In addition to the many penetration aids and tactics discussed in this chapter and in chapter 3, a number of additional considerations apply for the special case of city defense.

Recall that preferential defense was an important factor in enhancing the effectiveness of silo defenses: as the attack intensified, the BMD focused its resources on defending a smaller fraction of the silos, abandoning the others to the attacker. In no case did the defense aim to intercept a large fraction of the attacking RVs. Though preferential defense can be effective for preserving a small core of the retaliatory ICBM force, it is obviously useless in city defense. Indeed, the offense can adopt the tactic of *preferential offense,* concentrating attack on large cities or avoiding well-defended areas. In city defense the BMD must engage all or most of the attacking RVs. Working at the 90 percent, 99 percent, or even 99.9 percent survival level on the drawdown curve is totally different from working at the 10 percent level.

A force of ICBMs designed to inflict maximum damage on cities and population at low cost might abandon high accuracy; carry a payload of many low-yield warheads (possibly conserving special nuclear materials in the interest of large numbers); be fused for groundburst; or have warheads designed with special materials to maximize radioactivity. Since only a fraction of the warheads must get through in order to defeat the defense objective, the offense could try different tactics with portions of its force. Furthermore, if BMD raised the cost per delivered RV of ICBM attack, the offense would always have the alternatives of SLBMs, bombers, cruise missiles, or other means of delivery.

Historically the cost-exchange ratio has been considered an important analytical measure of population defenses, expressing the outcome of a spending race between offense and defense to maintain their levels of penetration and protection, respectively. An important question in constructing such a ratio is when to begin the race. One starting point would be the present, when the offense has a substantial advantage by virtue of two decades of missile deployments. Another would be some hypothetical future date at which the defense had established its objective against the offense and both sides had begun competing, missile-for-interceptor, to maintain or improve their positions.

Reckoning in rough orders of magnitude, the cost of development and procurement of 100 MX missiles (1000 RVs) is about $10 billion. If about half of this amount is nonrecurring development costs, the cost for each RV after the first 100 missiles are produced must be a few million dollars at most. To this must be added the cost of basing the missiles, which multiplies the cost for each RV by something between two (for silo basing) and three or more (for "survivable" basing). Most proposed basing modes for 100 MX missiles have cost $30 billion and up. This points up the difference in cost between relatively cheap silo-based ICBMs for first strike and survivably based missiles of greater cost. The incremental cost for each RV to an ongoing U.S. ICBM program is therefore somewhere between $1 million and $10 million. If it is meaningful to define the cost for each intercept of an RV (or boosters, where each booster equals ten or so RVs) to the BMD (after the initial investment in the defense is made, so that costs are computed from an ongoing BMD program), then this cost must be in the range of a few million dollars for the BMD to compete with an expanding offense.

The State of Technology for City Defense

Traditional endoatmospheric systems for city defense suffer most obviously from the limited geographical coverage of a single battery. Since the attacker can avoid defended cities (except perhaps certain unique or symbolic cities), the batteries must be everywhere; since the attacker can concentrate attack preferentially, the defensive coverage must be thick everywhere. The defense must therefore buy and field several times as many interceptors (and accompanying radars) as the offense has RVs. In silo defense, by contrast, a small fraction of survivors could be secured with a relatively small defensive arsenal and the tactic of preferential defense. In city defense virtually every RV must be intercepted.

The usual litany of penetration tactics for traditional defenses is even more daunting in the context of city defense than that of silo defense, since the attack price sought is very high. For instance, the attacker could pay the price of a number of RVs to blackout the vicinity of the defense in order to get an RV through to New York City. A MaRV (particularly one willing to sacrifice yield and accuracy for high maneuverability) can dissipate its large energy of reentry in high-acceleration dodging that an interceptor missile would not be able to follow. These penetration tactics and others limit the defense in a way that is fundamental and cannot be overcome at any cost. No radar, whatever its cost, can see through an early fireball. Technical experts are unanimous in their judgment that traditional endoatmospheric defenses standing alone cannot be adapted to the city defense role with any amount of modification or expenditure.

Exoatmospheric intercept systems can provide the nationwide coverage from a few batteries needed to cope with defense avoidance and with concentrated attack. All ICBM corridors approaching the United States could be defended from just a few bases housing advanced midcourse Overlay infrared-homing interceptors.

All of the technical complexities and uncertainties of exoatmospheric intercept systems described in this chapter apply to their use in city defense. Of particular interest is the susceptibility of infrared sensors in space to being fooled by decoys, multiplying the cost-exchange ratio in favor of the offense. The short flights and potentially low trajectories of SLBMs would make them difficult or impossible for the Overlay to intercept. Besides attacking the cities directly, SLBMs could attack the defense bases as well. Attack on cities can be stretched out over a longer period than attack on silos (silo-based missiles not destroyed on a first wave can be launched rather than await a second wave). The rocket-launched infrared probe used in the silo defense version of the Overlay only remains aloft for a few tens of minutes, so some other long-range acquisition and battle management sensor would be needed for efficient city defense operation.

To get a feeling for the kinds of calculations that go into the cost-exchange ratio for an Overlay defense of cities, consider an attack of the Soviet ICBM force of 10,000 RVs or so on the largest 100 U.S. cities. Suppose that the defense is to be sized to preserve 50 percent of the cities unscathed, with the remaining cities suffering one or more detonations. If P is the probability that each of the 100 RVs approaching a city will be intercepted successfully, then P^{100} must equal 0.5 in order to preserve 50 percent of the cities under attack. This means that P must be 99.3 percent. Since less than 1 percent failure is too much to ask of each Overlay homing vehicle, several would need to be directed independently at each RV. For example, if each homing vehicle were 80 percent reliable, four of them would be needed to keep the probability that at least one intercept would succeed at 99.3 percent. (This assumes statistical independence of the failure modes of the four vehicles, in reality an unlikely circumstance.) If a way could be found to assess which intercepts failed, there might still be time to allocate new kill vehicles to the RVs missed on the first try. This amounts to making a layered defense out of the Overlay itself, in which case fewer than four kill vehicles would need to be deployed for each Soviet RV. Another way of layering, of course, is to deploy a traditional underlay. The underlay would again need to be nationwide and thick enough every-where to catch the leakers from the concentrated attacks. The cost for each intercept of the two layering schemes would need to be compared.

At any rate (and leaving aside decoys, defense suppression, and other problems) between one and several Overlay homing vehicles would need to be built, deployed, and boosted into space for every attacking Soviet RV built, deployed, and boosted into space. It would seem unlikely that the complex Overlay homing vehicles could win this cost competition, especially if the offense sacrificed accuracy for extra RVs in the payload or deployed smaller RVs.

Since the defensive technologies whose technical characteristics are fairly well understood and can be displayed for analysis appear unequal to the special requirements of city defense, attention turns to other technologies that are less well understood. The current focus is on space-based directed-energy systems. The point is not that such schemes are known to be better in leakage or cost effectiveness than the traditional and Overlay intercept systems. They are simply not known to be worse. There is no sound basis for comparing the intercept cost of a laser defense to the Overlay's or for plausibly computing a cost-exchange ratio. Schemes that intercept boosters rather than RVs obviously have fewer objects to concern themselves with, but this advantage could be offset by the greater cost of making a booster intercept. Like the Overlay, laser systems could be supplemented with underlays, in this case midcourse intercept systems as well as traditional terminal systems.

As more is understood about advanced BMD concepts, some will appear less plausible and others will receive sharper definition. Since some decades seem to be involved in the maturing of these schemes, it is likely that in the interim entirely new technologies will make an appearance as well. And dramatic advancements in *offensive* technology should be regarded as just as likely as advancements in defensive technologies.

Space-Based Directed-Energy BMD

Of the host of directed-energy technologies seeking research funding today with a hypothetical BMD application in mind, two are most often discussed. The first is a constellation of large chemical laser battle stations, operating at invisible near-infrared wavelengths and heating the walls of ICBM boosters as they make their way through the atmosphere. The second, more recent concept consists of nuclear-weapon-pumped X-ray lasers deployed in orbit and causing destructive shock waves to be generated in the upper stages of missiles shortly after they leave the atmosphere. In the present state of understanding, these schemes appear less implausible than some others. These others involve particle beams and microwaves, as well as light and X rays; they call for ground, airplane, or space basing and variously attack boosters, buses, or RVs. Even the two most plausible schemes simply cannot be analyzed today in meaningful detail because, to a degree much greater than traditional defenses or the Overlay, these schemes lack engineering specificity. The examples earlier in this chapter make clear that the most difficult problems with a BMD system often arise at the point where the technology devices are embedded in an actual architecture in a wartime environment. The following discussion assumes that the technological devices work (a circumstance by no means ensured) and identifies a few generic issues pertaining to the system as a whole.

The proposed constellation of orbiting chemical laser battle stations must provide for coverage of the Soviet ICBM fields at all times. There also must be enough battle stations over the Soviet silo fields at a given time that all missiles can be handled if they are launched simultaneously. A satisfactory outcome of laser development would be a laser capable of destroying boosters at slant ranges of a few thousand kilometers by devoting 5 sec. or so of search, track, and illumination to each one in sequence. A constellation totaling twenty-five or more battle stations can provide coverage, by one satellite at a time, of all launch areas in the

USSR (and indeed worldwide) at all times. But a single battle station can handle only forty or so simultaneous launches, because a missile is only in its vulnerable boost phase for about 200 sec. Since the Soviet Union has some several hundred ICBMs that could be launched simultaneously, ten or so battle stations would have to be in position over the USSR at any one time, giving a worldwide total of 250 or more. This total does not include on-orbit spares to prevent a broken battle station from creating a gap in the coverage. Every time the Soviet Union adds forty boosters (perhaps small, single-warhead ones of the "Midgetman" variety being discussed in the United States today), a new battle station would have to be added overhead, meaning a total of twenty-five new battle stations worldwide. A cost-exchange trade of almost one battle station for each deployed offensive booster is clearly a losing proposition for the defense.

A second issue for the laser battle stations is their susceptibility to attack. Attack could come from ground-based or space-based lasers or from conventional or nuclear space mines attached to other satellites, disguised as space junk, or detached covertly from other spacecraft. The laser station could presumably defend itself against homing interceptor missiles. As a system architecture took shape, no doubt new counter-measures would be explored which are virtually impossible to address with any concreteness at this time.

The proposed X-ray laser BMD would consist of a smaller battle station, since its power source would be a compact nuclear weapon instead of tanks of chemicals. Sensing and pointing mechanisms would be similar. X rays cannot penetrate much below altitudes of 100 km because they are absorbed by air much more readily than the infrared light from the chemical laser. They would therefore have to wait until the upper stages of the missile appeared above the atmosphere, some 2 min. after launch. Since RVs are much harder than missile stages to kill with X rays, the X-ray laser would seek to destroy the upper booster stage or the bus before RV deployment. RV deployment lasts for several minutes after exit from the atmosphere, but it begins soon after burnout. The X-ray laser therefore has a short time to act if RVs are not to leak through. Missiles designed to fly depressed trajectories, staying below 100 km at least until RVs were deployed, would be immune to the X-ray laser. So too would be single-warhead missiles that presented only an RV (possibly inaccurate) as a target above 100 km.

A single X-ray laser detonation is alleged to be capable of directing beams at and destroying several ICBMs, like the chemical laser. But whereas the chemical laser fires at objects serially and can interrupt its fire, the nuclear explosion that generates the X rays destroys the entire station. Relying on one laser bomb to destroy several ICBMs might therefore result in a system susceptible to launches strung out over about 30 min.: by the time the last attacking Soviet ICBM lifts off, all the X-ray laser battle stations have blown themselves up. The X-ray lasers cannot defend themselves against antisatellite attack because self-defense means self-destruction. Without details (at this time known to no one) about the ultimate characteristics of this device and of the sensor, command-and-control, self-defense, and other systems accompanying it, together with a dedicated effort to devise countermeasures, it is pointless to analyze this scheme in further detail.

Another scheme would seek to avoid the self-defense problem by placing the laser devices on high-acceleration missiles on submarines in northern waters. In the first few minutes after ICBM launch, warning would somehow be communicated to the submarine, and it would launch the lasers very quickly to within range of the boosters just as they left the atmosphere. This scheme raises questions about the practicality of getting the laser device in position in time and about the high costs of submarine basing.

Other ideas for systems will no doubt appear in the future. It is possible that if any directed-energy system for BMD is ever deployed, it will look fundamentally different from the schemes discussed today.

The Question of Net Long-Term Benefit

The foregoing sections have described the benefits—however great or meager—accruing to the defense by investing in various types of BMD. If either the United States or the USSR makes a move toward major BMD deployments, the other is very likely to follow suit with its own BMD. Each will also react with changes to offensive forces or to the way they plan to use them. To merit approval, a proposed BMD must therefore result in *net* benefit to the nation contemplating deployment, considering the prospect of facing an opposing BMD, and the net advantage must also be shown to exist not just in the near term against a static opponent, but in the long term against an opponent determined to overcome the defense. This section considers military factors that should ideally go into a U.S. or Soviet BMD deployment decision besides technology assessment and unilateral mission analysis.

Models of Mutual BMDs

An obvious question to ask of a BMD proposal is whether the military advantage sought in the deployment is preserved when reactions of the other side are taken into account. Mutual BMDs mean that the survivability achieved with ICBM defense is purchased at the price of reduced ability to attack enemy targets. Take, for example, the use of BMD to defend the proposed deployment of MX missiles in the United States. MX is presumably being bought and made survivable in the first place because it is thought necessary to be able to threaten targets in the Soviet Union with retaliation. But if these targets are defended, the extra MX survivors obtained through BMD might not increase retaliatory capability. Would there in fact be a net military gain over the situation that existed without BMD, or even without both BMD and MX?

Analysis of this kind of question using exchange calculations and quantitative models, wherein nuclear strikes are simulated and the results totaled, can be complicated by inessential detail, and the results are generally dominated by the assumptions made and by the criteria of judgment. Clearly, assessments of the future strategic situation will differ as much from observer to observer as assessments of the adequacy of the present posture. Consideration of a few simple models highlight the features that drive the outcome of these calculations.

MODEL 1. In this model, both the United States and the USSR deploy identical BMDs in defense of their missile silos. Suppose that before BMD deployments, both sides have 1000 ICBMs, each with three MIRVed warheads. This would be thought to be an unstable situation, since each side could destroy the other's missiles in a first strike and have some left over. Suppose now that each side deploys with each silo a BMD capable of charging a price of three RVs. Now it takes a missile to destroy a missile: the world has been de-MIRVed!

Differences in offense and defense perceptions might complicate the picture. Suppose the United States, aware of the hidden failings of its system, reckons that in fact its BMD is capable of a price of only two RVs and is sure the Soviet Union is aware of these failings. Suppose, at the same time, the United States believes the Soviet BMD capable of exacting a price of four RVs. If so, the United States would figure that its missiles are still vulnerable to a Soviet first strike but that it is unable similarly to threaten Soviet missiles. The peculiar thing about the perceived asymmetry is that the Soviet Union could have the same perception, only reversed.

MODEL 2. In this model, the United States defends its ICBMs and the Soviet Union responds with a defense of C^3/OMT targets, deploying the 1000-interceptor nationwide BMD described in this chapter. Suppose a U.S. deployment of 100 MX missiles plus BMD, together with Minuteman, requires the entire arsenal of modern Soviet ICBMs to destroy—a high price. According to one view, the benefit of the U.S. deployment has been obtained for free, since the Soviet BMD is totally irrelevant: after a Soviet first strike the United States has no ICBM RVs for the nationwide BMD to intercept anyway, but the U.S. bombers, cruise missiles, and possibly SLBMs penetrate unharmed to do adequate damage to Soviet C^3/OMT targets. In a U.S. first strike, the Soviet BMD is overwhelmed or defeated by stylized attacks; or bombers, cruise missiles, and SLBMs are again used against Soviet C^3/OMT targets.

Yet, a small shift of the facts (or perceived facts) and emphasis seems to produce a catastrophe: a Soviet first strike virtually eliminates the U.S. ICBM force; the few surviving ICBMs are unable to penetrate to their targets; the Soviet BMD *can* intercept SLBMs; air defense improvements threaten bomber and cruise missile penetration; the United States is in fact relying on only bombers and cruise missiles to damage Soviet C^3/OMT targets, whereas the whole point of the BMD was to provide survivability for the ICBM component of the U.S. triad of strategic forces.

Formal "measures of merit" can be defined for assessing the outcome of these exchange models.[26] Exchanges are first simulated with each side taking turns initiating the exchange, and the damage to C^3/OMT and cities is totaled. The model probes "arms race stability" by comparing the damage the United States can do to the USSR in retaliation with the damage it suffers itself. If retaliatory damage to the USSR seems inadequate, pressures to build more U.S. offensive forces are assumed to develop. "Crisis stability" is examined by comparing the damage to the United States if it strikes first with the damage it suffers if it allows the Soviet Union to strike first. Large differences in these quantities

---

26. The author acknowledges the work of Ellery Block and Larry Sealy of Science Applications, Inc., in Huntsville, Alabama, in this area.

represent unwanted incentives to limit damage by initiating a nuclear exchange. It is clear that analysis of such measures of merit should precede decisions on the future of BMD.

Side Effects of New BMD Deployments

Strategic programs have developed for decades now in the absence of large-scale BMD deployment. A move to substantial BMD deployments would have a number of strategic side effects that should also be thought through before decisions are made.

CALCULATIONS OF THE STRATEGIC BALANCE. BMD represents an effective reduction in the opponent's offensive arsenal. In the world today without BMD, each nuclear weapon included in assessments of the balance of power between the United States and the Soviet Union implicitly represents potential destruction. It is unclear how such "bean counting" would or should be changed by BMD. Should the Soviet Union be credited with fewer SS-18s and SS-19s if the United States defends against them?

NEW PROGRAMS AND PLANS. Penetration aid programs and changes to offensive forces to counter opposing BMDs would obviously receive new attention, and their costs should be charged to the BMD deployment decision. The war plans of the superpowers are presumably drawn up today on the assumption that a targeted aimpoint is (usually) destroyed. The planning process would be much more complicated with BMD, since destruction of a given target would no longer be made certain just by allocating a weapon to it.

OTHER STRATEGIC DEFENSES. Serious consideration of BMD would doubtless inspire further discussion of strategic air defenses, civil defense, and perhaps even antisubmarine warfare.

HEDGES. That only small BMD deployments are allowed under the ABM Treaty is believed to make it harder for the Soviet Union to conceal stockpiled BMD components or large-scale preparations to "break out" of the treaty. Would the United States feel comfortable with its understanding of the nature and scope of Soviet BMD deployments, or would pressures develop for new "hedges" against failures of intelligence to detect and interpret BMD deployments? Would missile defense lead to added reliance on cruise missiles and bombers? What hedges against failures of these forces could be provided?

THE ALLIED AND CHINESE MISSILE FORCES. These forces represent an added threat to the Soviet Union that is generally thought to act strongly in the U.S. favor. Reduced penetration of these forces is another military penalty of BMD.

Alternatives and Opportunity Costs

After assessing the net long-term military benefit (if any) of the proposed BMD deployment, including in the assessment the costs of all the side effects, the planner (and the nation as a whole) must compare the proposed course with its alternatives, assessing the opportunity costs. For instance, silo defense would be compared with alternative ICBM basing modes, using the same criteria of analysis. Some observers maintain that ICBMs should not depend on warning for survival as bombers do, since that would mean both would be susceptible to the same type of failure. But BMDs depend on warning; does that rule them out? Alternatives to BMD might in some views include air defenses and civil defenses. Yet another alternative to BMD deployment to "fix" a perceived strategic problem is to reconsider the importance of the problem. Another approach is to seek solutions in arms control. A proposed BMD deployment would presumably have to prove itself better than all these competitors.

A BMD of measurable utility will cost *at least* $10 billion, and the cost of side effects could be high as well. BMD systems would be major and long-lasting additions to the strategic arena, the inevitable follow-ons and improvements making for continuing cost. Can the strategic forces budget encompass a major new program? Is investment in BMD worth forgoing improvements in conventional forces?

A New Complexity

The performance of any BMD is subject to uncertainties about myriad technical details. How will this uncertainty be encompassed by the strategists, politicians, and diplomats who will decide the future of BMD—and who attach great importance to quantitative measures of the strategic balance? Could they arrive at a judgment about the effectiveness of BMD and maintain confidence in that judgment? Would they require unrealistically precise statements of BMD capabilities and "proofs" that "parity" existed? Could the United States balance the weaknesses of its own defense system against the problems it would pose to a Soviet attacker? Would excessive importance be attached to exotic and subtle attack strategies? Would new scenarios proliferate to replace the old ones supposedly made less worrisome by BMD? How would arms control, which usually comes down to counting things, absorb the new complexity? These questions are certain to arise and in the end are probably much more important to the future than the scientific or military analyst's careful assessments.

CHAPTER FIVE

The Soviet BMD Program

SAYRE STEVENS

IT IS appropriate that a chapter dealing with Soviet ballistic missile defense activities be included in this book. The Soviet Union and the United States are partners in the ABM Treaty of 1972 that limits mutually the BMD deployment activities they can pursue. Consequently, the fate of BMD development in either country depends to some extent on where both partners want that course to lead.

The need to look Soviet BMD in the face derives more importantly, however, from the tremendous power of the BMD factor in affecting perceptions of the strategic balance between the United States and the Soviet Union. It was recognition of these effects that generated much of the support for the ABM Treaty. A means was sought to tamp down the arms race instabilities caused by perceptions of a hostile defense that could undermine deterrence by preventing the penetration of retaliating ballistic missiles. To be sure, that argument has become less compelling with the development of multiple independently targetable reentry vehicles (MIRVs) and the great increase in the number of missile-delivered weapons now available to both sides. Moreover, in the absence of offensive arms limitations (or reductions, as in the strategic arms reduction talks), even larger numbers, apt to overwhelm any near-term defense, could be deployed. But offensive weapons reductions are on the agenda of both the United States and the USSR, and overwhelming offensive force capabilities may not be available in all circumstances.

The unsettling effect of an extensive Soviet BMD deployment on U.S. thinking is encapsulated in the possibility of having to retaliate after a Soviet first strike, when many of our land-based intercontinental ballistic missiles (ICBMs) have been lost, command and control are uncertain, and generating a tailored attack against the Soviet BMD is no longer possible. BMD deployments that threaten to deny the workings of assured retaliatory response—and hence deterrence—are of course unsettling and tend to force both sides to react. The reactions are complex and involve the full range of strategic forces; this feature makes the consideration of Soviet BMD essential in any broader strategic analysis.

The ABM Treaty has served to diminish these concerns, but its continued credibility depends heavily upon the nature of Soviet BMD activities and the threats that they may pose now and in future years. Heavy emphasis is being given to reducing offensive arms arsenals to substantially lower levels in the ongoing START negotiations. Success in this endeavor can only once again heighten the significance of any disparities in the two sides' defenses and increase the importance of the perception of a "balance" in defensive forces. Whether or not the ABM Treaty can by itself maintain this perception depends on its ability to contain the pressures for change that are almost certainly building both in the United States and in the USSR, as improving technology makes effective BMD appear more feasible and easier missions such as hard target defense grow in importance.

Two other factors serve to amplify the importance of Soviet BMD activities. The first of these is the threatening growth of Soviet strategic capabilities in general. Now that the Soviet Union has improved the capabilities of its counterforce weapons, the U.S. retaliatory forces have become increasingly vulnerable. This effort has been pursued with commitment and persistence over the years. A Soviet first strike might result from a judgment by leaders in the USSR in a mounting crisis that nuclear war was imminent and inevitable and that preemption was essential if important strategic advantage was not to be lost. Soviet doctrine calls for the disruption of command and control along with the destruction of offensive nuclear forces in the critical first stages of nuclear war. In these circumstances, as noted above, Soviet BMD forces-in-being could weaken the deterrent effect of a much-reduced and "ragged" retaliatory attack.

The second factor has to do with the rather large gaps in what we know about Soviet BMD activities. There are and always have been many uncertainties about the Soviet BMD program, its achievements, technical objectives, and overall intent. As a result, our judgments about Soviet activities and the threat that they embody are far more often a matter of conjecture than of established fact. The discussion that follows will make this amply clear. The characteristics ascribed to the Soviet BMD program can affect perceptions of the overall strategic balance; also, characterization of the program can be the result of perceptions of the balance. For the pessimist anxious to support contentions of U.S. inferiority, bleak perceptions are a useful device. For those more sanguine about the balance or less concerned about its state than about provocative U.S. initiatives likely to fuel the arms race, a far less alarming interpretation of Soviet BMD activities serves a useful purpose. What is alarming to one set of viewers is perfectly explainable in benign terms to another. Uncertainties allow latitude for both persuasions and prevent one group from conclusively gainsaying the other.

As a result of this uncertainty, it is important that the differing perceptions of the Soviet BMD program, and their excursions from some central point, be laid out for those who are considering the future of BMD for the United States. The questions to be asked involve not only the characteristics and capabilities of the deployed Soviet BMD systems, but also Soviet intentions in developing new ones and Soviet plans for ultimately deploying them. Questions also arise about their augmentation with other weapons systems—principally air defense systems—that might serve to enhance ballistic missile defenses limited by treaty. There are also questions about Soviet perceptions of U.S. technology and the capability of the United States to gear itself up to take on the BMD job once again, forcing the Soviet Union into a defensive weapon systems race. What the Soviet Union is doing in ballistic missile defense development is important to the United States not only in terms of decisions about its own BMD program, but also in terms of decisions about other forces and policies it might use to face the Soviet threat.

BMD in Soviet Strategic Thinking

The Soviet BMD program is but a part of a much broader effort by the Soviet Union to develop the capabilities to pursue major strategic objectives. The BMD program must thus be considered against this broader backdrop.[1]

1. This treatment of Soviet strategic thinking benefits from access to unpublished work of Howard Stoertz and Mark Miller, long-time students of and writers about the strategic balance and Soviet perceptions of it.

For the most part, Soviet strategic objectives are political. The Soviet Union wishes to sustain the regime, to maintain its superpower status, and to expand its influence. It tends to see the value of military power and strategic forces in terms of their contribution to an overall, favorable "correlation of forces" (that is, a concatenation of military, economic, political, and social circumstances giving the Soviet Union the latitude to pursue its international goals) that will help the USSR dominate a crisis or a local conflict, and, most important, deter the imperialists—the United States and the North Atlantic Treaty Organization (NATO)—from initiating strategic nuclear war. Although the Soviet Union believes the ability to wage nuclear war is essential, it does not see nuclear war as desirable. The Soviet Union is averse to war but is determined that we shall be even more averse to it. Moreover, mutual vulnerability appears to be unsatisfying to the Soviet Union because such a doctrine inevitably leaves its fate in the hands of others.

To accompany these political objectives, a body of doctrine has been developed providing guidelines for the conduct of strategic nuclear war. It is important to note that Soviet doctrine is almost entirely the product of the military itself. Thus, it is not surprising that it supports the provision of the weapons the military wants. Soviet doctrine has a much narrower and more military focus than that of the United States, whose doctrinal approaches tend to be defined in broader terms by commentators outside of the military forces. As a result, Soviet military doctrine seeks to fulfill objectives that are significant to the military and to the military mission. Broader considerations, economic considerations, for example, do not play as significant a role in Soviet military doctrine as they do in that of the United States. Compatibility of military equipment with the demands of overall strategic doctrine is virtually ensured in the Soviet case by the fact that both doctrine and weapons acquisition requirements are defined by the same community.

Soviet national security policy thus has two distinct aspects. One constitutes an effort to prepare to fight and to survive a nuclear war; this is the domain of the military and produces the "military science" or doctrine underlying the selection of strategic weapons and plans for their use. The other, the domain of the political leadership, is the conduct of a peace policy intended to prevent war and to limit the threat to Soviet national security through political means. It is the responsibility of the political leaders to preserve peace and that of the military to ensure the capability to punish an aggressor and survive war. Viewed in this light, the often-conflicting statements about strategic policy that emerge from the USSR are easier to understand.[2]

In these circumstances, it is not surprising that there is some contention in the West as to the significance of the substance of Soviet military doctrine. Some believe that although it may reflect the thinking of the military, it is not a good guide to the thinking of the Soviet political leadership, which has been far more circumspect in its views of nuclear war. But there is evidence, too, that the Soviet political leadership has been more influenced by the views of the military than has the political leadership of the United States, and that the Soviet leadership has tended to defer to the military on technical defense issues.[3] Thus, the military's own doctrine is a significant consideration in searching for an understanding of Soviet BMD activities.

Soviet strategic doctrine is predicated on having the capacity to fight and to win a nuclear war to deter the imperialists.[4] The Soviet Union takes the possibility of nuclear war seriously, seeking to endure the consequences of strategic nuclear warfare if it should occur. In such circumstances the Soviet Union would employ all of the strategic means available: both tactical and strategic military forces and political, diplomatic, and economic means. Principal among defined Soviet military goals of nuclear conflict would be destruction of the enemy's capacity and will to fight, maintenance of firm control over the Soviet state and its forces, preservation of a basis for military and economic reconstitution, and domination of the postwar era. The capability to achieve such goals is believed to constitute the best deterrent. Although deterrence might be less costly, the Soviet Union appears to be highly confident that, if it can meet these warfighting requirements, it will indeed deter

2. David Holloway, *The Soviet Union and the Arms Race* (Yale University Press, 1983), pp. 29–58.

3. John Newhouse, *Cold Dawn: The Story of SALT* (Holt, Rinehart, and Winston, 1973), p. 105; Carnegie Panel on U.S. Security and the Future of Arms Control, *Challenges for U.S. National Security: The Soviet Approach to Arms Control; Verification; Problems and Prospects; Conclusions* (Washington, D.C.: Carnegie Endowment for International Peace, 1983), p. 8.

4. Much has been written on Soviet military doctrine. For its particular relationship to BMD, see chapter 8 herein, as well as Sidney Graybeal and Daniel Gouré, "Soviet Ballistic Missile Defense (BMD) Objectives: Past, Present and Future," in Ballistic Missile Defense Advanced Technology Center, *U.S. Arms Control Objectives and the Implications for Ballistic Missile Defense,* Proceedings of a Symposium at the Center for Science and International Affairs, Harvard University, November 1–2, 1979 (Puritan Press, 1980), pp. 69–90.

war. Unquestioned capabilities in this regard would be best, but it recognizes that full confidence can only be achieved in the future. The continuing improvement and extension of forces-in-being provide the route for getting there.

Since all the goals of Soviet doctrine are not yet fulfilled and deterrence is uncertain, the Soviet Union has given high value to a capacity to preempt and to launch on warning or launch under attack should it fail to preempt an enemy attack. The Soviet view of preemption is neither one of preventive war nor one associated with a "bolt-from-the-blue" attack. The Soviet Union sees general nuclear war emerging from a long period of crisis in which local conflicts may be under way in various parts of the world. War is most likely to emerge as the natural outgrowth of such a crisis and conflict, and the problem is not so much one of choosing between peace and war as of recognizing the point at which the failure of deterrence becomes inevitable. The Soviet Union would expect to monitor the emerging situation and detect signals indicating that the United States was preparing to attack.

Because the Soviet Union has adopted a combined-arms approach not only in the use of ground forces but also in planning for the use of strategic forces in the early stage of a war, all elements of military force would become involved. It is critical in Soviet thinking to dominate this early phase of the war, to sow confusion, to interfere with the lines of command and control, to employ surprise in the hope of achieving quick success, and, finally, to limit damage to the Soviet Union from U.S. retaliation to a Soviet preemptive strike. Even with successful preemption, the Soviet Union could not escape all damage. But damage might indeed be reduced. The Soviet approach to the reduction of damage is to use not only the counterforce capability of offensive weapon systems, but air defenses, civil and passive defenses, and ballistic missile defenses. The role of these strategic elements would be to limit the damage to the Soviet Union that would be caused by the forces remaining to the United States *after* a preemptive strike. Such a mission could significantly reduce the technical requirements put upon a BMD system. BMD does not have to carry the entire brunt of thwarting an enemy attack. It also enjoys the benefits of other, complementary defenses. Air defenses reduce the consequences of aerodynamic attack; passive measures such as dispersal make targeting uncertain if not impossible; other passive civil defenses provide protection to the leadership and to vital military and industrial cadres. Because BMD only has to contribute to the limitation of damage, whatever job it can do is a worthwhile one; absolute effectiveness may be sought but is not essential. The reduction of damage to any degree is seen to have value, fitting into a picture of nuclear war in which the consequences are recognized but the conflict is nevertheless seen as a real possibility. Because that possibility is taken seriously, plans must be made to endure the consequences of a war. Thus, when one side buys a BMD system, it does not buy total defense in Soviet eyes, but instead some limitation of damage in circumstances that virtually deny the possibility of surviving unscathed. What might appear useless to the United States, with its much more demanding perceptions of what ballistic missile defense must provide, might have significant incremental value in Soviet military eyes. A system that is fully effective but can be made even more effective over time would not be so ridiculous an investment as it might appear to us. Unless this view is understood, many things that have occurred in the Soviet BMD program appear to be remarkable, if not incomprehensible.

Although the Soviet Union has been committed for some time to the development and deployment of active defenses, it has concluded that, in general, the offense will overpower the defense.[5] In a sense, Soviet achievements in establishing such defensive momentum are the more noteworthy because of the view embodied in Marshal V.D. Sokolovsky's definitive work on Soviet doctrine that "one must recognize that the present instrumentalities of nuclear attack are undoubtedly superior to the instrumentalities of defense against them."[6] This perception serves to heighten the importance of counterforce weapons in "destroying the enemy's nuclear weapons where they are based."[7]

In summary, Soviet strategic thinking cannot be explained in terms of the effects of BMD alone, but these effects must be seen in conjunction with strategic counterforce strike capability and with passive defenses that play their own part in reducing the effects of nuclear attack. This view allows the Soviet Union to recognize the predominant significance of offensive forces in the nuclear era and at the same time to establish the need for active defenses as part of its overall strategic force capabilities.

The Soviet Union enjoys as well some advantages in terms of weapons

5. Thomas W. Wolfe, *Soviet Strategy at the Crossroads*, RM-4085-PR, prepared for the U.S. Air Force Project Rand (Santa Monica, Calif.: Rand Corp., 1964), pp. 243–46.
6. Quoted in ibid., p. 243.
7. Ibid.

acquisition and defense expenditures that the United States does not. Because of different priorities, different methods of defining them, and a different degree of openness in the debate, the United States and the Soviet Union face different imperatives in making weapons acquisition choices. In the United States, major defense initiatives must be justified in terms that are significant to the public debate that will ensue over most large programs. In the Soviet Union this is obviously not the case. Moreover, the doctrine that has been discussed here greatly reduces the justification required for deploying and continually improving weapons systems of initially limited effectiveness. Soviet success in persistently deploying new and modified weapons systems year after year reflects this doctrinal predisposition.

Early Days in the Soviet ABM Program

Quite apart from all these doctrinal trappings, it appears that the Soviet Union took to BMD research and development like a duck takes to water. It is now clear that shortly after the end of World War II, the Soviet Union first began to investigate the possibility of ballistic missile defense. In many respects this is not surprising. The terrible air raids that the Russian people suffered during World War II, particularly in Moscow and Leningrad, made it clear that the technical means for coping with attack from above was going to become an essential part of war in the future. This judgment was coupled with the commitment by the Soviet leadership to protect the homeland from the terrible ravages that it had suffered in World War II, a commitment probably made stronger by perceptions of Soviet unpreparedness at the outset of the war. The concern about air attack was accompanied by a growing awareness of the impact of the V-1 and V-2 weapons developed by Germany and used against Britain in the latter stages of the war. There was little doubt that these weapons represented a glimpse of the future. Clearly the Soviet Union felt the need to provide itself with defenses against such threats.

An opportunity to develop a technical approach was provided by the German scientists who had been rounded up in the aftermath of the war and sent to the USSR to work on Soviet systems. These were the same scientists who had developed the V-1, the V-2, and advanced German aerodynamic systems. Most important, the group also included a number of scientists who had worked on Germany's Wasserfall antibomber missile system. Upon their return to Germany many years later, they confirmed other indications that Soviet efforts to develop an air defense missile system of its own had become a very high priority. The extension of capabilities against bombers to a capability against ballistic missiles in space became an obvious goal.

The fruits of early efforts to design air defenses were fairly quick in coming. First came a remarkable deployment of jet aircraft interceptors and anti-aircraft artillery.[8] The latter development is perhaps more important because it established a basic tie between the air defense forces and the Russian artillery, which has a long heritage. The air defense forces *PVO Strany (Protivovozdushnaya Oborana Strany)* in large part grew out of the artillery forces. The PVO, which now is responsible for all aspects of air, antisatellite, and ballistic missile defense, has become a major branch of the armed services, a separate service in its own right.[9] This development established an institutionalized military service dedicated to the development and operation of active defenses. The PVO was not a Johnny-come-lately but an accepted, credible player with important military credentials. Over the years, the PVO has been extremely effective in getting a large share of the military budget and acquiring more than its share of new weapons systems.[10]

By 1952 surface-to-air missile (SAM) technology was reportedly available to the PVO.[11] The SA-1 SAM system was under deployment around Moscow by 1956 and was capable of providing defense against mass raids on Moscow by contemporary bombers using tactics of the kind that were employed in World War II. The SA-2 SAM system soon followed and was widely deployed throughout the USSR in the 1960s and early 1970s. Subsequently a whole series of improvements and new surface-to-air missile systems have been fielded in great numbers across the Soviet Union. Together with the extensive air-warning and command-and-control network that supports them, these SAM systems and

8. Johan J. Holst, "Missile Defense: The Soviet Union and the Arms Race," in Johan J. Holst and William Schneider, Jr., eds., *Why ABM? Policy Issues in the Missile Defense Controversy* (Pergamon, 1969), pp. 146–47.

9. Ibid., p. 147; and Harriet Fast Scott and William F. Scott, *The Armed Forces of the USSR* (Westview Press, 1979), pp. 147–53.

10. For comparisons of strategic defense expenditures with those of other mission areas, see U.S. Central Intelligence Agency, *A Dollar Cost Comparison of Soviet and U.S. Defense Activities, 1966–1976,* SR77-10001U (CIA, 1977).

11. Holst, "Missile Defense," p. 147.

a vast inventory of interceptor aircraft make up the most formidable air defense system in the world.[12]

In the early stages of this development there could have been little debate within the Soviet Union about the value of defense or of its significance in broader strategic terms. To a people who had gone through World War II, the importance and the basic justice of having defenses in place were obvious. Work on an actual BMD program evidently began in the late 1940s or early 1950s.[13] Claims have been made that the decision to pursue ICBMs was accompanied by the decision to develop ballistic missile defenses.[14] Whether or not so simple-mindedly rational an approach was in fact taken can be questioned, but it is clear that by the mid-1950s the Soviet Union must have begun the development of its first BMD.[15]

German scientists and engineers returning to the West reported that such activities were under way and that their Soviet counterparts were working hard. The United States officially recognized the existence of such a program before 1960.[16] Moreover, there were reports that the Soviet Union was developing a major missile test range where these activities would be conducted when they reached the testing stage. In what must be considered a stroke of extreme good fortune, the West had its first clear look at these BMD activities in April 1960 when a U-2 reconnaissance plane was able to take pictures of the activity under way in the region of Sary Shagan, a small village on the edge of Lake Balkash in Central Asia.[17] It was the next U-2 mission, one month later, that ended in the shooting down of Gary Powers and that marked the end of all U-2 overflights of the Soviet Union.

It was clear from the pictures returned in April that a major program was indeed under way and that a considerable amount of progress toward

12. Ibid., p. 147–48.

13. Raymond L. Garthoff, *Soviet Strategy in the Nuclear Age* (Praeger, 1958), pp. 228–31.

14. C. L. Sulzberger, "Khrushchev Says in Interview He is Ready to Meet Kennedy," *New York Times*, September 8, 1961; cited in Michael J. Deane, *The Role of Strategic Defense in Soviet Strategy*, Advanced International Studies Institute, University of Miami (Current Affairs Press, 1980), p. 26.

15. Graybeal and Gouré, "Soviet BMD Objectives," p. 70.

16. Lawrence Freedman, *U.S. Intelligence and the Soviet Strategic Threat* (London: Macmillan, 1977), p. 87.

17. Ibid.

the development of BMD components had already occurred. Most striking perhaps was the Hen House radar, a very large radar the size of which prevented it from being identified as a radar for some time.[18] But a number of other installations as well gave evidence of the intensity and commitment of the Soviet program. The size and scope of the entire undertaking impressed everyone who saw the pictures with the progress the Soviet Union had made in its BMD endeavor.

Sary Shagan proved to be the development and testing center of the PVO. Although it was early labeled as a BMD center and was long associated principally with BMD development, it does in fact support the development of advanced strategic air defense systems and probably antisatellite systems as well. Its early identification as a BMD range later complicated the sorting out of the missions of new weapons systems developed there.[19]

Sary Shagan represented a natural choice for a test range for BMD systems. It lies about a thousand miles downrange from Kapustin Yar, the Soviet Union's first ballistic missile test range, and provides coverage of the impact area for missiles launched from there. It is accessible by way of the Trans-Siberian railroad line but at the same time is in a remote region of the Soviet Union, quite off the beaten track for Soviet citizens, let alone for foreign visitors. It lies deeply enough within the USSR to make it difficult to monitor from peripheral intelligence-gathering sites along the border. Because flight test operations at Sary Shagan can be conducted well below the radio-horizon from such external monitoring locations, the Soviet Union has been able to conceal the details of its activities at Sary Shagan for many years.

Among the disparate elements of BMD activities that were seen at Sary Shagan in April 1960 were pieces of at least three systems that were later to have BMD implications.[20] These included a system (Griffon) that later appeared briefly at Leningrad and that may well have had BMD capabilities designed into it; the beginnings of the system that was to go around Moscow and is now known as the Moscow or Galosh BMD system; and finally a progenitor of one or the other of these two systems (precisely which one still remains a matter of debate).

This early coverage of Sary Shagan was important in providing a basis

18. Ibid.
19. John Prados, *The Soviet Estimate: U.S. Intelligence Analysis and Russian Military Strength* (Dial, 1982), p.155.
20. Ibid., pp. 152–55.

for understanding other developments that were beginning to emerge in the 1960s. One was the beginning of deployment of a whole network of Hen House radars providing coverage of space to monitor satellites in orbit and to provide early warning (and some tracking information) of ICBMs launched from the United States.[21] As the system grew, it provided a span of radar coverage that could provide a foundation of long-range acquisition sensors for a nationwide BMD system involving terminal or local area defenses. This radar infrastructure is the basis of much of the concern about "rapidly deployable" Soviet BMD capabilities. It has also been contended that the network may provide necessary radar support to less capable systems, such as air defense SAMs upgraded so as to have some BMD capabilities.

The next occurrence of significance for Soviet BMD in the early 1960s was the series of nuclear tests that occurred at the Sary Shagan–Kapustin Yar test ranges in October 1961 and again a year later. During these tests, missiles were launched from Kapustin Yar into the impact area in conjunction with BMD activities at Sary Shagan.[22] Also associated with these events was the detonation of a number of nuclear weapons at high altitude, presumably to assess the effectiveness of BMD systems in a nuclear environment.

In the same general time period, a beginning was made on the deployment of a defensive missile system around Leningrad; the elements of this system had been seen at Sary Shagan in 1960 and it was believed to be the beginning of a nationwide Soviet BMD deployment.[23] More will be said about that system shortly.

Within several years a second deployment effort began in the Moscow area. Critical components of this system were also related to installations that had been seen at Sary Shagan. With these activities, Soviet BMD efforts more or less came out of the closet. There was much commentary in the Soviet press about the BMD program, and prominent spokesmen indicated that the Soviet Union was on its way to the actual deployment of a BMD system. In October 1961, at the Twenty-Second Party

21. Freedman, *U.S. Intelligence*, p. 157. For the coverage currently provided by this early warning network as it has been extended and improved over the years, see U.S. Department of Defense, *Soviet Military Power*, 2d ed. (Government Printing Office, 1983).

22. Freedman, *U.S. Intelligence*, p. 87; and Prados, *The Soviet Estimate*, p. 152–53.

23. Freedman, *U.S. Intelligence*, p. 91.

Congress, Marshal Rodion Malinovsky noted that "the problem of destroying enemy missiles in flight has been successfully resolved."[24] Shortly thereafter, Chairman Nikita Khrushchev made his famous statement that the Soviet missile defense forces could "hit a fly" in space.[25] Given this lead, the popular press on defense technology was filled with articles both tutorial and hortatory dealing with the problems of ballistic missile defense in general and the accomplishments of the Soviet Union in particular.[26]

Even in the early days, some conclusions could be drawn about Soviet BMD design proclivities. One of the most remarkable was the clear difference between the approach taken by those who designed the system around Moscow and those working on the Leningrad system and its successors in later years.

The Moscow system used very large components, particularly large radars with a large power-aperture product that enabled them to search for and track missile reentry vehicles at very long ranges (see chapter 3). Adequate for dealing with individual targets, the radars lacked the sophistication to deal with many targets at one time. When we first saw the Galosh missile (the interceptor used with the Moscow ABM system) paraded in 1964, we found it to be huge.[27] In fact, the Galosh interceptor was larger than the Minuteman ICBM it was presumably to counter. Thus, one Soviet approach to BMD, perhaps the product of one development group, addressed the problem by building equipment that was especially designed to deal with the extraordinary difficulties of intercepting small missile reentry vehicles at very long ranges.

The other development line took a very different approach, characterized by the attempt to improve air defense technology to the point where it could cope with missile intercepts. Whether the early products of this design approach had significant BMD capabilities has long been debated.[28] In any event, this line of development has continued to the

24. *Pravda,* October 25, 1961.
25. Theodore Shabad, "Khrushchev Says Missile Can 'Hit a Fly' in Space," *New York Times,* July 17, 1962.
26. There were a large number of such articles. A serious contribution to popular articles in this general line was that of Major General Nikolai Talensky, "Anti-Missile Systems and the Problems of Disarmament," *Mezhdunarodnaya zhizn',* no. 10 (October 1964), pp. 28–34. See chapter 8 herein and, for a rather full bibliography, see Deane, *The Role of Strategic Defense in Soviet Strategy.*
27. Freedman, *U.S. Intelligence,* p. 89.
28. Ibid., p. 91.

present day.[29] All of the systems produced by this approach have a strong air defense look and seem to seek an antiballistic missile capability through the strengthening of a basic anti-aircraft approach.

Other characteristics of Soviet BMD technology were evident in this early period: it was clearly limited and unsophisticated by U.S. standards. Nevertheless, the Soviet Union had made a genuine commitment to the development, testing, and even deployment of the systems that it produced. These systems were "radar heavy"; the Soviet Union was not at all reluctant to add whatever elements were required in order to do the job, proliferating radars at heavy cost. In the Moscow system in particular, the costs associated with the very large radars must have been terrific. The Soviet Union was willing to meet that radar challenge without a visible flinch.

It was also evident that the Soviet Union was concerned about dealing with the operational realities of BMD. The nuclear tests of 1961 and 1962 revealed a concern for the operation of the system in conditions representative of nuclear war. This attempt to replicate the conditions under which the systems might be used went far beyond the U.S. approach of gathering data in the hope that a wide range of specific operational conditions could then be derived from more basic data.

The Leningrad system with its Griffon missile constituted the first deployment effort of the group approaching BMD along the air defense line; whether or not the system actually included a BMD capability remains uncertain. The first indications of its deployment occurred in the form of clearings that appeared in the early 1960s.[30] A number of elements went in. By 1962 as many as thirty launch positions had been observed in the process of deployment.[31] The elements used were similar to those first seen at Sary Shagan. Moreover, they were deployed in position not only to give protection to Leningrad as part of the Russian center and a key target area within the Soviet Union, but also to cover the flight paths into the western USSR of missiles or aircraft launched from the United States. There was, from the start, a good deal of skepticism about the system's having a significant BMD role, but its origins at Sary Shagan, and its association in time with the rash of Soviet statements about new-found BMD capabilities, fueled the fires of those

29. The "rapidly deployable" ABM-X-3 system shows a greater similarity to more recent Soviet SAM system developments than to the Moscow system.

30. Graybeal and Gouré, "Soviet BMD Objectives," p. 70.

31. Prados, *The Soviet Estimate*, p. 153.

who argued in favor of such a role.[32] Nonetheless, the elements that went into the system showed little promise of being able to cope with the rapidly developing offensive missile threat. Whatever the case, the Soviet Union quickly concluded that the system lacked the capabilities it sought, and deployment was stopped a year or so after it had begun.[33] The system was never to be seen again. Such a decision was not as surprising as it might appear, for in that period the Soviet Union on occasion undertook the concurrent deployment and developmental flight testing of strategic weapons systems.

The Leningrad system might be left in historical peace were it not for the fact that it became a significant element in the later debate about whether or not new strategic defensive weapons systems that appeared to have an air defense role also embodied by design a capability for dealing with some ballistic missiles. This debate first centered on the Leningrad system itself and set the stage for later debates about other systems.[34] There were those who argued on the basis of its capabilities as derived from the analysis of imperfectly seen and understood system components, and those who put greater importance on early Sary Shagan connections, its deployment location, and so on. In neither case was sufficient information available to make a conclusive argument. It may never be known for sure whether or not the system did have a designed BMD role. It is possible that under pressure from Khrushchev, who was not unwilling to demand the fulfillment of his bluffs by his military forces, the designers were obliged to produce a system with nominal BMD capabilities, and did the best they could, but that they were unable to complete deployment when the greater capabilities of the Moscow system became available. If such were the case, it is likely that the Leningrad system was in fact designed to intercept high-altitude aircraft targets and given a limited capability against ballistic missiles. The ballistic missile intercept capability might have given promise against a very limited threat, but it was incapable of dealing with emerging new ICBM developments. The dismantlement of the system at Leningrad might have been due to dissatisfaction with its capability as a high-altitude air defense system as well. In the aftermath of the U-2 experience,

32. Ibid., pp. 153–54.
33. Ibid.; and Graybeal and Gouré, "Soviet BMD Objectives," p. 72.
34. Prados, *The Soviet Estimate*, pp. 155–71; and Freedman, *U.S. Intelligence*, pp. 90–96.

the demands for such a defense were beginning to wane, and it may have appeared wise to wait until the follow-on SA-5 system, which by that time was being developed, came on the scene.

The Moscow ABM System

Whatever uncertainty may have existed about the Leningrad system and its Griffon missile, there was never any doubt about the design intentions of the Moscow system. On the eve of the conclusion of the ABM Treaty, the system consisted of the Hen House, Dog House, and Cat House search and target acquisition radars; mechanically steered dish antennas for tracking targets and for tracking the interceptor missiles and guiding them to their targets; and Galosh nuclear-armed interceptor missiles. The broad network of Hen House radars around the periphery of the Soviet Union was capable of providing early warning and missile acquisition information to the defenses around Moscow. The Hen House network was vulnerable to nuclear attack itself, chiefly because its operation in the very high frequency (VHF) region made it susceptible to nuclear blackout.[35] The installations themselves were very soft, indeed were so large as to make nuclear hardening unthinkable. Nevertheless, they did provide a base for detecting incoming ballistic missiles at extremely long ranges and could characterize, at least roughly, the approaching attack. A very large A-frame radar (which came to be known as the Dog House) was built in the Moscow area. It is believed to provide battle management for the totality of the Moscow defenses, assigning targets to the tracking radars and interceptors, and providing target acquisition information to the tracking radars. In the 1970s, a second battle management radar much like the first and imaginatively labeled the Cat House was added to the system.[36] It provided coverage in additional sectors, though it still did not close all of the attack corridors to Moscow. Both the Dog House and the Cat House are immense phased-array radars capable of handling a number of targets simultaneously. The exact number is not known, but the use of phased-array technology

35. Mark B. Schneider, "Russia and the ABM," *Ordnance*, vol. 56 (March–April 1972), p. 374.
36. Jacquelyn K. Davis and others, *The Soviet Union and Ballistic Missile Defense* (Cambridge, Mass.: Institute for Foreign Policy Analysis, 1980), p. 55.

to provide this type of coverage was almost surely dictated by the need for multiple-target-handling capability. Since the principal limitation on target handling is probably the data-processing capacity available, which is virtually impossible to deduce, the uncertainty is not likely to be removed. Undoubtedly the system incorporates a large computing center able to process the data taken and to provide battle management guidance to the terminal defensive locations.

Standing behind this impressive radar front end were the defenses themselves. When finally developed, each of the four defense complexes consisted of a set of two identical installations, each containing a large target-tracking radar, two smaller but similar missile-tracking radars, and launching facilities for eight Galosh interceptors.[37] The target-tracking radars were large dishes the design of which appears to have been taken from the antennas used in earlier years for radio astronomy. Similar installations were later seen as satellite communications ground stations. The use of mechanical steering limited their effectiveness to the tracking of one or possibly two targets at a given time.[38] It was also clear that the radars had to be given target acquisition information by either the Hen House network or by the Dog House or Cat House battle management radars, which were able to scan electronically. Without acquisition by these radars, the capabilities of the Moscow system were limited.

The missile-tracking radars were similar to but smaller than the target-tracking radars. The fact that they were limited as well in the number of intercepting missiles that they could track and guide simultaneously probably explains why there were two in association with each target-tracking radar and with eight Galosh interceptor missiles. The arrangement suggested that two Galosh missiles could be launched against a single target and tracked by the two missile-tracking radars. The computer center at the facility would calculate the guidance required by the interceptors in order to close with the incoming target reentry vehicle.

The Galosh missile was first seen in the November 1964 parade. Its very size indicated it was an exoatmospheric interceptor capable of carrying out engagements at extremely long ranges. The Soviet Union itself announced this capability to be in the range of hundreds of miles

---

37. Freedman, *U.S. Intelligence*, p. 88; and Gerard Smith, *Doubletalk: The Story of the First Strategic Arms Limitation Talks* (Doubleday, 1980), p. 302.
    38. Freedman, *U.S. Intelligence*, pp. 89–90.

from the launch point.[39] For intercepts at such ranges, the use of a nuclear weapon was required in order to ensure kill. The Galosh was able to carry a weapon of very large yield.[40]

The range of the Galosh and the capabilities of the radars associated with the system enabled the Moscow ABM system to cover an area of many thousands of square miles. Its footprint of coverage extended well beyond the limits of Moscow itself. When operating at its outermost limit, the system could in effect provide defense for much of the European USSR, though such calculations ignore operational requirements that might have constrained the actual performance of the system. The defensive complexes themselves were located around a ring some 40–50 mi. from the center of Moscow.[41]

The extremely long range of the system made it possible to use a shoot-look-shoot tactic of defense. One Galosh could attempt an intercept at very long ranges, the radar could detect the success or failure of that intercept, and a second intercept could be attempted in the high endoatmospheric region. Such tactics would of course make fairly high-confidence intercepts possible, a capability of some significance in dealing with third-country or accidental attacks.

For taking on the full brunt of a U.S. attack, however, the Moscow system was extremely limited. Saturating the radars with more targets than they could handle was an obvious penetration tactic. By the time the ABM Treaty was signed, the United States had been deploying MIRVs on its ICBMs for two years, thus increasing the number of weapons available for saturation. The system was also vulnerable to the use of exoatmospheric decoys and particularly to the use of chaff to conceal the location of actual reentry vehicles (RVs) from radars required to detect and track them at long ranges while they were still outside the atmosphere. Long trains of chaff clouds, each of which might contain an RV, effectively saturated the system. Finally, the system as a whole was extremely vulnerable to nuclear effects. Any leakage of attacking missiles through the defense might eliminate the Hen House radars on the periphery of the Soviet Union and the Dog House and Cat House radars, which were vital elements to the effective working of the defense.

39. Ibid.

40. Norman Polmar, *Strategic Weapons: An Introduction* (Crane, Russak, 1975), p. 60; *Scope, Magnitude, and Implications of the United States Antiballistic Missile Program*, Joint Committee on Atomic Energy, 90 Cong. 1 sess. (GPO, 1968), p. 66.

41. Freedman, *U.S. Intelligence*, p. 88.

Perhaps even more important, those radars were susceptible to blackout caused by bursts within their viewing sectors. The defensive interceptor complexes themselves were (and are) also soft, though the tracking radars operate at higher frequencies and in locations that could reduce blackout effects. As noted above, some attack corridors were not entirely closed by the forward radars. Ballistic missiles could be fired into the Moscow area without being detected by the defenses at all, unless the target-tracking radars were able to operate in a very clumsy mechanical scan mode. Were they to do this, they would be occupied with the search function and would be unavailable for intercept operations against attacks in other corridors.

The question of why the Soviet Union chose to deploy the system in view of all these limitations is an interesting one. No fully satisfying answer can be given. Early Soviet enthusiasm was followed by later doubts. It was clearly a major decision and one that involved substantial costs. The Soviet Union was nevertheless undeterred either by the shortcomings or by the high costs. It chose to deploy and to maintain the system until recently, when it undertook a program of improvement.[42] The Moscow system did have some importance in coping with accidental launches or, perhaps, with very limited attacks from the United States. It had some utility against the Force de Frappe of France and the British deterrent force, providing a limited defense to the target that obviously counted most, Moscow. It would have been an effective system against the small portion of the Chinese missile force able to reach Moscow.

The Moscow ABM deployment decision is by and large compatible with the Soviet weapons acquisition approach. High premium is given to forces-in-being—that is, to forces in the field, even those with limited capabilities. Such forces are a base upon which improvements can be made, so as to provide in the long run a capability that could not have been obtained without making a modest start. It is compatible as well with the Soviet damage-limiting doctrinal mentality discussed above. Most important, it would limit damage to the area that is essential to the continuation of the Soviet political regime—Moscow, the heart of the motherland and an economic, military, industrial, and political center.

Construction of the Moscow system began in the early 1960s. It was clear by 1965 that the Soviet Union was deploying a BMD. The elements of the system once again could be related to some seen at Sary Shagan. Work on the system continued, accelerating during 1966 and 1967.

42. Department of Defense, *Soviet Military Power,* p. 28.

Originally, it appeared that the defenses were to involve eight complexes accounting for a total of 128 interceptor missiles. In 1967, however, only six of the eight were under active construction. Work continued, and initial operational capability (IOC) of the system was probably achieved in the late 1960s. In 1968, work on two of the six complexes stopped, leaving the system with a total of four complexes and 64 interceptor missiles. By 1970 or 1971, the system was probably fully operational.[43]

The termination of two of the six complexes planned can only have indicated a change in heart by the Soviet Union with regard to the efficacy of the Moscow system. At the same time there was a general shift in the treatment of BMD by the Soviet press, and the earlier glowing accounts of the BMD capabilities of the USSR were toned down. Debates about the costs and benefits and effectiveness of BMD systems also appeared to be under way.[44] The question of whether or not the Moscow system would be extended beyond Moscow undoubtedly had been debated, and a decision was made not to do so. This decision was probably the result of a growing recognition of the shortcomings of the Moscow system, particularly with the appearance of MIRVed ICBMs in the U.S. arsenal. The high cost of the radars and the installation must have had an effect as well. On the eve of the ABM Treaty it appeared that the Soviet Union was waiting for significant improvements in technology before proceeding further with BMD deployments.

In 1972 the Soviet Union and the United States signed the ABM Treaty constraining the deployment of BMD to 200 interceptors at two locations. In 1974 an agreement reduced this to 100 interceptors at one location in each country. The United States deployed the Safeguard BMD at Grand Forks, deactivating it as soon as it had become operational in 1975. There was never any serious doubt that the Soviet location would remain at Moscow.

The Soviet Union and the ABM Treaty

It is not the purpose of this chapter to unravel the intricacies of the first round of the strategic arms limitation talks (SALT I) that led to the

43. Freedman, *U.S. Intelligence,* pp. 88, 90.

44. There are indications of a running debate within the Soviet Union relating to the efficacy of ballistic missile defense. These seem to have existed as early as 1963–64 and as late as 1973–74. See Wolfe, *Soviet Strategy at the Crossroads,* p. 242; Thomas W. Wolfe, *Soviet Power and Europe: 1945–1970* (Johns Hopkins University Press, 1970), pp. 439–41; and Holloway, *The Soviet Union and the Arms Race,* p. 167.

conclusion of the ABM Treaty in 1972. That has been done elsewhere and in far better fashion than this author could possibly do.[45] But the treaty and Soviet adherence to it raise a number of interesting questions. The significance of BMD to the Soviet Union and to its underlying doctrine of damage limitation has been discussed at some length here. The question left, then, is, Why was the Soviet Union so anxious to reach agreement on an ABM Treaty with the United States? Certainly the Soviet Union started out on its ABM venture in the aftermath of World War II with great insouciance. It seemed a natural thing to do in the light of a long-standing Soviet proclivity toward the development of massive defenses. Little thought surely was given in those early days to the destabilizing effects of BMD, which later became a central part of the debate surrounding SALT I and the ABM Treaty.

The Soviet Union resisted U.S. enthusiasm for limiting arms control to defensive systems in 1967. Nevertheless, it did give a generally positive response conditioned on linking offensive and defensive controls in proposed arms limitation talks. It came as a real surprise to some when, at the first session of SALT I in Helsinki in November 1969, the Soviet representatives themselves spoke enthusiastically about a limitation of BMD systems. They even began to speak of the destabilizing effects of BMD in terms that had become popular in the United States. At Helsinki in 1969 they took the initiative to note the possibility of a total ban on deploying BMD systems.

Most Americans assumed that the Soviet Union would be unwilling to give up the Moscow defense, and this contributed to the decision to adopt a position giving the Soviet Union the opportunity to preserve the defense elements already in place. Thus in the next round of SALT I in 1970 the United States proposed limiting deployment to a single site for defense of the National Command Authority (NCA) in Washington or Moscow. The Soviet delegates quickly accepted the proposed NCA defense, permitting retention of the Moscow system. In all too typical fashion, the United States then had second thoughts about the whole matter, fearing that the lack of congressional enthusiasm for ABM deployment in populated areas would, in effect, prevent the United States from implementing that option itself. As a result, the Soviet Union would emerge from the negotiations with the Moscow defense and the United States with none at all. The United States then proposed a complete ABM ban as an alternative. When the Soviet Union reaffirmed

45. Newhouse, *Cold Dawn;* and Smith, *Doubletalk.*

its acceptance of the NCA-level ABM limits, the United States replied to the Soviet Union, in effect, "We've given you a choice but you made the wrong one—now pick again." The Soviet delegates continued to express a preference for NCA defense. Later, the United States introduced still other ABM deployment options, including a disparity of 4-1 (then 3-1, then 2-1) in favor of a U.S. defense deployment to protect its ballistic missiles. In the end, the treaty allowed for two deployments on each side, one to protect the National Command Authority and one to protect a limited portion of its ICBM forces. In 1974 that agreement was modified to allow each side only one site.

With the ABM Treaty, the Soviet Union accepted constraints that would limit its opportunities to carry its BMD program beyond the deployment at Moscow. What had begun several years before as Soviet objection to the suggestion of constraining defensive weapons system deployment alone in the interest of stability and an appropriate strategic balance had now become a vigorous Soviet effort to "snare the cherished ABM agreement."[46] Alternative explanations for the change have been offered. On the one hand, the Soviet Union may have been responding to the interests of expediency, limiting the capabilities of the United States to pursue its better BMD technology. On the other hand, the Soviet Union might, indeed, have been convinced by the strategic concept of mutual assured destruction and the destabilizing effects of widespread BMD deployment.[47]

There seems to this author to be little doubt that the Soviet Union was, in fact, behaving in an expedient manner.[48] The Safeguard and the Site Defense BMD programs, well under way in the United States in the early 1970s, embodied substantially more sophisticated and powerful technology than did the Moscow system. Moreover, there were clear indications on the part of the United States that, despite a lack of public acceptance, the defense community had plans for the fairly broad expansion of BMD deployments in the future. Possession of such a BMD capability by the United States would constitute a threat to important elements of Soviet doctrine. The deployment of defenses to protect U.S.

---

46. Newhouse, *Cold Dawn*, p. 214.

47. Thomas W. Wolfe, *The SALT Experience: Its Impact on U.S. and Soviet Strategic Policy and Decisionmaking*, R-1686-PR, prepared for the U.S. Air Force Project Rand (Santa Monica, Calif.: Rand Corp., 1975), pp. 116–21, for a discussion of these differing explanations of the causes for change in Soviet views toward BMD limitation.

48. For a different view, see chapter 8 herein.

ICBM sites would threaten the Soviet Union's capability to acquire the preemptive counterforce capability that was the key to their damage-limitation doctrine and the element of that doctrine that seemed most achievable in the near term.

Other factors were important in this decision as well. Undoubtedly, it was a difficult and pragmatic decision that the Soviet Union had to make. A political rationale for the decision could be found in a belief that the time was right to make gains through détente. From a military point of view, it was important to avert the threat to Soviet strategies that might emerge from giving U.S. ICBMs carrying MIRVs BMD protection against a preemptive strike. The ABM Treaty ensured penetration by the Soviet Union's own future MIRVs to meet damage limitation objectives. It might well have seen the other defenses—which it alone was establishing in depth, such as air defenses, civil defenses, and dispersal practices—as providing partial compensation for the limitation of BMD that resulted.

It seems clear that the Soviet Union had by this time a growing appreciation of the weaknesses of the BMD technology it had available and had concluded that the Moscow system was not really suitable for widespread deployment throughout the USSR. Assessments of Soviet BMD technology in this period showed that it lagged behind that of the United States by about ten years. In economic terms, the decision to accept the ABM Treaty avoided the very heavy expenses associated with widespread deployment of the Moscow system. The treaty was undoubtedly easier for the United States to accept, particularly in the aftermath of the bitter ABM debate of the late 1960s, which made it clear that widespread ABM deployment was going to find rough sledding.

SALT I served to focus one of the great debates relating to Soviet BMD activities. This debate involved the so-called SAM upgrade controversy turning on whether the Soviet Union could somehow enable its widely deployed SAM air defenses to serve a useful BMD role. The Soviet Union had at the time nearly 10,000 surface-to-air missiles deployed throughout the country, which unquestionably provided a formidable base could such a weapon really be "upgraded." This matter had a peculiar significance in terms of perception of the Soviet ABM threat in the eyes of the United States.[49]

The origins of the debate really lay with the inability of the intelligence community to establish conclusively the mission of the SA-5 system

49. Newhouse, *Cold Dawn*, pp. 11–12.

being deployed throughout the Soviet Union during this period. Known in the West as the Tallinn system because of its initial deployment near the capital of Estonia, it represented a substantially improved weapons system that appeared at the outset to be either a product of the "Leningrad approach" to achieving BMD through air defense technology, or to be an improved air defense system somewhat more capable than the SA-2, or to be some combination of the two.[50]

That the SA-5 was developed at Sary Shagan constituted something like prima facie evidence of a BMD role. The SA-5 missile appeared to have some relationship with the Griffon interceptor used by the Leningrad system. Moreover, a relationship between these two systems had been noted at Sary Shagan. Some U.S. analysts further argued that the location of the early deployment of the system, in the Baltic region, was in the corridor of attacking U.S. missiles.[51] On the other side of the question, the SA-5 system looked very much like an air defense system, not unlike the SA-2 and SA-3 systems in many respects. Moreover, an assessment of the capabilities of the system (as it was so imperfectly seen and understood) raised serious doubts that it had the capacity to do a significant BMD job. The debate between those who emphasized one or the other set of considerations raged for many years and is not yet entirely dead. There are many who still believe that some BMD capability is embodied in the SA-5 or could be achieved rather easily if the Soviet Union chose to do so. Most, however, recognize the SA-5 as a widely deployed surface-to-air missile system providing defense against aircraft at long ranges and up to very high altitudes.

One difficulty in making the air defense story for the SA-5 was that there simply was no requirement for an air defense with these capabilities at the time it was deployed. On the other hand, it could be shown that when the SA-5 was being conceived and developed, the United States was preparing to develop and had in its defense plan the B-70 bomber, a high-altitude bomber that was to replace the B-52. The long lead time to deployment that characterized Soviet systems and the inertia of the Soviet weapons acquisition process might explain the continuing commitment to the SA-5 after the B-70's demise.

In broader terms, the entire SA-5 debate served to focus attention on the possible use of air defense systems to provide BMD protection. Many in the United States were deeply concerned that, because of its

50. This debate is discussed in detail in Freedman, *U.S. Intelligence,* pp. 90–96, and Prados, *The Soviet Estimate,* pp. 164–71.

51. Prados, *The Soviet Estimate,* p. 160.

extensive SAM deployment, the Soviet Union would have actual ABM capability despite the ABM Treaty, while the United States had none. There was no broadly deployed SAM defense in the United States that could provide the basis for a comparable upgrade.

In the course of investigating the validity of these concerns, the SA-2 and even the SA-1 systems were examined in detail to establish what capabilities the Soviet Union had in dealing with U.S. ICBMs. For any SAM system there are some major problems in performing the BMD mission. Searching for and detecting reentry vehicles (which even by 1970 were able to achieve very low radar cross sections) at long enough range to effect intercept was a serious problem for a surface-to-air missile radar designed to operate against much larger aircraft. Acquiring the target was another problem, as the acquisition radars used with SAM systems also normally operate against targets with higher radar cross sections flying at much lower speeds. Circularly scanning radars, requiring several scans to detect the target in its approach to the defenses, were simply inadequate to detect strategic ballistic missiles that could come from almost any direction. Quite apart from the radar problems, the surface-to-air missiles that were used for air defense generally were not fast enough to deal with the high speeds of reentering missile warheads. In order to achieve a kill at all they almost certainly required a nuclear warhead, and it was not so clear in that period that nuclear warheads were available for all these SAM missiles. Finally, the intercept timelines and the limitations on missiles and radars resulted in a requirement for extremely rapid reaction times, which normally can only be accomplished through automated processing and decisionmaking. Soviet SAMs used a manual system with reaction times substantially longer than were suitable for coping with the ballistic missile threat.

The general view was that SAM systems were marginal at best. Even so, there were always reasons why they could function against specific U.S. reentry vehicle targets. It was characteristic of some U.S. ICBMs, for example, that the tank closely followed the reentry vehicle, so that the problem of acquiring very small reentry vehicles was obviated by the opportunity simply to track the very large tank. Like the accompanying tanks, the higher cross sections of reentry vehicles at particular stages of reentry—such as the windshield burnoff point for the Mark II reentry vehicle—might serve to ease the radar problem as well. Other comparable difficulties with the U.S. force turned out to have similar effects; and so the debate raged as each side developed new arguments to overcome the objections of the other. The peripheral Hen House radars, for example, conceivably could have reduced significantly the acquisition problem for widely deployed SAM systems by providing handover data that would have enabled them to avoid having to search for incoming RVs. The density of deployed Soviet air defense radars and SAM systems was such that the coordinated use of several radars within a cluster of SAM sites could provide another mechanism for acquiring targets.

The underlying concern in all of this discussion of the SAM upgrade problem was that the improvements at issue could be made to particular SAM sites without being detected. One could not, for example, provide assurance to those who were worrying about this problem that the SA-2 had not been specially configured in some locations to provide the engagement radar with greater power, automated target-handling equipment, and so on. In these circumstances there simply was no way to rule out the possibility that the widely deployed Soviet SAMs could not offer some degree of protection against a ballistic missile attack. Most who worked on the problem thought the likelihood of this was low, and indeed the systems could have provided very marginal protection at best. But their numbers were large enough to have made a significant contribution, particularly in view of the Soviet doctrinal commitment to damage limitation.

Concerns about SAM upgrade had a substantial effect on the ABM Treaty negotiations. A number of provisions were sought that would protect the United States against the possibility. The most important of these provisions established a basis for the identification of ABM radars and limited them both in terms of numbers and allowable radiated power. They also limited the radiated power of most non-ABM phased-array radars that might be widely deployed. The objective of these provisions was to prevent the widespread deployment of a radar base that might be used in conjunction with other missile systems. A provision of the treaty specifically prohibited the testing of air defense weapons systems in an ABM mode, though no precise definition of "testing in an ABM mode" could be agreed upon. Most important, each party undertook "not to give missiles, launchers, or radars, other than ABM interceptor missiles, ABM launchers, or ABM radars, capabilities to counter strategic ballistic missiles or their elements in flight trajectory, and not to test them in an ABM mode."[52]

52. Article VI of the ABM Treaty, in U.S. Arms Control and Disarmament Agency, *Arms Control and Disarmament Agreements: Texts and Histories of Negotiations*, USACDA Pub. No. 105 (GPO, 1980), p. 141.

A significant loophole was left in the protections against SAM upgrade: antitactical ballistic missile (ATBM)—as opposed to strategic ballistic missile—defenses. Because the United States was in the process of developing the SAM-D air defense for deployment with ground forces in Europe, and it was hoped that SAM-D could be given the capability of intercepting short-range Soviet ballistic missiles deployed with their tactical forces, no specific constraints against this class of BMD system were included in the treaty provisions. More must be said about the whole problem of SAM upgrade below, but the SAM-D safety net that was employed during the negotiations of the ABM Treaty may prove to be one of our more worrisome problems in the future.

The Soviet negotiators were tough in SALT I and in the ABM Treaty discussions. The negotiations were adversarial, and it was understood by both sides that they were acting in pursuit of their own national interests. Thus, it is not surprising that the Soviet Union has employed a strict and literal interpretation of the treaty in developing a pattern of compliance with its provisions. The Soviet delegates were not forthcoming with the technical details of their systems or their plans about future ones. The United States had little reason to expect anything else. In the aftermath of the treaty, however, it is notable that the Soviet Union and the United States have had substantially different attitudes with regard to compliance with the treaty. As noted above, the Soviet Union has approached the problem of compliance in a narrow, legalistic way in which the letter of the treaty has been interpreted to Soviet advantage. The Soviet Union has operated in such a way as to be constrained only by positively expressed prohibitions included in the basic language of the treaty. It has felt little compunction in pursuing BMD-related activities not specifically excluded by explicit and unambiguous treaty provisions. For its part, the United States has tended to be affected far more by the spirit of the treaty. The sense of urgency in investigating the technology of ballistic missile defense, in gaining experience in the operation of BMD systems, and in preparing for the possibility that the treaty may at some point become untenable, has given way to the cautious avoidance of setting in motion BMD activities that might threaten the treaty in years ahead.

In the Soviet case, there have been no indications that the political leadership has restrained the military in the pursuit of its defensive weapons developments well short of the bounds of treaty compliance as has occurred in the United States. There was little doubt at the time the treaty was signed that the Soviet Union would not forgo the research and development program that it had maintained for so long. During the Supreme Soviet session that ratified the treaty, Minister of Defense Andrei A. Grechko noted that the treaty "does not place any limitations on carrying out research and experimental work directed towards solving the problems of defense of the country against nuclear missile attack."[53] The Soviet Union continues to work in that direction. The disparity between the approaches of the two countries in dealing with the problems and opportunities of ballistic missile defense in the aftermath of the treaty has now become a significant factor in perceptions of the strategic balance.

Soviet BMD in the Aftermath of the Treaty

In the years since the signing of the ABM Treaty, the Soviet Union has substantially improved both its offensive and defensive strategic forces. During this period, Soviet overall strategic goals have remained very much the same. The Soviet Union has worked hard and with great success at improving its quick-reaction counterforce capabilities by deploying the fourth generation of ICBMs, arming them with MIRVed warheads, and providing some with significantly improved accuracy.[54] As a result of this accomplishment, the Soviet Union appears to have put the entire U.S. ICBM force at risk. At the same time it has preserved the survivability of its own offensive forces through silo hardening and through the development, and recently the testing, of mobile ICBMs[55] that could become available as soon as the MX ICBM with its improved counterforce capabilities enters the U.S. force. Through an aggressive program of steadily expanding the use of passive defenses, population and industrial dispersion, and hardening, the Soviet Union has enhanced the endurance of strategic command and control elements and reserve military forces. Bunkers have been built in many locations for the political and military leadership as part of the civil defense program.[56]

53. *Pravda*, September 30, 1972.
54. Department of Defense, *Soviet Military Power*, pp. 18–20.
55. Ibid., p. 21.
56. 1983 U.S. Air Force Posture Statement, quoted in *Soviet Aerospace*, vol. 37 (February 28, 1983), p. 55; Central Intelligence Agency, *Soviet Civil Defense*, N178-10003 (CIA, 1978), p. 1; and Davis, *The Soviet Union and BMD*, pp. 6–7.

Increased emphasis on civil defense has strengthened the capabilities for postattack reconstitution by protecting vital industrial cadres and segments of the population. The goal of damage limitation runs through all these activities.

Nor has the Soviet Union ignored active defenses. In its relentless way, the Soviet Union has continued to improve its air defenses and to introduce new systems. The SA-10 is now being widely deployed throughout the country to provide strategic air defense against low-altitude bombers and cruise missiles. This process of continual air defense improvements and augmentation includes interceptor aircraft as well. In the past ten years many new aircraft have been introduced with increasingly sophisticated technology, including more recently a look-down, shoot-down capability. The massive radar infrastructure supporting air defenses has been maintained and enlarged; new and improved radars have been fielded.[57]

A Soviet nonnuclear, orbital antisatellite system has been repeatedly refined and tested attacking low-altitude satellite targets under various circumstances. It is now presumably in an operational status.[58]

It is not so surprising, then, that the Soviet Union has continued to seek improved antiballistic missile defenses. It appears to have been little deterred by concerns that the BMDs it develops could not be widely deployed, as seemed to be the case in the United States. The treaty provisions do indeed allow such an effort to be made by the Soviet Union. The wonder is that the effort has been undertaken with such apparent purposefulness and direction in the presence of a treaty that precludes the ultimate payoff. But in so dynamic an arena as strategic force development, an agreement reached about appropriate behavior at one time cannot be expected to remain acceptable in changing circumstances for so long into the future as to obviate the need to press ahead with R&D. This dichotomy of views about compliance with the ABM Treaty reflects a more basic difference of opinion between the Soviet Union and the United States about the meaning of such agreements. Hugh Seton-Watson has urged that Western democrats understand that while they are apt to look upon treaties as the solution of a dispute achieved through bargaining and ultimate compromise, the Soviet Union, rejecting compromise, sees them as but a halt or momen-

---

57. Department of Defense, *Soviet Military Power*, pp. 28–30.
58. Ibid., pp. 67–68, and Department of Defense, *Soviet Military Power* (GPO, 1982), p. 68.

tary retreat "in an unending, unrelenting march."[59] Soviet BMD activities are compatible with this observation.

Much has been made in the literature about alleged Soviet violations of the ABM Treaty. Certainly there are many who genuinely believe that these violations occurred with deliberate intent. Most seem to believe, however, that the activities objectionable to the United States were slips that occurred in the workings of a huge mechanism not everywhere attuned to the esoteric demands of the ABM Treaty.

The level of activities at Sary Shagan continued much the same as before the treaty was signed. The Moscow system has been filled out to become an operational system of sixty-four interceptors with four defensive complexes, each containing two sets of engagement radars and eight missiles. The apparent shortcomings of the Moscow system suggested to many that it would soon be improved and the vulnerable, mechanically scanned radars replaced. The Soviet Union made no moves in the 1970s to do so, however, despite a decision to maintain the current system. Neither did it make any effort to increase the number of interceptors associated with the system up to the limit of 100 allowed by treaty provisions. Work on the peripheral network of early warning and acquisition radars continued. Slowly but surely the Soviet Union continued to fill existing gaps in the coverage it provided. In general, this activity had a flavor of steady, unfrenzied progress toward defined development goals.

Some new BMD equipment began to emerge by the end of the 1970s. It included a new transportable, phased-array radar that seemed to be a product of the air defense technology approach rather than of the approach employed in the design of the Moscow system. In this case, however, there was no doubt at all that the radar had a BMD role. New BMD interceptors were also tested. They included a long-range missile that appeared to represent something of an improvement over the Galosh and, more important, a high-acceleration missile very much like the U.S. Sprint.[60] With this missile, the Soviet Union was for the first time in a position to employ atmospheric sorting to discriminate real reentry vehicles from penetration aids. Without such an interceptor, it had previously been forced to make the launch commitment while the

59. Hugh Seton-Watson, "The Long View from Red Square," *Washington Post,* April 3, 1983.
60. Davis, *The Soviet Union and BMD,* p. 13.

attacking reentry vehicle was still outside or in the very upper reaches of the atmosphere.

The combination of the new radar and one or the other (or both) of the missiles would seem to constitute a BMD system (now designated the ABM-X-3 system) suitable for fairly rapid deployment because of the transportable nature of its components.[61] To those who perceive the Soviet BMD program as a vigorous undertaking only searching for the right technology and the right strategic opportunity to abandon the treaty, this development appeared provocative indeed. To those less persuaded about the capabilities of the new system, it appeared that the Soviet Union still had a long way to go before it would really be ready to make a choice for further deployment. But from either point of view, the Soviet Union had made a significant step forward: it now had a system that appeared to have characteristics appropriate for widespread deployment. In addition, some of the basic shortcomings of the Moscow system had been addressed. The use of a phased-array as the engagement radar relieved the single-target constraint of the Moscow tracking radars. A high-acceleration interceptor allowed launch commitment to be delayed until atmospheric sorting of penetration aids could occur. Little can be said, however, about how the data-processing capacity incorporated in the system affects the degree to which both of these improvements can be exploited.

It is unlikely that a truly transportable radar can do an adequate job of long-range search and acquisition against the very low radar cross sections that characterize newer U.S. ICBM reentry vehicles. Presumably, wide deployment of the system would require the addition of search and acquisition radars like the Dog House or Cat House radars in the Moscow area. Failing that, the job of handing over incoming targets to individual ABM-X-3 sites might be performed by the peripheral radars. The old Hen House radars can certainly provide the necessary alerting information required and may be able to provide pointing data to guide the search of the ABM-X-3 radar, but it is doubtful that the Hen House can predict reentry vehicle trajectories with enough precision to make a direct handover of incoming targets to the ABM-X-3's transportable engagement radars.

But the peripheral network has been improved through the addition of new, large phased-array radars to augment the old Hen Houses, which

61. Department of Defense, *Soviet Military Power,* p. 28.

might result in substantially improved tracking.[62] These radars might strengthen the ability of the peripheral radars to provide target acquisition support to a large number of defenses that could be deployed behind them. The major shortcoming of such an arrangement would remain, however: these large VHF radars are vulnerable to blackout and to destruction. To ensure their neutralization would nevertheless require a tailored attack that might be difficult to mount with U.S. ICBMs after a Soviet counterforce strike.

This recitation of theoretically derived implications of the ABM-X-3 is simply that—theoretical. Whether the Soviet Union has in mind using the ABM-X-3 in the form of deployment described is not known. Nor is it known whether the system really has the capabilities to perform all the functions ascribed to it here, though it certainly can be expected to have some significant BMD capabilities if suitable acquisition information can be made available. The likelihood of Soviet deployment of the ABM-X-3 in the presence of the ABM Treaty is discussed below. As yet it apparently remains in the development test stage.

In addition to developing the ABM-X-3 system in "rapidly deployable" form, the Soviet Union has begun the upgrading of the deployed Moscow system.[63] As noted above, this step appears to be overdue. The removal of half of the sixty-four Galosh launchers at the Moscow BMD sites in 1980 marked the beginning of the upgrade program. It can only be assumed that the remaining thirty-two Galosh missiles and their associated dish radars will remain a part of the modified system.

The main feature of this improvement effort—the Pushkino radar—has been portrayed in remarkably dramatic pictorial form in the U.S. Defense Department's most recent popularized publication on the Soviet threat, in which it appears as a strong competitor for the Eighth Wonder of the World.[64] It is a very large, pyramidal radar structure some 500 ft. on a side and 120 ft. high, looking very much like the Missile Site Radar (MSR) developed for the U.S. Safeguard system. Each of the four faces of the huge structure contains a circular phase array about 60 ft. in diameter. Presumably the Pushkino radar will perform the engagement radar function for a major part of the Moscow system.

It must be assumed that with these modifications to the Moscow defense, the Soviet Union will bring the interceptor component up to

62. Ibid., p. 68.
63. Ibid., p. 28.
64. Ibid., p. 5.

the 100 allowed by the ABM Treaty. The type of missiles to be added is a matter of conjecture. The deployment of the high-acceleration missile associated with the ABM-X-3 would seem to be a good choice. It would provide the Moscow system with an endoatmospheric capability that could function as a second defensive layer below the long-range, exoatmospheric Galosh. Whatever missiles are deployed, it is clear that the three large radars now emplaced within the Moscow defenses—Dog House, Cat House, and Pushkino—will themselves have to be defended by the system, since without them the system would be crippled.

Although these improvements to the Moscow system will significantly enhance its limited capability, these defenses cannot seriously hinder a U.S. attack on Moscow, given the very large weapons inventories that currently exist. The susceptibility of the large radars to leakage attack, and saturation of the system with large numbers of attacking RVs, remain key areas of vulnerability. Against more limited attacks, however, the military value of the Moscow system could be significantly improved. Moreover, the upgrading of the Moscow system represents a significant step in strengthening the base of defenses in the Moscow region; these might be augmented in the future. Substantial expansion of the Moscow defenses beyond treaty limits could occur rapidly. If such an expansion could allow a preferential defense of certain critical components such as hardened command bunkers, a militarily significant capability could be achieved.

In a less conventional vein, continuing Soviet work on strategic defenses appears to have included research, development, and possibly the testing of directed-energy weapons, almost certainly with an eye toward their possible future utility for BMD purposes. Reportedly, both high-energy lasers and particle beams have been investigated.[65] The uncertainties in this area are great. They are not just uncertainties about what the Soviet Union is doing, but also about the likelihood of finding real BMD utility in these technologies, about which concepts are likely to have the greatest payoff, and even about how best to go about resolving these uncertainties.

Finally, in bringing Soviet BMD activities up to date, another word must be said on the subject of SAM upgrade. In some respects, developments in this area constitute the most disturbing change in the balance

65. Ibid., p. 75.

of U.S. and Soviet strategic defenses. Continuing Soviet effort at improving air defenses has been emphasized earlier. An aggressive U.S. program to improve strategic aerodynamic attack capabilities has been responsible for the vigor with which the Soviet Union has sought increasingly capable air defenses. A series of U.S. weapons systems, progressing from Hound Dog through the short-range attack missile (SRAM), and now low-observable aerodynamic attack vehicles, has put increasing pressure on Soviet air defense technology.

SAM upgrade was worrisome at the time of SALT I; that worry has grown and become more credible with the improvement of Soviet SAMs. U.S. improvements to its aerodynamic weapons have stressed the reduction of radar cross sections and the use of flight profiles that generate difficult intercept conditions, especially reduced reaction times available to the defenses. As Soviet designers have responded to these improvements, they have built into new SAM systems the attributes required to counter them. These SAM improvements are in substantial measure—though not entirely—applicable to the BMD intercept problem. This means that the likelihood of newer Soviet SAMs having some embodied BMD capability is higher than it was for earlier systems, and that the route to providing greater capabilities through improvements is shorter. The density and extent of Soviet SAM deployment remain high, and the improvements to the peripheral radar network have increased its capability to provide acquisition support. All of these points suggest that the problem of SAM upgrade is substantially more credible than it was ten years ago. The Soviet Union could have, with its new SAMs, a BMD capability able to enhance damage limitation that is not controlled by the ABM Treaty, whereas the United States, with no strategic SAMs, has none.

Reports that the Soviet Union is now developing an ATBM system give cause for even greater concern.[66] Such systems, designed to handle short-range ballistic missiles, must include in their design many of the features apt to be missing and requiring upgrade in SAM systems. Very short reaction times and automated launch commitment processes, for example, must be included in ATBM systems. Soviet development of such systems constitutes a qualitative change in the nature of SAM upgrade concerns, for although these weapons systems are not specifi-

66. "Report of the President's Commission on Strategic Forces," April 1983, p. 5.

cally constrained by the ABM Treaty, they will almost surely possess some significant capability against long-range strategic ballistic missiles (see chapter 3). This is particularly true in the case of submarine-launched ballistic missiles (SLBMs), the RVs of which generally have larger radar cross sections and reenter at lower speeds than ICBMs. Defense against SLBMs is, of course, particularly important to the Soviet Union since those at sea are not subject to counterforce attack.

The widespread deployment of ATBMs to Soviet tactical forces in the future could only produce a serious concern about their possible employment by the PVO in a strategic role. Soviet tactical defensive forces are normally mobile, so it can be assumed that ATBM systems will be mobile as well. If so, their rapid deployment in large numbers (possibly from covert storage) would constitute another means whereby the Soviet Union could extend its defensive forces, very possibly within the provisions of the ABM Treaty. Although the treaty does prohibit giving non-ABM systems the capability to intercept strategic ballistic missiles, it would be extremely difficult to make an airtight case that it had occurred if the Soviet Union denied the allegation.

Whither Soviet BMD?

The previous section outlined a number of opportunities apparently available to the Soviet Union for improving its strategic position relative to that of the United States. These opportunities derive from the significant disparity in the momentum of strategic defensive activities in the two countries. None of these opportunities can be exploited by the Soviet Union, however, without cost or without concern about the reaction it may generate. While there might be some military appeal to taking one or another of these BMD initiatives, that appeal is not likely to carry the day by itself. A key factor in assessing the likelihood of a major Soviet BMD initiative is its impact on the ABM Treaty. Most of the initiatives discussed here would require the Soviet Union to take the major step of abandoning the treaty—or at least of threatening to do so in the case of SAM upgrade or the strategic use of ATBMs—and of beginning the long and costly course of widespread BMD deployment and competition with the United States.

Consideration of all the factors apt to influence a Soviet decision to abandon the ABM Treaty reveals few powerful incentives for them to do it in the near term.[67] While the Soviet BMD program has momentum and has made significant technological progress over the past decade, it really has only now achieved the level of technology that was available to the United States ten years ago. The major difference now is that Soviet technology is much closer to application. The Soviet Union continues to fear the consequences of turning U.S. technology loose and probably still finds the ABM Treaty desirable as a means of constraining the application of U.S. prowess to BMD. It is noteworthy that areas in which the United States has more or less clear superiority (for example, microelectronics in general, large-scale integrated circuits, phased-array radars, compact and high-speed data processors, and the like) are particularly important to the development of advanced BMD systems.

Expressions of U.S. concern about the vulnerability of its ICBM forces have surely led the Soviet Union to expect that any near-term deployment of BMD in the United States would be for ICBM defense. As in SALT I, the Soviet Union would view this as an undesirable threat to its preemptive counterforce capabilities.

From a political perspective, abandoning the ABM Treaty in the near term would seem to threaten a vigorous Soviet propaganda effort to weaken Western European commitment to a revitalized NATO armed with intermediate-range nuclear forces. Nonetheless, the Soviet belief that there are gains to be made through the reestablishment of détente is likely to be weakening as U.S. and Soviet rhetoric becomes increasingly harsh. The heavy costs of extensive BMD deployment could pose a problem for the Soviet Union at a time when its economy is under much tougher strains than it was ten years ago. Finally, the Soviet Union enjoys some advantages in the current situation. The treaty regime has left it running virtually alone in the pursuit of effective BMD systems, as the United States has allowed its own efforts to diminish and be buffeted by changes in direction during the search for an acceptable basing scheme for the MX missile. Certainly this is a better arrangement than having to compete. Moreover, the Soviet Union enjoys an unparalleled opportunity both to preserve the ABM Treaty and to establish a damage-limiting force through SAM or ATBM deployment.

However unlikely, some military imperatives for BMD could conceivably carry the day. One possibility is that the Soviet Union might

67. A debt is again owed to Howard Stoertz for his work on possible Soviet BMD initiatives.

conclude that the situation is ripe—because of the vulnerability of U.S. ICBMs, the hiatus before new U.S. forces come on line, and a significant Soviet advantage in lead time to BMD deployment—to effect a dramatic shift in the strategic balance that would produce great political leverage. That initiative might consist of a nationwide deployment of several thousand interceptors. Although such a move might trigger a U.S. response, it could not be a rapid one. The Soviet Union might also feel the need to deploy defenses if it sees Pershing II, MX, and the Trident D-5 threatening its offensive forces in ways that it finds unacceptable. A more likely possibility is that, while the Soviet Union may consider its current BMD systems not yet effective enough to warrant a major deployment, further efforts to improve them might result at some point in strategic advantages that outweigh those of the treaty regime.

While all of these represent nontrivial possibilities, none appears to be likely in the near term. The advantages enjoyed under the ABM Treaty, Soviet concerns about energizing the application of U.S. technology to the BMD problem, the economic and political advantages of avoiding such an effort now, and fear of an all-out arms race with the United States all argue to this effect.

An entirely different possibility is that a U.S. initiative might trigger a Soviet deployment response. President Ronald Reagan's BMD announcement urging the search for an answer to the threat of ballistic missiles might be interpreted by the Soviet Union as the inception of a major BMD program that will ultimately lead to U.S. withdrawal from the treaty. Even with this perception, however, no near-term Soviet response is likely. In fact, it is not at all clear that defining so long-range a goal in the United States has not had the effect of driving a final stake through the heart of the U.S. Army's small BMD system development program, as it becomes subordinated to the search for the grand solution. In any event, major effects of such a U.S. program are not likely to be felt for many years. Since the Soviet Union apparently is pursuing such solutions in their own right, it is not apt to have illusions about the ease with which such a goal can be reached.

U.S. deployment of a treaty-limited defense for the protection of a clustered ICBM deployment, such as the closely spaced basing or Densepack scheme, would not be likely to evoke a Soviet position that would weaken the ABM Treaty. Rather, the Soviet Union will be difficult in demanding strict and literal treaty compliance when faced with such issues as moving the single allowed U.S. BMD site from Grand Forks to another location.

It is less clear how the Soviet Union would react to a U.S. proposal for treaty modification. The Soviet Union has indicated that it sees no need for modification, though undoubtedly there are modifications in which it would have an interest. A modest increase in the number of allowed interceptors might strike a receptive chord, for example, as it would provide an opportunity for thickening the Moscow defenses. If the proposal allowed the United States to deploy a fairly effective defense of its ICBM force, on the other hand, the Soviet Union would face a difficult choice. It is likely to conclude that preserving the current treaty regime and a predictable future is the preferable option.

In the event of deployment beyond treaty limits, it is clear that Soviet and U.S. priorities in the choice of targets to be protected will differ. In general, the Soviet Union will want to defend clusters of high-value leadership, communications, military, and economic targets, striving to limit damage and preserve those elements important to warfighting and reconstitution. Soviet programs for wartime dispersal, hardening of facilities, and civil defense contribute importantly to the achievement of those goals. The Soviet Union appears to have little interest in ICBM defense. The United States, on the other hand, currently puts highest priority on defending strategic retaliatory forces, principally ICBMs but also other critical military targets such as command-and-control centers, Strategic Air Command reconstitution bases, and so on. Because the United States has thus far not viewed damage limiting as an adequate objective and lacks the complementary passive and air defenses to support it, defense of cities and their incorporated soft targets can be achieved only through the development of multiple-layered, very low leakage systems like that called for by President Reagan.

Given the opportunity to improve its defenses, the Soviet Union is likely to put highest priority on augmenting the Moscow system. Next, it is likely to seek a regional defense of military and industrial concentrations in the western USSR. Such a choice is consistent with the long-standing focus of air defenses. Defenses in this region would greatly complicate targeting of the region by the United States and other countries, would preserve essential facilities in the area most critical to warfighting, and would add to overall damage limitation. The next step would be to extend this approach throughout the nation (see chapter 4).

Defense of ICBMs is a possible but not very likely choice. Such defenses have not been a focus of Soviet BMD R&D. Moreover, other options are available to provide protection for these weapons: hardening, mobility, preemption, and launch on warning (or under attack). Some

ICBM protection is provided by the long-range Galosh interceptors of the Moscow system, but that is at best a very thin defense. With the exception of the SS-18s, which are deployed in Central Asia, Soviet ICBMs would probably enjoy some protection in any nationwide deployment, because they are generally near the type of industrial concentrations that would be defended.

The defense mission most apt to be chosen by the Soviet Union is a difficult one to implement—more difficult than the defense of clustered hard targets like ICBMs—and will require large numbers of interceptors and radars. Leakage will remain a problem, particularly if penetration aids are employed. But since damage limitation is the goal, and complementary passive and air defenses can augment the effects of BMD, Soviet doctrinal preferences attach significance even to a technically limited defense.

This portrayal of Soviet BMD activities and predilections emphasizes their disturbing characteristics. The purpose is not to assert that such forbidding futures are certain to ensue, but to make clear the provocative interpretations that can be given to Soviet BMD efforts uncertainly perceived and understood. It is one thing to take comfort in the greater likelihood of less upsetting outcomes when one is an observer, but quite another to bear responsibility for ensuring that the less likely possibilities do not result in strategic disadvantage. Those in the latter category are designing the BMD programs of both the United States and the Soviet Union. A Soviet paper on the U.S. BMD program would surely find worrisome activities under way. Ballistic missile defense is intrinsically unsettling to the strategic balance, but it is much more unsettling in the context of our current uncertainties.

CHAPTER SIX

The ABM Treaty Today

GEORGE SCHNEITER

THE TREATY signed in 1972 by the United States and the USSR on the limitation of antiballistic missile systems has had and will continue to have a major effect on the debate regarding ABM systems. Coming into effect after a highly publicized and emotional debate within the United States regarding deployment of an ABM system, the ABM Treaty is considered by many the crowning achievement of the U.S.-Soviet arms control process. Others view the treaty as part of a successful Soviet strategy to impede U.S. programs while letting Soviet developments proceed apace.

This chapter explains the terms of the ABM Treaty and its 1974 protocol, discusses the results of the two five-year reviews that have taken place, analyzes certain issues with respect to the interpretation of the treaty, and discusses possible options for changing the treaty.

Provisions of the ABM Treaty

The ABM Treaty was signed by the United States and the USSR in May 1972, after some two and a half years of negotiation. The two countries also signed the Interim Agreement on strategic offensive arms at the same time. The negotiation of these limitations on defensive and offensive arms was closely linked.

In 1974 the United States and the USSR further agreed to reduce the number of ABM deployment areas permitted each side from two to one when they signed the ABM Treaty Protocol. The ABM Treaty entered into force on October 3, 1972; its Protocol entered into force on May 24, 1976. The text of the ABM Treaty and its Protocol appear in the appendix along with related interpretative statements and understandings derived from the negotiations.[1]

The Overall Nature of the Treaty

The climate in which the ABM Treaty and its Protocol were negotiated—a climate in the United States of deep suspicion that such strategic defenses were destabilizing—is reflected in the nature of the limitations. In short, the ABM Treaty first "takes everything away," that is, prohibits *any* ABM systems or components, and then "gives back" a limited number of specific systems and components, subjecting them to qualitative constraints.

The thrust of the treaty is to ensure that neither the United States nor the USSR can field, or proceed very far toward fielding, a "defense of its territory," that is, a capability to defend effectively a major part of its territory against a significant attack mounted by the other side's ballistic missile forces. The approach to achieving this is to ban outright such a widespread defense, and to limit severely the deployment of ABM systems that defend an individual region of the country. Article III of the treaty begins, "Each Party undertakes not to deploy ABM systems or their components" and then goes on to "give back" certain systems and components by adding exceptions, which are described below. But first it should be noted that what is forbidden to be deployed—ABM systems and their components—is defined for the purpose of the treaty in a very general way: "an ABM system is a system to counter strategic ballistic missiles or their elements in flight trajectory." Article II goes on to provide a description of the components of which ABM systems consisted in 1972—ABM interceptor missiles, ABM launchers, and ABM radars—terms that are used later in the treaty to describe what is permitted to be deployed, or even developed.

To repeat this important point: the treaty consists of a general ban, and some limited, specific exceptions to that ban. And there are stringent constraints with regard to those exceptions.

---

1. U.S. Arms Control and Disarmament Agency, *Arms Control and Disarmament Agreements: Texts and Histories of Negotiations,* 1982 ed. (Government Printing Office, 1982), pp. 137–63. Unless the context makes clear that such is not the case, the term ABM Treaty is used here to mean both the treaty and its Protocol.

What the Treaty Permits

The treaty permits the deployment of a specific type of ABM system, one consisting of ABM interceptor missiles, ABM launchers, and ABM radars. It distinguishes these components from non-ABM interceptor missiles, launchers, and radars by stating that ABM components are either constructed and deployed for an ABM role or are of a type tested in an ABM mode. It is clear that an ABM role would relate to the countering of strategic ballistic missiles or their elements in flight trajectory. And the context of the companion Interim Agreement makes it clear that strategic ballistic missiles comprise intercontinental and submarine-launched missiles (ICBMs and SLBMs). It is less clear what constitutes testing in an ABM mode. Although such definitional issues may appear tedious, they are of paramount importance, and in fact many of the concerns regarding the ABM Treaty derive from such issues, as will be seen.

Under the treaty and its Protocol each side has a choice between two locations for its permitted ABM system deployment, and the numbers and types of components it is permitted to have depend on which choice it makes. Each side can have either a deployment area centered on its national capital (Washington or Moscow) or a deployment area distant from its national capital and containing ICBM silo launchers.[2] Not surprisingly, the choices made by the sides reflected their 1972 emphases: the Soviet Union had deployed an ABM system around Moscow, and the U.S. ABM program was directed toward protecting the U.S. Minuteman ICBM force.

NATIONAL CAPITAL AREA. If a side chooses a national capital deployment area, the following restrictions (see figure 6-1) apply:

—It may have no more than 100 ABM launchers and no more than 100 interceptors at launch sites.

—It may have ABM radars within no more than six ABM radar complexes, each complex having a diameter of no more than 3 km. (Additionally, the Soviet Union was permitted to retain those non-phased-array ABM radars operational within its national capital deployment area on the date of signature of the treaty.)

—These components must be located within 150 km of the side's national capital.

2. Before the signing of the Protocol, each side was permitted deployments at both locations. The Protocol restricted each side to one location.

Figure 6-1. *ABM System Deployment Permitted for a National Capital Area*

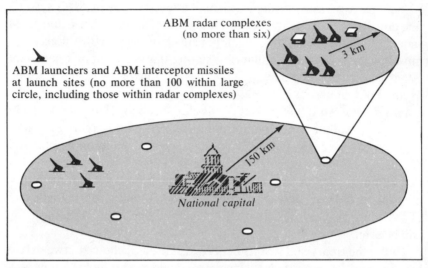

ICBM SILO LAUNCHER AREA. If a side chooses an ICBM silo launcher deployment area, the following restrictions (see figure 6-2) apply:

—It may have no more than 100 ABM launchers and no more than 100 ABM interceptor missiles at launch sites.

—It may have two large phased-array ABM radars having power-aperture products comparable to those of the U.S. Perimeter Acquisition Radar and Missile Site Radar.

—It may have no more than eighteen ABM radars, each having a power-aperture product less than that of the U.S. Missile Site Radar. (The sides agreed this limit was 3,000,000 wm².)

—These components must be deployed within an area having a radius of 150 km and containing ICBM silo launchers.

—The center of the deployment area must be no less than 1300 km from the side's national capital.

MODERNIZATION AND REPLACEMENT. The treaty is generally negative toward deployments of ABM systems and components. This negativism, however, does not carry over to the maintenance and updating of a side's permitted ABM forces. On the contrary, the basic statement in this regard is permissive. The treaty provides that, subject to its other provisions, "modernization and replacement" of ABM systems and their components may be carried out. Thus, research, development,

Figure 6-2. *ABM System Deployment Permitted for an Intercontinental Ballistic Missile Launcher Area*

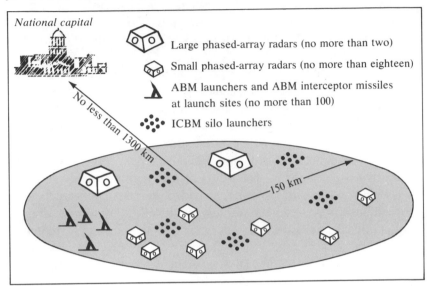

testing, and production may in general continue. And, consistent with this thrust, the deployment limits discussed above do not apply to ABM systems or components used for development or testing and located at test ranges. However, each side is limited to a total of no more than fifteen ABM launchers at "current or additionally agreed test ranges."

What the Treaty Bans

There are three classes of prohibited activities:
—Prohibitions of certain activities associated with the *permitted* ABM systems and components.
—Prohibitions of certain activities relating to *other kinds* of ABM systems or components or to non-ABM systems or components.
—Prohibitions of *transfers* of ABM hardware or know-how to other countries.

MOBILE SYSTEMS AND COMPONENTS. Development, testing, and limited deployment of certain ABM systems and components are permitted. However, the treaty provides that such systems and components must *not* be sea based, air based, space based, or mobile land based. This restriction bans, for example, any of the following.

—A mobile land-based launcher or radar, such as has been considered by the United States as part of a LoADS (low-altitude defense) or Sentry MX defense applied to various MX-basing schemes. This would be the case regardless of whether the mobility resulted from, say, a component being mounted on a wheeled vehicle or from a component being relocated from time to time.[3]

—A space-based ABM system or component, such as the space-based interceptor vehicles proposed for the High Frontier ABM system.

This restriction would not ban, for example:

—A rocket-launched infrared probe, such as is being considered by the United States in its Overlay advanced exoatmospheric concept, provided the probe's launcher is a fixed, land-based launcher.[4] (Note that it is the *basing* that is determining. The treaty clearly permits interceptor missiles, which fly when they operate, provided their launchers are fixed.)

—A component that can be "rapidly deployed," say, in a matter of months (unless it is also capable of being relocated in, say, a matter of days).[5]

A U.S. Arms Control and Disarmament Agency publication states

3. During the negotiations the United States stated, and the Soviet Union apparently agreed, that a prohibition on the deployment of mobile ABM systems and components would not rule out the deployment of ABM launchers and radars that were not *permanent fixed types* (Common Understanding C). Three other terms often used in the context of the ban on mobile systems and components are "transportable," "relocatable," and "rapidly deployable." *Transportable* generally means able to be carried from one location to another. For example, mobile missiles are often deployed on a vehicle called a transporter/erector/launcher. In this case, transportable is mobile in the treaty sense. However, one might build a fixed ABM component from elements transported to the site, rather than fabricated on site. Although such a component conceivably could be moved to another site in the same manner, this component would not necessarily be considered mobile in the treaty sense. Components might be considered *relocatable* in the same two ways. In general, the time scale should be the determining factor regarding whether transportability or relocatability qualify as mobility in the treaty sense. If the time scale is small enough to be tactically significant, the component should be considered mobile. If not, it should be considered fixed.

Rapid deployability is a different concept, although certainly a system composed of transportable or relocatable components is also a prime candidate for being rapidly deployable, perhaps in large numbers. Of course, some "truly" fixed components can be deployed rapidly, too. The ABM Treaty contains no prohibition on rapidly deployable systems or components, although the expressed concern regarding providing a base for a nationwide ABM defense implies some contradiction between rapid deployability and the objectives of the treaty.

4. Other aspects of the treaty might ban deployment of such a probe, however, as is discussed under "New Physical Principles," below.

5. Rapid deployability is defined further in note 3.

that the reason for these limitations is "to decrease the pressures of technological change and its unsettling impact on the strategic balance."[6] Of course, technological change can also have a "settling" impact on the balance, but apparently in 1972 the known current situation was judged to be safer than the unknown future. Other concerns that may have contributed to the ban on mobile components include: the greater difficulty in monitoring the number of mobile (as opposed to fixed) components; the ability of mobile components to avoid being targeted; and the ability of mobile components to be moved from defense of one set of targets to another.

RAPID RELOAD. The treaty also prohibits developing, testing, or deploying (including by modification) an ABM launcher that can launch more than one ABM interceptor missile at a time. And it prohibits developing, testing, or deploying systems for rapid reload of ABM launchers. These restrictions reinforce the one-missile-per-launcher concept of the treaty, banning actions that could raise concern that a side could quickly augment its 100 launchers by fielding several hundred readily launchable missiles. This is necessary because production of missiles is not controlled (primarily because of the difficulties in monitoring such production).

NEW PHYSICAL PRINCIPLES. Consistent with explicitly permitting modernization and replacement of the types of ABM components it allows (and the implied continuation of research and development), the treaty addresses future discovery of new ways to counter strategic ballistic missiles, ways not covered explicitly in the treaty text itself. When the treaty was negotiated, it was anticipated that one day directed-energy devices, such as lasers or particle-beam generators, might reach a stage of development that would permit their use as ABM components. The treaty permits only certain kinds of ABM components—interceptor missiles, launchers, and radars. Should ABM systems using lasers rather than missiles be allowed to substitute for the permitted traditional systems?

To whose advantage would permitting such systems be? It was not possible in 1972 to answer such questions, and their answers are not clear even today. Accordingly, a formula was found that neither precluded nor permitted such systems in the future. The sides agreed in the negotiating record (Agreed Statement (D) in a document initialed by the

6. ACDA, *Arms Control and Disarmament Agreements*, p. 138.

heads of the delegations) that, "in the event ABM systems based on other physical principles and including components capable of substituting for ABM interceptor missiles, ABM launchers, or ABM radars are created in the future, specific limitations on such systems and their components would be subject to discussion in accordance with Article XIII [dealing with the Standing Consultative Commission] and agreement in accordance with Article XIV [dealing with amendments] of the Treaty." Certain aspects of this statement deserve special note. It is particularly important to recognize that the statement applies only in cases where the new components (based on new physical principles) *substitute* for one of the three *permitted* types of components.

There appears to be some confusion regarding the extent of the limitations on new physical principles. Some have argued, for example, that it would be permissible to develop and test a space-based ABM system and that only subsequent deployment would be banned. Their interpretation is based on the argument that Agreed Statement (D) is the only "provision" that deals with systems based on new physical principles, which are not otherwise constrained by the treaty. In particular, the argument goes, the ban on the development and testing of space-based ABM systems and components does *not* apply to such systems, but only to those systems of the 1972 type, consisting of interceptor missiles, launchers, and radars. The only limitation, they argue, is on deployment of the new system, because Agreed Statement (D) makes reference to the obligation not to deploy ABM systems and components except as explicitly provided in the treaty.

In fact, there is no basis for such an interpretation: the treaty language makes clear that the treaty's constraints apply to *all* ABM systems and components, both of current and future types. Hence, the development and testing of a space-based ABM system is prohibited, as is its deployment.

Obviously, definitions of terms play an important role in the meaning of the ABM Treaty. The term "development" is key to the precise meaning of the ban on space-based systems: How far *can* a side proceed toward building such a system? The negotiating history and the ratification record make clear that development and testing refer to "field testing" as opposed to "laboratory" development and testing, a key distinction here being that the banned activity must be able to be monitored by national technical means (NTM) of verification. Thus a side could perform laboratory development of a space-based ABM system or component, so long as field testing of a prototype or breadboard model was not carried out. Also, a side could develop a fixed, land-based ABM system that used a high-energy laser as a substitute for the traditional interceptor missile. And such a system might have components in common with a space-based ABM system. Development and testing would be permitted, so long as the system were not *deployed* in *any* form, which is prohibited by Article II and reinforced by Agreed Statement (D), or *tested* in a *space-based* form.

The definition of an ABM system is also critical to the interpretation of these provisions. For example, a side could develop, test, and deploy a space-based antisatellite weapon system or a space-based anti-aircraft weapon system, *so long as that system were not capable of serving also as an ABM system*. That is, it must not be capable of countering strategic ballistic missiles or their elements in flight trajectory. In practice, such determinations may be extremely difficult to make, not only by the other side, but even by the deploying side. Key elements in making such a distinction would be: the characteristics of the lasers, particularly how much energy they could deposit on a target per unit area per unit time and how long they could operate; the number of satellites and the location of their orbits; and the testing program. In general, the required system capability increases significantly as one goes from the antisatellite to the anti-aircraft to the ABM mission. However, it might be difficult to distinguish a very capable system of one category from a limited-capability system of the next one.

A final example of a definitional issue relates to the use of an optical sensor in place of a radar in an ABM system, as described in chapter 3 under advanced exoatmospheric defense. Is such an optical sensor "based on other physical principles"? Some argue it is not, on the grounds that in both cases electromagnetic radiation coming from the target is detected, the major difference being the part of the electromagnetic spectrum being used (optical sensors using shorter-wavelength, higher-frequency radiation). Others argue that the physical principles *are* different, on the grounds that the optical sensor in question (which transmits no radiation) detects the thermal radiation *emitted* naturally by the target by virtue of its temperature, whereas a radar receiver detects a portion of a pulse that it *transmits* and that is *reflected* from the surface of the target.[7] In fact, the definitional issue is irrelevant in the case in question: it matters not whether the sensor is said to be based on

---

7. There are "optical radars" that detect the reflection of a transmitted pulse of optical or near-optical wavelength, but this is not the type of device proposed for replacing the radars in an ABM system.

"other physical principles." According to Article III of the treaty, ABM launchers, ABM interceptor missiles, and ABM radars are the only components for which deployment is permitted, and the sensor in question is clearly not a radar. However, it certainly is an ABM component in the sense of Article III, since it can substitute for an ABM radar. Therefore it may not be deployed without amendment of the treaty.

SAM UPGRADE. Perhaps no issue was, or continues to be, of as much concern to the United States as the so-called SAM upgrade issue—that the Soviet Union might give its widely deployed, anti-aircraft, surface-to-air missile (SAM) forces an ABM capability, thereby quickly placing the United States at a strategic disadvantage. (Such a sudden breach of an agreement's limitations is termed a "breakout.") Thus the United States insisted on the inclusion of a provision in the treaty that prohibited the sides from giving non-ABM missiles, launchers, or radars ABM capabilities, or testing them "in an ABM mode." This last phrase was not defined, but the U.S. delegation made a statement describing events that would in its view constitute testing in an ABM mode. (See Unilateral Statement B in the appendix.) Key events cited in that statement include:
—flight testing an interceptor missile against a target vehicle having a flight trajectory characteristic of that of a strategic ballistic missile (as noted earlier, by implication an ICBM or an SLBM);
—flight testing an interceptor missile in conjunction with the test of an ABM interceptor missile or an ABM radar at the same test range;
—making radar measurements on a cooperative target vehicle of the kind referred to above during the reentry portion of its trajectory or in conjunction with the test of an ABM interceptor missile or an ABM radar at the same test range.

However, certain radars—those used for purposes such as range safety or instrumentation—were exempted from the foregoing.

The major concern at the time the ABM Treaty was signed was anti-aircraft missiles. However, that is not the only concern at the present time. The Soviet Union has been modernizing its large force of short, medium, and intermediate-range ballistic missiles, and this has prompted increased U.S. interest in defensive missiles to counter such Soviet systems. On the other hand, the U.S. intent to deploy the Pershing II ballistic missile in Europe would be expected to increase Soviet interest in developing a missile to counter it. Both sides might want to begin the development of a generation of antitactical ballistic missiles (ATBMs) that could be even more difficult to distinguish from ABMs than are air defense missiles.

BALLISTIC MISSILE EARLY WARNING RADARS. Another area of U.S. concern was the ABM potential of certain very large radars located on the periphery of the Soviet Union, presumably for the purpose of providing early warning of a U.S. ballistic missile attack. (The United States has similar radars located in Alaska, Greenland, and England.) Were these radars only for early warning purposes, or were they in fact part of a present or future ABM system? Unfortunately, it is not possible to determine the exact capability of these radars to support a Soviet ABM system. It is possible, however, to tell that these large radars are themselves vulnerable to attack. This vulnerability derives in large part from their peripheral location—there is no place to put self-defense batteries in front of them. Therefore, the solution arrived at to allay the U.S. concerns was to require that any such radars deployed in the future be located along the periphery of a side's national territory and oriented outward. (An inward orientation on the "far side" of a country would permit defense against attacks from the "near side.") The United States went a step further, stating that it would regard any increase in the defenses of Soviet ballistic missile early warning (BMEW) radars by surface-to-air missiles as inconsistent with the treaty. (Note that this statement could be taken as an expression of concern about the ABM potential of the SAMs as well as the BMEW radars.) The Soviet Union has continued to upgrade its BMEW system, deploying more modern radars and closing gaps in their coverage, at least until recently in accordance with the restrictions noted above (see the later discussion on compliance).

The general concern regarding the ABM potential of large, phased-array radars also prompted Agreed Statement (F). It provided that, aside from those radars permitted in ABM deployment areas, at test ranges, or for ballistic missile early warning, phased-array antennas having a power-aperture product greater than 3,000,000 wm^2 could only be deployed for the purposes of tracking objects in outer space or for use as national technical means of verification.

TRANSFERS TO OTHER COUNTRIES. The potential exists in a bilateral agreement for a side to circumvent its obligations by arranging for actions to be taken by third parties. To inhibit this in the case of the ABM Treaty, one article states that neither side is permitted to transfer to other states, nor to deploy outside its national territory, ABM systems or their components limited by the treaty. Agreed Statement (G) makes clear that the nontransfer obligation also covers applicable technical descriptions and blueprints.

Administration of the Treaty

The treaty (Article XII) provides that, "for the purpose of providing assurance of compliance with the provisions of this Treaty, each Party shall use national technical means of verification at its disposal in a manner consistent with generally recognized principles of international law." It was, in fact, the recognition that such national technical means could satisfactorily monitor the relevant actions of the other side that made each side willing to undertake such an agreement.

Verification by National Technical Means

What are NTM? The treaty does not define them. However, a glossary published in 1979 by the U.S. Arms Control and Disarmament Agency defines NTM as follows:

> Assets which are under national control for monitoring compliance with the provisions of an agreement. NTM include photographic reconnaissance satellites, aircraft-based systems (such as radars and optical systems), as well as sea- and ground-based systems (such as radars and antennas for collecting telemetry).[8]

Obviously, means that are inconsistent with generally recognized principles of international law, such as espionage, are not included within the definition. Nor are legitimate means that are used in a manner inconsistent with international law, such as aircraft overflight of the other side's territory. Also, assets similar to NTM but *not* used for monitoring compliance with the provisions of an agreement are, for purposes of that agreement, *not* considered to be NTM.

The agreement to use NTM for monitoring compliance is strengthened by prohibitions against interference with the NTM of the other side, and against the use of deliberate concealment measures that impede verification of compliance with the treaty provisions. Note that all interference

8. U.S. Department of State, Bureau of Public Affairs, *SALT II Agreement: Vienna, June 18, 1979*, Selected Documents 12B (GPO, 1979), p. 62.

is banned, whereas deliberate concealment measures (such as camouflage or the encryption of radio signals from test vehicles) are banned only if they impede verification by NTM.

The Standing Consultative Commission

It was recognized when the treaty was signed that the sides would need to continue a dialogue regarding it. Procedures had to be developed so that the activities under the treaty's terms could be carried out to the satisfaction of both sides. Questions of compliance were almost certain to appear. The treaty might need to be updated as new technological developments appeared. To accommodate such needs, the sides established the Standing Consultative Commission (SCC). (Article XIII deals with the SCC and its functions.) The SCC has met at least twice a year since its establishment. Of particular interest has been its function as a forum for addressing questions of compliance, discussed further below.

Duration, Reviews, and Amendments

The ABM Treaty is of unlimited *duration;* that is, barring action by one or both of the parties, it will remain in effect indefinitely. However, the treaty provides for its review, modification, and possible termination. The sides are obligated jointly to conduct a *review* of the treaty every five years. Two such reviews have been held, in 1977 and in 1982. The results of these reviews are discussed below. Either side may propose *amendments* to the treaty. The SCC would be a logical forum for proposing, discussing, and possibly agreeing to amendments, but ordinary diplomatic and other channels could be used.

Withdrawal and Linkage to an Agreement on Strategic Offensive Arms

The withdrawal clause (Article XV, paragraph 2) acknowledges the sovereignty of the sides and provides that each has the right to withdraw (with six months' notice) from the treaty if it decides that extraordinary events related to the subject matter of the treaty have jeopardized its supreme interests. This clause, which was based upon a similar one in the 1963 Limited Test Ban Treaty, was included in the ABM Treaty with little debate. However, shortly before signing the ABM Treaty, the

United States noted that if an agreement providing for more complete strategic offensive arms limitations (that is, more complete than the five-year freeze on ICBM and SLBM launchers provided by the Interim Agreement) were not achieved within five years, U.S. supreme interests could be jeopardized, and this would constitute a basis for withdrawal from the ABM Treaty.

Such limitations on strategic offensive arms were in fact not achieved in the specified five-year period. At the end of that time, however, the Carter administration was in the midst of the SALT II negotiations and eventual agreement seemed almost certain. The *current* ramifications of that 1972 U.S. statement are less clear. One might argue that more complete strategic offensive arms limitations have been achieved, given the signing of the SALT II Treaty and the sides' current policies of compliance with many of its provisions (as well as all of the provisions of the SALT I Interim Agreement). Or the United States could take the position that even though the stipulated agreement has not been achieved, U.S. supreme interests have not, as yet, been jeopardized. Or the United States might claim that its supreme interests are jeopardized, but that it chooses not to withdraw from the treaty.

Note that such a withdrawal clause does not constitute the only grounds whereby a side might cease to be a party to an agreement. International law provides that, should a side determine that the other party is not complying with the agreement, it can declare the agreement no longer to be binding on its own actions. To be accepted by the international community, however, such a declaration would almost certainly need to be accompanied by convincing evidence that such a violation did occur and that it was of major significance.

Results of the 1977 and 1982 Reviews

Although neither of the two reviews resulted in a change to the ABM Treaty, they provide insight into the views of the respective U.S. administrations regarding the treaty.

Little public attention was paid to the 1977 review, which occurred during the negotiation of the SALT II Treaty, when there was little doubt that the ABM Treaty would continue in force. The Carter administration was always supportive of the ABM Treaty, and it was not in its interest, in the context of its negotiation and generation of public acceptance for the SALT II Treaty, to raise questions regarding the wisdom of continuing the ABM Treaty. The communiqué released by the United States and the USSR at the conclusion of the 1977 review reflected this view. It said in part:

> The parties agree that the treaty is operating effectively, . . . serves the security interests of both parties, decreases the risk of outbreak of nuclear war, facilitates progress in the further limitation and reduction of strategic offensive arms, and requires no amendment at this time.
>
> . . . consultations and discussions [in the SCC] have been productive and useful in clarifying the mutual understanding of the parties concerning certain provisions of the treaty, in working out appropriate procedures for implementation of its provisions, and in resolving a number of questions related to complete and precise implementation of the provisions of the treaty.
>
> . . . The parties reaffirm their mutual commitment to the objectives and provisions of the treaty and their resolve to maintain and further increase the viability and effectiveness of the treaty.[9]

The 1982 review took place under considerably different circumstances. The SALT II Treaty had been signed but not ratified. It was stated to be a bad agreement by the Reagan administration, which had embarked on its more ambitious strategic arms reduction talks (START). ABM systems were being actively considered as part of a possible solution to the U.S. ICBM vulnerability problem. Although administration spokesmen made clear that no immediate changes to the treaty were contemplated, they acknowledged that amendment might be required in the future to accommodate ABM systems that had, for example, mobile components. Also, there had been considerable publicity associated with an administration review of Soviet compliance with arms control agreements, including the ABM Treaty.

These factors, combined with a popular misconception that the ABM Treaty could be amended only during the five-year reviews (in fact, like any such agreement, it can be amended at any time) caused considerable attention to be focused on the 1982 review, particularly in 1981 and early 1982. Curiously, as the review approached, the attention it commanded decreased, and hardly any note was made, either in official statements or in the public press, of its occurrence!

The second review, like the first, was conducted in a session of the SCC convened for that purpose. Like all proceedings of the SCC, those of the second review were not released. However, that the tone of the review was almost certainly less supportive of the treaty than the first

9. "U.S.-USSR Communiqué on Antiballistic Missile Systems," *Department of State Bulletin*, vol. 77 (December 1977), pp. 856–57.

seems evident from its communiqué. Paragraphs from the 1982 communiqué, corresponding to those quoted above from 1977, read as follows:

> During the course of the review, the Parties carefully examined the Preamble and Articles of the Treaty and Protocol and evaluated their implementation in the period covered by the review.
>
> The United States and the Soviet Union each reaffirmed its commitment to the aims and objectives of the Treaty, and to the process of consultation within the framework of the Standing Consultative Commission to promote the implementation of the objectives and provisions of the Treaty and the Protocol thereto of July 3, 1974.[10]

Missing were such phrases as "the treaty is operating effectively," "consultations and discussions in the SCC have been productive and useful," and "the parties reaffirm their mutual commitment to the . . . provisions of the treaty."

Thus the second review resulted in a much less enthusiastic endorsement of the treaty. Yet it remains intact—there has been no evidence of efforts by either side to change it. And President Ronald Reagan, in his speech announcing a U.S. commitment to develop an effective defense against ballistic missile attack (completely inconsistent with the underlying premises of the ABM Treaty), made clear that U.S. actions would be "consistent with our obligations under the ABM Treaty" (at least for the near term).[11]

U.S. and Soviet Behavior under the Treaty

In the final analysis, the criterion by which an agreement should be evaluated is the effect that it has on the behavior of the two sides. There may be other reasons for having an agreement—for example, Henry Kissinger's attempt to enmesh the Soviet Union in a series of relationships with the United States and thereby positively influence its general behavior. However, history has shown that such attempts may be outlasted by the arms control agreements that are a part of their framework. Accordingly, the agreements should stand or fall on their own merits.

10. "SCC Completes Review of ABM Treaty," *Daily Bulletin* (U.S. Mission, Geneva), December 16, 1982.

11. "President's Speech on Military Spending and a New Defense," *New York Times,* March 24, 1983.

Research, Development, and Deployment of ABM Systems

What difference has the ABM Treaty made? How is the situation now different from what it would have been in the absence of the treaty? Views will differ on the answers to these questions. Some may point to the imminent deployments of large numbers of strategic missile forces, both offensive and defensive, that were forestalled by the SALT I agreements. Others will claim that those deployments were unlikely to occur in any event and that the ABM Treaty, like the Interim Agreement and the SALT II Treaty, did little besides ratify what the sides would have done unilaterally in any event. Yet others will argue that the treaty and the SALT process generally have been to the Soviet Union's advantage, allowing its programs to proceed essentially unabated, while significantly inhibiting U.S. efforts in strategic arms.

One problem the United States has in negotiating arms control agreements with the Soviet Union is that, because of the closed nature of Soviet society, we know much less about Soviet force planning than we do about our own. (Unfortunately, we also know too little about our own force planning over the five- to ten-year period of time typically covered by agreements.) The Soviet Union, in contrast, gives every indication of planning its forces well in advance, and the relative snugness with which its forces fit the constraints of the agreements it signs indicates it takes full advantage of this. This effect appears to have been particularly pronounced in the case of SALT agreements on offensive forces.

Also of importance is the degree to which the sides take advantage of the flexibility permitted within the terms of an agreement. The Soviet Union gives no indication that it recognizes or acts in accordance with the "spirit" of an agreement, as opposed to its letter. On the contrary, the Soviet Union seems to take advantage of the ambiguities that are inevitable in such agreements. Of course, this is closely related to their knowing (and our not knowing) what evolving weapons programs they want to protect. In some cases the United States has presumed that the Soviet Union would be bound by the U.S. interpretation of a key provision. The best example of this is the SS-19 case of the Interim Agreement. In negotiating the Interim Agreement, the Soviet Union had refused to accept a U.S. proposal that the distinction between light and heavy ICBMs be based upon missile volume, with the volume of the Soviet SS-11 being the upper bound for light ICBMs. Yet some members of the U.S. administration argued during the congressional hearings on

SALT I that the Soviet Union would in effect be bound by this definition. The Soviet Union subsequently deployed the SS-19 ICBM, which is significantly larger than the SS-11. It later became evident to all that the Soviet Union never intended to be bound by the U.S. interpretation and had made sure that the Interim Agreement's restrictions on light ICBMs would have no effect on its planned SS-19 program.

Another aspect of a side's behavior under an agreement is the effect that the mere existence of the agreement has on the side's perceptions of the strategic situation and on the emphasis given to programs covered by the agreement. Again, there is no evidence to indicate that, for example, Soviet research and development (R&D) activities in ballistic missile defense or air defense were in any significant way curtailed by the existence of the ABM Treaty. Soviet R&D programs in these areas appeared to flourish and led in the air defense case to extensive deployment of new systems. The Soviet Union has developed and is now deploying upgrades to its Moscow ABM defenses, including additional ABM sites, new silo launchers, and a new phased-array ABM radar with 360° coverage; and it has deployed the SA-10 air defense system. In the United States, the existence of the ABM Treaty not only inhibited ABM R&D (why develop what you will never be able to deploy?) but also resulted in the virtual abandonment of strategic air defenses, the logic being that it made no sense to try to protect the nation from bomber attack when the ABM Treaty precluded protecting the nation from a much more threatening ballistic missile attack.

Would the Soviet Union have deployed more or better ABM systems in the absence of the treaty? Would the United States have done so? The latter seems unlikely, considering the prominence given in this country to the technical difficulties of deploying a ballistic missile defense that would be effective with high confidence. The United States had in hand means for penetrating then-current ballistic missile defenses, and there was no reason to believe that the Soviet Union would not eventually duplicate that progress, thereby rendering ineffective the kind of ABM system we were then capable of deploying.

It is also questionable whether the Soviet Union would have gone far beyond the ABM program it has carried out under the treaty. For many years it has not even taken full advantage of the numbers permitted under the treaty, deploying only 64 of the permitted 100 ABM launchers in its Moscow defense. (It later reduced this deployment to 32, but it has recently built some additional ABM sites, as part of its upgrading of the

Moscow system.) The Soviet Union, too, must recognize the difficulties in successfully defending against a large attack by ballistic missiles, particularly if they carry sophisticated penetration aids. The Soviet R&D efforts have shown essentially no interest in defense of ICBM complexes with ABM systems, so it is also unlikely that without the treaty the Soviet Union would have deployed systems for that purpose. The Soviet ABM system would have some effectiveness against attacks by third countries, and the current program could in part be a response to increased third-country capabilities.

Compliance

Questions are frequently raised with regard to Soviet compliance with the terms of the ABM treaty, and such concerns are appropriate. Violations not only might grant one side a significant military advantage but also would raise serious questions with regard to the side's longer-term intentions.

According to published reports, the Reagan administration's initial studies of the record of Soviet SALT compliance identified at least three potential ABM Treaty violations: (1) Soviet testing of SAM air defense radars such as the SA-5 in an antiballistic missile role; (2) Soviet deployment of large ABM battle-management radars; and (3) Soviet development of a rapidly deployable ABM system known as the ABM-X-3.[12] These charges have been echoed more recently by Senator Jim McClure, who has additionally charged that the Soviet Union has tested the SA-12 SAM in an ABM mode.[13] Others give the SA-12 at a minimum an antitactical ballistic missile capability, reporting that it has been successfully tested against the Soviet SS-4 medium-range ballistic missile[14] (which has a 2000-km range).

More recent reports of potential Soviet noncompliance have dealt with the construction of a new, large phased-array radar in central Siberia

12. Clarence A. Robinson, Jr., "Special Meeting on SALT under Study," *Aviation Week and Space Technology,* vol. 114 (February 2, 1981), pp. 16–17; and David R. Griffiths, "SALT Compliance Termed Threat to U.S. Security," *Aviation Week and Space Technology,* vol. 114 (May 11, 1981), pp. 24–25.

13. Jim McClure, "Covert Strategic Reserve ICBM Force: Another Soviet SALT II Violation" (attachment to a press conference release, "Preserving the Integrity of the Arms Control Process," April 25, 1983), p. 26.

14. "New Soviet missile defenses," *Foreign Report,* April 14, 1983, p. 3-E, published by the *Economist.*

(not on the periphery of the Soviet Union, as early-warning radars of that type are required to be) and the rapid-reload testing of an ABM launcher.[15]

Some aspects of these compliance issues coincide with those addressed publicly by the Carter administration in 1979 in a report having the stated intention "to provide a brief account of the background, discussion, and status of those questions related to compliance with the SALT agreements of 1972 . . . which have been raised by the United States and the USSR."[16] (In more political terms, the purpose of this paper was to provide assurance to the public and the Congress that Soviet behavior had been good enough to permit the United States to become party to the SALT II Treaty.) The Reagan administration has not made public its finding with regard to these issues, nor what if any actions it has taken regarding them. However, it does refer to some of these systems in the Department of Defense publication, *Soviet Military Power*.[17] A brief discussion of three of these compliance issues follows.

TESTING OF AIR DEFENSE RADARS AND MISSILES IN AN ABM MODE. The concern here is that such testing could provide the breakout potential for a nationwide ABM defense, since the Soviet Union already has a nationwide air defense system in place. The 1979 State Department paper stated that certain Soviet testing of an SA-5 air defense *radar* could have been part of an effort to upgrade the SA-5 system for an ABM role or to collect data for use in developing ABM systems or a new dual SAM-ABM system; or the Soviet Union could have been using the radar for range instrumentation purposes.[18] The paper went on to state that shortly after the United States raised this issue in the SCC, the radar activity of concern ceased. It also noted that close monitoring by the United States had not indicated that ABM tests or any tests against strategic ballistic missiles have been conducted with an air defense *missile*. No information on such testing or regarding a possible ABM capability for the SA-5 has been subsequently released by the United States, nor has any information regarding the SA-12 been released.

15. Rowland Evans and Robert Novak, "New Soviet Radar Violates SALT Pact," *New York Post*, July 27, 1983; Philip J. Klass, "U.S. Scrutinizing New Soviet Radar," *Aviation Week and Space Technology*, vol. 119 (August 22, 1983), p. 19; and "Soviets Test Defense Missile Reload," *Aviation Week and Space Technology*, vol. 119 (August 29, 1983), p. 19.

16. U.S. Department of State, Bureau of Public Affairs, *Compliance with SALT I Agreements*, Special Report 55 (GPO, 1979), p. 1.

17. U.S. Department of Defense, *Soviet Military Power*, 2d ed. (GPO, 1983).

18. Department of State, *Compliance with SALT I Agreements*, p. 2.

BUILDING NEW LARGE ABM BATTLE MANAGEMENT RADARS. Here again, the concern is a nationwide ABM defense breakout potential. The 1983 edition of *Soviet Military Power* reports that the Soviet Union has made a major commitment to improving its network of Hen House radars near the borders of the USSR by constructing new phased-array radars which, when finished, will close gaps in Hen House radar coverage.[19] That publication makes no mention of the "battle-management" potential of such radars, that is, their ability to provide to ABM batteries in the interior of the USSR information permitting the Soviet Union to assign specific targets to individual interceptor missiles and to discriminate actual warheads from penetration aids such as chaff and decoys. It does note that such radars will provide Soviet leaders with better information about the size and objectives of any enemy missile attacks, but this is consistent with the BMEW role. Given the locations of these radars (apparently consistent with the ABM Treaty requirement that they be facing outward and located on the periphery of the USSR) and characteristics, they would be able to perform a battle-management function only while the warheads were outside the atmosphere (when discrimination is particularly difficult) and only for as long as the radars would themselves survive. Whether or not they are *intended* to play an ABM role is difficult, if not impossible, to determine, since that would depend in large part on such unverifiable characteristics as their computational capability and how they are connected electronically with the rest of the Moscow ABM system (or a hypothetical future nationwide system). In any event, the location of these radars means their survival in the early stages of an attack must be considered unlikely, particularly as viewed by the Soviet Union. A much more likely battle-management candidate is the new Pushkino ABM radar, located near Moscow, which evidently is accepted as being consistent with the ABM Treaty constraints (that is, it is located within 150 km of Moscow and does not cause the Soviet Union to exceed six ABM radar complexes). The reported new radar in central Siberia is potentially of more concern in the ABM Treaty context, in that it is reported to be neither on the periphery of the Soviet Union nor within 150 km of Moscow.

DEVELOPING A RAPIDLY DEPLOYABLE ABM SYSTEM. *Soviet Military Power* states that the Soviet Union has continued to pursue extensive ABM research and development programs, including a rapidly deployable ABM system. However, it gives no indication of the meaning of

19. Department of Defense, *Soviet Military Power*, p. 28.

"rapid" deployability. The 1979 State Department publication does provide some insight into this question. In refuting the alleged Soviet contravention of Article V of the ABM Treaty, which prohibits the development, testing, and deployment of *mobile* ABM systems and components, the publication observes that one of the types of radars associated with an ABM system in development at that time (1979) could be erected in a matter of months (rather than years, as had been the case for ABM radars that both sides had deployed in the past) and that another type could be emplaced on prepared concrete foundations. It concluded that, although a single complete operational site would take about half a year to construct, a nationwide ABM deployment based on that new system would take a matter of years to build. Presumably this is because a large number of sites would be required and resource limitations (manpower and equipment) would dictate a phased construction program.

The United States also has raised at least two other ABM Treaty issues with the Soviet Union, but they are of less potential significance: (1) inaccurate Soviet reporting of dismantling of excess ABM test launchers (the United States apparently viewed this as a procedural matter); and (2) placement of a Soviet ABM radar on Kamchatka Peninsula (there was apparently a misunderstanding as to whether Kamchatka was an ABM test range and thus a permissible site for locating ABM radars). These two issues, although not of strategic significance, do illustrate some of the definitional and administrative matters that the sides encounter when they are parties to an arms control agreement. The other three issues are more central to the question of the value and risks in such agreements.

The United States is careful in its defense activities to ensure that they are consistent with not only the letter but also the (U.S.-understood) intent of all agreements to which it is a party. The continual scrutiny to which U.S. defense programs are subjected (by the public, the Congress, and mechanisms such as arms control impact statements) would seem practically to guarantee U.S. compliance. Nevertheless, according to the 1979 State Department publication, the Soviet Union has not been at a loss in finding instances to raise regarding U.S. compliance with SALT agreements, although it is likely that some of these were raised as a tactical counter to U.S. allegations regarding Soviet behavior.[20] Three of these instances relate to the ABM Treaty:

20. Department of State, *Compliance with SALT I Agreements*, pp. 4–5.

1. In 1974 the United States notified the USSR in the SCC that the United States had completed dismantling activities at the Malmstrom Air Force Base, Montana, ABM deployment area, where ABM defenses had been under construction when the treaty was signed in 1972. Later in 1974 the Soviet Union raised a question about one aspect of the dismantling of an ABM radar at the Malmstrom site. The United States subsequently reviewed with the Soviet Union the dismantling actions taken at Malmstrom and showed it some relevant photographs of the site.

2. The Soviet Union in 1975 suggested in the SCC that a new phased-array radar constructed by the United States on Shemya Island, Alaska, was an ABM radar, which would not be permitted at that location. The United States explained that the radar was used for national technical means of verification, space tracking, and early warning.

3. In 1978 the Soviet Union expressed concern that the U.S. Pave Paws radars (two large, phased-array radars then under construction for early warning of SLBM attack) along with the other large, phased-array radars in the United States could enable the United States to have a radar base for an ABM defense of U.S. territory. The United States advised the Soviet Union that the Pave Paws radars were to be used for early warning of strategic ballistic missile attack, with a secondary function of space tracking. The United States also provided the Soviet Union technical information on the radars.

The Symbolic Role of the Treaty

The ABM Treaty is the principal bilateral agreement between the United States and the USSR. Successful negotiation of the treaty as a part of SALT I helped to strengthen U.S.-Soviet relations in the early 1970s, and it can be argued that the treaty helped restrain the deterioration of those relations in the 1980s. As noted earlier, it is not evident that the treaty has had a major effect on the ABM forces of the two sides. Nonetheless, an element of predictability has resulted, and the reluctance to give that up in exchange for the uncertainty that the absence of the treaty would bring has no doubt helped to keep it in force, as well as to inhibit programs that would require its being scrapped or significantly modified.

Another aspect of stability brought about by the treaty relates to the United Kingdom and France, which rely on it to give credibility to their own ballistic missile deterrent forces. President Reagan acknowledged this factor in "recognizing the need for close consultation with our allies"[21] in connection with his program of defense against strategic nuclear missiles.

Would the pursuit of other arms control agreements be undercut by the abandonment of the ABM Treaty? The answer is almost certainly yes, both for substantive and perceptual reasons. Efforts at further controlling and reducing strategic *offensive* arms would unquestionably be more difficult in the absence of the ABM Treaty. Given unlimited defenses, who will be willing to agree to major reductions in deterrent forces? Even given the current reliance on offensive weapons for deterrence, limitations of offensive forces must be accompanied by limitations on the most important elements of strategic defense (although the SALT II limitations on heavy bombers without limitations on air defenses tend to undercut this assertion).

Negotiations on a comprehensive nuclear test ban also are related to success in strategic arms control negotiations. A side's requirements for new or modified nuclear warheads, the development of which is one of the reasons for nuclear testing, will depend in part upon the weapons systems permitted by arms control agreements.

Possible Changes to the Treaty

The final issue to be discussed is the desirability of the ABM Treaty as it currently exists. This can best be addressed by considering possibilities for change.

Before discussing specific changes, it is worth noting potential advantages and disadvantages of the United States' proposing *any* change to the ABM Treaty. What would be the effect on public opinion, on U.S.-Soviet relations, or on arms control in general?

Public awareness of ABM-related issues is relatively low. President Reagan's speech of March 23, 1983, emphasizing defense against ballistic missile attack generated some interest within the defense community, but appeared to have only a passing effect on the general public. The public has appeared more responsive to the nuclear freeze movement. Hence, an ABM approach that would seek to reduce the number of

---

21. "President's Speech," *New York Times*, March 24, 1983.

weapons (as opposed to President Reagan's March promise of more security through a new class of weapons) would likely strike a more responsive note. Accordingly, seeking changes to the treaty that would make it more restrictive could gain more notice and acceptance by the public.

Over the past few years the U.S. defense community has paid sufficient attention to possible changes to the treaty (particularly with regard to potential MX basing modes) that U.S. proposals for changes to the treaty would come as no surprise to the USSR. The Soviet Union has come to expect sudden and major swings in U.S. policies and negotiating positions, particularly as a result of changes in administration. In general, the Soviet tactic has been to stand firm and wait until the perturbations die down and the U.S. position reverts to one closer to what it had been previously. One would expect a similar Soviet response (accompanied, of course, by loud shouts of dismay) were the United States to seek changes to the ABM Treaty, unless the Soviet Union itself wanted some particular changes. However, there have been no reports that the Soviet Union wants to modify the treaty.

The effect that seeking changes to the treaty would have on arms control would by and large depend on the ultimate outcome. The successful negotiation of changes would provide evidence that a permanent treaty could in fact be modified to take account of changing circumstances. Such a result should provide a boost to arms control efforts generally. Failure to succeed in negotiating the changes and a resulting stalemate or abandonment of the treaty would have the opposite effect of reducing expectations and efforts in seeking solutions through arms control.

Changes to the treaty might be sought in a number of areas. These fall generally into two categories: those that make no change to the treaty's basic limitations and those that do. The first category includes changes aimed at improving the means of verifying compliance, or at clarifying ambiguities by more precisely specifying what the sides can and cannot do under the terms of the treaty. This last could include activities relating to new technologies. A change in the second category could make the treaty more restrictive. For example, it could seek to eliminate the currently permitted ABM deployments, either to reduce strategic arms generally or to minimize the chances of ABM breakout. Alternatively, a change could seek to permit additional or more effective defenses of particular types. This could run the gamut from permitting more extensive defense of ICBMs to a situation where relatively unconstrained defenses were permitted, so as to facilitate the achievement of defense dominance over offensive missile forces. However, the latter case might in practice mean having no ABM Treaty.

Aiding Verification

It appears that in the areas of major concern for compliance, the question that arises is more the intended use of systems having potential ABM capabilities than those capabilities themselves. Accordingly, short of knowing Soviet intentions or, for example, having details of their command, control, and communication network, it is hard to conceive of areas where merely better intelligence would allay the concerns. Therefore, the current verification mechanisms appear to be adequate, at least to the extent that can be determined from unclassified sources.

What could be beneficial, however, is more exchange of information regarding the activities of each side, including the capabilities and functions of certain questionable components. The Soviet Union is reluctant to do this, although such exchanges appear to have come far since SALT's early days. Of course neither side can take what is said at face value, but the exchanged information provides a useful comparison for data obtained by NTM. It also provides a modicum of constraint, in that the exchanged information in effect sets up additional numerical (and perhaps geographic) bounds within which the sides' forces are expected to be.

Minimizing Future Ambiguities

Two potential future problem areas are often discussed: ATBMs and space-based ABM systems. In neither case is a satisfactory "fix" to the treaty evident.

The United States is developing, and the Soviet Union is reported to be developing, new surface-to-air missiles that have some potential to defend against tactical ballistic missiles. Drawing a technical distinction between an ATBM system and an ABM system would be difficult to do, and in fact may not be practical. It is hard to imagine an ATBM system that the Soviet Union might design and field to counter, say, the U.S. Pershing II tactical missile (which has a range of 1800 km) that would not also have some capability to counter the shorter-range SLBMs (the

Soviet SS-N-6 Mod 1 SLBM has a range of only 2400 km). This is because the trajectories of the reentry vehicles in these two cases will be approximately the same, with relatively small differences in speed and radar cross section. Of course under SALT SLBMs are considered to be *strategic* ballistic missiles, and hence systems capable of countering them must be considered ABM systems. An even more difficult case would be a U.S. ATBM system designed to counter the 5000-km Soviet SS-20 IRBM!

It is clear that one cannot draw a precise line between ATBMs and ABMs. One approach to minimizing problems in this area from the treaty standpoint would be to try somehow to eliminate the overlap zone between ATBMs and ABMs, for example, by constraining ATBMs to a capability well below ABM capability. However, it is not clear whether there exists a range of capabilities whereby a missile could perform a useful ATBM role while not having ABM capability. ATBMs intended to counter shorter-range ballistic missiles (such as the Soviet 120-km SS-21, 500-km SS-23, or perhaps the 900-km SS-22) but not medium- or intermediate-range ballistic missiles might conceivably meet such a criterion. Yet ambiguities would still exist. Added to this is the problem of the increasing overlap between air defense systems and ABM systems, as airborne targets become faster and less observable. In SALT the Soviet Union adamantly resisted all U.S. efforts to limit air defenses. And, of course, the United States might not be willing to accept the degree of restraint that would remove or limit the ambiguities just discussed, because it may want advanced air defenses or an ATBM capability of its own.

Given the aforementioned difficulties, it may well be that there is no choice (if either side wants to retain the ABM Treaty) but to live with the problems cited. That would mean relying on the "tested-in-an-ABM-mode" criterion for establishing ABM capability and simply accepting that borderline systems, if deployed, may provide a significant ABM capability.

A similar area of concern exists in the development of space-based directed-energy weapons, such as high-energy lasers. If such weapons are developed for antisatellite or, more important, for air defense purposes, it could be difficult to determine that they do not also have inherent ABM capability. Again, definition of a precise dividing line between ABM and other systems could be very difficult. Since directed-energy systems are now in their infancy, another possibility would be to try to prevent the development of space-based versions. (In fact, it could be argued that the recent Soviet proposals in the United Nations to ban all weapons in space takes this approach.) Whether such a prohibition would be in the U.S. interest would depend on an assessment of the relative value of such weapons to the two sides. The United States has in the past opposed such a ban (in large part for verifiability reasons), and the March 1983 Reagan speech in effect endorsed the goal of developing just such systems for ABM purposes.

Eliminating ABM Systems Entirely

The United States currently has no deployed ABM system; nor is there much prospect for near-term deployment of such a system. The surge in interest that accompanied the search for a survivable MX deployment mode appears to have waned, given the decision to place a limited number of MX missiles in modified Minuteman silos and to pursue a small ICBM as a long-term solution to the ICBM basing problem. The Soviet Union, by contrast, is modernizing and expanding its Moscow ABM system. Might it not therefore be in the U.S. interest to seek a total ban on ABM systems? On the surface this would appear to be the case, with the benefits being to decrease the chances of Soviet breakout by expansion of the Moscow system, to improve the effectiveness of the U.S. deterrent forces, to ensure the effectiveness of the deterrent forces of France and the United Kingdom, and to support arms reductions in general.

However, there are obstacles and there may be disadvantages to such an approach. Certainly a major obstacle would be Soviet acceptance of such a modification. Although the Soviet Union indicated some willingness to consider a zero-ABM solution early in SALT I, it clearly preferred to accept the U.S. proposal permitting defense of Moscow. There is no reason to believe that it has changed its mind since then, particularly in view of its significant investment in maintaining and more recently upgrading the Moscow system. The lack of any U.S. program for near-term ABM deployment would only reinforce this Soviet position.

The disadvantages of zero ABMs are somewhat less clear. Views on the subject will in part depend upon the perception of the contributions ABM systems can make to strategic stability. If it is believed that eventual defense dominance is feasible and desirable—or that ABMs can contribute to the survivability of one side's retaliatory forces without the other side's ABMs diminishing the penetration capability of those forces—then ABM systems should continue to be permitted (and in fact should be permitted in large numbers, although in the latter case they should still be subject to significant constraints). However, if it is believed that ABMs reduce stability by making effective damage limitation possible and thereby removing the threat of retaliation as an inhibition to a side's striking first, then it would be desirable to eliminate ABMs completely.

Allowing ICBM Defense

The principal U.S. incentive to relax treaty constraints has been to permit a more effective defense of ICBMs. ICBM defense has been the dominant reason for the U.S. interest in deploying ABMs throughout the period of SALT (up until President Reagan's recent pronouncement). Although the interest in this option appears to have waned within the U.S. government, it is nevertheless worthwhile (particularly in view of the frequent changes in U.S. intentions regarding ICBM deployment) to examine the implications of seeking treaty changes to permit the deployment of an ICBM defense more substantial than is now permitted under the treaty.

Let us assume that the parties intend to preserve the fundamental objective of the treaty—that is, to minimize the possibility of the deployment of a nationwide defense or the creation of a base for such a defense. In general, a nationwide defense requires a combination of large numbers of interceptors and broad area coverage. Without both of these, existing ballistic missile forces can overwhelm the defense. Thus the permitted ICBM-only defense must be constrained to either low numbers (the current ABM Treaty approach) or limited area coverage. In addition, the characteristics of the system should be such that rapid expansion to a nationwide defense would be detected well in advance.

An example that was the focus of the U.S. ABM system efforts for several years is the LoADS system designed for use with the multiple protective shelter (MPS) basing mode for MX. This system is described in chapter 4. It consists primarily of mobile defense units, each consisting of a radar and a few interceptors and each housed in the same type of shelter used to protect the ICBMs. Mobility is required so the defense units can be rehidden periodically. The deployment of one ABM radar and three interceptors per ICBM would be necessary to have the effect of doubling the number of protective shelters. (The treaty permits twenty radars and 100 interceptors, both fixed.)

The following changes to the treaty would be required to permit such a system with a deployment of 100 ICBMs hidden in some larger number of shelters: (1) increase the number of missiles and launchers to 300; (2) increase the number of radars to 100; (3) permit mobile launchers and radars; and (4) permit the United States to change its ABM deployment area from Grand Forks, North Dakota, to wherever the ICBM deployment area was (if different from Grand Forks). Two questions arise: (1) Would the Soviets accept such changes? and (2) To what extent would the changes (or other changes required to get Soviet acceptance) undercut the objectives of the treaty?

Were the United States to propose such changes to the Soviet Union, the latter would likely object (seeing them to be in the U.S. interest). The Soviet Union might eventually permit such changes in exchange for modifications it might want, say, to strengthen its Moscow ABM system.

It could be argued that the LoADS-type defense provides little base for a territorial defense, as its intercept footprint is very limited. Because it is a close-in defense optimized to defend hard targets, it is unsuitable for defending area targets such as cities. Changes the Soviet Union might want, in contrast, might significantly strengthen Soviet protection of a major part of the Soviet Union, which would arouse concern in the United States. Some are concerned already whether those U.S. ballistic missiles remaining following a Soviet first strike would (with their degraded coordination) be able to penetrate Soviet defenses successfully. Increasing the permitted number of Soviet ABM interceptors could only exacerbate these concerns.

CHAPTER SEVEN

The Small Nuclear Powers

LAWRENCE FREEDMAN

IN MANY WAYS, the development of ballistic missile defenses by the United States and the USSR could pose a far greater challenge to the small nuclear powers than it would to the superpowers. This chapter examines the way that Britain, France, and China have dealt with this fundamental threat to the credibility of their nuclear deterrents in the past, and the types of problems they would face if there was a revived antiballistic missile race.

The Equalizer

In the 1950s it was widely believed that thermonuclear weapons were the "great equalizers." They allowed massive damage to be done even by small-scale attacks. This meant that merely purchasing extra capabilities would not bring proportionate military effect. Great wealth could not buy overwhelming power. Any state that could acquire even a small number of nuclear weapons would be, in effect, on a par with the greatest states.

In varying degrees, this thought animated the nuclear programs of the three countries under consideration in this chapter. In Britain in 1956 Julian Amery observed that: "It would seem that the hydrogen bomb, when we have it, will make us a world Power again . . . the hydrogen bomb is a great leveller. It cancels out the disparity between population and big areas of territory and smaller ones."[1] More than a decade later General D'Armée Charles Ailleret was proclaiming the values of a missile capable of intervening "tous azimuts"—"a system which, during

1. *Hansard Parliamentary Debates* (Commons), 5th ser., vol. 549, cols. 1091–92.

future crises that may rock the world, would place France in a position where she could freely determine her own destiny."[2] China consistently stressed the importance of breaking the nuclear monopoly of the super-powers, not only for itself, but on behalf of the progressive peoples of the world. After its first atomic bomb test in 1964, China declared: "The mastering of the nuclear weapons by China is a great encouragement to the revolutionary peoples of the world in their struggles."[3]

In a negative sense nuclear weapons were potential equalizers. It was unlikely that one nuclear power would take on another unless put under mortal threat. In a positive sense, however, the mere possession of nuclear weapons did not guarantee great power status. Other factors, from classical military capabilities to economic strength, have been equally important as sources of power in everyday international affairs. Even in the negative sense, equalization has not turned out to be as straightforward as was at first hoped. Until the late 1950s the common assumption was that a nuclear stockpile adequate for deterrence con-sisted of only enough weapons to destroy the likely enemy's major cities. However, it soon became apparent that such a simple calculation was wholly inadequate. The stockpile had to be judged against criteria such as the proportion likely to survive an enemy first strike or to penetrate enemy defenses.

Survival and Penetration

At the start of the 1960s there was reason to believe that the standards of effective deterrence were becoming excessively demanding for a medium power. Not only were the two superpowers actively discour-aging their allies from acquiring their own nuclear arsenals, but they could also point out the probable futility of the exercise.[4] A small force, especially if composed of long-range bombers concentrated in a few, known bases on land, was vulnerable either to destruction in a surprise

2. General D'Armée Ailleret, "Directed Defènce," *Survival*, vol. 10 (February 1968), p. 43.

3. Quoted in Leo Yueh-Yun Liu, *China as a Nuclear Power in World Politics* (Taplinger, 1972), p. 61.

4. This point was made most forcibly by Secretary of Defense Robert S. McNamara. He observed that a relatively weak national nuclear force might be unable to function as a deterrent: "If it is small, and perhaps vulnerable on the ground or in the air, or inaccurate, it enables a major antagonist to take a variety of measures to counter it." See Robert S. McNamara, "Remarks by Secretary McNamara, NATO Ministerial Meeting, 5 May 1962, Restricted Session." The speech was declassified on August 17, 1979.

THE SMALL NUCLEAR POWERS

attack (by bombers or missiles) or to interception by the growing air defenses of the superpowers.

Even Britain, which had been in on the development of nuclear weapons at the start and was the third country to explode its own nuclear device, began to find the going tough. Strategic logic forced it away from bombers to missiles. But the national program was extremely expensive and technically difficult, and promised only a greater likelihood of beating enemy defenses without improved chances of survival against surprise attack. Even when in 1960 pride had to be swallowed and a U.S. missile—Skybolt—ordered, the new system would still be carried on aircraft that would be vulnerable in their bases. It was in part this thought that prompted the U.S. government to scrap the Skybolt program in 1962, thereby threatening the future of the British nuclear force.

The hurried compromise of December 1962 between Britain and the United States not only rescued the British force but put it on a much sounder basis.[5] The purchase of a submarine-launched ballistic missile (SLBM)—Polaris—meant that the deterrent would be located under the sea where an enemy was least likely to catch it unawares. Britain soon felt confident about this sea-based capability. When in the late 1970s the government was considering the most appropriate capability for the successor to the aging Polaris, it put "survivability" as the chief criterion and came out unequivocally for a submarine-based replacement.[6]

France, too, soon came to prefer submarines, despite having begun as a nuclear power in a typically grandiose fashion, with a triad in microcosm of bombers, plus ground and submarine-launched missiles. Today the Mirage IV bomber force is to be phased out while the land-based force is now only likely to be sustained if it can be made mobile at reasonable cost. Meanwhile there are already plans to increase the number of submarines to seven by the mid-1990s.[7] Even China, which

5. For background, see Lawrence Freedman, *Britain and Nuclear Weapons* (London: Macmillan for the Royal Institute of International Affairs, 1980), pp. 10–18.

6. "The Government believes . . . that we must maintain in a new force the standards of immunity to surprise and pre-emptive attack which the Polaris force has achieved so successfully since the 1960s." "The Future United Kingdom Strategic Nuclear Deterrent Force," Defence Open Government Document 80/23 (Ministry of Defence, 1980), p. 7.

7. On October 30, 1981, at a meeting of the Defense Council, President Mitterrand officially approved construction of a seventh nuclear ballistic missile submarine (SSBN) and the development of the SX mobile intermediate-range ballistic missile (IRBM). International Institute for Strategic Studies, *Strategic Survey, 1981–1982* (London: IISS, 1982), p. 63. The 1983–88 Defense Plan confirmed these decisions. "France Sets 1983–88 Defense Funding," *Aviation Week and Space Technology*, vol. 118 (April 25, 1983), pp. 22–23.

has seemed content with something that would barely pass for a second strike capability among its nuclear peers, has begun to test an SLBM.[8]

The small nuclear powers reckon that they can live with a possible threat of antisubmarine warfare (ASW), and it would take a dramatic breakthrough to shake their confidence in the survivability of their deterrents. As for penetration, for the last decade the small nuclear powers have been able to comfort themselves by pointing to the ABM Treaty. These powers rely on ballistic missiles. The treaty effectively restricts ballistic missile defenses. Thus, there is no problem of penetration.

Such a happy syllogism makes it possible to avoid the question of whether there would be a serious problem of penetration even if the ABM Treaty did not exist and the USSR was strengthening its defenses. There is no ASW treaty, and the USSR has devoted substantial efforts to its ASW program, yet these circumstances do not undermine confidence in the long-term prospects of submarine-based deterrents. Is it therefore the case that a Soviet ABM program unconstrained by treaty would pose a dire threat to the long-term credibility of the small nuclear forces? That is the question that this chapter seeks to answer.

Thin Defenses against Small Threats

Before the missile age there was no reason for any nuclear power to believe that it would be allowed an unopposed run at the enemy. It was assumed that air warfare was marked by a permanent duel between offense and defense and that the offensive force could only expect to reach its targets if it pursued regular modernization to keep ahead of ever improving defenses. This was certainly true of any country thinking of taking on the Soviet Union with its known determination to maintain

8. In October 1982 China tested its first submarine-launched ballistic missile. Michael Weisskopf, "China Fires a Missile from a Sub: Country Is Moving to Protect Forces," *International Herald Tribune,* October 18, 1982. In August 1981 China announced that it had developed an oceangoing submarine that "can remain submerged for tens of days." Not long afterward there were reports, denied by China, of an explosion associated with an SLBM test. See Gerald Segal, "China's Security Debate," *Survival,* vol. 24 (March/April 1982), p. 75. It is generally agreed that technical and resource constraints will mean that it will take many years before a significant SLBM capability is available.

robust defenses. The assumption led not to despondency but to an expectation of frequent modifications of long-range bombers.

The advent of the missile altered these calculations, although the true significance of the new situation was obscured for some time by the attachment of air forces to piloted aircraft and the strategic bombing mission, the scarcity and inaccuracy of the first long-range missiles, and the possible value of such factors as dispersal and continual airborne alert. However, by the early 1960s the advantages of missile forces, protected either in hardened silos or through mobility, became apparent. As we have seen, the small nuclear powers came to follow the logic that led to reliance on submarine-based ballistic missiles. It was not only the survivability of this type of weapon that impressed: the possibility of a truly effective antiballistic missile defense seemed remote. It was not assumed that the defensive problem was insuperable, but at the very least a useful breathing space would intervene before a new generation of offensive systems would be needed.

This confidence was short lived. In the mid-1960s it began to appear as if the superpowers were actually willing and able to construct substantial networks of antiballistic missiles. The Soviet Union was the first off the mark. In November 1966 U.S. Secretary of Defense Robert McNamara confirmed in public a development that intelligence agencies had been describing in private for a few years, that the USSR was constructing an ABM.[9] The U.S. administration was much more skeptical of the merits of ABMs and more reluctant to invest large resources in their production. However, this attitude was, if anything, even more worrisome to the small nuclear powers. The U.S. doubt was based on the improbability of being able to block a large-scale nuclear assault, especially if the potential enemy was able to introduce countermeasures such as penetration aids and multiple warheads to overcome defensive systems. There was far less doubt over the possibility of dealing with small-scale nuclear attacks—McNamara explained this as early as 1965. After noting the possibility of a small nuclear attack on the United States by a nation possessing only a primitive nuclear force in the 1970s, he reported a preliminary conclusion from studies on this matter that "a small, *balanced* defense program could, indeed, significantly reduce

9. See "Remarks by Secretary of Defense McNamara and General Wheeler at Presidential News Conference [Extracts], November 10, 1966," in U.S. Arms Control and Disarmament Agency, *Documents on Disarmament, 1966*, USACDA Publication 43 (Government Printing Office, 1967), pp. 728–33.

fatalities from such an attack."[10] This view prevailed in September 1967 when McNamara acceded to congressional and military pressure to construct a U.S. ABM system known as Sentinel. He attempted to deflect the system away from protection against the USSR, which he believed both futile and likely to stimulate an arms race, and toward China.[11]

Thus it seemed likely that ABMs were going to become a substantial source of inequality among nuclear powers. Britain, France, and China did not have the resources to develop nationwide defenses, and the short flight from Soviet territory would allow little time for detection, tracking, and interception.[12] All had opted for a policy of nuclear deterrence precisely because they were convinced of the hopelessness of true defense in the nuclear age. Although defense remained hopeless for them and problematic for the superpowers against each other, superpower defense against a small-scale attack was within the bounds of possibility. A large question mark was put against the future of small deterrent forces.[13] In 1968 France's Prime Minister Pierre Messmer found it necessary to point out to doubters in his own country that deterrence would still prevail as long as France's warheads had a chance of penetrating Soviet air defenses.[14]

It was, however, no more than a possibility. In Britain and France it stimulated research on new types of missiles designed to penetrate

10. *Hearings on Military Posture and H.R. 4016 to Authorize Appropriations during Fiscal Year 1966,* Hearings before the House Committee on Armed Services, 89 Cong. 1 sess. (GPO, 1965), p. 208 (emphasis added).

11. See chapter 10 herein.

12. See, for example, the discussion of the French government's decision against a ballistic missile defense in Michel Debré, *French White Paper on National Defense,* vol. 1: *1972* (New York: Service de Presse et d'Information, 1972), pp. 20–21.

13. For a discussion of this possibility in its most positive light see Herman Kahn, "The Case for a Thin System," in Johan J. Holst and William Schneider, Jr., eds., *Why ABM? Policy Issues in the Missile Defense Controversy* (Pergamon, 1969), pp. 73–75. Kahn argued that "it seems both imprudent and unreasonable for the U.S. and the Soviet Union to be completely without protection against almost any N^{th} (nuclear) country, including, of course, China." He suggested that there be at most two "superpowers" as a shared national interest. Without a "thin" ABM any country could become a virtual "superpower," at least in terms of political perceptions. Yet, "it probably would prove fairly easy for the Soviet Union and the United States, if they are in the ABM business, to keep their defenses overwhelmingly ahead of any Chinese offense, and perhaps ahead of the French and the British (or Japanese, or German?) offenses as well, and thus perhaps preempt or weaken those nations' desires to acquire or improve nuclear establishments."

14. "Les missiles antimissiles ne sont pas encore assez efficaces pour condamner la force de dissuasion," *Le Monde,* February 25, 1968.

ABMs. But, despite some gloomy commentary in the newspapers, it did not encourage fatalism in either of these countries. Britain completed its Polaris program, and France persevered with the development of its land- and sea-based missiles.

Having been singled out, China, of course, faced a specific problem. It had at the time only recently tested its first thermonuclear device and lacked any offensive nuclear capability. There had been persistent rumors that an ICBM test was imminent.[15] A convenient reassessment of what would constitute a significant Chinese ICBM force by the early 1970s served in the United States to justify the expenditure of billions of dollars to match it.[16] Of course many people, including McNamara, did not take the China rationale seriously, but the articulation of it set the terms of subsequent debate. Some opponents of Sentinel argued that it was well within China's grasp to develop means to penetrate this thin defense of U.S. cities.[17] A more promising line of criticism was that the

15. The construction of a launching facility in China for an ICBM had begun in 1965 and was completed in 1966, leading U.S. intelligence to conclude that either an ICBM test or a satellite launch might be attempted during 1967. See William Beecher, "Analysts Say China Will Have Operational ICBM in 3 Years," *New York Times*, February 5, 1967; and Charles H. Murphy, "Mainland China's Evolving Nuclear Deterrent," *Bulletin of the Atomic Scientists*, vol. 28 (January 1972), 28–35.

16. According to McNamara, in early 1967 there was no need to make a decision on an anti-China ABM because of the time it would take before China could get a "significant" ICBM capability. It was unlikely, he explained, that China "could deploy a significant (i.e., 50–100) number of operational ICBMs before the mid-1970s." See *Military Procurement Authorizations for Fiscal Year 1968*, Statement before a Joint Session of the Senate Committee on Armed Services and the Senate Subcommittee on Department of Defense Appropriations, 90 Cong. 1 sess. (GPO, 1967), pp. 48–49. By September 1967 no Chinese ICBM test had taken place, yet McNamara considered it prudent to press forward with a "thin" ABM deployment. What had changed was the criterion of "significance." A congressional report of July 1967 observed, "Perhaps most significant for the United States is the fact that a low order of magnitude attack could possibly be launched by the Chinese Communists against the United States *by the early 1970s*" (emphasis added); Joint Committee on Atomic Energy, *Impact of Chinese Communist Nuclear Weapons Progress on United States National Security*, 90 Cong. 1 sess. (GPO, 1967). It was this less permissive view of "significance" (a "few" missiles) that was used by the Systems Analysis Office to justify the anti-China system.

17. One supporter of the U.S. deployment noted that to design and build high-confidence penetration aids China would need research radars comparable in sophistication and complexity to those of the system to be penetrated. This was well beyond the Chinese capability. See Charles M. Herzfeld, "Missile Defense: Can It Work?" in Holst and Schneider, *Why ABM?*, pp. 31–32. However, it is of note that the U.S. Sentinel program as planned in 1967 was only expected to hold down U.S. casualties to a minimal level until China developed seventy-five or more ICBMs. *Scope, Magnitude and Implications of the United States Antiballistic Missile Program*, Hearings before the Subcommittee on Military Applications, 90 Cong. 1 sess. (GPO, 1967), p. 17.

rationale was based on an exaggerated view of China's capabilities. A third was that by drawing attention to China's capabilities in this way, its strength was exaggerated and its prestige would be boosted. At any rate, the "Chinese ICBM threat" did not materialize and in 1969 the U.S. program was reoriented to protect U.S. missile silos against Soviet attack (although the anti-Chinese rationale was not wholly jettisoned). It took until May 1980 for the first test of a Chinese ICBM and by then the political circumstances had altered so drastically that the event was not quite as alarming as it would have been a decade earlier.

The ABM Treaty

Britain and France's refusal to be panicked by the trends of the late 1960s toward ballistic missile defenses was rewarded in 1972 with the signing of the U.S.-Soviet ABM Treaty. Even France overcame its customary hostility to arms control treaties. This had been based on the not unreasonable suspicion that the test ban and nuclear nonproliferation treaties had been in part designed to keep it out of the nuclear business. The 1972 treaty had the opposite effect. Lord Carrington, Great Britain's secretary of state for defence, observed in early 1973: "We have a very direct interest . . . in the continuation of the ABM Treaty."[18]

One indication of the overall benefit that Britain and France believed themselves to be gaining from the treaty was the fact that they did not press their objections to its noncircumvention clause. This clause (Article IX) states that: "To assure the viability and effectiveness of this Treaty, each Party undertakes not to transfer to other States, and not to deploy outside its national territory, ABM systems or their components limited by this Treaty." In an agreed statement both sides accepted that this included an obligation "not to provide to other States technical descriptions or blue prints specially worked out for the construction of ABM systems and their components limited by the Treaty."[19]

18. *Nuclear Weapon Programme,* Twelfth Report from the Expenditure Committee together with the Minutes of the Evidence taken before the Defence and External Affairs Subcommittee, House of Commons, sess. 1972–73 (London: Her Majesty's Stationery Office, 1973), p. 26.

19. U.S. Arms Control and Disarmament Agency, *Arms Control and Disarmament Agreements: Texts and Histories of Negotiations,* USACDA Publication 105 (GPO, 1980), pp. 141, 144.

Such a clause was inherently objectionable to U.S. allies. Even if they had no intention of acquiring an ABM capability of their own, this clause made it possible for the USSR to interfere with Atlantic military relations and created a precedent for limitations on offensive arms where such a clause could make a real difference (for example, in the transfer of U.S. SLBMs to the United Kingdom).[20] To help allay this fear, the U.S. delegation to the negotiations made a statement for the record in April 1972 that Article IX did not set a precedent for a treaty on offensive arms, noting: "The question of a transfer of strategic offensive arms is a far more complex issue, which may require a different solution."[21] This, plus the absence of any such clause in the Interim Agreement on Offensive Arms and the importance of the ABM Treaty itself, allowed the noncircumvention clause to pass.

China was, at least in public, not so enthusiastic about the treaty. This was to some extent because of its natural distrust of any U.S.-Soviet deal. As one commentator observed, "China is the only major nation in the world to condemn publicly and strongly the SALT I agreements as a sham."[22] China objected more to the weakness of the actual limitations on offensive arms than to the ABM Treaty, about which remarkably little was said; this reaction indicated that there might be something in it for China. After all, Henry Kissinger had made clear that he believed the United States was forgoing some anti-China protection.[23] Even in Beijing some comfort could be derived. The preoccupation at the time was in building up a substantial regional capability. Moscow was, for the time being, well beyond reach. The treaty could only help China keep the Asian USSR under threat. China may have had confidence in its own capacity to organize passive defenses. It was about this time that Chairman Mao Zedong delivered his injunction to dig deep and store grain!

20. Ian Smart, "Perspectives from Europe," in Mason Willrich and John B. Rhinelander, eds., *SALT: The Moscow Agreements and Beyond* (Free Press, 1974), pp. 191–94.

21. ACDA, *Arms Control and Disarmament Agreements*, p. 147. The literature on SALT I contains a strikingly small amount of discussion on this issue. Gerard C. Smith recalls how early on in the negotiations the noncircumvention issue was raised and how much this was bound up with concerns about offensive rather than defensive arms, in *Doubletalk: The Story of the First Strategic Arms Limitation Talks* (Doubleday, 1980), pp. 97–98.

22. Morton H. Halperin, "The Perspective from China and Japan," in Willrich and Rhinelander, *SALT*, p. 210.

23. Quoted in ibid., p. 213.

After 1972 the ABM Treaty became generally regarded as the savior of the small nuclear forces. Since the treaty virtually eliminated the penetration problem, it was easy to assume that without the treaty these forces would have been faced with carefully designed defenses that they would have otherwise been unable to overcome. For this to be true, however, the USSR would have to have been able to protect all key targets and the small powers would have to have been unable to overcome these defenses. Neither statement is necessarily true.

The Cruise Alternative

The problems that might have been posed had the treaty not been signed and ratified are illustrated by an alternative mode of delivery—the cruise missile. The cruise missile was actively considered by both Britain and France in the late 1970s. Because of its versatility and relatively low cost, it appeared at first glance to be an attractive alternative to the ballistic missile. Soon a number of drawbacks were identified that modified the early enthusiasm. Among these, the likely susceptibility of cruise missiles to Soviet air defenses loomed large, despite the fact that the USSR was still some way from solving the anticruise problem. When calculations took into account the need to saturate enemy defenses, the numerical requirement shot up. The demand for strict survivability, which implied submarine basing, further increased costs. Submarines are far more expensive to buy and operate than the missiles on board. When the number of boats needed to ensure there is one on station at all times was considered, a force of cruise missile submarines started to look much larger and more expensive than one of ballistic missile submarines.[24]

This argument compared cruise missiles unfavorably with ballistic missiles but did not rule them out. The prospect of serious Soviet air defenses imposed a potential further penalty, but not a prohibition. This penalty would have taken two forms: first, a larger and more expensive force would have been necessary than with ballistic missiles; and second,

24. This issue is discussed in detail in Lawrence D. Freedman, "The European Nuclear Powers: Britain and France," in Richard K. Betts, ed., *Cruise Missiles: Technology, Strategy, Politics* (Brookings Institution, 1981), pp. 454–55. See also "Future United Kingdom Strategic Nuclear Deterrent Force," p. 15.

new generations of cruise missiles would have had to be developed to keep pace with evolving Soviet air defenses.

In the same way, renewed Soviet ABM activity might impose a penalty but not a prohibition on the maintenance of small ballistic missile forces. This possibility can be examined further by considering not only the extent to which the existing and planned capabilities of Britain, France, and China make allowances for Soviet ABM activity, but also the form that this activity might take.

As will be shown below, the form of Soviet ABM activity against which the small powers are best prepared to cope represents an extension of existing Soviet capabilities as exhibited by the Moscow system or incremental qualitative improvements. The question is whether there might be more substantial Soviet ABM activity that would be sufficient to deny the small powers their deterrents while being of only marginal relevance to the United States. The extreme case of a true breakthrough in Soviet defenses effective even against the United States would obviously sweep up the small powers along with a much bigger fish.

Britain

Both Britain and France have taken steps to deal with the "ABM threat." In particular both have developed or are developing missiles with warheads hardened so that each one will have to be intercepted by a separate ABM missile, equipped with penetration aids and decoys, and capable of dividing into multiple reentry vehicles (MRVs).

After being obscured for many years by great secrecy, Britain's program has now been fully revealed. This was largely the result of a parliamentary inquiry designed to uncover the causes of the overruns and the delays in the program.[25] The history of the program, as traced by the inquiry, begins with a research effort at the Atomic Weapons Research Establishment (AWRE) at Aldermaston in 1967 supported by intelligence estimates of the likely scale of the Soviet ABM effort. In 1970 the decision was taken to move to a feasibility study. In 1972 the Conservative government authorized full development, a decision that

25. *Ministry of Defence: Chevaline Improvement to the Polaris Missile System*, Ninth Report from the Committee of Public Accounts, House of Commons, sess. 1981–82 (London: HMSO, 1982). See also Freedman, *Britain and Nuclear Weapons*, pp. 41–51.

was confirmed by the new Labour government in 1974. Throughout this period policymakers apparently found it difficult either to be decisive about the basic features of the proposed new system or to make a long-term commitment to its success. It was not until 1976, after surviving a major defense review, that the program was finally put on a firm basis with defined objectives, agreed funding, and a proper managerial team at its head. The program was originally intended to reach operational capability in 1979. In 1981 it was reported that it had run into difficulty,[26] but by the next year the problem had been sorted out and operational trials began.[27]

That system became known as Chevaline. It was a replacement front end for the A-3 reentry system with which the U.K. Polaris SLBMs were originally equipped. In fact, the choice of the A-3 hardened, shotgun MRV warhead as against the A-2 was one of the first decisions of the Labour government in October 1964. The decision was in part influenced by reports of Soviet ABM advances. The fullest public description of Chevaline reads:

> The essential characteristics of the improved missile system [designated A3TK to distinguish it from the existing U.K. Polaris A3T], are that it carries re-entry vehicles which have been hardened to resist the effects of Anti-Ballistic Missile warheads. The improved system is mounted on a Penetration Aid Carrier, the payload of which includes a large number of penetration aids designed to confuse the Anti-Ballistic Missile radars. The Penetration Aid Carrier deploys the elements of its payload on different trajectories all of which, however, terminate in one target area; consequently Chevaline does not provide a multiple independently targetted re-entry vehicle (MIRV) capability. The Penetration Aid Carrier is, nevertheless, a sophisticated space craft which, after separation from the second stage of the missile, manoeuvres itself in space so that its payload can be correctly deployed.[28]

The sophistication of the spacecraft appears to have been the cause of many of the development problems. It is believed that many of the penetration aids take the form of decoys. The objective of this system is to swamp enemy defenses with the arrival into the target area of decoys

26. Peter Hennessy, "£1000m Nuclear Deterrent Suffers Setback in Trials," *Times* (London), June 30, 1981.

27. "The highly successful series of missile test firings, carried out from HMS *Renown* off Cape Canaveral earlier this year, represented an important final milestone in the programme. The new system will enter operational service shortly." U.K. Secretary of State for Defence, *Statement on the Defence Estimates 1982*, vol. 1, Cmnd. 8529-1 (London: HMSO, 1982), p. 7.

28. *Ministry of Defence: Chevaline Improvement to the Polaris Missile System*, Commons, p. 1.

and reentry vehicles coordinated in such a way as to pose maximum difficulty to the defender.

After many tribulations the Chevaline program is now deemed to be a technical success. The question is why such a complicated development effort, of a sort that even many in the U.S. nuclear laboratories considered exceptionally difficult, was attempted. In particular, why did Britain bother in the first place, especially as the vital decisions on funding were not taken until after the ABM Treaty had been ratified? To the extent that some system was necessary, why not simply follow the U.S. line of development and purchase the MIRVed Poseidon?

The answer to the first question lies in the "Moscow criterion," which appears to be the organizing principle of Britain's targeting philosophy. This criterion requires an independent deterrent to be able to mount a convincing threat to the elements of state power in and around the enemy's capital. To the extent that this policy was discussed at all, it became highly controversial, critics asking why it was necessary to threaten anything more than a substantial portion of the Soviet economy and society located outside of Moscow.[29]

The issue was never fully aired; with so few privy to the relevant decisions, the Moscow criterion was adopted. Once adopted, and given the existence of the Galosh system protecting the Moscow area, it created a requirement for a system capable of coping with the Moscow ABM. This requirement was unaffected by the 1972 ABM Treaty because Galosh was unaffected, and indeed was allowed to expand from 64 to 100 launchers (though the Soviets initially did not take advantage of this allowance). Further, the United States had warned that failure to agree on a full treaty limiting offensive arms by 1977 could serve as grounds for abrogating the ABM Treaty, and also that development and qualitative improvement of ABMs were not forbidden.[30]

As early as 1967, a well-informed report in the *Economist*, though generally gloomy about the eventual impact of Soviet ABM improve-

29. Michael Quinlan, deputy undersecretary of state (policy and programmes), stated before the Defence Committee: "There is a concept which Chevaline makes clear, that Governments did not want to have a situation where the adversary could expect sanctuary for his capital and a large area around it." *Strategic Nuclear Weapons Policy,* Fourth Report from the Defence Committee, House of Commons, sess. 1980–81 (London: HMSO, 1981), p. 107.

30. Lord Carrington suggested in 1973 that the ABM Treaty would only last until 1977 and a clarification had to be inserted into the record. See *Nuclear Weapon Programme,* Commons, p. 34.

ments, had given Polaris no longer than 1975, but still suggested that against the then-current Moscow system it would be effective much longer, "after some modifications." The reason was that the radars of the Soviet defense would be blinded by the nuclear explosions of their own ABMs for a few minutes. Because the Polaris missiles could be fired at the rate of one per minute, this effect would allow the second and third to get through even if the first had been stopped.[31] A government report has since stated that Polaris, even without Chevaline, would probably have been effective against the Galosh system. Hardening of reentry vehicles (RVs) *seems* to have been the first priority of those concerned with the implication of the Moscow system for Polaris.[32]

An improved Moscow system, including improved radars that make it possible to handle more than one RV at a time, would become too much for one boatload of sixteen Polaris missiles to handle. Two boats permanently on station would have made this problem manageable. However, the total submarine force of four boats could support only one boat on station for much of the time, given in-port time and long periods of refitting.

Still the British government considered it necessary to plan to penetrate the Moscow defenses, even if the rest of the USSR was to be left defenseless. Acquisition of Poseidon missiles was one option actively discussed with the United States. London ruled it out on four grounds. First, the fact that the Galosh system was exoatmospheric meant that a system based on decoys could make as much sense as one based on MIRVs (the point being that exoatmospheric systems are potentially much less capable of discriminating between decoys or penetration aids and warheads). Second, there was a certain enthusiasm for an innovative national program attempting for once to do something that the United States had not yet tried—even though the original concept had come from the United States. Third, there were doubts about whether the U.S. Congress would authorize the sale, especially if the MIRV "bus" was transferred along with the rest of the missile (Britain would always fabricate the actual nuclear warheads), and about whether the administration would accept the complications such a transfer might introduce into SALT. It was widely believed in Washington that, with the ABM Treaty in place, small nuclear forces were quite secure without their

31. "Polaris Afternoon," *Economist,* vol. 225 (October 28, 1967), pp. 368–71.
32. See, for example, David Owen, *The Politics of Defence* (London: Cape, 1972), p. 182.

having to resort to anything quite so provocative as MIRVs. Lastly, Britain was not sure that it even wanted MIRVs.[33] Although it was generally agreed that Poseidon, even without MIRVs, would be more expensive than Chevaline, the cost itself was not prohibitive, and there were some in London who felt that it might make sense to modernize with the already available Poseidon missile in advance of submarine replacement. If a drawn-out Chevaline project forced all components of the system to be replaced at once, then the concentrated burden on the budget in the 1980s might be too severe (as turned out to be the case!). Another reason was that even the Conservative government responsible for the basic choice of system was nervous about opting for Poseidon because it might be politically divisive. The previous Labour government had explicitly ruled out Poseidon, and the Conservatives worried that a future Labour government might do the same[34] and might thereby jeopardize the whole future of Britain's nuclear force. MIRVs had a reputation for being destabilizing. Hence the choice of Chevaline.

By the late 1970s, however, just as London began to consider options for replacing the Chevaline-equipped Polaris boats and missiles when they reached the end of their active life sometime in the 1990s, MIRVs had become an accepted feature of the strategic environment. Their acquisition by Britain would not attract great comment (although the possible arms control consequences did concern the State Department before the Carter administration agreed to the transfer in 1980). Furthermore, the cost and difficulty of the Chevaline project had so sobered Britain into recognizing the advantages of buying "commonality" with the United States in system production and operation that it abandoned its first choice of the Trident C-4 SLBM when it became clear the United States would soon opt for the newer D-5 version. Once the criterion of survivability was adopted, the choice of a successor system was almost

33. For further background, see Freedman, *Britain and Nuclear Weapons*, pp. 46–51.

34. As early as March 1965, in a parliamentary debate, Prime Minister Harold Wilson had implied that Soviet ABM development (combined with a rather gloomy view as to the shelf life of Polaris) might push Britain out of the nuclear business because the follow-on Poseidon would be prohibitively expensive. "Ten Years' Life for Polaris?" *Times* (London), March 8, 1965. In June 1967 Wilson formally rejected Poseidon in a parliamentary answer. *Hansard Parliamentary Debates* (Commons), 5th ser., vol. 748, col. 299. When justifying Chevaline (not described in so many words) to the Labour cabinet on November 20, 1974, Wilson emphasized that there would be no "Poseidonization." Barbara Castle, *The Castle Diaries, 1974–76* (London: Weidenfeld and Nicolson, 1980), p. 227.

wholly driven by the quest for commonality rather than by such matters as targeting requirements.

The Trident D-5 offered an embarrassment of strategic riches, far in excess of Britain's conceivable requirements. It was chosen not because the government wanted a 6000-mi. range or up to fourteen warheads, but because calculations suggested that the missile would provide the most cost-effective option over the lifetime of the force. In order to placate critics and also to save some money, the government stressed that "the move to Trident D-5 will not involve any significant change in the planned total number of warheads associated with our strategic deterrent force in comparison with the original intentions for a force based on the C-4 missile system."[35]

With 14 warheads per missile, the new force of four boats with sixteen launch tubes could have a maximum of 896 warheads. Given the expectation that always two, and sometimes three, Trident boats will be on station at any one time (because of the extended intervals between long periods of refitting made possible by a more durable propulsion unit), this makes for a maximum of 672 warheads on station. Holding it down to the equivalent of a Trident C-4 force with 8 warheads per missile would mean a maximum of 384 warheads on station. Either way this would be a drastic increase over the 16 to 32 warheads on station with the current Polaris A-3.[36]

With the maximum warhead count presumably still available if the unilateral constraint was to be removed,[37] it can be seen that a massive protective screen would be needed around the Moscow area for this basic target to be denied to Britain. Extremely comprehensive area defenses would be needed for Britain to be denied any substantial targets at all, given the flexibility the Trident force will enjoy in both launch and aim points. Following the 1983 general election, the United Kingdom will almost certainly go ahead with Trident. It should then have no trouble with any conceivable Soviet area defenses based on the technol-

35. "The United Kingdom Trident Programme," Defence Open Government Document 82/1 (London: Ministry of Defence, 1982), p. 6.

36. See the note by Lawrence Freedman appended to *Strategic Nuclear Weapons Policy*, First Special Report from the Defence Committee, House of Commons, sess. 1981–82 (London: HMSO, 1982), pp. 24–25.

37. The Ministry of Defence has stated that having sixteen rather than twelve launch tubes on the new U.K. Trident SSBNs, even if not all of them are to be filled, "would provide flexibility to cope with any possible improvements in Soviet ABM defences throughout the life of the force." "The United Kingdom Trident Programme," p. 6.

ogy of the 1980s or 1990s. It was officially stated that even with the C-4, Trident was "a system which has within it, and could have to a further degree, a very considerable capability to counter an ABM defence even if that were significantly extended beyond what is currently allowed under the ABM Treaty."[38]

Whether Polaris-Chevaline could cope with dramatic improvements in the Moscow system is moot. An increase in numbers within obvious limits would be manageable because of the many realistic decoys involved in Chevaline. The most dangerous development would be a Soviet move to a new endoatmospheric system, because such a system is much more capable of discriminating between real warheads and decoys.[39] However, it is still important to remember that, even if some way was found to deny Moscow as a target, there would still be many others available.

France

Far less is known about France's decisionmaking in this area, although a certain amount can be discerned from trends in weapons development. It is likely that the ability to attack Moscow has a similar priority although there has not been a public debate on the Moscow criterion. Nor is there much evidence of a private debate. It is possibly of relevance that as the French force has matured there have been doubts as to whether Moscow would be available as a target. The issue in France has been more a question of the ability to inflict a general level of damage rather than to attack specific targets. French pronouncements tend to talk of attacks on Soviet cities (in the plural). French doctrine stresses "proportionality," that is, ensuring that the cost to the Soviet Union of its aggression always exceeded the potential benefit; the cost to the USSR of an attack on France need not be made as great as the cost of attack on the United States. The main issue when it comes to targeting has been whether it is necessary to threaten anything other than cities to achieve the necessary deterrent effect.[40] The issue has involved not only military targets (to

38. Michael Quinlan in *Strategic Nuclear Weapons Policy*, Fourth Report, Commons, p. 108.

39. See chapter 6 herein, which suggests this is a real possibility.

40. See chapter by David Yost, "French Strategic Nuclear Targeting," in Desmond Ball and Jeffrey Richelson, eds., *Strategic Nuclear Targeting* (forthcoming).

which France has a doctrinal aversion) but the need to strike administrative as well as economic or population centers.

France's official position has been that it can manage with the level of Soviet defenses permitted under the treaty but that it would have problems if the treaty were revised. One senior official has warned that this "would weaken the technical credibility of our striking force with respect to the USSR."[41] France has taken steps to improve the capacity of its missiles to penetrate existing Soviet defenses. France's force has developed incrementally with a succession of new missiles that have gradually extended the range and yield of the land- and submarine-based forces.[42] There has been a gradual improvement in the capacity for penetration.[43]

Before it came into service in 1977 the M-20 missile that is now deployed on all submarines was said to be "hardened" and to have "improved penetration aids."[44] In 1985 the M-20 is to be replaced by the M-4 in a new submarine, and four of the five existing submarines will also be refitted with M-4s. The M-4 has been designed to penetrate Soviet defenses. The system has been reported to contain six hardened reentry vehicles, each of 150-kT yield, and also decoys and perhaps chaff. Although the reentry vehicles are not independently targeted, they separate sufficiently early and to a sufficient extent to force the enemy to use up at least one ABM to deal with each RV.[45] It is possible that the

---

41. Jean-Louis Gergorin, quoted in David S. Yost, "Ballistic Missile Defense and the Atlantic Alliance," *International Security,* vol. 7 (Fall 1982), p. 148.

42. Thus with the SLBM (or MSBS—*mer-sol balistique strategique*) force, the pattern has been:

Date	Missile	Range	Yield
1971	M-1	1350 NM	500 kT
1974	M-2	1650 NM	500 kT
1977	M-20	1650 NM	1 MT

43. Raymond Tourrain, *Rapport d'information par la Commission de la Défense Nationale et des forces nucléaires françaises,* no. 1730 (Paris: Assemblé Nationale, October 1980), p. 108.

44. "French Emphasizing Nuclear Weapons," *Aviation Week and Space Technology,* vol. 105 (August 2, 1976), pp. 43–45.

45. Jacques Isnard, "Les nouvelles armes nucleaires à l'ordre du jour," *Le Monde,* June 11, 1980; G. Chambost, "France and NATO: An Ambiguous Relationship," *International Defence Review,* vol. 12, no. 4 (1979), pp. 526–30; and Edward W. Bassett, "French Push Strategic Missile Plan," *Aviation Week and Space Technology,* vol. 113 (July 28, 1980), p. 15.

next generation of SLBMs (the M-5) that may appear in the 1990s will be MIRVed.

The penetrability of the land-based intermediate-range ballistic missile (IRBM) force has also steadily improved. The new SSBS-3, deployment of which was completed in early 1983, incorporates decoys and improved hardening and safety devices.[46] Considerable interest now focuses on the successor to the SSBS-3, the S-X, a mobile missile to be developed during the 1980s. The S-X needs a smaller warhead than the M-4. One report has suggested that the general staff advised that the S-X be equipped with "a single so-called revolving nuclear warhead, that is, one capable of independent movement at the end of its journey and thus able to escape a surface-to-air defense attacking it during the last stage of its flight." The nuclear engineers suggested that it might be possible to have as many as three of these maneuverable warheads on each missile.[47]

France is confident of its ability to cope with present Soviet defenses. In the late 1970s a senior French official argued: "So long as ABM defenses remain at the current level, the multiple-warhead system that will be in service with the M-4 should be able to exhaust these defenses without too much difficulty and to assure the penetration of a significant portion of our strategic missiles. Moreover, what is called the hardening of warheads and missiles can make our missiles more invulnerable to the effects of ABM warhead explosions."[48] The official went on to note the possibility of expanding numbers to meet an expanded threat. France certainly has a number of options available for dealing with improvements in Soviet ABM defenses, and the Soviet Union would have to go substantially beyond existing levels before France would be required to alter its plans.

China

Even less is known about China's efforts to develop warheads. With scarce resources, China has found it necessary to establish a clear set of

46. Chambost, "France and NATO," p. 526. There are eighteen SSBS-3 in place.
47. *Le Monde*, March 17, 1980.
48. Ivan Margine (pseudonym), "L'avenir de la dissuasion," *Défense Nationale* (April 1978), p. 28.

priorities. The first priority was to develop a serious regional capability. Only then was it possible to work toward an anti-Moscow capability, something that was met only late in the program.[49] It is possible that the ABM capability surrounding Moscow could cope with a Chinese threat to the capital. However, the USSR would have considerable trouble in any attempt to deal with a Chinese regional missile capability if China's goal was to hit a handful of medium- to large-sized cities out of many in the Far East. Thus China should continue to be able to pose a regional deterrent threat even if a specific threat to Moscow will remain problematic for some time to come. An improvement in the Moscow system would put back further the date when China could be confident about an attack on the capital. Although China's recent actions and statements indicate that it is unhappy with the quality of its nuclear capabilities, there has never been any suggestion that the relative crudity of these capabilities meant that China did not have any deterrent capabilities in operation.

China now has a few ICBMs available. One report from China has claimed that it will eventually have eight to ten MIRVed warheads.[50] There is no evidence that China is even close to such a capability. However, there is evidence that it is working on a MIRV system. One such piece of evidence was the use of a missile to launch three space research satellites.[51] It may well be that the leadership in Beijing is hoping to raise the quality of China's deterrent by developing a full anti-Moscow capability. If so, then this effort could be blown off course by significant improvements in the Moscow defense.

    49. A table provided by Gregory Treverton in his "China's Nuclear Forces and the Stability of Soviet-American Deterrence," in *The Future of Strategic Deterrence*, pt. 1, Adelphi Paper 160 (London: IISS, 1980), p. 39, illustrates the difficulty that the International Institute for Strategic Studies has faced in keeping track of China's nuclear weapons development. It suggests that Moscow came under threat somewhere between 1974 and 1976. At that time the United States was also expecting imminent deployment. However, in 1978 the chairman of the Joint Chiefs of Staff was reporting that the relevant missile, the CSS-3, having been flight-tested in 1976, had yet to be deployed, and when it was this would only be in "limited numbers." *United States Military Posture for FY 1979*, p. 42. It was not until the start of 1980 that limited deployment was confirmed. *Department of Defense Annual Report, Fiscal Year 1981*, p. 84. (This report contains a map showing the range of Chinese strategic systems.) IISS, *The Military Balance, 1982–83* (London: IISS, 1982), p. 80, gives the range of this missile, now called the T-3, as 4800 to 5600 km. It suggests that ten are deployed.
    50. Quoted in Segal, "China's Security Debate," p. 75.
    51. IISS, *The Military Balance, 1982–1983*, p. 78.

Conclusion

The fundamental question facing defense planners has always been, How much is enough? The answer in an age of deterrence depends as much on a judgment concerning the perceptions of the adversary as it does on detailed calculations as to military needs. There has been a tendency in American strategic analysis to suppose that the potential adversary is liable to remain unimpressed by all but the most pointed or devastating of threats: either to obliterate his society or else to point at some clearly defined Achilles' heel—the higher political command, the security services, key industrial sectors, or even the dominant national groups.

Such options are not available for the small nuclear powers. The threat they pose is one that might have appeared "total" in earlier times, before comparisons needed to be made with a superpower capacity for complete and utter destruction, but now is "limited." The natural tendency for these countries has been to raise the terror quotient by maximizing the ability to hit the great centers of enemy population. This threat might be moderated or refined by talking of "centers of state power" (as in Britain) or "administrative networks" (as in France), but nothing really moderate or refined is described.

The question then becomes one of how minimum can a minimum deterrent be? In France's formula for proportionate deterrence presumably the value of the prize is relevant. The degree of pain that an enemy might tolerate to remove a strong and active France is larger than that acceptable to deal with a France that was shrinking away from involvement in a European crisis. So the answer cannot solely be found in the degree of violence that could be inflicted on the USSR. It is even possible to argue that the loss of even one major city would be unacceptable to a leader contemplating aggression. In the debate in Britain over the successor to Polaris, some argued that adequate deterrence operated as long as there was a possibility that a few nuclear weapons might explode on Soviet soil. China has had to trust in what has essentially been a regional threat posed by weapons that themselves might not be able to survive a surprise attack.

However, for national leaders having to contemplate some future cataclysm in which current notions of pain and suffering might be swept away in some furious clash of ideologies and arms, the absolute minimum may not seem sufficient. Does sufficiency then come once a particular quantity of destruction is threatened, or is there a qualitative element involved? The strategic force decisions of Britain and France imply that the quality of the destruction is relevant, but only Britain appears to believe that the ability to destroy Moscow is much more important than the ability to destroy any number of other Soviet cities. In a centralized society such as the Soviet Union, get the center and everything else collapses, as industry, the apparatchiks, and the military all become leaderless.

Moscow is undoubtedly crucial to the functioning of the whole society, while other cities may be less important. But that would not make the loss of these other cities inconsequential and it seems hard to believe that deterrence would fail simply because one vital target was properly defended while 100 lesser, but important, targets remained exposed. For a small power wishing to make the greatest impression on Soviet thinking, the Moscow criterion makes sense but might not be absolutely essential to the viability of the deterrent. Therefore, even if Moscow were properly protected, Britain, France, and China would not be out of the deterrent business. (Indeed, on this basis China has never been in!)

As it is, Britain, France, and to a lesser extent China, have all engaged in major programs to develop or sustain a threat to Moscow by improving their ability to penetrate Soviet defenses. They certainly have not relied entirely on the permanence of the 1972 ABM Treaty, and they might not be as inconvenienced as is often supposed by a collapse of the treaty. The offense still enjoys substantial advantages over the defense. The 1972 treaty may have been a definitive judgment on the offense-defense balance, which remains valid with or without the treaty, rather than a cap on the arms race.

This is true at least regarding area defenses, with which the USSR seemed, in the past, to be most concerned. The judgment is likely to be invalidated only by dramatic breakthroughs in area defense technology. The author lacks the expertise to assess such possibilities but tends to follow those who are highly skeptical. It is of note that defense officials in Britain have also shared this skepticism.[52] When President Ronald Reagan announced his initiative of March 1983 to encourage space-

52. Secretary of State for Defence John Nott has doubted the potential of the more exotic systems. Philip Webster, "Nott Says Cost of Chevaline 'Has Gone Bananas,'" *Times* (London), July 9, 1981.

based missile defenses, the reactions of Britain and France were negative to say the least. British officials, who had not been consulted in advance, were horrified. The prime minister took care to stress that only "research" was involved. The basic hope was that as the announcement had so obviously slipped through the policy filter, the machine would now correct the mistake and the plan would soon die without a trace.

If the ABM Treaty is to be abrogated, then the most common reasons suggested for such a move, at least in the United States, revolve around the requirements of hard-point, not area, defense. Although Trident D-5 is often described as a first-strike weapon, there is no reason to believe that Britain is at all interested in preparing for counterforce attacks. France has an explicit policy of countervalue targeting. China is tied by doctrinal and resource constraints to a small-scale deterrent. The dedicated protection of high-value military targets by a superpower would therefore be of only marginal relevance to a small nuclear power.

If the removal of the ABM Treaty would not undermine the credibility of small nuclear forces, why do these powers worry about the loss of the treaty? In part, at least in the case of Britain and France, it is because of the association of this treaty with the process of arms control, which in turn is part of the greater process of détente. With the unsettled state of public opinion, any abrogation of the treaty, especially if initiated by the United States, would be seen as a dangerous omen.[53] The collapse of what is still taken to be a major achievement of arms control might strengthen calls for unilateral disarmament.

A second factor is that all military planners like the future to be as predictable as possible. However manageable the ABM threat would be if it materialized, at the moment it is one less thing to worry about. With recurring reports of new types of directed-energy weapons and other "exotics" about to enter the realm of the feasible, any uncertainty would encourage speculation over the long-term viability of the forces, however unjustified. Furthermore, if extra insurance were needed to guard against some unexpected Soviet improvement, then this would add to the cost of national strategic programs that are already criticized for their expense.

The main reason why the loss of the treaty would raise questions about the future of the small nuclear forces is that the treaty has been

---

53. I have dealt with the role of ignorance and prejudice in shaping Europe's response to the ABM issue in "Europe and the ABM Revival," *Arms Control* (November 1982).

cited often as something that helps guarantee this future. However much a government might insist that it could manage perfectly well against Soviet ABMs, there would be inevitable concern that such insistence merely represented inertia and a refusal to bow to the inevitable. This would be particularly true in Britain, where the national consensus supporting the nuclear force is far less securely based than in France and China. For the small nuclear powers, therefore, the advantage of the ABM Treaty is not that it is absolutely necessary to guarantee the viability of their deterrents. Rather, it provides a recognized and straightforward confirmation of the vulnerability of the USSR to attack that avoids the complexities of strategic analysis.

CHAPTER EIGHT

BMD and East-West Relations

RAYMOND L. GARTHOFF

THE ISSUE of deploying ballistic missile defenses in the 1980s will affect East-West relations in important ways. Perceptions both of the intended purposes and of the expected results of any proposed BMD deployment would be key elements influencing the course of East-West relations, depending on the political context, the initiative and stimulus for a proposal, and the texture of allied as well as East-West relations. Western European and Soviet views must be considered. In particular, an understanding of Soviet thinking on BMD, of the existing ABM Treaty, and of possible changes in BMD is crucial to assessing the impact of BMD on East-West relations. Effects of a BMD proposal on third countries, particularly potential nuclear powers, also might affect East-West relations.

The Context of East-West Relations Today

Today in the West there is a serious gap between widespread aspirations for a détente in East-West relations and widespread disillusionment over the efforts in the 1970s to establish such a détente. Aspirations remain higher in Western Europe; disillusionment is deeper in the United States. Europeans (West and East) continue to accept détente both as a reality, albeit seriously weakened, and as an aim. Many in the United States, including those in the present administration, do not accept it as either.

The Soviet Union not only expresses a continuing support for détente, but in fact does wish to see a return to the détente of the 1970s. The problem is that the Soviet Union pursues policies and takes actions that many in the West regard as threatening and as incompatible with détente, as they envisage it. And the Soviet leaders see some Western, especially U.S., policies as threatening and as incompatible with their conception of détente.

Nebulous as the term "détente" is, and uncertain as the prospects for reducing tension in East-West relations are, the divergence in expectations on this central question cannot help but affect reactions to any agitation of the BMD issue. It is not a simple case of being for or against détente; efforts in the United States to depict the question in this way and to oppose détente can alienate important segments of Western European opinion. The fact that different parties have differing concepts of détente, as well as differing assessments of its attainability, compounds the problem. Moreover, there are divided public and official views in the West, and very likely differing emphases among participants in the Soviet policy process as well.

Much the same kind of difference characterizes attitudes toward arms control. The current official attitude in the United States is nominally supportive of arms control but at best holds only modest expectations— and in the eyes of most people in Europe and many in the United States, the United States puts forth no more than modest, if not purposefully stalling, efforts. The more intense European interest in arms control is based both on higher expectations of its efficacy and on stronger wishes to see arms control succeed—both on its own merits and as a means of contributing to détente.

At the same time, a substantial number in the United States (ranging on particular issues from a small minority to a majority) would agree more with the "European" view, and at least some Western Europeans (in particular in official circles) would agree more with the U.S. administration on some of these issues. For some purposes, it is enough that a given government takes a particular view; for others, we must distinguish between official and public attitudes.

The central political fact, however, is that the ABM Treaty of 1972 is widely seen not only as the crowning—and principal surviving—achievement of U.S.-Soviet strategic arms limitation efforts, but also as a symbol that détente between the United States and the Soviet Union is not completely dead and may be revived.

Only in the context of these political considerations is it appropriate to look at the military aspects of BMD. It would take a strong military rationale today to propel BMD forward in the United States, and a still more powerful one would be required to gain a favorable reaction in Europe. From an analyst's perspective, a range of military considerations for and against various BMD possibilities can be identified, but the international political context poses a formidable obstacle course that any advocacy of BMD would have to run.

Many in Europe today see the greatest danger arising not from possible Soviet aggression and attack, but from the risk of nuclear war and the arms race. A growing "green" antinuclear movement rooted in concern for the environment and social priorities has emerged and become a new element in the political landscape of Europe. But a much more sizable element of the population, with more moderate political views, also shares a significant concern over nuclear war. This antinuclear sentiment, which is currently focused above all on the North Atlantic Treaty Organization (NATO) deployment of the intermediate-range nuclear force (INF), is to some extent becoming an anti-NATO and anti-U.S. sentiment, stimulated in part by discrepant U.S. and European evaluations of the source of the greatest danger, in part by insensitive statements in the United States, and in part by Soviet efforts to capitalize on these feelings and turn antinuclear sentiment into anti-alliance and anti-U.S. positions. In the United States, concern over the course of the arms race has also led to wide public support for a nuclear weapons freeze, but without the divisive anti-alliance aspect of the more militant European movement and also with a greater acceptance of a continuing need for nuclear deterrence.

The Importance of the Circumstances of Initiative

The impact of BMD on the East-West relationship depends on who takes the initiative in raising the subject and on the circumstances as well as the nature of any proposal. Any Soviet initiative would meet with skepticism from those in the United States who are suspicious of any Soviet action in arms control; it would also perplex those in the West who have taken Soviet adherence to the ABM Treaty for granted and have been more concerned about any possible U.S. initiative. Any Soviet proposal to revise the treaty (unless it were to call for a complete ban on BMD) would undoubtedly be seized upon by advocates of BMD in the United States as offering an opportunity to advance their own preferred modifications without suffering the onus of having reopened the issue. Concrete reactions would, of course, also depend on the proposed terms and on whether the proposal was advanced tentatively for consideration or as a necessary change foreclosing the option of retaining the ABM Treaty as it stands.

That said, however, Soviet initiative in the 1980s to reopen the question of BMD deployment or to amend the ABM Treaty is highly unlikely. As indicated in chapter 5, despite the strong continuing efforts in research and development in the USSR, the Soviet leaders see no prospect of improving their relative military position by launching a competition in BMD deployments. The same considerations that over-rode the traditional Soviet proclivity for coupling strong strategic defen-ses with strong offensive forces in the late 1960s, and that led to Soviet acceptance of the ABM Treaty in 1972, continue to hold today and almost certainly will for the foreseeable future as well. These consider-ations were based not only on recognition of possibly ephemeral U.S. advantages in BMD technology, but also on a new appreciation of the dynamics of the offensive-defensive arms interaction. Moreover, despite its continuing efforts over the past decade, Moscow—compared with the United States in terms of level of scientific-technological achieve-ment—has at best only redressed its previous shortcomings. While any new "race" in BMD deployment would see an initial Soviet advantage in ability to field a marginal operational BMD system, it could not yield a significant strategic advantage and might serve only to unleash superior U.S. scientific-technological potential. In short, the Soviet military and political leaders see more danger than promise in reopening a competition in BMD deployment. Similar considerations with respect to the overall strategic relationship promote a serious Soviet interest in strategic offensive arms limitations as well, but because the problems are complex, to date only minimal and precarious restraints have been agreed upon. In the realm of strategic BMD, while the Soviet Union continues its efforts to remain abreast of the state of the art, it wishes to maintain the established severe limitations.

Soviet defense requirements against nuclear powers other than the United States were a factor in the original Soviet decision in 1969 to accept limitations on BMD deployment, but they were overridden then by other military and political considerations. Despite the rising capa-bilities of other potential nuclear adversaries, especially China, the

Soviet leaders continue to pursue a variety of political, diplomatic, and military measures to reduce the threat from such powers. This consideration weighs heavily against giving up the Moscow BMD deployment, and in favor of modernizing it and improving its capabilities within the limits of the ABM Treaty; it does not, however, outweigh the disadvantages of reopening an all-out BMD competition with the United States.

Political considerations complement these conclusions on the net military advantage of maintaining the ABM Treaty. Arms control as a political, as well as a military, instrument leads the Soviet leaders to wish to preserve the ABM Treaty—and, by extension, not to tamper with it for possible marginal changes even if limited amendments of interest to the Soviet Union were conceived. There would be too great a risk that the United States would use such an opportunity to kill the ABM Treaty while avoiding the costs of having reopened the issue. Finally, the ABM Treaty is regarded in Moscow as a symbol of past and possible future détente with the United States, and this is considered by the Soviet leaders to be an important additional reason for maintaining it. In short, the Soviet Union is highly unlikely to take any initiative to amend, abrogate, or violate the ABM Treaty.

It is, therefore, far more likely that further general statements of direction and purpose, such as those made by President Ronald Reagan on March 23, 1983, and any concrete proposal for amending the 1972 ABM Treaty would all come from the United States. The purported aim of any proposal would be relevant, but not necessarily central. Whatever the concrete terms, it would undoubtedly be described by its advocates as serving purposes of greater stability (or deterrence)—and it would undoubtedly be scrutinized for other objectives, or in any case other effects on the military balance and stability, by the Soviet Union and others.

Real progress in other areas of arms control, especially a strategic arms reduction or INF agreement, would provide a more receptive climate than the present situation, where the most recent U.S. action has been the decision not to ratify the SALT II Treaty. Merely proposing arms reductions, as the United States has done since 1981, has gained some time from European public opinion and may suffice to ensure at least the start of the NATO INF deployment, but even if effective for that purpose, the transparently nonnegotiable arms reductions proposals advanced to date are less and less credible as signs of real interest by the U.S. administration in reaching agreements.

Any U.S. proposal for modifying the ABM Treaty would, under these prevailing circumstances, be seen by many in the West as endangering the treaty and possibilities for further arms control—as well as prospects for revived détente. The terms of the proposed modifications would probably have only marginal influence. A proposal for renegotiation that expressed a readiness to maintain the treaty unless there were agreement on amendments would considerably soften adverse reaction. Such a position is, however, unlikely. It would be perceived as undercutting bargaining leverage; moreover, a decision to propose amendments would probably (although not necessarily) only be made if the administration had decided to go ahead on a BMD course even in the absence of Soviet acceptance of an amended treaty.

The one thing that *would* importantly affect the Western reaction, and could defuse much opposition, would be a receptive Soviet reaction. Arms control and détente then, for most people, would not seem to be threatened. Such a Soviet reaction, however, is highly unlikely. Even if the Soviet Union at some point wished to modify or even to abandon the treaty, it would probably let the United States take the heat for proposing changes and endangering the treaty, the constraints of which it could then escape, or which it could later take credit for "rescuing" if agreement could be found on modifications acceptable to it.

From this broad overview of the context of East-West relations today, and the crucial significance of any initiative to reopen the issue of BMD deployment, it is useful to turn briefly to the relevant recent history before considering the future.

Western Alliance Perspectives

Apart from the general reactions based on beliefs about the negative impact on East-West relations of reopening BMD issues, more concrete interests and concerns within the Western Alliance would be based on political, military, and deterrence considerations. A useful way to understand these interests and concerns is to look back at the experience of the late 1960s.

On September 18, 1967, Secretary of Defense Robert S. McNamara delivered a speech in which he set forth at length prevailing U.S. views on deterrence and strategy. He described the "action-reaction" interplay of offensive and defensive arms, and a "mad momentum" in the pressures of the arms race to deploy new technologies and weapons.

And he argued strongly against any attempt to create a defense against Soviet ballistic missile attack. He again urged strategic arms limitation talks (SALT), but said that even if such negotiations should not lead to agreed limitations, any U.S. or Soviet attempts to create BMD would be "foolish" and could not succeed. Only after eloquently and forcefully arguing against the value of BMD—and, indeed, stressing its harm and dangers owing to "the action-reaction phenomenon"—did McNamara conclude his speech by announcing the decision to deploy a "light" ABM defense not against Soviet attack on the United States, but against a prospective small Chinese strategic ballistic missile capability in the early and mid-1970s. He also noted that such a "Chinese-oriented ABM deployment would enable us to add—as a concurrent benefit—a further defense of our Minuteman [ICBM] sites against Soviet attack," and "protection of our population against the improbable but possible accidental launch of an intercontinental missile by any of the nuclear powers." The planned ABM deployment was called the Sentinel system.[1]

A host of alliance concerns promptly emerged: (1) the absence of consultation; (2) an avowed anti-China orientation of the system; (3) suspicions that the anti-China rationale was a pretext for an eventual defense against Soviet missiles; (4) political concerns about the implications of defense of the United States but not of Western Europe; (5) uncertainty as to public reactions in Europe; and (6) concern about the effects on deterrence.[2]

The first indication of a contingent U.S. decision to deploy an ABM defense had in fact been made in early 1967. In his budget message on January 24, 1967, President Lyndon B. Johnson had included a request for $375 million funding for an ABM, but said he would "take no action now to deploy an antiballistic missile defense." He also stated his intention to "initiate discussions with the Soviet Union on the limitation

1. "Text of McNamara Speech on Anti-China Missile Defense and U.S. Nuclear Strategy," *New York Times*, September 19, 1967. See also an interview with McNamara that repeated his main arguments, but with greater stress on defense of ICBM silos— which also disturbed our allies. Richard B. Stalley, "Defense Fantasy Come True," *Life* (September 29, 1967).

2. See Lawrence W. Martin, *Ballistic Missile Defence and the Alliance* (Boulogne-sur-Seine, France: Atlantic Institute, 1969); David S. Yost, "Ballistic Missile Defense and the Atlantic Alliance," *International Security*, vol. 7 (Fall 1982), pp. 144–46; and Lawrence Freedman, "Europe and the ABM Revival," *Arms Control*, vol. 3 (September 1982), pp. 75–77.

of ABM deployments."³ In fact, these confidential discussions were already under way. And on March 2, 1967, the president announced that the Soviet leaders had "confirmed the willingness of the Soviet government to discuss means of limiting the arms race in offensive and defensive nuclear missiles."⁴ There had been no advance consultations with or even relaying of information to our allies before these announcements.⁵

Consultation began with a meeting of the permanent representatives of the North Atlantic Council and a special experts meeting in early March 1967. The focus of these consultations, and of allied interest, was on the proposed strategic arms limitation talks with the Soviet Union, rather than on possible U.S. deployment. The consultations with leading experts from the State and Defense departments and the Arms Control and Disarmament Agency did, however, address the strategic relationship and military technological prospects (including, inadvertently, the first official disclosure and description of the U.S. MIRV program!).⁶ SALT did not, however, begin.

In April, at the first meeting of the new Nuclear Planning Group (NPG) of selected NATO defense ministers, Secretary McNamara reported on the efforts made to begin talks and reiterated the promise to keep the allies fully advised on the subject. The NPG defense ministers also discussed the technical and strategic (and financial) aspects of BMD and agreed to keep this subject under review. A study was begun on ABM issues, including those involved in possible ABM defense in Europe. There was, however, no subsequent advance consultation before the

3. "The President's Message to the Congress Transmitting the Budget for Fiscal Year 1968, January 24, 1967," *Weekly Compilation of Presidential Documents,* vol. 3 (Government Printing Office, 1967), p. 89. In his State of the Union Message on January 10, President Johnson had mentioned the start of placement of "a limited antimissile defense" around Moscow, and the need for arms control, but he had not then referred to possible U.S. arms limitation or deployment decisions, although both had been taken. Ibid., p. 35.

4. "The President's News Conference of March 2, 1967," *Weekly Compilation of Presidential Documents,* vol. 3 (GPO, 1967), p. 353.

5. The president had, however, in his announcement of March 2 referred to an expectation of "further discussions of this subject in Moscow and with our allies" (ibid.), thus publicly flagging our intention to consult with our allies. The Soviet leaders had, of course, been advised that the president planned to announce their readiness for talks, although they were not provided the exact text.

6. This account is based on the author's participation as the Department of State representative at the NAC and Experts meetings, March 7–8, 1967.

sudden U.S. announcement in September concerning ABM deployment.[7]

Following an outcry at the second NPG meeting in late September over the absence of consultation, the study of ABM issues being carried out under the auspices of the NPG became more active and led to a final report in April 1968.[8] In this study, the effects of various U.S.—and Soviet—ABM deployments and also of possible European NATO ABM deployment were examined.

The NPG study concluded that the reasons leading the United States to deploy a "light" ABM defense against China were not relevant to European defense. Moreover, no feasible ABM defense for Western Europe could prevent the Soviet Union from "inflicting catastrophic damage" on NATO Europe. In addition, it was recognized explicitly that European ABM deployment (by NATO or by European members of NATO) could have significant adverse political implications for East-West relations. The conclusion was that in the light of the current (and foreseeable) technological circumstances, the deployment of ABMs in NATO Europe was not "politically, militarily or financially warranted."[9] Perhaps the most important result of the consultation was that the European NATO members had the opportunity, with a forthcoming but not directing U.S. participation, to reach their own decisions.

The NPG study also concluded, admittedly in some deference to a U.S. decision already made and announced, that U.S. and Soviet ABM deployments, provided they remained "light," need not affect adversely either the military balance or political relations and arms control.[10] The

---

7. Although not disclosed publicly or to our allies, the United States had informed the Soviet leaders in advance of the McNamara speech in September also renewing the proposal for SALT.

8. The following account is based on the author's participation in the NPG Staff Group study of ABM issues in 1967–68. The study was submitted to the NPG from the North Atlantic Council on March 26, and approved by the NPG on April 19, 1968. See also Paul Buteux, *The Politics of Nuclear Consultation in NATO, 1965–1980* (Cambridge University Press, 1983).

9. There was concern that the major costs involved would draw European resources away from other defense needs, a concern shared by both the European and U.S. participants. It was also recognized that both serious political issues (predelegation of authority to fire) and resource problems would be posed by command-and-control requirements for such a system.

10. A "heavy" deployment, on the other hand, was expected to stimulate pressures for an ABM in NATO Europe, or resentment if NATO Europe had none.

study, and the NPG ministers in April, also urged that U.S. efforts to negotiate limits on strategic defensive and offensive arms be continued.

The anti-China orientation of Sentinel was both perplexing and troubling to the Europeans. An anti-China rationale for BMD deployment had not figured in the March and April consultations. Many saw in it another example of a long-standing U.S. obsession with China, which had contributed to U.S. overinvolvement in Vietnam. Others, correctly suspicious of the genuineness of the anti-China rationale, incorrectly saw it as screening a desire to build a base for a "heavy" anti-Soviet ABM defense.[11] In fact, it was neither; it was a device by McNamara, to whom President Johnson had given authority to use any rationale he wanted in meeting what the president saw (probably incorrectly) as growing congressional and public pressure for ABM deployment. McNamara, despite State Department efforts to tone down the anti-China rationale, instead raised it to the fore precisely as a foil to support his strong *opposition* to a heavy, anti-Soviet ABM deployment.[12] There were those in the U.S. Army, the Joint Chiefs of Staff, and elsewhere in the U.S. government in 1967–68 who did hope later to build the thin nationwide Sentinel deployment into a heavy anti-Soviet one[13]—and it was to counter this pressure that McNamara had been led to his anti-China rationale.[14]

The most elusive considerations concerned the impact of ABM deployment in the United States on deterrence of the Soviet Union and on implementation of the NATO strategic concept. NATO had but recently formally adopted the concept of flexible response. Would U.S.—and Soviet—ABM deployment enhance the credibility of extended deterrence by making the U.S. strategic forces more secure, or would it reduce deterrence by dividing undefended Europe from a defended United States facing a defended Soviet Union? The question was not posed so sharply, of course, in part because the United States

11. See the accounts by Martin, *Ballistic Missile Defence and the Alliance*, p. 31; and Freedman, "Europe and the ABM Revival," p. 75.

12. This is based on the author's involvement as a representative of the Department of State in work on the subject, which included reviewing the draft of McNamara's speech.

13. See chapter 9 herein.

14. For a very useful account of the whole decision and surrounding bureaucratic byplay by a participant in the Defense Department at the time, see Morton H. Halperin, "The Decision to Deploy the ABM: Bureaucratic and Domestic Politics in the Johnson Administration," *World Politics*, vol. 25 (October 1972), pp. 62–95.

was stressing that it would not be seeking or obtaining defense against all-out Soviet missile attack. But there was also a European concern over what some regarded as a greater U.S. concern with waging war, rather than with deterrence.[15]

The U.S. reorientation of its ABM defense deployment plan from a thin nationwide anti-China deployment (Sentinel) to a concentrated defense of ICBM forces (Safeguard) in March 1969 should have posed these questions about the effects of BMD on deterrence more sharply, but it did not.

The initiation of strategic arms limitation talks in 1969, and the eventual success of those negotiations with respect to BMD in the ABM Treaty of 1972, did have a major impact, both on alliance views of the military balance and on expectations of improving East-West relations. The ABM Treaty was seen as a major step toward stabilizing the strategic arms race and removing any questions of differentiation in vulnerability between NATO Europe and the United States. Furthermore, the ABM Treaty was not an isolated phenomenon; it came as the United States and the Soviet Union launched a wide-ranging détente, removing the previous discrepancy between a developing East-West détente in Europe and a lingering U.S.-Soviet confrontation.

After the somewhat ragged start in 1967, U.S. consultation with its NATO allies (and a few other close allies) during SALT was exemplary. From January 1969 through June 1972 there were forty-five meetings or formal communications describing the course of the negotiations, including twenty-two meetings of the North Atlantic Council Permanent Representatives in Brussels attended by senior members of the SALT negotiating delegation. Moreover, issues of particular concern to the NATO allies were discussed and decided in accordance with the consultations. Most issues, by the way, concerned the negotiations on strategic offensive limitations. In addition, the earlier NPG study of the ABM question played a major part in averting what might otherwise have been more confused and complicating questions with respect to

---

15. Martin, *Ballistic Missile Defence and the Alliance*, pp. 29–36. See also Johan J. Holst, "Missile Defense: Implications for Europe," in Johan J. Holst and William Schneider, Jr., eds., *Why ABM? Policy Issues in the Missile Defense Controversy* (Pergamon, 1969), esp. pp. 190, 196; and Theodore C. Sorenson, "The ABM and Western Europe," in Abram Chayes and Jerome B. Wiesner, eds., *ABM: An Evaluation of the Decision to Deploy an Antiballistic Missile System* (Harper and Row, 1969), pp. 179–83.

the ABM issues in SALT I. The value of having made this joint study, apart from the proprieties of consultation, thus proved considerable.

Steps toward BMD deployment in1967–69 particularly concerned Britain and France because of their small national strategic establishments.[16] The ABM Treaty was quite a boon to the French and British strategic forces.[17] By limiting Soviet ABM defenses to Moscow, and to a level of not more than 100 interceptor launchers, the credibility of the separate national deterrents was greatly enhanced. This factor continues to give both Britain and France a strong stake in keeping the ABM Treaty as it is.

Soviet Perspectives

Notwithstanding traditional and continuing Soviet interests in defense of their homeland, the Soviet leaders by 1969 had decided to accept limitations on BMD deployment. The ABM Treaty of 1972, of indefinite duration, was a product of a Soviet as well as a U.S. desire to curb strategic defenses that could have placed deterrence in question through challenging strategic offensive missile forces. The Soviet Union was even prepared to consider giving up its Moscow defense altogether (although not without appropriate compensation), but the possibility of negotiating a "zero ABM" agreement was prejudiced by an early U.S. proposal, and prompt Soviet acceptance, of a limitation to ABM defense of the National Command Authorities (NCA) in the national capitals.

Soviet acceptance of sharply constrained BMD was certainly facilitated by the fact that the United States had a much superior BMD defense technology and thus capabilities for an important lead in BMD

---

16. See chapter 7 herein.

17. The U.S. decision early in the negotiations to propose limiting ABM deployments to the national capitals was in fact made with little attention to how this would affect the British and French forces. The interests of these allies would of course have been best served by a complete ban on ABM deployments, and this argument for such a position (among others) was raised by the advocates of a complete ABM ban in the Department of State and the ACDA. The decisions in the White House were, however, driven by other considerations. For a summary of the evolving negotiating positions on ABM limitations, see Raymond L. Garthoff, "Negotiating with the Russians: Some Lessons from SALT," *International Security*, vol. 1 (Spring 1977), pp. 10–13. A fuller account can be found in Gerard Smith, *Doubletalk: The Story of the First Strategic Arms Limitation Talks* (Doubleday, 1980).

deployment in the 1970s.[18] That may even have been an important factor contributing to the Soviet decision, but it was not the only one. The ABM Treaty and continuing negotiation on limitations on strategic offensive systems in SALT were also the result of a serious and active new interest (not universally shared in the Soviet military establishment) in arms control as an important element in political-military strategy.

Soviet détente policy in the 1970s also included as an important element the establishment of parity with the United States. The U.S. acknowledgment of strategic parity, reflected in SALT, was part of a broader Soviet objective to gain political parity. The ABM Treaty was seen as a key contribution toward stabilizing a strategic deterrent balance. Efforts to reach an effective limitation on strategic offensive forces were much less successful, principally because the issues were more intractable.

The ABM Treaty was thus valued by the Soviet leaders not only because it foreclosed a U.S. BMD deployment that could have shored up U.S. superiority in the strategic balance for a while longer, but also because it contributed, they felt, to Soviet control over the strategic offense-defense interaction. As offensive limitations proved more elusive in the late 1970s and early 1980s, the ABM Treaty also stood as a remaining restraint on an unbridled strategic arms race and as a symbol of resolve and early achievement in joint efforts at restraint. As other ventures in détente with the United States were abandoned, the ABM Treaty also acquired for the Soviet leaders something of the symbolic significance attributed to it by adherents of détente in the West. It has consistently been accorded such treatment in Soviet commentary, including statements by the Soviet leaders.

This is a considered assessment of the Soviet political and strategic interests underlying Soviet attitudes toward BMD. It is not, however, an assessment that is prevalent in the West at this time. Western, and especially U.S., views have tended to fluctuate widely, more because of hopes and fears than because of analysis of the data bearing on Soviet views. Thus, in the late 1960s and early 1970s there was both suspicion of Soviet political and military designs and substantial doubt as to the likelihood of Soviet agreement to limit BMD. Then, during the heyday of détente and in the wake of the ABM Treaty, from 1972 until 1976, it was widely believed that the Soviet Union had joined the United States

18. See chapter 5 herein.

in subscribing to a doctrine of mutual assured destruction (MAD) and had more generally espoused a policy of détente significantly mitigating the East-West competition and confrontation. Finally, a sharp shift of view took place in the late 1970s and became dominant after the Soviet occupation of Afghanistan at the very end of the decade. This change has reflected suspicions of the reasons behind what has widely been perceived to be a relentless Soviet military buildup, as well as apparent Soviet readiness to use its growing military power as a shield behind which to advance in the world by diplomatic pressures, and by support for and manipulation of "national liberation struggles," including use of "proxy" forces (the Cubans and Vietnamese, in particular) and even Soviet military forces (in Afghanistan). Assumptions as to Soviet interest in arms control have tended to vary with the perceptions of Soviet investment in military power and expectations as to Soviet readiness to use that power. U.S. views of Soviet positions on BMD have tended to be derivative of these broader shifts of attitude—from doubt to hope buoyed by détente, and then to fear spurred by disillusion in détente.

In fact, while Soviet attitudes, expectations, military doctrine, and political action have changed over time in significant ways, the actual development has borne little resemblance to the caricature in fluctuating popular—and for that matter official—views. It would not be possible in the scope of this discussion to deal with the broader flow of Soviet policy, but we do need to examine in some detail changing views on BMD in order to evaluate the impact of future changes on the status of BMD. And to do so we must begin with the change in Soviet political and military thinking that led to the Soviet acceptance, and indeed espousal, of the ABM Treaty.

Soviet military doctrine, as conceived by the Soviet military and political leaders, has two levels or aspects: the governing political or political-military level, and the so-called military-technical level.[19] The former represents state policy and is established by the leadership of the Communist party. The latter is the province of the professional military leadership; it is based upon military science and is elaborated in military strategy. The military-technical level is subordinate to the political level, which establishes the aims and allocates the resources that the military leadership then manages. Military strategy is an arm of political strategy;

19. For example, see "Military Doctrine," *Sovetskaya voyennaya entsiklopediya* (The Soviet Military Encyclopedia), vol. 3 (Moscow: Voyennoye ministerstvo, 1977), p. 229.

military policy is a component of national policy. This is scarcely a unique Soviet conception; to the extent that the U.S. approach and practice differ, it is actually the Soviet conception and practice that are closer to the modern historical norm and are identified with the classical descriptions and prescriptions of Karl von Clausewitz and others.

Soviet military doctrine readily assimilated the technological prospects for BMD. Indeed, to the extent that Soviet military doctrine had a bias, it was to emphasize the importance of strategic defense, rather than to rely upon a strategic offensive capability for deterrence as the United States has done. BMD was thus pressed by the Soviet leaders, just as strategic air defense had been ever since the 1950s.[20] So Soviet efforts were carried forward with the only modestly effective Galosh ABM deployment around Moscow in the mid- to late-1960s.[21] These efforts were not affected by the ouster of Nikita S. Khrushchev in 1964, although bluster and bluff in claims of military capability were sharply curtailed. Although Khrushchev had claimed that the Soviet Union had developed an ABM missile that could "hit a fly in outer space,"[22] such flamboyant claims were dropped by the political and top military leadership; however, some of the Soviet military leaders (particularly those charged with strategic defense) did continue until the late 1960s to claim a growing capacity to fulfill the BMD mission.

Soviet military doctrine also developed a strategic defensive concept for the use of the growing Soviet offensive forces. As military thinking was permitted to surmount the confines of an artificially delimited "Stalinist military science" in the mid-1950s after the dictator's demise, one important development was a belated acknowledgment of the greatly increased importance of strategic surprise in the nuclear age. Coupled with this development was articulation (in 1955) of the concept of a Soviet "preemptive strike" *if* the United States were to attack. A

20. For example, in the mid-1950s the Soviet Union spent $1 billion in then current value to deploy a massive but only marginally effective surface-to-air missile defense (based on the SA-1 missile) around Moscow and Moscow alone.

21. See chapter 5 herein. As noted there, the earliest deployment was begun with the Griffon system around Leningrad in the early 1960s, but that incomplete deployment was abandoned.

22. See Theodore Shabad, "Khrushchev Says Missile Can 'Hit a Fly' in Space," *New York Times*, July 17, 1962. Marshal Rodion Malinovsky, the minister of defense, had made the first comprehensive claim some months earlier, stating more carefully: "the *problem* of destroying ballistic missiles in flight has been successfully solved." *Pravda*, October 25, 1961 (emphasis added).

preemptive strike was not a euphemism for a preventive or deliberate first strike. The concept was set forth in the confidential pages of the General Staff journal (where it appeared only after intervention and approval by Minister of Defense Georgy Zhukov) and was explicitly distinguished from a preventive strike, which was rejected as a Soviet option. The concept of a preemptive (literally, "forestalling"; in Russian, *uprezhdaiushchyi*) strike was to deny the enemy the fruits of successful surprise by launching the Soviet offensive force before it was struck— and, if possible, in time to strike all or part of the enemy offensive forces before they were launched. It was, in short, an operational concept for force employment under certain very limited circumstances: enemy initiative in deciding to attack and sufficient Soviet warning to permit above all preemptive salvage and use of its own striking force and, if possible, also preemptive decimation of the enemy strike force. It was a damage-limiting and retaliatory measure to be employed, if possible, at a time of attack chosen by the enemy.[23]

This is the only kind of preemptive action ever endorsed in Soviet military literature—and explicitly only in the confidential General Staff journal in the 1950s. After all, not even the first tests of strategic missiles had yet taken place in 1955, and the bomber force was just reaching its stride. Warning and response, even preemptive response, against bombers using foreign bases and refueling were not so unfeasible in the 1950s. The coming of a missile age was, however, foreseen.[24]

The Soviet concept of preemption has *not* been the determinant for the size, capabilities, or posture of the Soviet strategic force; it is a possible defensive resort to deny the enemy success in a first strike and would thus be a mode of response to ensure retaliation and to blunt the attack at the time of the enemy's decision to attack.[25] It is, in short, an

23. The initial, and most complete, exposition of this Soviet concept was by Marshal Pavel Rotmistrov. In his words, "The duty of the Soviet armed forces is to not permit a surprise attack by an enemy on our country, and *in case an attempt is made,* not only to repulse the attack successfully, but also *to deal to the enemy simultaneous or even preemptive surprise strikes of terrible crushing power."* Marshal P. Rotmistrov, "On the Role of Surprise in Contemporary War," *Voyennaya mysl'* (Military Thought), no. 2 (February 1955), p. 20 (emphasis added).

24. The most complete review of the Soviet writings on surprise and preemption in the 1950s, with extensive direct quotations, is in Raymond L. Garthoff, *The Soviet Image of Future War* (Public Affairs Press, 1959), pp. 60–85.

25. For example, Marshal Rotmistrov, in his seminal discussion, made clear he was referring only to "preemptive (or forestalling) *actions,"* and stated explicitly that the Soviet armed forces "have everything that is necessary for this." Rotmistrov, "On the Role of Surprise in Contemporary War," p. 20.

alternative to BMD for the purpose of preserving strategic offensive retaliatory forces.[26]

Counterforce capabilities for preemption, as a factor in establishing force goals and affecting force procurement, clearly have played a more important role in U.S. defense planning than in Soviet defense programming and planning. This was true even during the years in which the United States openly advocated a doctrine of mutual assured destruction in the 1960s. Defensive *damage limitation* became a lesser factor in U.S. defense programming after the mid-1960s, whereas in the Soviet Union it did not. Hence the much greater continuing Soviet efforts in strategic air defense, civil defense, and for a time BMD.

Soviet research on BMD began in the 1950s with Soviet military technologists investigating the possibilities of BMD, and it paralleled the early development of long-range offensive ballistic missiles.[27] Soviet discussions of BMD in the early 1960s continued to note the offense-defense interacting cycle and to assume BMD would develop—by 1962–63 the Soviet Union was claiming a lead but also stressing that BMD was "exceptionally expensive."[28]

In at least one case, a prominent Soviet scientist, Academician Pyotr Kapitsa, noted as early as 1956 that the eventual advent of ABMs as well

26. Regrettably, there has been a great deal of confusion and, frankly, misrepresentation of the Soviet concept of preemption in U.S. writings. It is pertinent to recall that the United States, too, had articulated a confidential national policy of preemption, but not preventive war, in the 1950s—as the Soviet Union either knew or (correctly) suspected. Thus NSC-68, adopted in 1950 as the basic U.S. political and military guidance for pursuit of the cold war, while rejecting "preventive war" (after a cool balancing of pros and cons), went on to state: "The military advantages of landing the first blow become increasingly important with modern weapons, and this is a fact which requires us to be on the alert in order to strike with our full weight as soon as we are attacked, *and, if possible, before the Soviet blow is actually delivered.*" See *Foreign Relations of the United States, 1950; National Security Affairs; Foreign Economic Policy,* vol. 1, H. Doc. 82-264, 82 Cong. 1 sess. (GPO, 1977), p. 282; italics added. See also David Alan Rosenberg, "The Origins of Overkill: Nuclear Weapons and American Strategy, 1945–1960," *International Security,* vol. 7 (Spring 1983), pp. 3–71.

27. For example, see the discussion in 1957 by Maj. Gen. G. I. Pokrovsky, a notable military technologist, in Pokrovsky, *Science and Technology in Contemporary War,* trans. and annot. Raymond L. Garthoff (Praeger, 1959), pp. 178–79.

28. For example, see M. N. Nikolayev, *Snaryad protiv snaryada* (Missile against Missile) (Moscow: Voyenizdat, 1960), pp. 145–46; and a retitled revision, M. N. Nikolayev, *Raketa protiv rakety* (Ballistic Missile against Ballistic Missile) (Moscow: Voyenizdat, 1963), pp. 195–96. See also M. N. Goncharenko, *Rakety i problema antiraket* (Ballistic Missiles and the Problem of Anti-Ballistic Missiles) (Moscow: DOSAAF, 1962). For a political reference to a Soviet lead, see General A. Yepishev, "Guarding the Peaceful Labor of the Soviet People," *Politicheskoye samoobrazovaniye* (Political Self-Education), vol. 7 (January 1963), p. 18.

as long-range ballistic missiles would pose new challenges to disarmament.[29] He therefore called for including BMD along with nuclear weapons and delivery systems in general disarmament. And in a suggestion never further pursued, he called for an "obligatory exchange of information concerning experimental work on defense measures" such as BMD.[30] But this was one man's statement, and a Soviet disarmament or arms control "line" on BMD was not developed until later.

In the mid-1960s, an important Soviet military theoretician assigned to study problems in the disarmament field developed an arms control doctrine pertaining to BMD. The author of this approach was retired Major General Nikolai Talensky, who had held important positions on the General Staff concerned with the elaboration of military doctrine.[31]

General Talensky set forth his views in 1964 in an article on antiballistic missile systems and disarmament.[32] He stressed the interaction between offensive and defensive weapons. Nonetheless, he argued that ABM systems are "defensive weapons in the full sense of the word," because by their very nature they go into action only when an attacker has already launched his attack. He also noted international political advantages that would arise because there would be "no difficulty at all in deciding who is the aggressor and who the attacked."[33]

Talensky recognized "the Western objection" to ABM because such defenses "upset the mutual deterrence based on the threat of a nuclear strike." But, he argued, an aggressive state may pursue policies that increase the risk of war whether it has BMD or not, so "the creation of an effective antimissile defense system by a country which is a potential

29. See Pyotr Kapitsa, "Scientists' Views on Preventing Atomic War: The Paramount Task," *New Times* (Moscow), no. 39 (September 1956), p. 11.

30. Ibid., p. 11.

31. General Talensky was editor of the classifed General Staff journal *Voyennaya mysl'* in the mid-1950s, and after Stalin's death personally led the first round of revivification of military doctrine in 1953–54. He also served as chief of the Military Historical Division of the Main Military Science Directorate of the General Staff. After retiring from active duty in 1960, he served as the arms control and disarmament liaison between the Ministry of Defense and the Academy of Sciences of the USSR and its institutes up to his death in 1967.

32. Dr. Sc. (Mil.) N. Talensky, "Anti-Missile Systems and Disarmament," *International Affairs* (Moscow), no. 10 (October 1964), pp. 15–19. (The title, in the original Russian, was *protivo-raketnye sistemy,* "antirocket" or "antiballistic missile" systems, and I have so rendered it in the text above; the English-language version of the journal is cited here for the reader's convenience.)

33. Ibid., p. 16. This passage also appears to represent an indirect criticism of the concept of a preemptive strike.

target for aggression merely serves to increase the deterrent effect [of its retaliatory forces] and so helps to avert aggression."[34] Talensky acknowledged the argument that "the international strategic situation cannot be stable where both sides simultaneously strive toward deterrence through nuclear missiles forces and the creation of defensive antimissile systems." But he rejected that argument: "From the standpoint of strategy, powerful deterrent forces and an effective antimissile defence system, when taken together, substantially increase the stability of mutual deterrence."[35]

General Talensky's final argument was that "the creation of an effective antimissile system enables the state to make its defences dependent chiefly on its own possibilities, and not only on mutual deterrence, that is, on the goodwill of the other side."[36]

Talensky argued for disarmament as the "one reasonable alternative to a race in antimissile systems." But in the meantime his prescription was clear and strong: "The Soviet state, its government and people have a vital stake in creating a reliable defence system" and should not "forgo the creation of its own effective systems of defence against nuclear missile aggression and make its security dependent only on deterrence."[37]

General Talensky's views on BMD and arms control are of interest because they were not challenged in the mid-1960s and because he was at that time an influential link between the Ministry of Defense and the civilian institutes and the Disarmament Committee of the Academy of Sciences of the USSR.[38]

34. Ibid., p. 17.
35. Ibid. This author has modified the translation of one particularly awkward phrase from "nuclear rocket power" to "nuclear missile forces," which more clearly renders the meaning. The present author personally argued this point with General Talensky in a private discussion five months before his article appeared, obviously to no avail. Later, in 1966, Talensky began to have doubts about his position, but he was never really convinced. He died in mid-1967, just as the Soviet leaders were deciding the issue.
36. Ibid., p. 18. In conversation on this point, Talensky readily acknowledged to this author that mutual deterrence depends on much more than "goodwill," but still stressed the element of dependence on the "intentions" and rational calculation by the other side. In this article he also stressed: "History has taught the Soviet Union to depend mainly on itself in ensuring its security and that of its friends."
37. Ibid., p. 19.
38. General Talensky's views were echoed as late as September 1967 in an "unofficial" paper presented at a Pugwash conference by Col. Gen. Anatoly A. Gryzlov, the Ministry of Defense/General Staff liaison with the Soviet Ministry of Foreign Affairs

The significant point is that when the U.S. proposal for BMD limitations was first being considered in Moscow, both military doctrine and "disarmament doctrine" favored BMD and other forms of active defense. However, the views on offensive systems were sharply divided: military doctrine called for very large forces, whereas Soviet disarmament theory, and proposals, called for very low offensive arms levels—in fact, a minimum deterrent "umbrella" (as had been proposed in the so-called Gromyko Plan in 1963)—on the way to "general and complete disarmament." There was also a growing divergence between the attitudes of the military (who recognized the offensive-defensive interaction) and the proponents of disarmament (who stressed sharply cutting offensive arms). Arms control had but a very limited place in Soviet considerations of basic force levels and was then seen mainly as applying to what later came to be called confidence-building measures.

When U.S. Ambassador Llewellyn Thompson told Soviet Ambassador Anatoly Dobrynin on December 6, 1966, that the United States wished to propose a serious discussion of mutually limiting ABM deployment, Dobrynin (and the Soviet government when apprised) reacted in a noncommittal but open way: What did the United States have in mind? In the earliest official exchanges of notes in January 1967, the *first* Soviet substantive position was to state that because of the action-reaction interplay of strategic offensive and defensive forces, both must be included in such discussions and limitations. The United States quickly agreed.[39]

The initial Soviet responses to the U.S. overtures in December 1966 and January 1967 were, in fact, based on a consideration of what the Soviet Union had *believed* to be a U.S. initiative a whole year earlier! When on December 6 Ambassador Thompson, fresh from President Johnson's Texas ranch, raised with Dobrynin the idea of a "mutual understanding" on limiting ABM systems, he was taken aback by Dobrynin's reply that the U.S. side had never responded to his statement the preceding March, under instructions, conveying the Soviet govern-

---

on disarmament matters. Gryzlov's paper defended the morality of ABMs in contrast to ICBMs, and he asked rhetorically, If the United States was so concerned about the Soviet ABM, why didn't it build its own ABM? That kind of argument dissolved when less than two weeks later the United States *did* announce an ABM deployment! General Gryzlov later served on the Soviet SALT delegation in 1969–71 in a minor role.

39. Based on the author's participation, as are other unreferenced details on SALT in this discussion. See also Raymond L. Garthoff, "SALT I: An Evaluation," *World Politics*, vol. 31 (October 1978), pp. 1–4.

ment's view that ABMs should be considered together with offensive systems. Moreover, he said that when Foreign Minister Andrei Gromyko had come to the United Nations that September he had asked Dobrynin about the matter, but that he had had to say that there had been no further word from the United States.[40] Dobrynin repeated the Soviet government's view that ABMs and offensive arms should be considered together.

The formal Soviet response on January 17 kept open the door for a retreat to the political defensive propaganda high ground of relating the whole matter to "general and complete disarmament." Such a line of retreat was considered necessary in case the United States attempted to impose a freeze on offensive forces at a time when it held a commanding superiority, or to demand politically and militarily intrusive on-site inspection as a condition.

When the first inkling of these exchanges reached the press, Prime Minister Aleksei N. Kosygin, away from Moscow on a trip in Western Europe, was asked by Western newsmen in London on February 9 about the Soviet view of limiting ABM defenses. Without special briefing and off-the-cuff, he replied, according to the *Pravda* account: "I think that a defensive system which prevents attack is not a cause of the arms race. . . . Perhaps an antimissile system is more expensive than an offensive system; but its purpose is not to kill people, but to save human lives."[41] Kosygin did not state a Soviet position on the question of negotiations. (In fact, a recording of the actual exchange showed that what he had really said was that a defensive system was "not a *factor in*," rather than "not a *cause of*" the arms race; that an ABM system was

40. In fact, the matter had first been raised by William C. Foster, director of the ACDA, in a meeting with Dobrynin on January 21, 1966, in which Foster expressed a personal interest in limiting the arms race by freezing ABM deployment before it began. Dobrynin had taken this to be an official probe, and on instructions had replied on March 17. Foster had immediately brought this to Secretary of State Dean Rusk's attention, and Rusk had mentioned it to Dobrynin when he happened to see him the very next day—saying we would be happy to discuss limitations of ABMs *and* ICBMs. Dobrynin said his government would be very interested. And there the matter died— Dobrynin and the Soviet government waiting for a new approach from Rusk or Foster, while Rusk did not realize the ball was in our court, and Foster had no instructions. Ambassador Thompson was unaware of the earlier exchanges, Rusk did not recall them, and Foster was not consulted, when President Johnson responded to McNamara's proposal for talks with the Soviet Union by authorizing the State Department to raise the matter with the Russians. This is a rather interesting, and previously undisclosed, wrinkle in the initiation of SALT, if not a model of policy management.

41. *Pravda*, February 11, 1967.

"probably," rather than "perhaps," more expensive; and he did not make the oft-quoted comment about the purpose being to save lives *at all*—rather, he said, "these questions [relative *costs* of offensive and defensive systems] are not related to each other"!)[42] Kosygin's London remarks had been poorly translated, but that translation was widely reported in the Western press and even in a partially revised (not fully corrected) version in the Soviet press. Kosygin's comments, as reported, were widely interpreted in the West not only as an endorsement of BMD, but also as an indirect rejection of the U.S. proposal for ABM limitation talks.[43]

Indications of possible disagreement, or at least of an unsettled view, within the Soviet leadership soon arose. In an article in *Pravda* on February 15, *Pravda*'s well-connected political observer, Fedor Burlatsky, cited Kosygin as having said in London that "the Soviet government is ready to discuss the question of the prevention of a further arms race both in the fields of offensive and defensive arms."[44] In fact, Kosygin had neither expressed Soviet readiness to hold such talks, nor rejected them (as much Western press speculation had interpreted his reported remarks in London). Members of the Western press corps in Moscow reported this article as indicating a "shift" in the Soviet position toward strategic arms limitation talks.[45]

A highly unusual thing then happened. A member of the Western press corps was told by a Soviet source, citing unnamed "high Soviet authorities," that the article in *Pravda* had been a "mistake" by the author, that there "was no change in the Kremlin's position" of opposition to such talks, that Burlatsky had been severely reprimanded, and that *Pravda* would soon run an article making the Soviet position clear.[46]

42. From a comparison with a recording of the actual interview by the London Voice of America representative. A British translator made the original errors (including errors in the translation of questions); *Pravda* did not correct the translation of questions *and* kept a revised version of the *mis*translation of Kosygin's reply on saving lives! It changed Kosygin's answers to more tentative comments on the relative cost of ABM systems. Most significant (if less striking) was *Pravda's* implicit acceptance of defensive systems as being a "factor" in the arms race, revising Kosygin to state only that it was not the "*cause*" of the arms race. The discrepancies did not become publicly known.

43. For example, see Dana Adams Schmidt, "Kosygin Is Cool to Missiles Curb," *New York Times,* February 10, 1967.

44. F. Burlatsky, *Pravda,* February 15, 1967.

45. For example, see "Soviet Hints Shift on a Missile Pact," *New York Times,* February 16, 1967.

46. AP and Reuters wireless files, February 17, 1967. See also "Soviet ABM Shift Denied," *Washington Post,* February 18, 1967.

The Soviet source also stressed the emphasis in Soviet military doctrine on defense, and the distrust of Johnson and McNamara by the Soviet leadership. No correction, however, appeared in *Pravda*. And although Burlatsky had indeed attributed to Kosygin a view that he had not expressed in London, the article was no "mistake." In fact, it reflected accurately the confidential exchanges then in progress. A positive reply from the Soviet government, conditioned on including offensive arms as well as ABMs, had been received in Washington on January 17, and a letter from Kosygin to Johnson confirming Soviet interest and expressing satisfaction at the U.S. acceptance of inclusion of offensive arms was transmitted on February 27, just a week after Burlatsky's article had appeared. It was this letter that led to President Johnson's public announcement on March 2.

For present purposes it will suffice to note that the Soviet Union continued to agree in principle to holding talks on strategic offensive and defensive arms limitations through 1967 and the first half of 1968, without, however, agreeing on a concrete time and place. (The United States had indicated flexibility on time, place, and level of representation.) The most notable discussion occurred when Prime Minister Kosygin met President Johnson at Glassboro, New Jersey, in June, at which time Secretary McNamara gave a spirited pitch for strategic arms limitations, to which Kosygin did not reply. Kosygin did reiterate the view that antimissile systems, intended to defend against attack, should not be singled out for limitation, while leaving an offensive arms buildup. But Kosygin did not withdraw (or advance) the Soviet position, which was positive in principle, but still reserved on when the talks could begin.[47]

Substantive issues with respect to the Soviet position on BMD limitations were undoubtedly one important reason for the Soviet delay in beginning SALT discussions. They were not, however, the only reason and may not have been the main one. One other reason known to be important was the continuing, but decreasing, difference in levels of strategic offensive forces.[48] From the outset, the Soviet side showed

47. The least ill-informed of the several public accounts of the Glassboro meeting is in John Newhouse, *Cold Dawn: The Story of SALT* (Holt, Rinehart, and Winston, 1973), pp. 94–95. The present author was briefed by both U.S. and Soviet participants in the exchanges. See also "Transcript of the News Conference Held by Premier Kosygin at the United Nations," *New York Times*, June 26, 1967.

48. In January 1967 the United States had 2280 ICBM launchers, SLBM launchers, and heavy bombers to the USSR's 750 (1200 if other missile launchers under construction are included). By September 1968 when the Soviet Union had agreed to begin negotiations,

concern that the United States would propose a freeze, which would (if accepted in 1967 or 1968) have perpetuated the great U.S. superiority in strategic offensive forces. That proposition, needless to say, was unacceptable to the Soviet Union. Nor was it central to the U.S. interest at the time, which continued to be a sharp limit on ABM deployments. (It was, in fact, the undisclosed U.S. position on offensive limitations at that time.)

Clearly there was also a debate under way in the Soviet Union in 1966–67 with respect to doctrine, technological prospects, and strategic implications of ABM deployment or constraints on ABM deployment.[49] Some differences in public evaluation had antedated the U.S. initiative on ABM limitation (and on ABM deployment). In particular, Marshal Rodion Malinovsky, the minister of defense, had toned down earlier claims as early as April 1966, when he said that Soviet defenses could cope with "any enemy aircraft" and "many"—that is, not "all"— ballistic missiles.[50] But the U.S. initiative stirred up much more intense debate.

In 1967, as the Soviet leaders were making their decision on the proposal for SALT, Marshal Malinovsky, his deputy (and soon successor) Marshal Andrei Grechko, Deputy Minister and head of civil defense Marshal Vasily Chuikov, and Commander-in-Chief of the Strategic Missile Forces Marshal Nikolai Krylov, all stressed that BMD could not be made completely effective. Army General Pavel Batitsky, the new commander in chief of the Air Defense Forces, with operational respon-

---

the United States had 2275 to the USSR's 1650 (including those under construction). By November 1969 when talks actually began the totals were 2235 for the United States to 2035 for the USSR. For a more detailed review see Raymond L. Garthoff, "The Soviet Military and SALT," in Jiri Valenta and William Potter, eds., *Soviet Decision-making for Defense* (London: Allen and Unwin, forthcoming).

49. Several senior Soviet officials have privately referred to an unofficial meeting of U.S. and Soviet scientists interested in arms control and disarmament in December 1967 as especially useful and significant in influencing Soviet thinking away from the "Talensky doctrine" on BMD and arms control toward the "McNamara doctrine."

50. Marshal R. Ya. Malinovsky, *Pravda*, April 3, 1966. He clearly meant some would penetrate, not that BMD would be effective against certain classes of offensive ballistic missiles but not others. This statement was made to the Twenty-Third Congress of the CPSU.

Soon after, Marshal of Aviation Vladimir Sudets was removed as commander in chief of the Air Defense Forces. Although the reason for his replacement has not been established, he may have been removed because of a dispute over BMD. Sudets (in *Sovetskaya Rossiya*, April 19, 1966) had implied criticism of Soviet efforts in the field of BMD, with development but not yet operational deployment, as "insufficient."

sibility for BMD, in contrast went so far as to claim that Soviet BMD could "reliably protect the territory of the country against ballistic missile attack."[51] And Lieutenant General Ivan Zavyalov, a leading military theoretician, on March 3 wrote an article on Soviet military doctrine in which he affirmed the need for strong strategic defenses, including BMD, as well as strong offensive forces.[52]

Similar signs of differences among military leaders continued in 1968.[53] Then, in June 1968 Foreign Minister Gromyko formally announced to the Supreme Soviet that "the Soviet government is prepared for an exchange of views" seeking "an understanding on the mutual limitation and subsequent reduction of strategic nuclear delivery systems, offensive and defensive, including antiballistic missiles."[54] Even as Gromyko made this formal (if cautious) announcement of readiness to begin SALT talks, there were signs of continuing disagreement. For one, in that same address, Gromyko lambasted unidentified "sorry theoreticians" "who

51. Marshal R. Ya. Malinovsky, *Pravda*, February 23, 1967; Marshal A. A. Grechko, *Izvestiya*, February 22, 1967; Marshal V. I. Chuikov, Radio Moscow, in Foreign Broadcast Information Service, *Daily Report: Soviet Union*, February 23, 1967, p. CC11; Marshal N. I. Krylov, "The Strategic Rocket Forces," *Voyenno-istoricheskii zhurnal* (The Military-Historical Journal), no. 7 (July 1967), p. 20; and Army General P. F. Batitsky, interview, Radio Moscow, February 20, 1967. Army General P. A. Kurochkin, head of the Frunze Military Academy, also stated that "detection and the destruction of missile warheads in flight are no problem," interview, Radio Moscow, in FBIS, *Daily Report: Soviet Union*, February 21, 1967, p. CC3.

52. Lt. Gen. I. Zavyalov, "On Soviet Military Doctrine," *Krasnaya zvezda* (Red Star), March 31, 1967.

53. In 1968 a number of military leaders again engaged in a series of public statements almost in open debate. To cite but the most prominent, Marshal Matvei Zakharov, the chief of the General Staff, and Marshal Krylov used the more guarded formulation on interceptability of "many [but not all] missiles," and Marshal Chuikov again stressed that enemy missiles would get through, while General Batitsky said the defense system could deal with "both air and space [missile] forces of an aggressor," and Marshal Kyril Moskalenko claimed "the means for antimissile defense." Moreover, they each stated their positions repeatedly. See Marshal M. Zakharov, in *Partinaya zhizn'* (Party Life), no. 3 (February 1968), and on Radio Tallin, February 23, 1968; Marshal N. I. Krylov, in *Trybuna ludu* (Voice of the People), Warsaw, February 6, 1968, and *Sel'skaya zhizn'* (Rural Life), February 23, 1968; Marshal V. I. Chuikov, *Pravda*, February 21, 1968; Army General P. F. Batitsky, in *Sovetskii voin* (Soviet Warrior), no. 1 (January 1968), pp. 2–4, and in an interview on Radio Moscow, February 21, 1968; and Marshal K. S. Moskalenko, in *Literaturnaya gazeta*, May 8, 1968, and in *Trud*, May 9, 1968.

54. A. A. Gromyko, "On the International Situation and the Foreign Policy of the Soviet Union," *Izvestiya*, June 28, 1968; an address to the Supreme Soviet on June 27, 1968. See Leonid Brezhnev's speech on July 3 confirming that agreement had been reached to begin the SALT talks; in *Pravda*, July 4, 1968.

try to persuade us . . . that disarmament is an illusion.''[55] In addition, even later there were instances of editorial interference with publication of such statements, in particular in the Soviet military press.[56] And in the most direct criticism of SALT from the military-political theoreticians, one outspoken officer, Colonel Yevgeny Rybkin, wrote that "it is impossible to agree that disarmament can be realized by a quiet discussion of this acute and complex problem by representatives of the opposing social systems," and said that hope of success in such talks was "an illusion"—the very charge Gromyko had castigated. Rybkin also attacked détente as a path to arms limitation and ridiculed "utopian 'tranquilization' of the class, political conflict in the international arena."[57] But the question of BMD itself receded from press attention.

In addition to a sharp curtailment of frequency and specificity of claims as to BMD during 1968, the annual military parade on the anniversary of the Russian Revolution on November 7, 1968, for the first time since 1963 failed to include media reference to an ABM missile. And there has never been such mention since then.

In addition to doctrinal reconsideration and bureaucratic maneuver over the issues of BMD, resource constraints and the unpromising nature of the available Soviet ABM system undoubtedly influenced political and military leaders. In 1968 the planned deployment of 128 launchers and interceptors around Moscow was curtailed to 96, and in 1969 cut back again to 64. These unilateral program changes were almost certainly not determined by the prospect of possible arms limitations, but by Soviet judgments on the limited value of the system and the worth of the investment.

During the period 1967 to mid-1968 there were also important political reasons for Soviet reticence toward entering the profferred strategic arms limitation talks. Consideration of these political aspects occasioned divergent views among the Soviet leaders. Initially in the forefront was Soviet reluctance to enter on a politically sensitive security collaboration with the United States at a time when the United States was escalating

55. *Pravda*, July 4, 1968.

56. For example, the military newspaper *Krasnaya zvezda*, in reporting a subsequent speech by Gromyko, pointedly deleted his positive reference to future strategic arms limitation negotiations. See *Krasnaya zvezda*, October 4, 1968. Reference to other arms control proposals were *not* deleted in the article.

57. Lt. Col. Ye. I. Rybkin, "A Critique of Bourgeois Conceptions of War and Peace," *Kommunist vooruzhennykh sil*, no. 18 (September 1968), p. 90.

its prosecution of the war in Vietnam. That was mentioned explicitly by Prime Minister Kosygin in his letter to President Johnson in February 1967.

Soviet readiness to hold a summit and to begin concrete SALT talks came precisely at the time that agreement was finally reached on the Nuclear Non-Proliferation Treaty (NPT), signed on July 1, 1968. From the Soviet standpoint, the accession to the NPT of West Germany was the ideal example of a political solution to a potential military problem; the absence of a German nuclear weapons capability removed one possible requirement for an antimissile capability. It was, as the Russians like to say, not by accident that West Germany signed the NPT and the SALT talks began within the same 24-hour period. Later, in SALT, the Soviet leadership also tried unsuccessfully to enlist the United States in a different kind of political solution to their strategic defense problem against China.

More broadly, although the Soviet leadership had decided in 1966 to open a détente with Western Europe, it was not until 1969 that General Secretary Leonid Brezhnev—and not definitively until 1971 that the collective leadership in Moscow—decided to seek an East-West détente with the United States as well as with Western Europe.

When the Soviet leaders finally moved to proceed with SALT in mid-1968, they had probably decided on the essentials of their position, including acceptance of long-term severe restraints on BMD.[58] By that time, the United States had publicly shifted to the long road of disengagement from Vietnam. And Soviet ICBM deployment programs had reached a point where attainment of parity was in view.

By the fall of 1968, although the opening of SALT negotiations had been sidetracked by the Soviet occupation of Czechoslovakia, confidential exchanges on the still-planned negotiations had led to agreement on the objectives of "stable mutual strategic deterrence" and recognition of an "integral interrelationship" between strategic offensive and defensive systems.[59] Soviet military doctrine and views on arms control had thus evolved considerably in just a few years—indeed, since the proposal

58. By the end of 1968, there were virtually no direct references to BMD, and none of the open sparring in the press by military leaders in support of contending views. Only briefly in mid-1970 was there a flurry of renewed comment, at a time of stalemate in SALT.

59. The exchanges have not been published, but the author is conversant with them from his participation in the process.

for SALT in December 1966. Views such as those of General Talensky favoring ABM active defenses on the grounds of a military contribution to political stability had been superseded by concern over the "arms race stability" of an ABM-offensive missile (and especially ABM-MIRV) interaction and the arms race.

In one of the first formal SALT meetings, in November 1969, Deputy Minister Vladimir Semenov, the head of the Soviet delegation, set forth the Soviet position on ABM limitation. He acknowledged indirectly the change in Soviet views by saying that, although initially it had seemed that ABM would serve humane goals and that the only problem seemed to be a technical one, it was later found that ABM systems could stimulate the arms race and could be destabilizing by casting doubts on the inevitability of effective retaliation by missile forces of the side attacked. In view of the strategic defensive-offensive interrelationship, ABM deployment could be strategically destabilizing. Deployment by one side of an ABM system, said Semenov, to a level that might give it confidence in its relative invulnerability to a retaliatory strike might generate a temptation to use strategic offensive arms against the other side.

Turning to arms limitations, Semenov outlined three alternative possibilities: a complete ban on deployment, a limited deployment, and "heavy" area defenses. The Soviet side wanted to sound out U.S. views before committing itself to a concrete position, much less a proposal, but it should not have been difficult to divine the range of Soviet interests and preferences. The Soviet Union would not have taken the initiative in raising a possible ABM ban unless it was prepared to consider such action. The Soviet side mentioned the "heavy" area option in negative terms, saying that it would involve "the highest levels" of both defensive and offensive strategic arms. Moreover, such a deployment could, it was said, even "facilitate" a first strike. In private discussions, members of the Soviet delegation made clear that by a "limited" ABM system in the middle option, they did *not* include a thin nationwide deployment (which, they stressed, could evolve in time into a destabilizing heavy ABM deployment), but one with strictly limited area and target coverage (that is, limited in terms of both geographic area and quantitative level of ABM defenses).[60]

For present purposes, we need not examine further the elaboration

60. This description of the Soviet presentation of views is based on the author's familiarity from participation as a member of the U.S. SALT I delegation. For an account by the head of the delegation, see Smith, *Doubletalk*, pp. 93–96.

of the Soviet view, except to note that at this opening stage the Soviet Union indicated a willingness to consider a complete ABM ban *if* another way was found to provide a defense against third-country provocative attack—laying the foundation for a later initiative on that subject. Nor is it feasible here to trace comprehensively the course of the SALT I negotiations leading to the ABM Treaty, although they were highly revealing of Soviet views. It is, however, useful to note a few aspects of particular relevance to this assessment of future Soviet interests in BMD and in the ABM Treaty.

The Soviet Union had, at least by late 1969, decided to seek the maximum ABM limitation consistent with maintaining a minimum Moscow defense against third-country attacks, and (as noted above) the Soviet leaders were even prepared to consider a complete ban if the United States was cooperative on assurances and arrangements that could substitute for an active BMD in protecting the Soviet Union from third-country provocative nuclear attacks. Given the conservatism of Soviet military doctrine and political outlook, this represented a remarkable degree of acceptance of arms control as a means of meeting vital Soviet security interests.

The Soviet Union from the very start in 1966 insisted on coupling limitations on strategic offensive and defensive arms. It also affirmed recognition of the interaction of defensive-offensive forces and of the importance of this factor to stability in further confidential exchanges in 1968, and again at SALT in 1969.

The Soviet attempt to reach agreement first on an ABM treaty, and only then to return to offensive limitations, did not begin until 1970 *after* significant differences in approach had made it clear that limitations on strategic offensive arms would be very difficult to reach and would probably not constrict the main lines of continuing offensive force improvement, including MIRV.[61] Hence the Soviet interest to move

61. The Soviet decision during 1970 to seek a separate initial agreement on ABM limitations did not reflect a change of the Soviet recognition of the interconnection of offensive and defensive forces. Rather, it grew from the Soviet Union's conclusion that the United States was not prepared to accept the Soviet approach based on considering as "strategic" for purposes of SALT limitation all forces capable of nuclear strikes on the Soviet Union, and was pressing to reduce the most advanced elements of the Soviet offensive arsenal (especially, then, the SS-9) without being prepared to curtail any existing or planned U.S. programs, in particular MIRV. Without arguing the merits of the respective sides' positions, in the Soviet perception this meant that, at best, strategic offensive limitations would be a long and drawn-out negotiation and would probably represent a lowest common denominator of compromise agreement, rather than a promise to effectively curtail the strategic offensive arms competition.

quickly to seize upon and stabilize low ABM limits before the strategic defensive side of the equation also got out of control.

No doubt calculations as to tactical bargaining leverage also led the Soviet side to wish to reach an ABM agreement first, as the U.S. side recognized. But the persistence of the United States in proceeding with an ABM deployment not consistent with its own SALT proposals (for ABM limitation to national capitals)[62] made the Soviet side wonder if it was simply being used as a foil—whether SALT was the "bargaining chip" to get the reluctant U.S. Congress to deploy an area ABM defense.

Although the fact is little known, it was the Soviet side that took the initiative in proposing Article I of the treaty providing the basic undertaking "not to deploy ABM systems for defense of the territory of the country."[63] After the agreements were concluded, Soviet spokesmen concerned with political-military and arms control matters stressed the prohibition on nationwide ABM deployment.[64]

It was the U.S. side, however, that finally proposed—despite divided views and after much controversy—the significant undertaking embodied in Agreed Statement (D) that, in conjunction with other provisions of the treaty, bans deployment of "exotic" future BMD systems,

62. The first U.S. proposal for ABM limitation, advanced on April 20, 1970, would have limited each side to a single site for defense of its NCA (Moscow and Washington). After only seven days, the Soviet delegation, on formal instructions, accepted. On August 4, the U.S. delegation proposed (as part of a new overall proposal) alternatives of NCA or "zero" ABM deployments. The Soviet delegates were perplexed; they had already accepted the NCA limitation. Meanwhile, they hinted and finally proposed going ahead first with an ABM limitation agreement alone. On March 19, 1971, they tabled a draft ABM treaty, limiting ABM deployment to NCA defenses. One week later, on March 26, the United States proposed a new third option, having "equal status" with the NCA and zero options; the new option was for four sites for defense of ICBMs for the United States, and only one site at Moscow for the USSR. By this time the Soviet delegation was astonished, and Moscow became highly suspicious as to U.S. intentions. This suspicion was reinforced when the U.S. delegation soon had to inform the Soviet side that it was instructed to withdraw the NCA and zero options. The main reason for the U.S. change was precisely in order to be able to say in Congress that the funding for the third and fourth ABM sites being requested in 1971 was "consistent" with our SALT negotiating position. See Garthoff, "Negotiating with the Russians," pp. 10–13.

63. Incidentally, the U.S. acceptance of this undertaking was *never* discussed in Washington at the policy level, nor was the delegation *ever* instructed on it. Ibid., pp. 17–18.

64. For example, see G. A. Trofimenko, "Questions of Strengthening Peace and Security in Soviet-American Relations," *SShA* (USA), no. 9 (September 1974), p. 13; and I. S. Glagolev, *Mezhdunarodnaya bezopasnost' i ekonomicheskoye razvitiye* (International Security and Economic Development) (Moscow: Nauka, 1974), p. 103.

substituting systems or basic components based on new physical principles (such as lasers).[65] Just as the principal objection to this undertaking within the U.S. government had come from the military, so the Soviet military initially objected. The spokesman for the Soviet delegation arguing against the proposal was the senior Soviet military delegate. However, after five and a half months the Soviet side accepted the ban.[66]

It is also significant that even after the United States had proposed, and the Soviet side had accepted, limiting ABM deployment to defense of National Command Authorities in the national capitals, the Soviet leaders were prepared to consider a complete ABM deployment ban. In the summer of 1971, while the United States was formally shifting from four to three sites for American defense of ICBMs and the Soviet Union was standing firm on NCA defenses, the White House did authorize a private probe at the heads-of-delegation level on Soviet reaction to a complete ABM ban. When, however, Deputy Minister Semenov on instructions reported positive interest in the idea in Moscow, Henry Kissinger (who had not expected or wanted a positive Soviet reaction) instructed the head of the U.S. delegation to state that the United States was no longer interested in an ABM ban in SALT I, but would raise the matter in SALT II. In fact, President Richard M. Nixon personally instructed Ambassador Gerard C. Smith to "impress" on the Soviet Union that in the SALT II negotiations the United States would "set as our goal a ban on ABMs." No such proposal, however, was ever made or even considered throughout SALT II.[67]

The Soviet Union also resisted U.S. arguments for placing limits on non-ABM systems as collateral constraints to reinforce the ABM limitations. It argued that limits on air defense systems, early warning systems, and other radars would unduly and unnecessarily limit other military (and in some cases even civilian) activities not the subject of the treaty. (Again, the Soviet position was in fact close to that of the U.S. Joint Chiefs of Staff.) Nonetheless, the Soviet Union did accede to U.S. pressures on those constraints (especially concerning non-ABM radars) on which the United States could make a strong case.

The Soviet Union was at all times prepared to agree on equal ABM

65. See chapter 6 herein.

66. For a discussion, particularly of the U.S. debate on the issue, see Smith, *Doubletalk*, pp. 263–65, 343–44. For a recent Soviet reaffirmation of this undertaking, see interview with Col. Gen. Nikolai Chervov, *Pravda* (Bratislava), April 29, 1983.

67. See Smith, *Doubletalk*, pp. 256–63, 485–86.

limitations at a level of one or two sites on each side (or none with other compensating or offsetting arrangements, or probably three sites if the United States had insisted). But it consistently opposed from the outset any nationwide deployment, even a "thin" one. Interest in maximum ABM limitation also led the Soviet Union to override the standard preference of the Soviet (and U.S.) military to avoid qualitative constraints and constraints on future systems. A wide range of significant qualitative limitations on ABM systems was incorporated in the treaty. If agreement had been reached on a ban on ABM deployment, Soviet negotiators informally indicated the Soviet Union was prepared to agree on even more severe limitations on all ABM development and testing. Finally, the Soviet Union also favored maintaining ABM limitations for indefinite duration.

These Soviet positions are not consonant with an interest limited simply to heading off a temporary U.S. lead in BMD technology or with preparing the groundwork for later Soviet BMD deployment. This was most striking in the Soviet readiness to consider a complete ban on ABM deployment but was also evident in the extensive qualitative limitations accepted, the complex of constraints as a whole, and the indefinite duration of the treaty undertakings. In line with these positions in SALT I were parallel developments in Soviet military doctrine on both the political and military-technical levels.

A prominent Soviet commentator with high political connections, Alexander Bovin, made the following statement in a eulogy to the ABM Treaty of 1972, in an article following the signing of the SALT II Treaty in 1979:

> This agreement introduced into the nuclear arms race for the first time some elements, albeit minimal of restraint, certainty, and predictability. . . . Let us suppose that a potential enemy—for us this is the United States, and for the Americans it is the Soviet Union—deploys an antimissile defense system which protects the country's basic vital centers, including the areas where ICBMs are based. . . . The other of course would not be reconciled to lagging behind strategically. As a result, instead of stability there is a forced arms race, both in defensive and in offensive arms. So in as far as the destabilizing significance of antimissile defense systems was understood, both the Soviet Union and the United States virtually gave up deploying them, or to be precise each side has the right to deploy only one such system [complex].
>
> Thus since 1972, the strategic situation has become somewhat more simplified: each side must reckon with the fact that he who decides on a first strike will have a counterstrike delivered against him which will be unacceptable in its consequences. In other words, it is precisely the preservation of a

retaliatory strike potential which is regarded as the best guarantee of security. This is that same balance of fear about which we have all read and heard, and under conditions of which we live.[68]

This statement could equally well have been made by a number of people in the United States (reversing of course the reference to the adversaries). It is also, as we have seen, directly in line with the Soviet declared view and negotiating positions in SALT.

Especially in the period after the SALT I agreements were concluded, but also earlier, a number of Soviet spokesmen for arms control and détente with connections to the Central Committee, the Institutes of the Academy of Sciences, and the Ministry of Foreign Affairs (MFA), stressed offensive-defensive system interaction as a controllable cause of the arms race. Thus in *Pravda* in June 1972, two leading Soviet SALT negotiators from the MFA (writing under pseudonyms) stated: "As is well known, strategic offensive and defensive systems are closely connected with one another. The development of one of these forms of armament inevitably entails the development of the other, and vice versa—the arms race is continually being driven forward by this process. In order, therefore, reliably to block the way to a further buildup of arms, a decision is needed which would limit both strategic offensive weapons systems and systems for defense against their attack."[69]

Beginning in early 1970, just as the MIRV issue was raised and quickly killed in the SALT talks, a number of Soviet spokesmen stressed the particularly destabilizing effect of the combination of ABM and MIRV deployments.[70] Nonetheless, there were indications that the Soviet

68. A. Bovin, FBIS, *Daily Record: Soviet Union,* June 20, 1979, pp. AA6–AA7.

69. O. Grinev and V. Pavlov, *Pravda,* June 22, 1972. "O. Grinev" is Oleg Grinevsky, and "V. Pavlov" is Viktor Pavlovich Karpov; both, especially Grinevsky, had played an important role in SALT I, and Karpov was later to be the chief Soviet negotiator in the later phases of SALT II and in START. See also V. Viktorov (pseudonym for Vladimir Viktorovich Shustov of the MFA), *Pravda,* July 7, 1971; V. Matveyev, *Izvestiya,* June 10, 1972; and for an early article see Yu. [Georgy] Arbatov, *Izvestiya,* April 15, 1969. Arbatov's article, keyed to a monograph by George Rathjens, discussed the U.S. debates in a manner intended also to influence developing Soviet thinking on the subject.

70. See, in particular, the important *Pravda* article under the Central Committee designator "Observor," titled "An Important Problem," *Pravda,* March 7, 1970—written while the United States was determining its position on MIRV limitation. See also the editorial "Between Helsinki and Vienna," in *SShA,* no. 1 (January 1970), p. 60; and G. A. Trofimenko, "Some Aspects of U.S. Military-Political Strategy," *SShA,* no. 10 (October 1970), p. 25, in which the author described U.S. programs for both ABM and MIRV as reflecting pursuit of a first-strike capability.

Union (like the U.S. administration) had decided in 1969 to give priority to seeking ABM limitation.[71]

More generally, numerous Soviet commentaries stressed the role of SALT in contributing to détente and of both SALT and détente in contributing to a reduction of tensions and of the risks of war. This accords with the Soviet stress on the *prevention* of war by political means—always given higher attention than by the United States, which stresses more the *deterrence* of war by possession of military means.

The Soviet agreement to the ABM Treaty *did* involve acceptance of a condition of mutual deterrence based on mutual vulnerability—although not in terms of the U.S. doctrine of mutual assured destruction (MAD) based on assured countervalue destruction denominated in percentages of industry and population. It is not only a question of *inferring* a Soviet view from the fact of the Soviet Union's acceptance of the ABM Treaty with its implied mutual vulnerability, but of the actual record of the Soviet definition of its own interests.

In addition, the Soviet pursuit of strategic arms limitations in general, as well as the ABM Treaty specifically, reflected the Soviet Union's developing political-military doctrine based on stabilizing strategic military parity and controlling the arms competition through seizing the key link in the interaction of offensive and defensive systems.

But what about the military-technical level of military doctrine? Did the professional military now accept the concept of controlling the strategic competition through radically limiting BMD? Or did the military hope to be able to resurrect it later and see an advantage in curtailing deployments during a period of U.S. advantage, which the military hoped to surmount? Or was the military simply compelled to accept it by the Soviet leadership?

Among those called upon to support the ABM Treaty in the ratification deliberations of the Supreme Soviet were Minister of Defense Marshal Grechko and First Deputy Minister and Chief of the General Staff, Army General Viktor Kulikov, then the two senior professional soldiers. Marshal Grechko declared that the treaty would "impede the development of the competition between offensive and defensive nuclear missile

71. In particular, the unofficial discussion between Soviet and U.S. scientists in the Pugwash conference in October 1969, on the very eve of SALT, left this impression. Two of the Soviet participants served on their SALT delegation: Academician Aleksandr Shchukin, and Viktor Komplektov (MFA), and other key Soviet figures were also there, including Georgy Arbatov and Vladimir Shustov (MFA).

arms," and Marshal Kulikov recognized the key significance of the ABM Treaty in "preventing the emergence of a chain reaction of competition between offensive and defensive arms."[72] Thus the top military leaders stressed the same "arms race stability" aspect of the ABM Treaty as did the political leaders and commentators.[73]

Even more revealing indications of the changes in Soviet military doctrine had appeared in internal military theoretical writings in the late 1960s, as the Soviet leaders were determining their position on SALT in general and BMD in particular. General V. I. Zemskov, editor of the confidential General Staff theoretical journal *Military Thought*, stated in a major article in May 1969 that a "nuclear balance" had been established, but that this balance could be disrupted either by a sharp change in offensive capabilities "or by the creation by one of the sides of highly effective means of antiballistic missile defense while the other side lags considerably in solution of these tasks."[74]

Other articles in *Military Thought* in the late 1960s stressed the existence of mutual deterrence, citing the fact that "with the existing level of development of nuclear missile weapons and their reliable cover below ground and under water it is impossible in practice to destroy them completely, and consequently it is also impossible to prevent an annihilating retaliatory strike."[75] In addition, a number of these articles from the late 1960s made clear that the Soviet Union had adapted its preemption concept of the 1950s to take account of the implications of the missile age. The new concept was missile launch under attack or on warning. With missiles capable of rapid readying to fire, and systems capable of detecting enemy missile launches and attack, an attacker "is

72. See Marshal A. A. Grechko, Session of the Presidium of the Supreme Soviet of the USSR, in *Pravda,* September 30, 1972; and Marshal V. G. Kulikov, Joint Session of the Foreign Affairs Commissions of the Council of the Union and the Council of Nationalities of the Supreme Soviet of the USSR, *Izvestiya,* August 24, 1972.

73. Clearly, the Soviet military leaders had to support the ABM Treaty, but the variations in individual statements indicate they had discretion in choice of the arms race stability theme.

74. Maj. Gen. V. I. Zemskov, "Wars of the Contemporary Era," *Voyennaya mysl',* no. 5 (May 1969), p. 59.

75. Army General Semyon P. Ivanov, "Soviet Military Doctrine and Strategy," *Voyennaya mysl',* no. 5 (May 1969), p. 47. General Ivanov was then commandant of the General Staff Academy and had recently served as deputy chief of the General Staff and chief of the Main Operations Directorate. See other references in Raymond L. Garthoff, "Mutual Deterrence and Strategic Arms Limitation in Soviet Policy," *International Security,* vol. 3 (Summer 1978), pp. 125–32.

no longer able suddenly to destroy missiles on the territory of the country subject to aggression before their launch. They will have time during the flight of the aggressor's missiles to leave their launchers and inflict a retaliatory strike against the enemy."[76] This particular statement was written in 1967 by Commander-in-Chief of the Strategic Missile Forces, Marshal Nikolai Krylov.

The Soviet shift to a launch-on-warning concept, reflected in many statements by Soviet military and political figures,[77] helps to explain the lack of Soviet interest in BMD for defense of ICBMs in silos. They would be protected from destruction in the event of enemy attack not by active antimissile defenses of one or another degree of effectiveness, but by being launched in retaliation before their silos were hit. This might be supplemented in the future by a gradual shift from fixed silo to mobile land-based missile systems.

The changes in Soviet military doctrine, at both the political and military-technical levels, were faithfully reflected both in statements by the Soviet delegation in the SALT negotiations and in the positions taken by the Soviet government. In the very first meeting, the Soviet delegation read a prepared statement which reaffirmed mutual deterrence: "Even in the event that one of the sides were the first to be subjected to attack, it would undoubtedly retain the ability to inflict a retaliatory strike of crushing power. . . . War between our two countries would be disastrous for both sides. And it would be tantamount to suicide for the ones who decided to start such a war."[78]

The Soviet SALT I delegation had been instructed, at the direction of Minister of Defense Grechko, not to discuss military operational doctrine or strategy in the negotiations. Nonetheless, one inadvertent exchange occurred when the Soviet delegation referred in passing to the fact that an attacker's ICBMs might find the defender's ICBM silos empty by the time they arrived. That comment led to an exchange on launch on warning, with the U.S. side arguing that such a policy would be

76. Marshal N. I. Krylov, "The Nuclear Missile Shield of the Soviet State," *Voyennaya mysl'*, no. 11 (November 1967), p. 20.

77. See Garthoff, "Mutual Deterrence," pp. 129–32. There have been a number of authoritative references in recent years as well. See, for example, Marshal N. V. Ogarkov, "In the Interests of Raising Combat Readiness," *Kommunist vooruzhennykh sil*, no. 14 (July 1980), p. 26.

As in the case of the concept of a preemptive strike, the general doctrinal acceptance has not been reflected in the strategic force posture, and the terms of contingent application in operational plans are not known.

78. Cited in Garthoff, "Mutual Deterrence," p. 126.

destabilizing and the Soviet delegation attempting to pin the whole question on discussions published in the United States. The Soviet delegation declined to express an official Soviet government view on the subject.[79]

Discussions of the mission of BMD in SALT were, of course, focused on the bargaining over specific limitations. Nonetheless, it was clear that while the Soviet side bargained hard for equality with any U.S. defense of ICBM silos, it was not really interested in that mission. Defense of the NCA in Moscow was clearly a real interest.[80]

Throughout the SALT negotiations, the Soviet military press had maintained a discreet silence on SALT. Following the agreements of 1972, favorable comments were made,[81] but not frequently. In fact, there are indications that many Soviet military men who had paid little attention to press references to ongoing SALT negotiations were rather surprised and even shocked by these agreements—not so much with respect to their content, as to the very fact of collaborative agreements with the United States in the field of military security.[82]

79. See ibid., pp. 130–31. It was this discussion of launch on warning that led General Ogarkov to remark to General Allison privately that "as a military man you should understand that question" and that the subject was neither appropriate nor necessary for the SALT arms limitation negotiations—it was not a question of keeping secrets on Soviet weapons or forces from civilians on the delegations, as erroneously implied in Newhouse, *Cold Dawn*, pp. 55–56, 192, and by many others citing or misciting Newhouse's account.

80. There was a curious Soviet reticence to define the treaty limitations in terms of defense of national capitals. (Neither side wanted to use the technical term "National Command Authorities.") The Soviet draft treaty had specified obscurely only "a circular area" to be defended, and the Soviet delegation proposed a separate understanding (which it would not need to publish) specifying Moscow and Washington. After a month of intermittent discussion in which the U.S. representatives refused to consider any such evasive circumlocutions, the Soviet delegation finally accepted the proposal to refer to national capitals. It appears that the Soviet leaders preferred not to make quite so explicit that they would be protected, while the populations of Leningrad, Kiev, and other cities would not. In these negotiations, the Soviet representatives initially argued that their proposal should help out the U.S. side with Congress. When this was rejected, they still argued that there had been some problems in the United States when it appeared some cities would be defended and others not. They finally admitted privately to concerns about Soviet views outside of Moscow.

81. Apart from the statements of Soviet military leaders cited earlier, see Col. M. Ponomarev, "Productive Results of the Leninist Foreign Policy of the USSR," *Kommunist vooruzhennykh sil,* no. 13 (July 1972), and Capt. First Rank G. Svyatov, "The Limitation of Strategic Arms: The Principle of Equal Security," *Krasnaya zvezda,* July 28, 1972.

82. The author was told by three senior retired officers with extensive military ties that such reaction was in fact widespread. The SALT accords brought home to many officers the reality that détente was *not* just political propaganda!

The sharp limitations on BMD posed a particular problem for the Air Defense Forces, which had responsibility for the BMD mission.[83] It seems quite likely that when the initial decision was made in 1969 to seek tight ABM limits, the Soviet political and overall military leadership directly or implicitly promised that the basic *air* defense mission would be maintained. There are of course other reasons why the Soviet Union, with other putative enemies around it, would not unilaterally decide, as the United States had, to cut back sharply on its air defenses. Traditional and institutional factors, and perhaps bureaucratic politics, also came into play. Marshal Grechko went the furthest by far in an unusual statement in his testimony before the Presidium of the Supreme Soviet in which he understated the actual constraints imposed by the ABM Treaty in saying that, despite the sharp limits on deployment, the treaty "does not place any limitations on the conduct of research and experimental work directed toward the solution of problems of the defense of the country from nuclear missile strikes." By also stressing, in the very next sentence, the contribution of the treaty to "preventing the development of the competition between offensive and defensive nuclear missile arms," Grechko seemed to be trying to have his bread buttered on both sides.[84] In the years following the ABM Treaty, its implications were noted, but only grudgingly, by some of the principal Air Defense generals.

Shortly before the beginning of SALT, the third edition of the basic Soviet text on *Military Strategy* was issued; it retained several paragraphs on BMD, including the statement that "one of the cardinal problems for Soviet military strategy is the reliable protection of the rear of the country from nuclear strikes—antiballistic missile defense."[85] The discussion conceded that "under contemporary conditions methods and means of nuclear attack undoubtedly predominate over methods and means of defense against them," but the BMD mission, along with anti-air and antispace defense (and civil defense) remained.[86]

83. The most extensive compilation of Soviet military statements on BMD, especially by PVO officers, is in Michael J. Deane, *The Role of Strategic Defense in Soviet Strategy* (Current Affairs Press for the University of Miami, Advanced International Studies Institute, 1980). Regrettably, although prodigiously researched, the analysis in the study is flawed.

84. Marshal A. A. Grechko, *Pravda*, September 30, 1972. Some Western commentators have incorrectly translated Grechko's statement as referring to "research and development"—a much broader area.

85. See Marshal V. D. Sokolovsky, ed., *Voyennaya strategiya* (Military Strategy) (Moscow: Voyenizdat, 1968), pp. 246–47. This edition went to press in November 1967.

86. Ibid.

After the conclusion of the ABM Treaty, any reference to the BMD mission virtually disappeared from Soviet military writings—with one significant exception. Many generals and other officers of the Air Defense Forces, particularly in their own service journal, continued in the 1970s to make general references to BMD or even to a need for defense against ballistic missiles as well as aircraft.[87] Most, however, simply stopped referring to BMD and continued to stress the air defense mission.[88]

The most explicit, indeed the only specific and informative, reference to BMD plans and programs was by Marshal Batitsky in the confidential General Staff organ *Military Thought* in 1973, in which he stated: "Within the framework of the agreements limiting ABM defense, such defenses will in all probability change only qualitatively, and will remain limited in capability, able only to cover the capitals of the countries against prospective means of ballistic missile attack."[89] This remains the most authoritative Soviet statement of prospects for BMD under the ABM Treaty.[90]

During the decade after the ABM Treaty the Soviet Union has, as we have seen,[91] carried forward an active research and development program on BMD, within the limitations of the treaty. It is of interest that as early as 1972 in the negotiations, and 1974 in its support of the protocol to the treaty, the Soviet Union showed no real interest in BMD for the defense of its strategic forces. This approach has also characterized the Soviet research and development program, although some aspects of it

87. See, in particular, Marshal of Aviation G. V. Zimin, chief of the Military Academy of the Air Defense Forces, in *Razvitiye protivovozdushnoi oborony* (The Development of Air Defense) (Moscow: Voyenizdat, 1976), pp. 100, 105, 192. In one notable exception, Marshal Viktor G. Kulikov, the chief of the General Staff, also wrote of the requirement "to ensure the protection of the country and the armed forces from air and nuclear ballistic missile attack," but in an article in the Air Defense Forces journal; Marshal V. G. Kulikov, "Air Defense in the System of Defense of the State," *Vestnik protivovozdushnoi oborony* (Herald of Air Defense), no. 4 (April 1973), p. 4.

88. For example, Marshal P. F. Batitsky, "Development of the Air Defense of the Country in the Years of the Great Fatherland War," *Voyenno-istoricheskii zhurnal*, no. 10 (October 1972), p. 30.

89. Marshal P. F. Batitsky, "Air Defense Forces of the Country," *Voyennaya mysl'*, no. 11 (November 1973), p. 36.

90. Thus, for example, a recent volume on military-technological developments and prospects by a leading Soviet military technical innovator makes no reference whatsoever to BMD in discussing the Air Defense Forces (and devotes only two sentences to civil defense, belying a routine reference to its "enormous significance"). See Lt. General Professor M. M. Kiryan, *Voyenno-tekhnicheskii progress i vooruzhennye sily SSSR* (Military-Technical Progress and the Armed Forces of the USSR) (Moscow: Voyenizdat, 1982), pp. 306–7, 310.

91. See chapter 5 herein.

could be adapted to such use. Similarly, the Soviet leaders showed themselves in no hurry to upgrade and fill out their defense of Moscow. A major new radar was added. In 1980 they cut by half the number of their old Galosh long-range interceptors and launchers from sixty-four to thirty-two before beginning in the early 1980s to build silos to deploy sixty-eight terminal defense endoatmospheric interceptors and thus fill out the allowed defense. By all indications, the Soviet Union sees this deployment as sufficient.[92]

Thus the Soviet Union has adjusted its military doctrine and concrete military programs to accommodate the major arms control restraint on the offensive-defensive arms competition established in the ABM Treaty of 1972. This treaty, in turn, represents not only a military-political decision, but also a political investment in a détente policy that features arms control as one of its principal elements. When feasible, actual limitations are established; when the West is not prepared to agree to terms that the Soviet Union sees as providing "equal security," it falls back on the propaganda advantages and possible later movement stemming from continued advocacy of arms control. While Soviet proposals— not unlike our own—are fashioned to their advantage, the ABM Treaty stands as witness to the fact that the Soviet Union is prepared to support balanced arms control agreements embodying substantial constraints on the military programs of both sides. This political dimension of the ABM Treaty should not be ignored in evaluating both Western stakes and Soviet reactions in considering the impact of possible future initiatives on BMD on East-West relations.

BMD, Other Countries, and East-West Relations

While Western European views of BMD are of some importance, Eastern European views have been less involved, or at least not taken into account very much. The Soviet Union has in general informed its Warsaw Pact allies of major SALT and BMD decisions only after they

92. The Soviet Union was prepared in 1972 in the SALT I negotiation to agree to a limit of 75, rather than 100, interceptors on launchers for the Moscow deployment. This would, however, have caused complications in the context of balancing equal numbers in view of the U.S. desired deployments for defense of ICBM silos, and was not given real consideration.

have been reached or even implemented. If, however, an ATBM (antitheater ballistic missile) defense were deployed in Western Europe, the question of one for Eastern Europe could arise. Short of such a direct relationship, the principal Eastern European interest is derivative of Soviet-U.S. and Soviet–West European relations. In that respect, the Eastern European communist allies of the Soviet Union strongly support East-West détente and therefore support the ABM Treaty.

Japan is, in most respects except geography, part of the West. Its defense relationship, however, is unique in that it rests on a bilateral tie with the United States and a self-limited nonnuclear military establishment. BMD has not, in the past, been a subject of much interest in Japan. Recent growing attention to Soviet SS-20 deployments in Eastern Siberia and to the INF issue in Europe has stirred some new concerns in Japan. The credibility of the U.S. deterrent, not greatly questioned in the past but crucial, might arise as an issue if the United States deployed BMD. Proposals to deploy a theater or "tactical" BMD in Europe, particularly a nonnuclear system, might precipitate the question in Japan.

China would be concerned about national BMD deployments by the United States and the Soviet Union or theater BMD deployments in Europe. Soviet deployment of a comparable theater BMD in relation to China would be the probable result of a theater BMD in Europe. A general BMD deployment by the two superpowers would threaten China's deterrent capabilities against the Soviet Union, and without alliance commitments from the United States this would be a more serious risk for China than for Western Europe or Japan.

The Chinese factor in Soviet and U.S. thinking is also important. In SALT I, the Soviet side hinted that its receptivity to a complete ABM ban might depend upon a Soviet-U.S. agreement to act jointly against provocative "catalytic" actions by China—a proposal rebuffed by the Nixon administration. Kissinger assumed Soviet motives in raising this latter issue were to preclude or spoil the initial steps toward U.S.-Chinese rapprochement then under way (1970) and to give the Soviet Union a free hand in China. He failed to consider that it might instead, or in addition, reflect a Soviet defensive concern. Moreover, the link between political reassurances against China's nuclear action and military reassurances as represented by the Moscow ABM was logical and plausible—but Kissinger failed even to see the connection, as is clear from his own memoirs, in which he misconstrues the Soviet linkage of an ABM agreement and an antiprovocative war agreement as meaning that "collusion against China was to be the real Soviet price for a summit."[93]

China opposed the ABM Treaty of 1972 as part of its opposition to U.S.-Soviet détente and arms control collaboration as a whole. At the same time, China no doubt appreciated the distinct advantage it provided in military, deterrence, and political-military terms by giving China's fledgling strategic missile forces a free ride (except against Moscow). This consideration remains valid and must affect China's attitude toward any revised BMD limitation. Whether that consideration would, in China's view, be offset by satisfaction over worsened U.S.-Soviet relations as the result of an acrimonious repudiation of the ABM Treaty is difficult to say.

Most Third World countries would react to a BMD initiative in terms reflecting their general attitudes toward East-West relations. Those favoring improvements in such relations would regret measures that worsened them, and the opposite would be true for those not favoring East-West détente.

Potential or actual Third World nuclear weapons states would probably not be overly concerned about U.S. and Soviet BMD. None of

93. Henry A. Kissinger, *White House Years* (Little, Brown, 1979), pp. 554–55, and see pp. 545, 547–48.

Kissinger has confused two separate matters: one was the Soviet proposal in the June 25, 1970, aide-mémoire from Dobrynin to proceed promptly with agreements on ABM limitation and on measures against accidental war; the other was the Soviet proposal in July in Vienna for an agreement on measures to counter possible provocative nuclear attack by a third power. The Soviet proposal in June may actually have been an overture for an early summit; it was, in any case, an attempt on the part of the Soviet Union to overcome our resistance to an initial agreement on ABM limitations alone by cosmetically tying it to a noncontroversial agreement on measures to avert accidental war, work on which was proceeding well. The "linkage" was not really helpful, but it was offered as a proposal to advance, not to slow down, agreement and a summit. The later separate probe in Vienna on measures to counter possible provocative attack was never related to the question of proceeding expeditiously toward a SALT agreement and toward a summit.

Kissinger's assumption was also belied by the fact that the Soviet Union promptly abandoned the antiprovocative attack proposal, concluded the accident measures agreement as soon as the United States was prepared to do so (prior to but not delaying a summit), and proceeded to work toward an ABM agreement and summit. Kissinger's account does not mention the specific tie of the possibility of a complete ABM ban to the antiprovocative attack proposition because it was never advanced as a formal Soviet proposal or through his "back-channel" with Dobrynin, so he ignored it (if, indeed, he was ever aware of it). He was, in any case, merely using the proposal for an ABM ban as a negotiating ploy, as he admits (pp. 548–49). I noted earlier the abrupt White House instruction to drop the idea, as soon as the Soviet leadership showed interest.

them (except perhaps for Japan and Sweden in the future) would pursue nuclear weapons primarily for deterrence against the Soviet Union or the United States. They would, nonetheless, be concerned about the possible spread of ATBMs to their adversaries—who, in turn, would by the same token be interested in acquiring such antimissile capabilities.

If the ABM Treaty were to be abandoned, any country that wished to justify withdrawing from the Non-Proliferation Treaty in order to pursue a nuclear weapons capability (or for other purposes, including needling the superpowers) could certainly interpret the failure of the ABM Treaty as the collapse of SALT and as proof of the inability of the principal nuclear powers to fulfill their responsibilities under Article VI of the Non-Proliferation Treaty of 1968 "to pursue negotiations in good faith on effective measures relating to cessation of the nuclear arms race at an early date and to nuclear disarmament"[94]

Effects of Possible Future BMD Initiatives

The question of the possible impact of BMD on East-West relations in the future can best be approached in terms of three propositions relating to U.S. BMD (they might be proposed courses or unilaterally announced decisions): (1) defense of strategic offensive missiles, (2) antitheater ballistic missile defense in Western Europe, and (3) defense of the United States and the Soviet Union.

Defense of Strategic Offensive Missiles

The U.S. concern over the growing vulnerability of its fixed land-based ICBM force led in the late 1970s and early 1980s to renewed consideration of BMD as a possible solution to this problem. BMD was sometimes seen as a possible complement to ICBM deployment either in mobile formations (such as a multiple protective shelter or "racetrack" deployment), or in closely spaced superhardened silos (Densepack). As U.S. attention shifted toward small, mobile single-warhead missiles, interest in BMD for this purpose subsided. Given the gyrations of U.S.

94. "Treaty on the Non-Proliferation of Nuclear Weapons," in U.S. Arms Control and Disarmament Agency, *Arms Control and Disarmament Agreements: Texts and Histories of Negotiations,* 1982 ed. (GPO, 1982), p. 93.

policy on this subject in recent years, however, it remains possible that BMD will be seen as having a potentially useful role, perhaps in defending MX in hardened Minuteman silos. A meaningful BMD deployment for ICBM defense would, however, require amendment or abrogation of the ABM Treaty.

The argument would be advanced by proponents of BMD for protection of ICBMs in silos that such a defense would be strategically stabilizng in that it would enhance the assurance of retaliation.[95] One problem with that argument is that, even if it were true, it ignores other effects of BMD deployment. For example, if an exoatmospheric "overlay" defense were part of the BMD system, its wide area coverage would involve area defense even if that were not its principal intended purpose. Even more difficult would be the attainment of comparable (and perceived comparable) BMD on the two sides, and at a comparable pace of development and deployment. Finally, there would be the political as well as technical problem of "getting from here to there."

Against any contribution that BMD might make to deterrence stability by protecting concentrated ICBM forces must be weighed not only the politically destabilizing effects of such a step, but also its probable sacrifice of the ABM Treaty. Proponents could argue that BMD for ICBMs would give a new lease on life for MIRV systems and would obviate the need for their replacement. For those who would seek an eventual shift from large MIRVed ICBMs to small single-warhead missiles, however, continuation of the ABM Treaty constraints would be essential, since the latter could never match MIRV systems in assured penetration of a heavy BMD.

The Soviet reaction would probably be very negative, partly owing to real concerns about subsequent expansion of U.S. BMD deployment, and partly in order to stir up a divisive issue in the United States and Western Europe. Soviet agreement to amending the treaty would be highly unlikely unless (1) an amended treaty could still effectively constrain the United States from a comprehensive BMD, (2) the Soviet Union feared that the alternative would be U.S. abrogation of the treaty and unconstrained deployments, or (3) the Soviet Union came to believe that BMD for its own ICBMs was both necessary and feasible. Otherwise, it would probably resist amending the treaty, even at the cost of seeing

---

95. The strongest case is made by Jan M. Lodal, "Deterrence and Nuclear Strategy," *Daedalus,* vol. 109 (Fall 1980), pp. 166–72.

the treaty abrogated by the United States. Indeed, it might initially declare a unilateral policy of abiding by the ABM Treaty for a time to allow U.S. "reconsideration," if there were a strong continuing domestic opposition to abrogation and a possibility of reversal of the decision.

In short, the impact of ICBM defense on East-West relations would probably be highly negative. The Soviet Union would object strongly. Moreover, the opinion of Western Europe (and the world) would probably not support U.S. action in abrogating or endangering the treaty.

Antitheater Ballistic Missile Systems

Although they are not yet a subject of wide public discussion, antitactical (or antitheater) ballistic missiles (ATBMs) designed to counter short, medium, and intermediate tactical and theater ballistic missiles—especially in order to protect one's own intermediate-range theater forces—are attracting interest. ATBM systems would necessarily be deployed in potential combat theaters, particularly Europe.

The idea of ATBM immediately raises a host of questions and serious problems. First of all, what would distinguish ATBM from *strategic* ABM—would ATBM be possible under the ABM Treaty? And would its qualities be such that deployment of the Soviet Union's own ATBM in the European USSR, matching NATO deployment in Western Europe, could affect the U.S.-USSR strategic relationship as well? In other words, would the United States be so confident that NATO ATBMs were compatible with the purposes of the ABM Treaty that it would have no objection to Soviet ATBMs, which might have different geo-strategic implications? These are questions better considered early than late.

What are the relevant provisions of the ABM Treaty? The treaty deals with ABM systems "to counter strategic ballistic missiles" (Article II), but it does not define "strategic ballistic missiles." This matter is crucial, because the treaty does bar the United States from deploying ABM systems outside its own territory or from transferring any ABM technology to other powers (Article IX). If ATBM is *not* an ABM covered by the treaty, those restrictions would not apply. The treaty also bans giving any *other* missiles, launchers, or radars "capabilities to counter strategic ballistic missiles." Thus even if ATBM is not *designed* to counter strategic ballistic missiles, if it did have the "capabilities" to do so, its deployment and testing in an ABM mode are prohibited (Article VI).

Both the United States and the Soviet Union are currently developing advanced tactical air defense systems (the U.S. Patriot and the Soviet SA-12) that might have some capability against short- and intermediate-range ballistic missiles. Can they be tested, developed, and deployed, even as air defense systems, if they have been provided with some degree of ATBM capability? The question is bound to arise soon. In the present discussion, however, it is important to address the related but clearer case of an avowed ATBM system with appropriate development and testing, whether based on the Patriot, the SA-12, or other systems.

Western European reaction to a U.S. proposal to develop and deploy ATBM in Europe would probably be highly negative.[96] Concerns over BMD in any form would apply, notably the threat to the ABM Treaty and détente, and concern that the Soviet Union would respond by deploying BMD systems negating the British and French missile forces and the new NATO Pershing II force. Although concern over a U.S. retreat to a "fortress America" would not arise, Europeans would be alarmed over U.S. interest in warfighting rather than deterrence, specifically warfighting in Europe. If, as would be likely, an ATBM required a nuclear warhead, the widespread antinuclear sentiment in Europe would certainly focus on a system that would, moreover, detonate its warheads largely over Western Europe (even if safely). Proposals justifying ATBM as necessary to defend the INF would intensify the continuing controversy over the INF deployment itself. Finally, there would be the need to negotiate, on the basis of political as well as military criteria, where in Europe to deploy the system. (If it were built on the basis of the long-planned improved air defense system, the deployment plan for modern air defense also would undoubtedly be distorted by such considerations and controversies.)

Soviet reaction would not only be predictably negative, but would undoubtedly impugn U.S. motives. The Soviet Union would seek to capitalize on differences within Europe (assuming there was some support) and differences between Europe and the United States.

The few direct Soviet commentaries on ATBM have attacked it as a

---

96. Much of the discussion of Western reaction closely follows the excellent article by Yost, "Ballistic Missile Defense and the Atlantic Alliance," pp. 143–74, which was based on extensive interviews in Europe in 1980 and 1981. Yost's findings of negative reactions to ATBM are particularly interesting because his own inclination is to favor such a system.

violation of the ABM Treaty. Within hours after NBC television news on March 12, 1983, reported that the Pentagon was developing the Patriot air defense system into an ABM (ATBM) system as well for deployment in Germany, TASS was broadcasting this report with a comment that such an action would be a "gross violation" of the ABM Treaty.[97]

Soviet military reactions might take several forms, apart from Soviet ATBM against the British, French, and Pershing II ballistic missiles. If in fact a U.S. ATBM in Europe compatible with the ABM Treaty could be fielded effectively against Soviet SS-20, SS-22, and SS-23 missiles, but not against distant Soviet ICBMs, some of the Soviet ICBMs could simply be retargeted on Europe. Moreover, the Soviet Union could deploy cruise missiles facing Europe, posing the question of additional costly new defense systems. A continuing offense-defense arms race would be certain.

Another possible Soviet reaction would be to propose inclusion of ATBM in the INF negotiations and to seek deferral of additional INF deployments pending negotiation of an agreement. Or, if the Soviet Union believed it could develop and deploy an effective ATBM with some strategic ABM capability while the United States limited itself to whatever European ATBM deployment it could gain Western European support for, the Soviet Union might—after squeezing political dividends from Western opposition to the idea—"reluctantly" acquiesce in interpretations that reaffirmed the ABM Treaty and allowed ATBM in Europe (including the European USSR).

Even though variations in the Soviet reaction, and in such aspects as whether the ATBM required a nuclear warhead, might affect Western reactions, it seems clear that the overall response would be negative, and possibly sharply negative. Even if some favorable sentiment were found, the issue at best would be divisive. It also seems clear that the Soviet reaction would be hostile, and the impact on East-West relations would be negative.

Defense of the Country

President Ronald Reagan, in his speech of March 23, 1983, mentioned in an unprecedented way the possibility of an eventual general defense

97. TASS, "Dangerous Plans of the American Military," Radio Moscow, in FBIS, *Daily Report: Soviet Union,* March 13, 1983, p. AA4; and Vladimir Bogachev, "The ABM Treaty and Stability," Radio Moscow, in FBIS, *Daily Report: Soviet Union,* March 16, 1983, p. AA4.

of the United States from ballistic missile attack.[98] The idea of a nationwide BMD has thus now been resurrected, and reactions to the president's initiative provide some recent data that assist in assessing Western European and Soviet attitudes toward the idea. Although there was for a time a great deal of speculation by the press, very little official clarification of the proposal followed. It would be unreasonable to expect a detailed outline for such a new general approach, but the inconstancy in the president's *aim* contributed to uncertainties and concerns, especially in Europe and the Soviet Union. Questions of feasibility aside, the goal of replacing deterrence by defense raises one set of questions; an aim of deterrence through powerful retaliatory offensive forces bolstered by effective BMD presents quite another set—and if unilaterally effected would pose a threat to the other side. President Reagan's candid if casual reference to a range of choices open to a U.S. president with such a combination of offensive power and defensive superiority *could* include a generous offer to give it to the adversary, but it could just as easily— and to the Soviet leaders far more probably—include ultimative threats to them.[99] This concern also stirred many in the United States and Europe. The president had, to be sure, included in his speech (reportedly in a last-minute insertion at the urging of the Department of State, when it belatedly was informed of the imminent initiative) reference to BMD of "our own soil or that of our allies." But he did not mention how such a defense could be mounted or what it would mean, especially in relation to the wide arsenal of weapons within range of Europe other than "strategic ballistic missiles." For Europe, the idea is even more improbable, reinforcing the impression that reference to the soil of allies was a cosmetic political addendum.

The reaction of the other members of NATO was also guarded and negative because once again, as in 1967 and 1969, there had been no advance consultations. Secretary of Defense Caspar W. Weinberger had met with the other NATO ministers of defense in the Nuclear Planning Group in a session ending the very day of the initiative—but had not been in a position even to prepare the way for it.

The initiative met widely with disbelief and dismay in Europe "as a setback to hopes that the superpowers can stabilize the nuclear bal-

98. Ronald Reagan, *Peace and National Security*, U.S. Department of State, Bureau of Public Affairs, Current Policy 472 (GPO, March 23, 1983), p. 7 (also the full text was printed in the *New York Times*, March 24, 1983).

99. "Transcript of Press Interview with President at the White House," *New York Times*, March 30, 1983.

ance."[100] In part, it reawakened fears of a U.S. interest in drawing back into a "fortress America," which were raised a decade or more ago in the earlier ABM debate.[101] But even more basically it appeared to reflect a U.S. desire to retreat from the complex realities of politics, strategy, and arms control in the nuclear age. There was heightened European concern at another sign of the United States' distancing itself from the task of reaching a compromise with the Soviet Union. Concern also was aroused over expected Soviet reactions. In short, Europeans saw the initiative, and the motivations that underlay it, as potentially destructive of East-West relations.

The Soviet reaction was predictable and swift. The Soviet Union denounced the U.S. motivation and intention and called attention to the political, military, and arms control impact. The nature of the critical reaction also reveals a great deal about Soviet thinking on BMD and related strategic issues.

Soviet reactions focused in part on the context and background to the initiative. Influential commentators stressed the fact that the president's stand on BMD followed closely on his attack on the Soviet Union as "the focus of evil" in the world, the latest manifestation of his anti-Soviet posture. The president's speech was contrasted with the Soviet unilateral initiative, and U.S. rejection, of a pledge on "no first use" of nuclear weapons. The Soviet Union argued that the U.S. rejection had transparent immediate aims of blunting the U.S. nuclear freeze movement and of gaining support for a military budget of unprecedented size. It was seen as part of a growing campaign for developing weaponry for war in space to accompany a host of new offensive strategic arms: MX, Trident II, B-1, Pershing II, and submarine- and ground-launched cruise missiles.[102] The U.S. aim was said to be to upset parity and to contribute to the quest for superiority.[103] In this respect, it was said to represent "a

100. Peter Osnos, "ABM Plan Spurs European Concern Over Timing, Defense Implications" [title varies with editions], *Washington Post*, March 30, 1983, citing a number of European officials and commentators.

101. See Holst, in Holst and Schneider, *Why ABM?*, pp. 190–94.

102. Many of these specific points are included in a major commentary by A. Tolkunov, "Washington's Skywalkers: On the New Militarist Venture by the White House," *Pravda*, March 30, 1983. On the context of American buildup of offensive weapons, and space weaponry, see also Lt. Gen. M. Mil'shtein, Ret., "Washington's Big Lie," *Komsomol-skaya Pravda* (Komsomol Pravda), April 13, 1983.

103. For example, see TASS, in FBIS, *Daily Report: Soviet Union*, March 24, 1983, p. AA2; and [Col.] L. Semeyko, Ret., "Counting on Impunity: On the New White House Militarist Concept," *Krasnaya zvezda*, April 15, 1983.

new intensification of global military preparations in both a geographic and a military-political sense."[104]

The most authoritative Soviet comment has come from General Secretary Yuri Andropov. He acknowledged that "on the face of it, laymen might find it even attractive as the president speaks about what seem to be defensive measures," but that is true only for those "who are not conversant with these matters." He noted that

> in fact the strategic offensive forces of the United States will continue to be developed and upgraded at full tilt and along a quite definite line at that, namely that of acquiring a first-strike nuclear capability. Under these conditions, the intention to acquire the capability of destroying the strategic systems of the other side with the aid of BMD, that is, of rendering the other side incapable of dealing a retaliatory strike, is a bid to disarm the Soviet Union in the face of the American nuclear threat. One must see this clearly in order to appraise correctly the true meaning of this "new concept."[105]

Although the American aim is portrayed—and probably seen—as hostile and dangerous, Soviet accounts also stress its unattainability, owing both to technical problems and to Soviet matching and countering measures. General Nikolai Chervov of the General Staff, for example, states that "as a matter of principle, there does not and cannot exist any absolute weapon. 'Absolutely reliable antiballistic missile defense' is just a mirage."[106] Owing to the fact that the powers "have reached approximately the same scientific-technical standards and have weapons that are roughly equivalent . . . neither side can overtake the other by a great margin. This is also true of BMD."[107] And others repeat "there can be no effective defense means in a nuclear war."[108] An unusual "Appeal to All Scientists of the World," signed by 243 prominent Soviet scientists and public figures, strongly opposed President Reagan's initiative and endorsed arms limitations. It included a statement that "there

---

104. Semeyko, *Krasnaya zvezda,* April 15, 1983.

105. "Replies of Yu. V. Andropov to Questions from a Correspondent of Pravda," *Pravda,* March 27, 1983. See also "Replies of Yu. V. Andropov to the Journal Spiegel (FRG)," *Pravda,* April 25, 1983. Among other Soviet accounts stressing these points, see the editorial, "Again the Big Lie," *Novoye vremya* (New Times), no. 14 (April 1, 1983), p. 1; Y. Soltan, Radio Moscow, FBIS, *Daily Report: Soviet Union,* April 12, 1983, p. AA4; Rudolf Kolchanov, Radio Moscow, FBIS, *Daily Report: Soviet Union,* May 3, 1983, pp. CC3–CC4; Vladlen Kuznetsov, "Washington's Dangerous Ambitions," *Sel'skaya zhizn'* (Rural Life), April 9, 1983; and many others.

106. Col. Gen. N. Chervov in an interview in *Pravda* (Bratislava), April 29, 1983.

107. Ibid.

108. Soltan, FBIS, *Daily Report: Soviet Union,* April 13, 1983, p. AA4.

are no effective defensive means in nuclear war and their creation is in practice not possible."[109]

Nonetheless, one effect of the U.S. decision (and most Soviet commentators, especially military ones, take the president's statement as a firm decision of the United States) has been to whip up the arms race and deal a serious blow to arms control. The U.S. pursuit of BMD, according to a Soviet commentator, "will open up the door for a tremendously intensive . . . arms race in both defensive and offensive weapons. It will be tremendously costly and tremendously dangerous. I think it will absolutely derail the whole process of arms control."[110] Moreover, that is said by another commentator to be not only its effect, but also its purpose: "The real purpose behind R. Reagan's space fantasies is to pave the way for renouncing existing accords and whipping up the arms race in all kinds of strategic weapons, offensive and defensive."[111]

From the first TASS account soon after President Reagan's speech, Soviet commentary has stressed that "the deployment of such antimissile defense systems would be a direct violation of the Soviet-American treaty."[112] Military spokesmen in particular have stressed the importance of the ABM treaty and its "important contribution to the limitation of strategic arms."[113] General Chervov has stressed the ban on developing BMD based on new physical principles such as lasers, as well as the ban on space-based BMD. He also notes the relevant constraints of the 1963 Limited Nuclear Test Ban Treaty and the 1967 Outer Space Treaty.[114]

More broadly, the Soviet discussions stress the destabilizing effects of BMD: "With all the differences in approaches of the USSR and the

109. *Pravda,* April 10, 1983.

110. G. Arbatov, interview on Radio Moscow, in FBIS, *Daily Report: Soviet Union,* April 13, 1983, p. AA2.

111. A. Bovin, "Fantasies and Reality," *Izvestiya,* April 21, 1983. See also V. Bogachev, "Illusory Calculation To Go Off with Impunity," TASS, Radio Moscow, in FBIS, *Daily Report: Soviet Union,* April 26, 1983, pp. AA5–AA6.

112. TASS, Radio Moscow, in FBIS, *Daily Report: Soviet Union,* March 24, 1983, p. AA2.

113. Semeyko, *Krasnaya zvezda,* April 15, 1983.

114. Chervov, *Pravda* (Bratislava), April 29, 1983; and on space-based BMD see also Semeyko, *Krasnaya zvezda,* April 15, 1983, and Tolkunov, *Pravda,* May 10, 1983.

The limitations imposed by the ABM Treaty are examined in chapter 5 herein; the Limited Nuclear Test Ban Treaty bans the detonation of nuclear explosives in space and would therefore ban testing or operation of nuclear-pulse explosions in space; the Outer Space Treaty bans the placing into space of any nuclear weapons or other weapons of mass destruction.

United States to problems of war and peace . . . former U.S. administrations still held that strategic stability . . . is in the interests of both the
USSR and the United States. The Reagan administration, adopting the
plan on establishing the ABM defence system, has demonstrated once
again that it either does not understand or ignores the dangers of military-
political destabilisation."[115]

Particular stress is placed by both military and political commentary
on the "inseparable linkage between defensive and offensive strategic
weapons,"[116] and the prospect, if BMD is pursued, of "an endless
escalation of measures, countermeasures, and counter-countermeasures
which would be more and more difficult to halt."[117] General Secretary
Andropov stressed this point in his comment on President Reagan's
BMD declaration. He noted that "when the USSR and the U.S.A. began
discussing the problems of strategic arms, they together acknowledged
that there is an inseparable interconnection between strategic offensive
and defensive arms." Later, the SALT accords in 1972, including the
ABM Treaty, reflected and affirmed that interrelationship, and the fact
that "only mutual restraint in the field of BMD can make it possible to
advance along the road of limiting and reducing strategic offensive arms,
that is, in controlling and reversing the strategic arms race as a whole."
He argued that "today, however, the United States has in mind to break
this interconnection. The result of such a concept, should it be realized,
would in fact open the floodgates of an unrestrained arms race in all
forms of strategic arms, offensive and defensive. Such is the real
meaning, the other side so to speak, of Washington's 'defensive concept.'"[118] And as another Soviet advocate of détente and arms control
commented on the new U.S. interest in BMD: "Whatever way you look
at it, the idea of 'absolute security' for one side becomes absolute
insecurity for the other."[119]

Agitation of the BMD issue by President Reagan has a somewhat
differing impact on different elements of the Soviet political establishment. For example, the reaction—the unusually strong and detailed
reaction—of Soviet military men with an interest in enhancing military
security through mutual arms control is obvious, but the reaction of

115. Bogachev, FBIS, *Daily Report: Soviet Union,* April 26, 1983, p. AA6.
116. Chervov, *Pravda* (Bratislava), April 29, 1983.
117. Semeyko, *Krasnaya zvezda,* April 15, 1983.
118. "Replies of Yu. V. Andropov," *Pravda,* March 27, 1983. Many Soviet
commentaries have repeated these views.
119. Bovin, *Izvestiya,* April 21, 1983.

those preparing threat assessments (those who, even before Reagan's initiative, had been predicting something along that very line as a logical step in U.S. pursuit of superiority and a first-strike capability) can only be surmised. The Ministry of Defense's official published assessment, *Whence the Threat to Peace,* included this passage:

> Intensive research is under way to produce effective antimissile weaponry.
>
> The main effort is concentrated on developing an in-depth antimissile system that would intercept objects in outer space as well as in dense atmosphere, involving the latest weaponry, including multiple warheads banned under the Soviet-American Treaty on the Limitation of Anti-Ballistic Missile Systems.
>
> The Pentagon has, indeed, set its sight on laying the requisite technical foundation for the deployment of this type of operational antimissile system already in the current decade.
>
> The agreed schedule of the Pentagon plans for building up strategic offensive armaments and deploying antimissile and space defense systems is timed to complete the development of a so-called first-strike potential in the 1980s.[120]

To those holding this view of U.S. intentions and military programs, the president's announcement, while dealing with more advanced long-term systems, merely confirmed their expectations and their viewpoint.

To those in Moscow who have continued to argue for the feasibility of general strategic arms limitations, even after the repudiation of the SALT II Treaty and the reluctant approach and transparently slow motion of the Reagan administration toward arms control, the prospect of U.S. repudiation of the ABM Treaty as well was a serious blow. There is a mix of suspicion and frustration in Soviet reactions to the change in U.S. official thinking. As one long-time Soviet advocate of détente and arms control put it,

> The President of the United States must know that all these problems have already been discussed, and most thoroughly, in the early seventies when the ABM Treaty was being worked out. Then the United States and the Soviet Union reached the conclusion that a reliable and extensive ABM system cannot be created. Then the United States and the Soviet Union agreed that attempts to create ABM systems destabilize Soviet-American relations and would impede agreement on limiting the strategic capabilities of both sides. What has changed since that time? In principle, nothing has changed.[121]

---

120. *Whence the Threat to Peace* (Moscow: USSR Ministry of Defense, 1982), p. 36; and in the second edition of the Russian language text, *Otkuda iskhodit ugroza miru* (Moscow: Voyenizdat, signed to press on July 14, 1982), p. 41.

121. Bovin, *Izvestiya,* April 21, 1983. Bovin had, in the 1960s and early 1970s, come under direct attack by conservative military commentators for his early endorsement of such views.

Indeed, it is clear—and in one instance explicit—that some Soviet commentators are concerned that the internal *Soviet* consensus on arms control hammered out in the late 1960s and early to mid-1970s might unravel. The offense-defense linkage was key to this development of compatible military doctrine and arms control doctrine, not only on BMD, in that earlier period and continuing since that time. Academician G. Arbatov has stressed that "all [this] was discussed and *discussed at length in a very heated way* at the end of the sixties and beginning of the seventies, and this *naive concept,* which was *shared by many people* in different continents, *maybe even some people on our side at the beginning, was that defensive weapons are not dangerous.*"[122]

Clearly, Arbatov recalls very well that this view, publicly taken more than once by Prime Minister Kosygin and initially dominant even in arms control circles in Moscow, was changed only after long and "heated" discussions. He does not want to see the question reopened. In his interview, speaking off the cuff, Dr. Arbatov went on to say this renewed talk about "such exotic and unknown means of annihilation like X-ray, laser, and many others" is "really like a bad dream," "the worst possible situation the arms race . . . could have."[123]

The unsettling nature of even the revival of the question of BMD, and its potential impact on Soviet military doctrine, on Soviet views of the prospects for arms control, and ultimately on détente may become clearer from pondering the Soviet reaction to President Reagan's initiative on BMD. Nor is it difficult to predict a substantial influence on Western thinking of possible changes in Soviet policy stirred by the issue of BMD for defense of the country.

Conclusions

It is difficult to reach any other conclusion but that under present and forseeable circumstances any intensified pursuit of BMD can only have a negative impact on East-West relations, ranging from moderately to disastrously negative in both its political and its military and arms control dimensions.

---

122. Arbatov, FBIS, *Daily Report: Soviet Union,* April 13, 1983, p. AA1 (emphasis added).
123. Ibid., p. AA2.

Paradoxically, the most favorable context for a U.S. national decision on BMD, especially on a nationwide BMD, and virtually a prerequisite for international "acceptance," would be a considerable prior improvement in East-West relations. In fact, the ideal circumstance would be a U.S.-Soviet agreement jointly to develop and deploy such defenses in order to ensure strategic stability, crisis stability, and arms race stability. It may well be questioned whether, under such idyllic political circumstances, there would be sufficient interest and readiness to make the necessary extensive commitment of resources to improve strategic stability further. There would, no doubt, also be a continuing controversy as to whether such a development would, in fact, enhance security. The posited political condition is, however, so remote as to remove the effort at analysis from the current agenda. It is, nonetheless, important to have in mind the need to plan and to accompany *any* initiative on BMD with appropriate considerations of how BMD could contribute to security in political as well as technical dimensions. That, in turn, would require an understanding and consideration of the important relationship of BMD to military doctrine as well as programs, to the regime of existing and possible future measures of arms control, and to U.S.-allied, U.S.-Soviet, and East-West political relations.

CHAPTER NINE

Past and Present:
The Historical Legacy

DAVID N. SCHWARTZ

As a policy issue ballistic missile defense is burdened with a particularly heavy historical legacy. The fact that it was the focus of one of the first "great debates" over U.S. national security policy in the late 1960s and early 1970s will be used by those on either side of the issue to make their particular points.

It will be tempting for opponents of BMD to argue that the ABM Treaty of 1972 rendered a definitive historical judgment that BMD, aside from its ineffectiveness, is highly destabilizing and must be kept to the barest minimum. They will argue that all the points made by opponents of BMD deployments during the 1967–70 period remain valid today and that any attempt to revisit the issue in 1983 is doomed merely to a prolonged, and ultimately futile, effort to avoid realities that were squarely faced in 1972.

Proponents of a renewed BMD effort can also make reference to history. They can argue the case for BMD that was made in the late 1960s with the rationale that the case is better than was realized at the time. Alternatively they can argue that while the judgments of 1972 seemed to be the best given the situation at the time, technology, strategy, and politics have moved significantly beyond the 1972 period and force us to reexamine our old judgments. In either case proponents of change will argue that it is a mistake to view the treaty, and the debate leading up to it, as rendering definitive historical judgments of any sort.

This chapter reviews the highlights of the events and decisions of more than a decade leading up to the 1972 treaty in order to give the reader a better sense of how to assess arguments that make use of history

330

in this way. No claims to definitiveness are made. Rather, a review of the most important aspects of this historical legacy can reveal the differences and similarities between then and now that are relevant to any assessment of current arguments based on history.

The Historical Record: An Overview

Interest in ballistic missile defense dates back to the era of the first operational ballistic missile, the German V-2.[1] Shortly after World War II, the U.S. Air Force, intrigued by the potential opportunities of offensive ballistic missiles, was also interested in exploring ways to shoot down enemy missiles. Two early projects, Thumper and Wizard, began in 1946 to examine the technical feasibility of ballistic missile defense. But relevant technology—rocket propulsion, guidance, target acquisition, and rapid data processing—was too primitive throughout the 1940s and early 1950s to offer much hope for the feasibility of BMD.

Developments in these technologies had, by the mid-1950s, changed technical assessments of BMD feasibility. The air force's Wizard project had begun to flesh out a feasible technical concept for BMD involving what are now considered standard elements of BMD: target acquisition and tracking by powerful, long-distance radar; and a nuclear-tipped interceptor missile that would be guided to its target by the target-tracking radar.

During this time the U.S. Army—eager for a bigger role in the nuclear mission—began to explore similar concepts in the framework of its Nike series of air defense missile programs. Noting the conceptual and

1. The best general history of BMD technology, upon which much of the following historical review is based, is by Edward Randolph Jayne II, "The ABM Debate: Strategic Defense and National Security" (Ph.D. dissertation, Massachusetts Institute of Technology, 1969). Unfortunately, this study has never been published. Nor has the fascinating biography of Nike-Zeus provided in Fred A. Payne, "A Discussion of Nike Zeus Decisions," a speech before a seminar on Science, Technology, and Public Policy, Brookings Institution, October 1, 1964. Of the many published sources, several are particularly useful: Ralph E. Lapp, "A Biography of the ABM," *New York Times Magazine*, May 4, 1969; Ernest J. Yanarella, *The Missile Defense Controversy: Strategy, Technology, and Politics, 1955–1972* (University Press of Kentucky, 1977); Benson D. Adams, "McNamara's ABM Policy, 1961–1967," *Orbis*, vol. 12 (Spring 1968), pp. 200–25; and Morton H. Halperin, "The Decision to Deploy the ABM: Bureaucratic and Domestic Politics in the Johnson Administration," *World Politics*, vol. 25 (October 1972), pp. 62–95.

technical similarity of BMD and air defense, the army in 1955 asked Bell Laboratories to develop a variant of the Nike-Hercules nuclear anti-aircraft missile that would be able to shoot down incoming ballistic missile warheads. The result was the Nike-Zeus system, which became the forerunner for virtually all U.S. BMD systems.

The period between 1955 and 1958 saw an intense competition between the air force's Wizard project and the army's Nike-Zeus program. The battle was over which service would be granted the BMD mission—the air force, which had already established service dominance in the strategic nuclear mission and had won the mission of defending wide expanses of territory ("area defense") against enemy aircraft, or the army, which lacked a major strategic mission but which had been given the air defense mission of defending specific targets ("point defense"). The interservice battle over BMD became part of a much broader competition for missions and defense resources.

In early 1958 Secretary of Defense Neil McElroy, forced by the Sputnik launch to make a quick decision on the BMD mission, authorized the army to proceed with operational development of Nike-Zeus. The air force was directed to scale down the Wizard effort and to focus on development of radar and data-processing capabilities for systems to warn of ballistic missile attack. In addition, to ensure effective civilian control over future research and development (R&D), McElroy created the Advanced Research Projects Agency (ARPA), a civilian scientific agency tied to the Office of the Secretary of Defense and charged with overall direction of advanced military research on space and missiles, including BMD. During the next three years the army would attempt, in each budget cycle, to persuade the secretary of defense and the president to authorize production funds for Nike-Zeus. Each time, the army's request was refused. These negative decisions were the result of a complex set of technical and political factors that led a broad coalition within the executive branch to oppose production funding.

There was a general argument, championed by the air force but shared by Pentagon civilians, that investment dollars were better spent on offensive missile forces. More important, scientists in the Pentagon, under the direction of Herbert York, and the President's Science Advisory Committee harbored technical doubts about the ability of Nike-Zeus to perform its mission. These doubts centered on the ability of the target-acquisition and tracking radars to discriminate between reentry vehicles (RVs) and decoys at altitudes above the atmosphere;

the problem of system saturation if RVs arrive at close intervals; the ability of Nike-Zeus radars to function properly in the face of nuclear blackout; the ability of guidance systems to bring the Nike-Zeus interceptor to within kill radius of the incoming RV; and the lack of performance testing against a realistic Soviet threat. Many of these issues were raised for the first time in late 1957 and early 1958 in a study by a technical panel called the Reentry Body Identification Group, which was headed by William E. Bradley and which reported to the Pentagon's director of guided missiles, William Holaday.[2] During the 1958–61 period the issues were sufficient to persuade McElroy, his successor Thomas Gates, and President Dwight D. Eisenhower to continue rejecting army requests for production funds. They did not, however, prevent the army from taking its case directly to Capitol Hill, where it gradually mustered enough support in the fiscal 1961 budget to persuade Congress to restore money for Nike-Zeus production that had been deleted by the president. Even then, however, the executive refused to spend it, so that at the start of the Kennedy administration the Nike-Zeus program had still not been given a production go-ahead.

The Pentagon under the stewardship of Robert McNamara took a similarly jaundiced view of the operational capabilities of Nike-Zeus, even after the army had conducted a series of tests at the Kwajalein missile range that indicated that Nike-Zeus could be used to shoot down incoming RVs from first-generation U.S. intercontinental ballistic missiles (ICBMs).[3] Of particular concern, initially, to McNamara and his staff was the army's tendency to argue Nike-Zeus's effectiveness against *current* Soviet technology; the new civilian planners insisted on measuring the system's effectiveness against the likely *future* Soviet ICBM threat, which might include sophisticated penetration aids and decoys. Against such a threat Nike-Zeus could not measure up.

But the technical issues were only some of the concerns of the new staff at the Pentagon. Among the new strategic concepts brought in by the Kennedy administration was the objective of damage limitation. In assessing the value of various defensive efforts in limiting damage to U.S. society and weighing the value against the relative costs, the Pentagon concluded that passive defensive measures—particularly an enhanced civil defense–shelter program—were far more cost effective

2. Payne, "Discussion of Nike Zeus Decisions," pp. 4–5.
3. Adams, "McNamara's ABM Policy," p. 211.

than BMD. As a result of analyses conducted by the Pentagon's Weapon System Evaluation Group, McNamara concluded that production of Nike-Zeus would make no sense if the United States had already invested in an effective shelter program.[4]

In the fiscal 1962 and fiscal 1963 budget cycles McNamara was able to resist army pressures to authorize Nike-Zeus production, for the reasons cited above. In the fiscal 1963 budget cycle, however, he chose a new tactic, which redirected the army program and virtually eliminated pressure for Nike-Zeus production. On the basis of an ongoing BMD study, Project Defender, ARPA had concluded that emerging technologies in radar, data processing, and rocket propulsion could be put to use in a new ABM system. ARPA Director Jack Ruina had been asked by Director of Defense Research and Engineering Harold Brown to consider possible alternatives for continued BMD development programs. Ruina outlined four options: NZ-0, which was the current Nike-Zeus system under development in the army; NZ-1, which was similar to NZ-0 except that it would use a much higher velocity interceptor missile, allowing for endoatmospheric target discrimination and intercept; NZ-2, another spinoff of NZ-0, which would use the faster interceptor missile and a phased-array radar to locate and track multiple targets in a short period of time; and NX, which would not rely on NZ-0 as a basis but would use the faster interceptor, phased-array radars, and new computers, integrated into a totally new system. Thus was born "Nike-X."[5]

Because Nike-X was conceived as an endoatmospheric system—its objective would be to destroy RVs after they had entered the atmosphere—its tracking radars could use the differing effect of atmospheric drag on RVs and decoys to help solve the problem of discriminating between the two. However, waiting this long for initiating interception would allow the RV to approach very near the target—at very high speed—before it could be destroyed. This imposed a requirement for an interceptor capable of extremely high acceleration to reach altitudes of several miles in several seconds. The technology needed to develop such a missile (which was the forerunner of Sprint) and to guide this missile to its target was on the horizon. Phased-array radars, the feasibility of which had been demonstrated by ARPA studies in 1963, would enable Nike-X to handle large numbers of incoming targets. With such technol-

4. Ibid., pp. 213, 218–19; see also Jayne, "The ABM Debate," pp. 183–84.
5. Interview with Jack Ruina, May 2, 1982.

ogy, the saturation problem would be less a result of slow radar acquisition and tracking than it would be a function of RVs in excess of interceptors.

Defense scientists believed the Nike-X concept was feasible. In fiscal 1963, McNamara authorized a dramatic shift in R&D resources to the Nike-X program, and the army—under General Austin Betts—spent the next eighteen months developing Nike-X to the point where a production decision looked reasonable.

The army, convinced that Nike-Zeus should be produced and deployed against the current threat, resisted this development. Nonetheless, the shift to Nike-X was a significant improvement in the prospects for BMD. McNamara had not relinquished his position that investment in ABM production would only make sense after the nation had invested in a civil defense program. But he had acknowledged that the technical and operational questions regarding Nike-Zeus were in principle rectifiable. More important, he was persuaded to fund research and development if only to keep open future options, and had authorized $350 million in 1963 to do just that.

But the battle for BMD was not over. While the army was developing Nike-X, McNamara became concerned about yet another aspect of BMD—its potential for stimulating an arms race. The logic of this concern, articulated in the civilian policy offices of the Pentagon beginning as early as 1962, was simple but compelling.[6] If the Soviet Union were intent upon maintaining a capability to inflict a given degree of damage on the United States, an ABM system that degraded that capability would stimulate growth in Soviet offensive capabilities to offset that degradation in capability. This would bring the offensive threat to the United States back to its pre-ABM levels; the United States would then respond by increasing its defensive systems to compensate for the growth in Soviet offensive capabilities. Such a ratcheting up of the arms race was considered to be a serious, almost decisive argument against BMD programs that were technically feasible.

Against such a critique, few ABM systems—not even the Nike-X, far superior from a technical standpoint to the Nike-Zeus—could meet the criterion of arms race stability imposed by McNamara. Nevertheless,

6. An early, comprehensive statement of this view was provided by Jack Ruina and Murray Gell-Mann in "Ballistic Missile Defense and the Arms Race," a paper prepared for the Twelfth Pugwash Conference on Science and World Affairs, Udaipur, January 27–February 1, 1964.

General Betts was successful in gaining full support from the Joint Chiefs of Staff for the program. In 1966, the army and the Joint Chiefs made a concerted effort to gain production authority from the president.

By this time many of the arguments McNamara had used to postpone Nike-Zeus production could no longer be used against Nike-X. Because of the development of phased-array radars, high acceleration rockets, and advanced data processing, the arguments regarding Nike-Zeus's inability to discriminate RVs from decoys in time to destroy the RVs and defend targets of value were not valid for Nike-X. Furthermore, although it could still be saturated, Nike-X was better able than Nike-Zeus to deal with RVs arriving at close intervals. Although the United States had not invested a substantial sum in civil defense preparations, McNamara had little hope of or inclination for getting more resources devoted to this area. Soviet improvements in strategic offensive forces, not evident in 1961, also argued for taking the BMD mission more seriously. Finally, there was evidence that the Soviet Union was proceeding with an intensive BMD effort of its own.

In sum, time had forced McNamara into a corner. As the debate over Nike-X moved into 1966—the fiscal 1968 budget cycle—McNamara was forced to rely less on his previous arguments against deployment and more on the implications of the action-reaction phenomenon. Analyses done in the Pentagon examined how two specific ABM postures, based on the Nike-X system, would affect the Soviet "assured destruction" capability, and how various Soviet responses would degrade the performance of these two postures.[7]

Posture A consisted of an area defense system of the United States, and a local defense of twenty-five cities. This was the posture advocated by the Joint Chiefs as an initial step. Posture B was more extensive, involving defense of some fifty-two cities, and probably reflected the ultimate goal of the services. (In addition, because of demographics, defense of more than fifty cities showed greatly diminishing marginal returns.) It was clear from Pentagon analyses that even posture A could result in a 90 percent degradation of Soviet assured destruction capabilities. Posture B would degrade these capabilities still further. Civilian analysts, supported by McNamara, argued that such degradation would not be tolerated by Soviet military planners, who would seek various

---

7. The following summary of Pentagon analyses is drawn from Alain C. Enthoven and K. Wayne Smith, *How Much Is Enough? Shaping the Defense Program, 1961–69* (Harper and Row, 1971), pp. 184–94.

means to offset it. If the Soviet Union invested in multiple independently targetable reentry vehicle (MIRV) technology and penetration aids and moved to a force that included 100 mobile ICBMs, it could regain 90 percent of its capability against posture A. Posture B might provoke the Soviet Union to increase investment in mobile ICBMs to some 500 systems; such a response, combined with MIRV and penetration aid technology, would regain 80 percent of its capability. Looked at in this light, either BMD posture being analyzed by systems analysts in the Pentagon stood a good chance of stimulating a destabilizing arms race with no foreseeable termination.

These conclusions were not shared by the armed services. Having spent several billion dollars in R&D money to develop an ABM system that looked as though it would actually work against Soviet offensive forces in being at the time, the armed services were reluctant to forgo the program on strategic grounds. They argued variously that there was little evidence that the Soviet Union sized its forces according to the assured destruction criteria that guided the civilian analysts; that the Soviet Union would not be able to afford a response of the type foreseen by these analysts; and that even if it could, it would be doomed to an unending game of catch-up with the United States that would be politically damaging and extremely costly. Thus, they pressed for an anti-Soviet ABM program along the lines of posture A, described above.

These arguments came before the president in a series of meetings on the 1968 defense budget in late 1966.[8] Both positions were argued forcefully, in particular at a December 6 meeting in Austin, Texas, where McNamara and his deputy Cyrus Vance put forward the case against Nike-X, and General Earle G. Wheeler and other service chiefs put the case in favor of posture A as an interim step toward eventual adoption of posture B. When President Lyndon Johnson indicated his decision to move ahead with deployment, McNamara offered a compromise that the president accepted. The 1968 budget would contain several hundred million dollars for production and procurement of long-lead items for Nike-X, but this money would be withheld pending efforts to explore bilateral, negotiated ABM limitations with the Soviet Union.

Many observers have remarked on the way in which this turn of events, however spontaneous, reflected McNamara's deep and growing

---

8. Several useful summaries of these crucial meetings exist. See Jayne, "The ABM Debate," pp. 333–43; and John Newhouse, *Cold Dawn: The Story of SALT* (Holt, Rinehart and Winston, 1973), p. 86.

concern about the U.S.-Soviet nuclear arms race. There can be little doubt on this score. Nevertheless, the proposal *was* spontaneous and conditioned in large part by the secretary's perception that he could no longer postpone production as he had during the previous five years. Time had run out for McNamara; in recognizing this, he was committed to keeping deployments as low as possible and to engaging Soviet cooperation toward this end.

Diplomatically, the six-month period between the Austin meeting and the June 1967 U.S.-Soviet summit at Glassboro, New Jersey, was a period of intensive activity, as the United States tried to engage the Soviet Union in arms control talks on ABM.[9] High-level, secret contacts in Washington and Moscow indicated that the Kremlin was interested in talking, although it insisted that talks include offensive weapons as well as ABM. In March, however, it was announced that the two governments had agreed in principle to begin discussions on both offensive and defensive systems, but no date was set. Work on the U.S. negotiating position, begun in January in a small working group of the State and Defense departments, continued, as did contacts in Washington and Moscow. But when the June 1967 Glassboro summit arrived, Johnson was unable to gain Soviet Premier Aleksei Kosygin's agreement on a timetable for talks. Indeed, Kosygin still seemed skeptical regarding the urgency of constraints on defensive systems, even after hearing the U.S. secretary of defense expound on the matter over a luncheon meeting.

Faced with Soviet unreadiness to proceed promptly with strategic nuclear arms control, Johnson saw no choice but to move ahead with funding for Nike-X, which had been renamed Sentinel. Johnson had been willing to postpone while McNamara sounded out the Soviet representatives. In January Johnson had also been treated to an extraordinary White House meeting, orchestrated by McNamara, to which were invited all past and present presidential science advisers and directors of defense research and engineering—in effect the leaders of the defense science establishment.[10] Their unanimous recommendation had been against deployment of a major anti-Soviet ABM deployment and only marginally more supportive of a smaller anti-China deployment. Still, that month Johnson had earmarked $375 million for Sentinel

9. Newhouse, *Cold Dawn*, pp. 87–89.
10. Ibid., p. 89. See also Yanarella, *Missile Defense Controversy*, p. 124.

production in fiscal 1968 pending contacts with the Soviet Union, in accordance with his decision of December 1966. Now that the contacts had failed to produce prompt agreement that talks should begin, McNamara's problem became how to justify the $366 million expenditure that Congress had agreed to in July.

The problem was difficult. Persuaded that expansion of a "thin" ABM system into a large anti-Soviet system would represent a tragedy of major proportions, McNamara was determined to find a rationale that was not keyed to an anti-Soviet deployment and that effectively precluded the later expansion of the system into an anti-Soviet one. Several such rationales had existed for years in the U.S. defense bureacracy; McNamara had suggested some of these in previous annual reports to Congress. In intensive debates within Pentagon staffs, and supported by some within the State Department, he eventually fixed on one of them— a system to defend in the medium term against the nascent Chinese nuclear threat.[11] In June 1967 China had detonated its first thermonuclear device; U.S. intelligence considered Chinese ICBMs to be inevitable, if several years away. Using work that had been previously done by the systems analysis staff, and updating it somewhat, the civilian Pentagon leadership fashioned an anti-Chinese rationale to fit McNamara's bill.

But more was needed. McNamara felt he needed something to constrain the enthusiasm of the Joint Chiefs. He had no doubts that, once construction had been authorized, the Joint Chiefs would continue to press for expansion of the system into one that could handle the Soviet ICBM threat as well. Determined to prevent this, he marshaled all the arguments he could find against a Soviet-oriented system, relying heavily on the action-reaction phenomenon that continued to trouble him.

The result of this intensive search for the safest rationale, the one that held the least danger in the future, was a remarkable speech McNamara delivered before the Press Club in San Francisco on September 18, 1967. In it he pleaded passionately against the feasibility, utility, and wisdom of an anti-Soviet Sentinel system, alluding at one point to the "mad momentum" of the arms race. Toward the end of the speech, however, he turned his attention toward China and announced the administration's plan to deploy a "thin" Sentinel system to defend against the predicted small Chinese ICBM threat and accidental launches.

11. Newhouse, *Cold Dawn*, pp. 95–96.

This speech marked a turning point in the history of the ABM issue. Over the next four years, until the U.S.-Soviet ABM Treaty was signed in May 1972, the ABM issue became the focus of intense public debate and equally intense diplomatic maneuvers between the United States and the Soviet Union.

The public debate found its locus in the U.S. Senate, where interest in ABM had been sporadic over the past decade. A small but influential group of senators on the Armed Services Committee, friendly to the services and fearful of the Soviet ABM effort to protect Moscow, had unsuccessfully but regularly pressed the administration to fund ABM production ever since the early 1960s. This group, led by Strom Thurmond, John Stennis, Richard Russell, and Henry Jackson, maintained a strong interest throughout the 1968–72 period in promoting Sentinel and its revised version after 1969, Safeguard.[12]

Opposition to ABM in the Senate was confined in these early years to a small group of liberal senators, such as J. William Fulbright, Albert Gore, and Edward Kennedy, who brought a general skepticism about defense spending, stimulated by opposition to the Vietnam War, to the particular issue of Sentinel and Safeguard.[13] In April 1968, however, they were joined by the powerful Republican senator from Kentucky, John Sherman Cooper, who began to organize opposition to Sentinel deployment in the summer of 1968.[14] The coalition he developed in mid-1968 attempted three times—in June, August, and October—to delay or cut funding of Sentinel production, relying on a set of arguments that included the action-reaction phenomenon, the danger of defense in a world of arms race instability, technical deficiencies in the system, and financial considerations. Each time it failed, but it was surprisingly strong; the first vote in June found thirty-four senators voting in favor of postponing Sentinel deployment for one year while renewed efforts could be mounted to reach agreement on strategic arms limitations.

The administration fought these efforts to delay or cut Sentinel and was generally successful. In addition, in the summer of 1968 the Soviet Union had agreed on holding arms control talks. Plans for a summit meeting and the opening of the strategic arms limitation talks (SALT) were scuttled, however, when the Soviet Union invaded Czechoslovakia

12. Yanarella, *Missile Defense Controversy,* p. 125; Jayne, "The ABM Debate," pp. 126, 184–91.
13. Yanarella, *Missile Defense Controversy,* pp. 145–57.
14. Ibid., pp. 149–52.

in August, and the Democrats had lost the 1968 election before they were able to put the talks back on the agenda.[15]

Public concern, quiescent until 1968, became widespread as it was revealed that the first phase of Sentinel—a population defense system—would involve missile deployments north of several major cities, including Chicago and Boston. When the full fiscal 1969 ABM funding of $1.2 billion was approved in October 1968,[16] the public took to the streets in these cities, and the major demonstrations of this period persuaded even sympathetic senators, such as Everett Dirksen, that Sentinel could become a serious political liability.[17]

These events, combined with the Nixon administration's desire to undertake a comprehensive review of U.S. strategic policy when it came into office in January 1969, made it relatively easy for the new secretary of defense, Melvin Laird, to suspend the Sentinel program in early February 1969, pending a full review. In mid-March President Richard M. Nixon made public his revised ABM program, Safeguard.[18] Using much the same technology as Sentinel, Safeguard would be reoriented away from population defense to a greater emphasis on point defense of ICBMs. At the same time, it would retain an area-defense mission, although no interceptors would be based near major cities. The system would be directed against the Soviet ICBM threat—the Chinese threat had failed to materialize at the pace predicted in 1967—and would be designed to take into account new offensive technologies, including MIRV.

This new proposal prompted a strong public reaction. The Senate Foreign Relations Committee held a series of intensive hearings on the subject and brought an array of nongovernmental expert witnesses to testify on the technical and political implications of ABM.[19] A broad spectrum of the U.S. scientific community now became embroiled in the controversy, and major figures carried on bitter debates before senators

15. Newhouse, *Cold Dawn*, pp. 131–32.

16. "Numerous Moves Fail to Kill Plans for ABM System," *Congressional Quarterly Almanac*, 90 Cong. 2 sess., vol. 24 (Washington, D.C.: Congressional Quarterly Service, 1968), p. 95.

17. Yanarella, *Missile Defense Controversy*, p. 152.

18. Ibid., pp. 143–86.

19. *Strategic and Foreign Policy Implications of ABM Systems*, Hearings before the Subcommittee on International Organization and Disarmament Affairs of the Senate Committee on Foreign Relations, 91 Cong. 1 sess. (Government Printing Office, 1969), 3 pts.

in these hearings and in parallel ones held by friends of Safeguard in the Armed Services Committee.[20] The Cooper coalition re-formed to do battle with the new proposal, but in the end—by a vote of 51–50, with Vice-President Spiro T. Agnew casting the tie-breaking vote—the Senate approved funding of the first phase of Safeguard.[21]

Throughout this debate and a similar one in 1970 over funding for expanding phase I of the Safeguard program, the administration used Soviet development of the Galosh ABM system around Moscow and the growth of the Soviet strategic offensive arsenal to justify deployment of the system. Another justification used was related to SALT, which began in November 1969. The administration argued that only by continuing to fund Safeguard would there be any incentive for the Soviet Union to agree to negotiated ABM limitations. This rationale became increasingly important as the negotiations dragged on. By May 1971 the United States and the Soviet Union publicly announced that an agreement on defensive systems, separate but loosely linked to one on offensive systems, would be in the interests of both sides.[22] By May 1972 the two governments had agreed on a treaty that put a cap—at a very low level—on the ABM capabilities of the superpowers.

Some have read into this treaty an endorsement by the superpowers of the strategic doctrine of mutual assured destruction, articulated by Secretary of Defense McNamara in the 1960s principally as a means of capping offensive arms expenditures. According to this doctrine, stability and deterrence are enhanced if the two superpowers leave their societies exposed to second-strike retaliation by each other and avoid posing a first-strike offensive threat to those retaliatory forces. Both sides seemed to understand that defensive preparations could inject an element of instability into the superpower relationship. If effective, a defense system could deny the enemy the capacity to retaliate after a nuclear attack and could conceivably increase the incentives of either side to preempt in a time of crisis, though obviously for different reasons. More likely, since the systems developed in the 1960s could be offset with a relatively marginal increase in offensive forces by the other side,

20. See, in particular, Anne Hessing Cahn, "American Scientists and the ABM: A Case Study in Controversy," in Albert H. Teich, ed., *Scientists and Public Affairs* (MIT Press, 1974), pp. 41–120.

21. "Nixon Missile Plan Wins in Senate by a 51–50 Vote; House Approval Likely," *New York Times*, August 7, 1969.

22. Newhouse, *Cold Dawn*, p. 217.

deployment of an ABM system could stimulate long-term pressures for an arms race—the action-reaction phenomenon McNamara had articulated in his various reports to Congress and in his September 1967 Sentinel speech.

At the same time, the actual behavior of the superpowers since 1972 leads to some serious question as to how deeply the mutual assured destruction doctrine was adopted by either side. In offensive programs both sides pursued, within the limits of the offensive force constraints imposed by SALT, vigorous programs to multiply the numbers of RVs on ICBMs and submarine-launched ballistic missiles (SLBMs) and to increase the accuracy of these RVs to the point where today each side could do substantial damage in a first strike against the other's strategic retaliatory forces. Nor has either side foresworn ABM. As table 9-1 shows, the United States has maintained an impressive level of funding for basic research and development since 1972. Many concepts have been examined on the blackboards of defense scientists. But since 1972 no operational prototypes of new systems have been built, in accordance with the treaty.

Lessons of the Past

Learning from history is never easy. But the fact that history is often used to buttress arguments regarding current policy choices requires us to attempt to learn what we can, in a discriminating and cautious way, from past experience. The BMD issue is no exception. The admittedly brief review of history in this chapter enables us to assess the claim that nothing has changed, that the arguments that won the day between 1968 and 1972 are as valid today as they were then, that the 1972 treaty reflects a definitive judgment that BMD is wasteful and destabilizing and therefore should be severely constrained on both sides. It should also enable us to assess the argument that considerations of politics, strategy, and technology are fundamentally different from those of the 1968–72 period and hence invalidate the arguments made then against BMD deployment. It would be surprising if there were not some important elements of truth in both claims. Take, for example, the assertion that all the old arguments are still valid. Who can deny that any responsible discussion of BMD today will have to take into account all the issues that were debated so hotly a decade ago? Strategically, the issue of the possible Soviet military

Table 9-1. *U.S. Spending on BMD after the ABM Treaty,*
Fiscal 1973–85
Millions of dollars

Year and type of funding	Continued deployment of Safeguard	Continued development of site defense	Development of advanced missile technology	Development of systems technology	Development	Procurement
1973						
Actual	599	80	93	. . .	. . .	. . .
1974						
Planned	341	110	62	. . .	. . .	. . .
1975						
Actual	a	. . .	95	117	. . .	. . .
1976						
Actual	. . .	. . .	97	100	. . .	. . .
1976[b]						
Planned	. . .	. . .	25	25	. . .	. . .
1977						
Planned	. . .	. . .	103	100	. . .	. . .
Actual	. . .	. . .	102.7	100	. . .	. . .
1978						
Planned	. . .	. . .	107.3	106.2	. . .	. . .
Actual	. . .	. . .	107.3	106.2	. . .	. . .
1979						
Planned	. . .	. . .	113.5	114	. . .	. . .
Actual	. . .	. . .	113.5	114	. . .	. . .
1980						
Planned	. . .	. . .	120.8	120.8	. . .	. . .
Actual	. . .	. . .	. . .	240.7[c]	. . .	. . .
1981						
Planned	. . .	. . .	. . .	268.2[c]	. . .	. . .
Actual	. . .	. . .	. . .	266.6[c]	. . .	. . .
1982						
Planned	. . .	. . .	. . .	. . .	462.1	57.3
Actual	. . .	. . .	. . .	. . .	462.1	. . .
1983						
Planned	. . .	. . .	. . .	. . .	519	. . .
1984						
Proposed	. . .	. . .	. . .	. . .	709.3	. . .
1985						
Proposed	. . .	. . .	. . .	. . .	1564	. . .

Sources: *Annual Defense Department Report, FY 1975*, p. 54; *FY 1978*, p. 127; *Department of Defense Annual Report, Fiscal Year 1979*, p. 129; *Fiscal Year 1980*, p. 131; *Fiscal Year 1981*, p. 139; *Fiscal Year 1982*, p. 119; *Department of Defense Annual Report to the Congress, Fiscal Year 1983*, p. III-66; *Fiscal Year 1984*, p. 228. Research by Nancy Ameen.
a. Safeguard system terminated in accordance with fiscal 1976 congressional directive.
b. July 1–September 30, 1976.
c. Includes both systems technology and advanced technology programs.

responses, and the long-term stability of a world in which BMD plays a greater role than it does today, is a legitimate concern. Indeed, whatever the validity of the action-reaction relationship when postulated by McNamara in the mid-1960s, the fact of a U.S.-Soviet treaty that would have to be amended or abrogated in order to accommodate most new BMD initiatives virtually guarantees that action-reaction will take place today. It is reasonable to assume that the treaty provides political and symbolic reasons, apart from any strategic reasons, for the Soviet Union to respond to any major new U.S. BMD effort with one of its own; if the United States acts in violation of the treaty, the Soviet Union will almost certainly follow suit. In this sense at least, arms race stability may be diminished.

In addition, much of the early strategic argumentation regarding the potential for crisis instability emerging from a BMD race may be relevant today. Will a BMD race make the superpowers more or less concerned about the ability of their offensive forces to provide an adequate deterrent in a time of crisis? Will the protection afforded by BMD persuade its possessor that nuclear war can be initiated with relatively acceptable losses from retaliatory attack? Will one of the superpowers feel so uncomfortable about the other's preparations, and its interaction with offensive capabilities, that it will be tempted to preempt in a crisis, fearing that its retaliation will be less than adequate if it attempts to absorb a first strike before trying to penetrate the other's BMD system? To some these concerns will be as compelling as they were in 1968, when they played an important role in the debate. Others will be skeptical, much as they were in 1968. In contrast to the issue of arms race stability, there is still little empirical evidence to back up claims on either side of the argument; this lack of data is perhaps one reason why strategic debates of this sort take on a theological tone.

But here, it seems, it is important to acknowledge the very real strategic differences between the world of the late 1960s and today's world. Of principal importance is the enormous growth of strategic arsenals since 1972. Until the early 1970s the United States was clearly ahead of the Soviet Union in most major numerical indexes of the strategic nuclear balance. The advent of U.S.-Soviet parity has, rightly or wrongly, altered perceptions of the stability of the U.S.-Soviet balance. The dramatic multiplication of RVs through MIRV technology on both sides, combined with more accurate delivery systems, has made the basic task of BMD more demanding by posing a far greater offensive threat. It has also threatened, in theory at least, to put at risk substantial numbers of each side's land-based ICBMs in a surprise first-strike attack. Indeed, by most calculations the Soviet capability in this regard has surpassed that of the United States. This development has led to a fear, justified or not, that Soviet leaders would be emboldened in peacetime to challenge U.S. interests across the globe and in a crisis to act in provocative ways that might lead to miscalculation and war.

More specifically, the growing vulnerability of the U.S. ICBM force, and the intensive effort since the mid-1970s to find a way to reverse this trend, have had a profound impact on the way BMD R&D has been pursued. President Ronald Reagan's March 23, 1983, speech notwithstanding, U.S. efforts in BMD research have been directed not at schemes for population defense, but at those for ICBM silo defense. The implications of this shift toward silo-defense missions have been elaborated in earlier chapters of this volume. Here it is sufficient merely to note that, to this extent at least, our approach to the strategic implications of BMD today must be tempered to reflect concerns that were not driving forces in the 1960s.[23]

But while there are many who would still see strong relevance in old strategic arguments for today's debate, few would argue that the political arguments of the past are nearly as relevant today. This is not to suggest that political controversy will be any less intense than it was in the late 1960s. Nor is it to suggest that none of the basic political concerns in 1968–72 are relevant today. The general tenor of East-West relations, an important political concern of opponents to BMD in 1968, will be a major consideration today. Opponents of a new BMD effort will also point to allied nervousness, much as they did in 1968.

But the single most dominant political fact in today's BMD debate—the presence of a ratified treaty between the superpowers severely constraining BMD efforts in perpetuity—was not a factor in the first BMD debate. As late as 1972, the existing state of affairs was open ended with respect to the eventual size of deployment. In 1972, however, the presumption of possible deployment was replaced with the presumption of nondeployment. The treaty has become an accepted part of national and international life. This means, in contrast to 1967, that those who would have the United States conduct BMD activities beyond the very

---

23. Whether the Scowcroft Commission report, with its deemphasis of the ICBM vulnerability problem, will have a long-term impact on interest in silo-defense missions remains to be seen.

low levels permitted in the treaty will have to argue either that the Soviet Union can be persuaded to agree to revise the treaty to permit such activity or that the military benefits of the program outweigh both the military costs of a Soviet military response with a program of its own and the political costs of abrogating a solemn treaty commitment in the absence of clear-cut Soviet violations. In effect, the existence of the treaty means that any advocates of a major new BMD effort will have to make a truly compelling case—more compelling than either Presidents Johnson or Nixon made in their advocacy of the Sentinel and Safeguard systems.

The rationale for any new U.S. efforts will be more difficult to sustain as a defense against China's nuclear forces than it was in 1967. China's ICBM force was far slower in developing than anticipated and will probably remain very small for the indefinite future. More important, the new political relationship that developed between the United States and China during the 1970s effectively precludes embarking on an anti-China BMD with quite the rhetorical enthusiasm demonstrated in 1967. To do so would jeopardize the delicate balancing act the United States has tried to pursue in its diplomatic relations with China. (At the same time, ironically, the growth of China's nuclear arsenal aimed at the Soviet Union, coupled with a decade of hostility between the two governments, may have given the Soviet Union new incentives to pursue an anti-China BMD deployment.)

This greater political burden carried by BMD advocates is reinforced by two related factors. One impact of the ABM Treaty has been to increase dramatically the perceived stakes of the NATO allies in the BMD issue. Before 1972, the allies had shown some interest in the BMD issue. Indeed, one of the first regular sessions of the NATO Nuclear Planning Group was devoted to this topic, as recounted in chapter 8. For the allies in those years, the issue was principally strategic, turning on the interaction of offense and defense in calculating the ability of the United States to "extend" its deterrent over its allies. This is still an issue today, but the treaty invests the issue with broader political stakes for the allies. It stands as the only ratified arms limitation agreement in force today as a result of the strategic arms limitation process. Viewing this process as the centerpiece of East-West détente, the allies are likely to be particularly difficult to convince of the merits of any initiative that places U.S. adherence to the treaty in question.

Second, to some extent there will be a domestic political constituency that finds these concerns equally compelling. The arms control process has developed a loyal following in this country, which is likely to take a rather dim view of any effort to tamper with the last remnants of the SALT process. But even here, the domestic politics are somewhat different from what they were a decade ago. In particular, the political— as opposed to strategic—consequence of U.S.-Soviet strategic parity, and of the concerns over Minuteman vulnerability, has been a growing nervousness about the Soviet threat and about the ability of arms control to deal effectively with that threat, and a significant strengthening of domestic political forces who view arms control and the broader objective of détente with deep skepticism. The political self-doubt of the late 1970s and early 1980s that replaced the confidence of the 1960s and early 1970s has given those who argued against the ABM Treaty in 1972 a stronger voice today; whether they will be able to use this new mood effectively to achieve a consensus behind revision or even abrogation of the treaty remains to be seen.

From the technological perspective, the claim that the situation today is far more promising than it was in 1968–70 is attracting the most attention, and thus requires more careful examination. The prominence of exotic technologies in the current debate—reflected in the fact that President Ronald Reagan's March 23 speech is widely referred to as the "Star Wars" speech—*is* a new phenomenon. As the historical review has suggested, the development of BMD technology through 1972 showed strong continuity. BMD concepts in the 1950s and 1960s were basically derivative of the first army BMD program, Nike-Zeus. The components of the Nike-Zeus system—radars for target acquisition and tracking, nuclear-tipped ground-based interceptor missiles, and data-processing capability to guide the interceptor to target—became the basis for all future BMD concepts, including Nike-X, Sentinel, and Safeguard. Although exotic technologies were explored, they were clearly not the focus of the U.S. effort.

Today the situation has changed, at least insofar as a constituency for exotic technologies has developed to the point where the president is persuaded to redirect R&D in this direction. Nonetheless, the same basic technical questions that were asked originally will be asked of any exotic system: Will it work to specifications? Will it be affordable? Can it be countered by the Soviet Union at reasonable cost? Unless the answers to these questions are significantly different from those that were offered for Sentinel and Safeguard in the late 1960s, it is difficult to imagine serious momentum developing in favor of moving beyond R&D permitted under treaty constraints. Moreover, it is difficult to imagine *any* confident answers to these questions being offered before R&D has moved far beyond the current advanced conceptual stage of research. In 1967 it was possible to support or oppose an actual system with relatively well-known characteristics, one that could be, and in fact was, deployed. Today's supporters and opponents will not be arguing about a system. For the foreseeable future, they will be arguing about plans and concepts, not about physical objects. This fact alone will give the technical debate a very different quality; if participants in the debate are honest, they will acknowledge far greater technical uncertainties on both sides of the issue than existed in the previous debate.

In summary, strategy, politics, and technology all show both significant continuities and discontinuities between 1972 and the present, which will have to be taken into account by informed participants in today's debate. It should also be clear that the fact of the 1968–72 debate—the fact that the issue was so hotly contested, that exchanges between participants were often bitter and left scars, and that the issue was resolved fairly clearly in favor of opponents to BMD—all this invests the current debate with a drama and intensity that it otherwise would probably not have. The victors in 1972 will fight hard to maintain the fruits of their victory, the ABM Treaty. The losers in 1972, with new high-level political support and new technologies to buttress their case, will seek to modify the judgment rendered in 1972. The potential for acrimony is high and difficult to appreciate without the perspective provided by history.

Yet, if the foregoing analysis is correct, and there is as much difference as similarity between the late 1960s and today, it would be a pity for parties on either side of the issue to slip into the polemics of the past. Just as a careful review of the history is essential for today's participants who were not engaged in the late 1960s, a careful review of the strategic, political, and technical considerations of today is essential for those who were deeply involved in the great debate of the past. If this is done, we can reasonably hope that polemics will give way to a constructive, rational exchange on the major policy issues raised by BMD.

CHAPTER TEN

Assessing Future Prospects

DAVID N. SCHWARTZ

THIS CHAPTER identifies the main options that will be available to policymakers as they face decisions about ballistic missile defense. The six options for BMD discussed here are broad categories of action, not specific future courses, much less predictions. The specific examples within each section have been chosen, somewhat arbitrarily, to illustrate the general problems each option might pose.

Status Quo

Even if the ABM Treaty remains in force and no significant deployments are made on either side, critical choices will face U.S. decisionmakers. One set of critical choices will be in the management of research and development programs. R&D funding maintained an annual level of about $200 million throughout the 1970s and has recently risen to about $500 million. Decisions will have to be made as to whether this is an appropriate amount; these in turn will be influenced by an assessment of how much is worth spending as a hedge against a Soviet breakthrough in BMD technology. Decisions will also have to be made about how to spend this money, whether to develop relatively well-understood traditional technologies that could be applied to a fieldable system in a short time or to redirect R&D toward the study of advanced technologies. The choice of investing in one direction more heavily than the other depends on an assessment of the "hedge" value of a quickly deployable BMD system, the promise of advanced technologies, and relative costs, to the extent that they can be predicted. Can enthusiasm for R&D of this dimension be sustained for an extended period, without the clear prospect of eventual deployment? It is difficult to instill scientists and engineers with a sense of purpose when they know that the fruits of their labor are forbidden by law. It is also important to examine the extent to which a long-term R&D program can be sustained politically, against either domestic or international pressures, if the program casts doubt on the ultimate intentions of the United States with respect to the treaty.

To pursue a serious R&D option for BMD, even maintaining the status quo, it will be necessary to pursue R&D on offensive technologies as well, particularly new RVs and penetration aids. Any U.S. R&D effort would have to take into account evolving offensive technologies; pushing these technologies to their limits, within reasonable cost constraints, can help the BMD planner to evaluate accurately the threat the United States might face years from today. It also has the added benefit of making Soviet BMD efforts more difficult and complex.

A final issue that would need to be sorted out in the course of long-term R&D would be the relative roles of the services, particularly the army and the air force. For the past twenty-five years the army has controlled the BMD mission and can be expected to do so indefinitely. Such an arrangement has advantages: the technical expertise of the army in this mission has grown over the years and now constitutes the only "institutional memory" in the government on the subject. The BMD Systems Command in Huntsville, Alabama, is a natural focus for the R&D effort.

At the same time, the air force is more familiar with the broader picture of strategic force planning and more accustomed to dealing with issues of strategic force posture than the army, though the air force has not always been supportive of BMD efforts in the past. In addition, the air force has a more traditional claim to the military use of space. Thus any reconsideration of the relative roles of the army and the air force is likely to be acrimonious.

Even if the current status of BMD is unchanged, there will be a continuing need to examine other solutions to the problems of vulnerability for intercontinental ballistic missiles (ICBMs) and command, control, communications, and intelligence (C³I) networks. The direction of R&D will be determined in large part by whether we continue to view current and probable future levels of vulnerability as a problem, and whether we can identify effective non-BMD solutions to the problem.

Though it still forces some difficult choices, continuance of the status quo is by far the least controversial—and thus the most likely—future for BMD. Its most important aspect is preservation of a treaty that still commands domestic and international support and permits the superpowers to engage in relatively active R&D programs with a reasonable expectation of no actual deployments by the other side.

MX Defense

The United States could decide to deploy a BMD to defend MX. This is the mission that has been most discussed over the past decade, the mission that has driven most R&D in the area, and the mission that— President Ronald Reagan's March 23, 1983, speech notwithstanding— has dominated the Pentagon's BMD agenda for the past decade. Furthermore, given the technical and strategic momentum behind the ICBM vulnerability problem, it is unlikely that the president's speech will significantly derail interest in this mission.

Of course, whether one believes that defense of MX is an important mission will depend in no small part on whether one believes that ICBM vulnerability is a particularly important problem. If vulnerability is thought to be a problem, then MX defense by BMD is a rational option that should be considered along with the many other defenses, active and passive, for ICBMs, including deceptive basing, mobility, and hardening. If vulnerability is not thought to be a problem, then the purpose of this option seems relatively unimportant.

Given the nature of today's defense debate, it is impossible to predict the future of the MX, with or without BMD. If, however, some MX missiles are eventually deployed, it is useful to assess the implications of a hypothetical deployment. For instance, assume that 100 MX are deployed in Minuteman silos, that the other 900 silos in the field contain Minuteman missiles, and that a traditional endoatmospheric BMD system is deployed to defend all 1000 MX and Minuteman missiles, with the goal of charging an attack price of five reentry vehicles for each silo, or 5000 RVs for the entire force. This is roughly comparable to the attack price imposed by the Carter administration's MX multiple protective shelter (MPS) basing system, which would have forced the Soviets to shoot some 5600 accurate, reliable RVs to attack the entire ICBM force of MX/MPS and Minuteman in silos.

Could such a system be deployed under the constraints of the ABM

Treaty? There would be two compliance issues. The magnitude of such a deployment would be the most obvious one. A defense of all 1000 ICBMs would involve deployment of far more BMD interceptors than would be permitted under the 1972 treaty. Mission ambiguity would be the second issue. Could such a system be deployed in such a way as to preclude ambiguity with area defense? The answer here is probably yes. Radars could be used to optimize sensing only for an attack on missile bases; endoatmospheric missiles could be designed and deployed so that their footprints preclude area or population coverage; radars and missiles could be mounted in fixed sites to prevent redeployment. All this is technically feasible, well within the bounds of traditional endoatmospheric technology, and would probably be necessary to ensure compliance with the 1972 treaty's injunction against area defenses. The more one departed from traditional endoatmospheric systems, however, the greater the danger of ambiguities with respect to mission: overlay systems and boost-phase systems, even in defense of ICBM silos, would possess inherent area defense capability.

Such an extensive deployment in excess of treaty limits, though perhaps less controversial than city defense, is not without significant consequences. The Soviet Union would probably be unreceptive to approaches for renegotiating the 1972 treaty to permit extensive ICBM defense. If the United States proceeded with such deployment in the face of Soviet opposition, it is likely that U.S. efforts would be in the direction of preferential defense of widely distributed military targets. U.S. silo defenses would also be expensive, on the order of tens of billions of dollars. Thus the United States would have to balance the consequences of such a deployment, both positive and negative, against the consequences of pursuing other ways of enhancing ICBM survivability, including mobile basing and deceptive basing.

Given the uncertainty of the consequences, it may be difficult to imagine a case so compelling as to persuade a broad segment of the public of the need to pursue MX defense irrespective of the treaty and Soviet reaction. Nevertheless, if such a course is chosen, even in pursuit of a relatively uncontroversial mission such as MX defense, the pattern of East-West relations will be dramatically altered. The diplomacy of arms control will have been dealt a severe setback. It would be virtually impossible to maintain momentum in other ongoing arms control negotiations. And U.S.-Soviet relations would be acrimonious for years to come.

Soviet Initiative

Most current discussions of BMD start from the premise that if any initiatives would be taken to modify or change existing arrangements, such initiatives would come from the United States. Analysts across a broad spectrum of opinion agree that the status quo serves near-term Soviet interests and that it would be almost inconceivable for the Soviet Union to approach the United States with an offer to amend the 1972 treaty. Some believe that the Soviet Union values the treaty because it has enough loopholes to allow the Soviet Union to position itself for a breakout (which will be discussed later). Others believe that the Soviet Union values the status quo because it has accepted the futility of an arms race in this area, because it views untrammelled competition in BMD as destabilizing, and because it believes the mutual hostage relationship reflected in the treaty is the best hope for stability in an admittedly imperfect world.

Even if a Soviet initiative of any sort is highly unlikely, what sort of motives could drive the Soviet Union to such a course? One such motive might derive from the results of the ongoing Soviet R&D program, which may convince the Soviet Union of the technical merits of their technologies. A second possibility, perhaps more likely, is the future growth of nuclear arsenals in Britain, France, China, and perhaps other countries as well (for example, Pakistan). Although Chinese nuclear programs have been extremely slow to mature, within the next decade the threat China poses to the Soviet Union will increase. British and French offensive nuclear forces are easier to predict; by the end of the decade they will have more than doubled their ability to strike targets in the Soviet Union. The Soviet Union is currently seeking to limit this growth through arms control, but if its efforts fail it may see benefits in increased active defenses.

The scope and nature of the initiatives the Soviet Union might take would depend critically on the threat it is defending against and the targets it is defending. Traditional Soviet proclivities toward widespread defenses are not likely to shift, all the more so since the most likely incentives for seeking change—third-country nuclear arsenals—will probably not pose a serious threat to Soviet strategic nuclear assets in the foreseeable future. The most likely Soviet initiative, therefore, would propose modifications to improve the efficacy of the Moscow defenses or the peripheral sensing capabilities essential to nationwide defense. Such changes, of course, would probably not prevent at least one warhead from reaching Moscow; however, if the changes were sufficient to force Britain, France, and China to increase their force requirements, the Soviet Union might well be satisfied.

Another point to remember in assessing the option of a Soviet initiative is that the Soviet Union will be sensitive to the political costs of upsetting the status quo. The Soviet Union's ability to portray itself as a champion of disarmament would be seriously weakened by such a move. It also would lose a valuable instrument for challenging U.S. commitment to strategic arms reduction negotiations. By taking the position of *demandeur*, the Soviet Union would be exposing itself to U.S. political attacks, which would in turn weaken political opposition in Europe to U.S. arms control and disarmament policies. In short, politically there is much for the Soviet Union to lose, and little to gain, in such a move.

Finally, any initiative by the Soviet Union would be tempered by its assessment of which superpower can more effectively exploit new technologies not currently permitted under the treaty. Here one can only guess, but it is far from clear that the Soviet Union would feel confident in deliberately unleashing U.S. technical know-how in this fashion.

Major U.S. Initiative

Any major U.S. initiative on BMD will necessarily be limited by what technologies and systems are available at the time the initiative takes place. If it were to take place today, it would be confined to a traditional high-altitude endoatmospheric system, using either a nuclear or a nonnuclear warhead for target kill. By the late 1980s or early 1990s, it might be supplemented with an Overlay system, if full-scale R&D on such an advanced concept could be undertaken simultaneously with the more traditional deployment. A boost-phase BMD could be planned as a follow-on, but not until the late 1990s and then only if R&D can provide an effective and functional system architecture.

Traditional endoatmospheric systems of the type deployable today could probably be made to charge an attack price of five RVs for each U.S. ICBM silo (or a total of 5000 RVs). This represents a substantial proportion of current Soviet RVs, but not necessarily future Soviet levels. Widespread deployment would also complicate Soviet attacks on bomber bases, C³I targets, and other military targets. By the early 1990s such a deployment could be supplemented by an overlay. Some 400 Overlay interceptors might be able to increase the attack price on U.S. ICBMs to ten RVs and offer further complications for attack plans against other military targets. Adding a third, boost-phase layer to this might deny confident attack options against a wide range of military targets or even serve to limit damage to cities.

Such a future would hold out the prospect of immensely complicating Soviet offensive force planning, reducing the incentives Soviet leaders might have to initiate a nuclear attack in a crisis, and protecting the United States quite well from attack by smaller nuclear powers and from accidental attacks. But the risks are equally impressive. The United States would be embarking down the path toward a defense dominant world, a path that no other power has traveled, one that may have numerous technical and strategic pitfalls that cannot be anticipated. Furthermore, it is at least an open question that deterrence would be strengthened, even if the systems worked as advertised. The Soviet Union may not ascribe such high performance qualities to the U.S. deployments and thus might be tempted to preempt in the belief that their first strike would fare better than a "ragged" retaliation.

A major U.S. initiative of the type described here could encounter serious problems in four ways. Most obviously, the Soviet Union could embark on an effort to neutralize the capability or significance of the U.S. deployments. A large increase in the number of Soviet ICBM RVs could make the Soviet Union more willing to pay a particular price. An associated increase in the capability of penetration aids could actually lower the attack price.

Another potential problem would be the failure of technology to live up to expectations. This is a problem even for the traditional endoatmospheric system because, although the technologies are relatively well understood, the system architecture is not. Even systems that are developed "off-the-shelf"—that is, using components that are already developed and tested—often present unexpected problems and delays. For Overlay systems, the problems may be greater, since the concepts and technologies are less well defined. For boost-phase systems, technologies are barely conceptualized. Much basic work needs to be done to determine if these concepts are in fact workable; only then can the task of system architecture, with all its inherent uncertainties, proceed. In any BMD program, there may be a particularly high premium on quick deployment, but the premium may be lost through technical problems that cause delay. Technical problems can also result in poorer performance than expected. Would the United States have gone ahead with a $15 billion endoatmospheric system advertised as extracting a five RV attack price for each target if it had known that the real attack price was somewhere around three RVs?

A third problem with a major U.S. initiative is that it may stimulate a more sustainable Soviet BMD effort. Consider the implications of a U.S. effort that ends after five years, because of lack of funds or political interest, while the Soviet effort continues at a rapid pace and results several more years down the road in a truly robust nationwide defense. The United States might then be forced to expand its offensive forces considerably to counter it. An unspoken assumption of advocates of a major U.S. initiative seems to be that the United States would retain the initiative over time. But a responsible decisionmaker must consider the consequences if this assumption is incorrect.

Finally, even if the systems work to specifications, deployments move ahead without delay, costs can be kept down, and the inevitable Soviet response can be managed, there would be profound political consequences to be reckoned with. U.S. allies would strongly oppose such an initiative, given both its effect on détente and its implications of a "fortress America"; the damage done to the alliance may be deep and permanent. The viability of British and French deterrents may be perceived to have been reduced, prompting major new strategic programs on their part at the expense of much needed contributions to conventional defense efforts. And finally, such an initiative would be a death knell to U.S.-Soviet arms control efforts across the board. In particular, it would derail efforts to achieve a negotiated balance in strategic offensive forces which could be to mutual advantage.

Soviet Breakout

Another vision of the future—a distinctly ominous one—is the Soviet "breakout" scenario. What distinguishes such a scenario from the Soviet initiative discussed earlier is the unilateral nature of the action, the speed with which it is accomplished, and the magnitude of its effect on the strategic balance.

Several such scenarios have been postulated. One involves the rapid deployment of large numbers of missiles in the new ABM-X-3 system, an advanced traditional BMD with an apparent endoatmospheric capability. Such a system has been developed and could even be deployed in small numbers under treaty constraints. But the breakout scenario would involve the rapid deployment of many such systems to provide an effective area defense, perhaps in coordination with the upgrading of the peripheral radar network of the Soviet Union to give the ABM-X-3 greater depth of vision in detecting incoming RVs.

Another breakout scenario often mentioned involves the upgrading of Soviet surface-to-air (SAM) missiles. The Soviet Union might quickly expand and improve its existing air defense to serve as an area defense, either functioning alone or working in coordination with other explicit BMD systems. A third such scenario would involve the development, testing, and deployment of antitheater ballistic missiles (ATBMs) in such a way that they would be unlimited by the treaty, but capable of rapid conversion to a strategic defense.

Such scenarios seem to hold out the prospect of a dramatic shift in the strategic balance over a relatively short period of time. But how likely are they? Under what circumstances would they occur? Would the Soviet Union risk taking such provocative acts? And would there be effective ways to respond to such acts? How much faith would the Soviet Union have in the effectiveness of its defenses? Would it be prepared to accept the long-term consequences of such acts for relations with the United States and with the North Atlantic Treaty Organization? How would the Soviet Union assess U.S. reactions in these circumstances?

These considerations are largely subjective, but more amenable to objective discussion is the question of whether such acts would provide effective protection against U.S. nuclear attack. A massive breakout, such as a Soviet deployment of the many thousands of SAMs in a BMD mode, by imposing even the relatively modest attack price of three RVs could significantly constrain U.S. offensive options. However, the integration needed to make such a large system effective would be unprecedented. Smaller breakouts would be easier to deploy and to operate, but they might also be easier to counter with offensive tactics or with simple saturation.

Another technical factor is that SAMs and ATBMs are not generally optimized for the BMD mission. They shoot at objects with trajectories very different from those of strategic RVs, and in the case of SAMs, objects that are much slower and easier to track. Modification of these systems to handle strategic RVs is probably technically possible, but there is at least a case to be made that the Soviet Union would choose to break out with systems that have been designed from the outset with BMD in mind.

On balance, the prospects for Soviet breakout depend greatly on three criteria—unilateral action, speed, and significant impact on the strategic balance—which are each highly problematic, largely because of the avenues of response open to the United States. Even a breakout could not be achieved overnight. While the breakout was occurring, a period of months, the United States could well detect such activity; and this possibility would not be discounted in Moscow. The receipt of such information would certainly prompt a U.S.-Soviet crisis of major proportions, during which the likelihood of U.S. preemption would probably increase. If such a crisis did not result in war, the United States would be free over the long term to pursue countermeasures to offset the Soviet deployments. It would seem likely that domestic U.S. political support could be sustained for virtually any long-term response to neutralize the Soviet advantage, including the massive increase of U.S. offensive forces, the development of new offensive tactics to exploit specific weaknesses of the Soviet system, and the deployment of a U.S. BMD program of similar scope and capability. Furthermore, this effort would probably have the support of most, if not all, U.S. allies.

These prospects would seem sufficient to deter the Soviet Union from the breakout option. At the same time, it is clear that the most difficult situation is not one of a clear Soviet breakout, but one of a more ambiguous nature, wherein Soviet activities are difficult to interpret but suggest that Moscow may intend to achieve the capability for a breakout, not in order to use this capability but to keep it in reserve for a crisis. It is difficult to offer concrete proposals to guard against such events or to guide decisionmakers facing such ambiguities. Perhaps the best that can be said is that the Standing Consultative Commission, created by the 1972 treaty, exists at least in part to offer both sides an opportunity to seek clarification in just such situations.

New Arms Control Arrangements

A final set of options to consider address BMD from the perspective of arms control. Of course, the status quo already severely constrains

BMD through an arms limitation agreement. But it is possible to imagine at least three other futures, different from the status quo, in which arms control arrangements impose new constraints on BMD.

Perhaps the easiest to imagine is a new agreement that simply plugs the gaps in the 1972 treaty. For example, the two parties might agree to additional measures limiting the capabilities of air defense systems in order to minimize the overlap with BMD. Another example might be a bilateral, explicit understanding regarding ATBMs.

Such a course may seem attractive to some arms control advocates in the United States, and it might even find a receptive audience in Moscow. However, there are two reservations against such a course. First, the Reagan administration, and perhaps future ones as well, will be more interested in keeping options open than in closing them off. They will view such a course as involving needless, even dangerous, mortgaging of future capabilities for what is at best a temporary solution. More important, perhaps, is the fact that the treaty addresses the fundamental problems it was directed at, as argued in chapter 6. Reopening an essentially sound treaty to deal with marginal problems may run the risk of creating new problems where none previously existed.

A second possibility for the future under arms control is more extreme. It would take the 1974 Protocol one step further and ban all BMD systems and tests of any kind, irrespective of form, function, mission, or location. The rationale for such an approach is that the continued R&D programs of both sides are sufficiently open-ended as to create damaging suspicions with respect to treaty compliance, suspicions that would be eliminated under an austere arms control regime. To gain acceptance, an outright ban on BMD would have to overcome the strong Soviet commitment to the Moscow defense, as well as the argument that the current level of deployments allowed by the treaty is so small as to produce the same result as a ban.

A third, longer-term possibility for a future arms control regime integrates an approach to offensive and defensive limitations. In order to appreciate it, one needs to recall that the dominant strategic concern over the past decade has been the vulnerability of ICBMs on both sides, as a consequence of the increasing numbers and the improved accuracies of offensive ICBMs. Concern over this trend has been a driving force behind the quest for a new basing mode for the follow-on missile to the Minuteman ICBM. It was a factor in criticism of the SALT II Treaty, because the treaty would have done little to solve this problem. And it has helped to guide current U.S. policy for strategic arms reduction talks (START).

The third possible arms control regime takes this concern as a point of departure. It envisions a strategic arms reduction process that would eventually reduce offensive nuclear forces on both sides to an extremely low level and then expand the role of BMD so that it could provide an additional, effective margin of safety for these forces, at an acceptable cost. In strategic terms, such an arms control regime would have to impose three stringent conditions on strategic offensive forces: they would have to be small in both launcher and warhead totals, sufficiently small to defend at an affordable cost; they would have to reflect a warhead-to-launcher ratio that would make it difficult, or extremely costly, to saturate the defenses of a given launcher; and they would have to be located quite far from major urban areas, to minimize the risk that a BMD deployment in defense of silos would be mistaken for a population defense.

The defenses deployed in such an arms control regime could be of the traditional type; endoatmospheric systems would be ideal because of their limitations in defending widely disparate targets. They could be of the more exotic variety, although Overlay and space-based systems would have the intrinsic ability to defend populated areas even when deployed in defense of ICBMs. The numbers would obviously be related to the numbers of ICBMs and RVs permitted under the agreement.

What relevance would ICBM defense have in such a world, so severely constrained by arms control? The conditions imposed on offensive forces would seem to minimize the vulnerability of either side's deterrent. BMD for these systems would appear redundant and wasteful.

The principal argument that would be made by advocates of such a course would be that a shift in the relative dominance of offense over defense in the strategic balance may undermine current interest in various offensive warfighting scenarios at the lower end of the spectrum of violence. These scenarios have proved politically controversial; more important, they tend to generate pressures for new offensive forces. In a defense-dominant world, such scenarios are unattractive.

The attractiveness of the single-warhead ICBM, at least in theory, is gaining in recognition. In fact, it seems to have been advocated by the Scowcroft panel, when it recommended stepped-up research and development on the so-called singlet or Midgetman single-warhead mobile

ICBM. The development of singlet, in an appropriately constrained arms control regime, could help to reduce the critical warhead-to-launcher ratio. A *mobile* singlet would be less vulnerable to attack than a fixed one, depending on just how mobile the system proved to be; presumably a fixed singlet would generate greater arguments in favor of BMD.

The feasibility of singlet aside, however, there are several obvious but important caveats with respect to this future. The first is that we are nowhere near the point in the drawn-out process of U.S.-Soviet strategic arms control where this future can be viewed as imminent. More than a decade of intensive negotiations between the superpowers has resulted in only the most modest, precarious constraints on the offensive arms race. Even under the provisions of SALT II, which are being observed by both sides even though they have not been ratified, developments in offensive weaponry are dynamic and troubling. Under the best of circumstances, it would take years before reductions in offensive arms could be achieved to a degree that would make renewed BMD appropriate. Under current conditions, with East-West tensions running high, the prospects are grim indeed.

A second problem, closely related to the first, is the "getting from here to there" problem. The process of moving toward offensive reductions and enhanced BMD deployments in a bilateral arms control setting would be extraordinarily delicate. At each stage of offensive reductions it would be necessary to maintain ratios of warheads to launchers that would enhance stability. It would also be necessary to initiate discussions and limitations on BMD at a point where neither side could gain unilateral advantage over the other through deployment of BMD. Finally, and most critically, it would be necessary to lock new BMD deployments firmly into the arms control process. Agreed expansion of BMD deployments in the absence of strict constraints on offensive forces would simply increase pressures for offensive buildups to offset defensive measures. Alternatively, deployments of new BMD without an agreement, even after major offensive reductions and limitations, could provoke an unrestrained defensive arms race and might even generate pressures to abrogate offensive limits. Clearly, in this future offensive and defensive limits must work hand in hand and must be tailored to each other in a way that not only optimizes the BMD deployment but preserves arms race and crisis stability.

A third caveat is that the deployment of singlet missiles may in itself increase pressures for BMD deployment, pressures that would have to be carefully managed. Offensive arms control limits that resulted in a relatively small number of singlet missiles on each side could persuade either party to adopt *area* defenses, given the small and manageable size of the threat. In practice, of course, such pressures could be offset by the characteristics of singlet RVs and by the cost-exchange ratio between these RVs and the new BMD deployments. But they are worth bearing in mind in any assessment of this future.

It is difficult to foresee how U.S. allies would react to such developments. The U.S.-Soviet amity upon which they would have to be based would be welcomed by the allies. But the allies would probably also harbor doubts about the ability of the United States to deter aggression against them, as much as a result of the offensive reductions as of BMD deployments.

CHAPTER ELEVEN

Reactions and Perspectives

THE CONTRIBUTORS to this chapter were asked to adopt an approach to their writing opposite, in a sense, from that of the authors of the previous chapters. The previous chapters addressed specific aspects of ballistic missile defense, and the authors were asked to present information and analysis without interjecting their personal views—to the extent possible. The authors of the present chapter, by contrast, were asked to address whatever aspect of the BMD question their experience and judgment convinced them was most important, representing freely their own opinions.

All of the contributors to this chapter either have had an important involvement with the national security programs of the U.S. government or frequently express views influential in shaping these programs. Though they represent a wide range of views within this strategic community, their judgments do not necessarily span the entire range of public discussion of BMD. Diverse as they are, however, they do have two common characteristics. First, none recommends that the United States deploy now, or in the near future, a BMD system in violation of the ABM Treaty. Second, none recommends a complete halt to BMD research and development in the United States. These commonalities suggest that the range of thinking about BMD, at least among experts, is bounded at both ends.

NORMAN R. AUGUSTINE

During the height of the great ballistic missile defense debate of the mid-1960s, a well-known opinion-surveying organization sought the public's attitudes regarding BMD. Approximately two-thirds of those polled believed that the system then deployed already afforded good protection to our citizenry. Of course, there *was* no system then deployed; just as there *is* no system deployed today. Yet it seems doubtful that a similar survey in the mid-1980s would evoke a much different response.

Nonetheless, a very great deal has happened in the intervening two decades, militarily, politically, and technically. In this context, it is inappropriate *not* to revisit ballistic missile defense to determine what, if anything, it might contribute in these waning years of the twentieth century to world peace and to the preservation of freedom. It may be that debates on the efficacy of strategic defense have in the past failed to stimulate the general public to take an active, informed role in deciding whether BMD is to be a major part of our national defense policy because many of the participants in the debates tend to discount *altogether* even legitimate considerations supporting the opposing point of view. The difficulty, of course, is that ballistic missile defense is an enormously complex issue, one that does not lend itself to simple solutions or to slogans.

It is, for example, relatively easy to obtain an arms control agreement with the Soviet Union, unless, that is, one wishes an equitably balanced, verifiable arms control agreement with the Soviet Union. It is relatively easy to match the Soviet military buildup, given the relative sizes of gross national products of the two nations, unless, that is, one wishes not to alter fundamentally the economic life-style our citizenry enjoys. It is relatively easy to reduce greatly the defense budget, unless, that is, one is genuinely concerned about declared and, unfortunately, rather evident expansionist pursuits of the Soviet Union.

The options available in ballistic missile defense, as but one element of a strategy to balance these objectives, range from making an immediate commitment to the deployment of a large-scale antiballistic missile (ABM) system on one hand to doing nothing on the other. Both these options, as is so often the case with extremes, are probably inadvisable, at least at this time.

What then *should* be the U.S. policy with regard to ballistic missile defense? The purpose of this commentary is to outline the rudiments of one such policy and to examine its underpinnings.

What's New?

A great deal *has* taken place since BMD was last scrutinized on a national scale. The Soviet Union has progressed from a position of clear strategic inferiority to one of clear equivalence (and, probably, tactical superiority in terms of general purpose forces). An ABM treaty has been placed in force that precludes deploying any meaningful measure of ballistic missile defense. (The Soviet Union obviously does not share this conclusion, any more than it shares the conclusion of the United States concerning the futility of intensive air defense of the homeland in the absence of widespread defense against ballistic missiles.[1]) During this same period, significant technological advancements have been made, but the technical infrastructure to support ballistic missile defense development and deployment in the United States (which is often overlooked even though it is of enormous importance) has largely been dismantled. That is not to suggest there is not a healthy base available upon which to build, or even that such a structure could not be reassembled given sufficient time and priority. However, few could confuse today's national BMD infrastructure with that in existence in the 1960s, which centered on the technical excellence of the Bell Telephone Laboratories (now out of the BMD business) and the sobering experience of having to build and demonstrate *operating* systems (now terminated).

Whereas the U.S. response to the ABM Treaty has been to dismantle its only deployed system (probably prudent), to cease for a time (at the direction of the Senate) all systems-oriented engineering activities, and to terminate all interceptor flight tests (probably unwise), the Soviet response has been to redouble its research and development (R&D) and testing efforts, to upgrade its deployed ABM system (presumably within the confines of the treaty), and to deploy extensive early warning radars that could be supportive of BMD objectives as well as other functions.

1. The Soviet Union might, of course, simply attach disproportionate value to the defense of a subset of the nation's citizenry against attack by nuclear powers having relatively modest inventories.

Technology in the 1980s

The technological building blocks available with which to assemble BMD systems today are as different from those of the mid-1960s as is the Space Shuttle from the Mercury capsule of that earlier era. Computers are now available that dwarf their earlier counterparts in capacity, speed, and cost per unit of capability. Surveillance satellites are available that can provide reliable and rapid alerting of ballistic missile attack. Aircraft platforms capable of carrying sensors and command-and-control elements may soon provide endurance aloft measured in days; directed-energy weapons and their associated pointing and tracking devices have made significant strides; and the payload of the launch systems needed to place such devices in orbit has been steadily growing.

In the exoatmospheric ballistic missile defense arena, infrared sensors that have been proved are sensitive enough to detect the heat emitted from a large ice cube located hundreds of miles away, as well as to track hundreds of objects simultaneously. Interceptor guidance is being refined to a point where, in the exoatmospheric case, not only will nuclear warheads be unnecessary, but *any* warheads might be unnecessary. Given miss distances measured in inches, relatively small interceptors need only collide with threatening objects, destroying them with the enormous kinetic energy associated with a closing velocity on the order of 6 mi. per sec.

As for the building blocks of endoatmospheric defense, advanced phased-array radars are now in general use for other missions, and interceptors having much-improved accuracy, time-of-flight, and maneuver-response are feasible. The possibility of constructing an interceptor with sufficient accuracy to permit engagement with a nonnuclear warhead *within the atmosphere* appears feasible, given adequate developmental support. The latter capability could be of enormous importance in circumventing the nuclear release problem that dominates the already difficult BMD command-and-control challenge, in reducing cost, and in alleviating some of the public opposition to BMD deployment.

The "ultimate" ballistic missile defense system, other than arms control, appears to be one capable of boost-phase intercept. In this context threats can be engaged before multiple warheads are released and before relatively inexpensive decoys are deployed. The challenge is the short period of time available from threat detection to required intercept, which usually demands large numbers of defensive satellites located in space with an "interceptor" having the speed of light, not to mention a superb command-and-control system. This is, of course, the concept of many directed-energy "beam" weapons. Such devices could play an important role in the next century, but in the near term major technical obstacles, countermeasure issues, and cost implications remain to be resolved.

As might be expected, just as defensive technology has progressed significantly in recent years, so too has offensive technology. The latter includes improvements in delivery accuracy, in the ability to undertake large maneuvers during reentry (for evasion or accuracy enhancement), and in the ability to fractionalize payloads.

The collision of these two flows of technology frequently occurs in the arena of countermeasures. For example, even when the progress made in infrared technology is recognized, significant questions remain unanswered about certain types of exoatmospheric decoys, particularly the impact-to-kill mini-interceptors of an overlay system. With respect to atmospheric intercepts the atmosphere itself provides a powerful filter by which decoys and reentry vehicles can be discriminated. This is particularly true of deep-in-the-atmosphere intercepts, which are, however, appropriate only to the defense of point targets and not to the defense of urban or industrial areas.

Overall, it would appear that defensive technology has, in fact, "gained" on offensive technology during the past two decades. Whether this gain has been sufficient to overcome some of the inherent advantages enjoyed by the attacker in the past can only be determined by examining the mission and system context into which the above technology is to be embedded.

System Considerations

In the mid-1960s, the fundamental arithmetic of the strategic offensive-defensive confrontation seemed to favor the offense. Many reentry vehicles could be launched from a single ballistic missile, each consuming an interceptor. Relatively lightweight decoys were available. Nuclear precursors were considerably more debilitating to the defense than to the offense because of the former's need to sense, communicate, and maneuver. In the late 1950s and early 1960s matters were even worse from the defense's standpoint: not only was it necessary to assign an individual interceptor (or two or three because of imperfect reliability) to each threatening object, but it was often necessary to assign a single mechanically scanned radar to each object.

With the development of electronically scanned phased-array radars capable of search, track, and engagement, and large solid-state digital data processors, endoatmospheric engagement became practicable, particularly deep within the atmosphere. And when precision guidance became possible, the small overlay homing vehicles previously described could be launched *severally* from a single interceptor missile. The defense thus realized the ability to "MIRV" (fractionize) its *own* launch vehicles, neutralizing yet another element of the offense's arithmetic advantage. Early-warning satellites made layered defenses feasible, wherein the defense could disrupt "stylized" attacks (such as a carefully timed "ladder" of reentry vehicles attacking a defense radar) and could gain, in some instances, enormous leverage through the ability of the second tier to engage only "leakers" through the first tier. Furthermore, in defending some types of *redundant* target sets (such as silos or duplicative command-and-control facilities), the defense can decide at the last minute to allocate its entire capacity to the defense of some subset of the overall target structure ("preferential defense"), whereas the offense, not knowing which targets will ultimately be defended, must allocate its resources (inefficiently) on the assumption that *any* target may be fully defended. Finally, in the case of the defense of the land-based intercontinental ballistic missile force, the objects being defended might themselves employ deception by offering multiple protective shelters among which ICBMs are covertly moved in a modern version of the circus shell game.

If all these factors are added together, or perhaps more properly multiplied together, the arithmetic for the first time seems to be reversed so that it might favor the *defense* in the protection of certain classes of redundant target sets such as land-based ICBMs.

Nonetheless the numerics of urban-industrial defense against large attacks appear as foreboding as ever. The target cities are large, soft, widely distributed, and of enormous individual value. Against an attack of, say, 5000 reentry vehicles (RVs), one would presumably seek a defense that provides a leakage of less than 1 percent. To do this with a single-layer defense obviously requires an intercept efficiency greater than 99 percent. Even in a two-layer defense (with independent layers and subtractive tactics), if that were feasible, *each* layer would have to be 90 percent effective.

Because of these factors, careful consideration must be given to the selection of missions for possible ballistic missile defenses. Further, what may be true of BMD for one mission will very likely not be true for some other application.

BMD Missions

At the not inconsiderable risk of oversimplifying, the missions of ballistic missile defense can be categorized in the following three general groups:

—Urban-industrial defense (for example, the defense of cities).
—Hard-point defense (for example, the defense of ICBM silos).
—Threshold defense (for example, the defense of certain command centers and air bases).

The defense of cities against large attacks, the most demanding of all BMD missions, still appears far from practicable in the foreseeable future. Furthermore, this form of defense must be considered in concert with defense against bomber and cruise missile threats—a capability that today is possessed to a very limited degree by the United States, that is probably feasible, but that is also very costly. The best investment of marginal dollars for defense of the population, and even elements of the industrial base, appears to be civil defense—not active defense. Unfortunately, the political climate in the United States, unlike that in the Soviet Union, is probably not compatible with such an undertaking. Yet civil defense could, given the unthinkable, one day suddenly become priceless.

Defense of cities against *limited attacks,* such as accidental launches and "*n*th-country" threats, presents a much different set of circumstances from that pertaining to defense of the urban-industrial complex against large-scale attacks. It is also the antithesis of the defense of ICBM silos, which permits a leaky defense of hard targets against enormous attacks; the defense of cities in this case is concerned with the near-perfect defense of soft targets against very small attacks. In a free society, the defense of cities probably requires defense of the entire country and is likely to take on increasing importance as a growing number of nations acquire nuclear weapons and the means to deliver them. But such issues cannot be addressed in the confines of ballistic missile defense, because of the many related issues that also have to be addressed: for example, how does someone contend with the threat of a nuclear weapon in the cargo bay of an nth-country commercial airliner, in the hold of a foreign ship in a U.S. harbor, or even in normal commercial mailing channels? And how does one obtain the confidence needed to release an antiballistic missile when only a single attacking missile appears to have been spotted, particularly if the antiballistic missile carries a nuclear warhead of its own? Perhaps bombs in cargo vessels would not be as effective instruments of international extortion as would be even a single nuclear-armed ballistic missile targeted at Washington, D.C. What does seem certain, however, is that the world will be a very different place in which to conduct international diplomacy when the United States and the Soviet Union face this type of threat. This prospect would seem to argue strongly that common interests are at stake in promoting U.S. and Soviet cooperation in nonproliferation.

Hard-point defense would appear to be the most likely form of BMD to be deployed in the next two decades, since it would provide a solid hedge against continued growth of the Soviet counterforce capability, particularly if it were coupled with a deceptively based, hardened ICBM deployment. The focus here should be on movable, nonnuclear terminal defenses, possibly with an overlay of infrared-sensing exoatmospheric probes and interceptors.

The third category of ballistic missile defense is "threshold defense," a term coined by the Defense Science Board to describe a moderate-to-light, preferential, wide-area defense that could be used principally to introduce uncertainty into an enemy's attack planning—uncertainty as to which resources would be defended with what intensity. Since deterrence is in the eye of the beholder, the cause of deterrence can be served merely by eroding the enemy's confidence in the success of an attack. Today a Soviet planner can calculate almost exactly how many reliable ballistic missiles are required to eliminate the strategic bomber bases, the command-and-control structure, the ICBM force, submarines in harbors, and so on. In contrast, a defense that can at the last minute be devoted in its full force to the protection of a specific subset of these assets makes high-confidence attacks difficult to carry out successfully, reduces the chance of "silver bullet" attacks against uniquely valuable targets, and makes surgical strikes much less plausible. Further, the requirements of such a defense are not, from a technical standpoint, inordinately demanding if it is deceptively based.

It should be noted that both threshold defense and light urban defense, while too weak to negate a concerted attack by U.S. or Soviet standards, could, if adopted by the Soviet Union, erode to a considerable degree the effectiveness of the strategic ballistic missile forces of our European allies. This obviously has important political connotations that might transcend the technical and targeting considerations involved in such defenses.

A BMD Program for the 1980s

The arguments of the 1960s that ballistic missile defense is destabilizing (that it will undermine the deterrence achievable through mutual assured destruction and that it will merely force the opponent needlessly to spend money to overcome the defense and thus reestablish the status quo) seem highly suspect. Certainly, if a strong defense of all nations could be provided, it would be difficult to argue that this makes a less safe world. It would seem that assured survival is an inherently better policy than assured destruction, if the former is indeed practicable. All things considered, an energetic but carefully focused ballistic missile defense program appears to be clearly worthy of pursuit. One such program might include:

—A technology program focused on discrimination, particularly exoatmospheric discrimination for Overlay-type systems.

—A low-altitude terminal defense prototype program, using nonnuclear interceptors and ground-based radars.

—An Overlay prototype program, concentrating on spaceborne sensors and high-precision homing interceptors.

—A highly selective research program on directed-energy systems.

—A family of system studies defining how various technological building blocks can be combined to provide useful overall *system* capabilities.

A Look at Arms Control

A few words specifically on the subject of arms control seem appropriate. In today's world, ballistic missile defense and arms control are inextricably related topics. Indeed, it is doubtful that the Soviet Union would have accepted the arms control agreements that are in force today had not the United States committed itself to the deployment of the Safeguard system. A strong BMD R&D program would seem to support the cause of peace and promote further arms reductions. Additionally, BMD itself becomes more practicable as overall force levels are reduced.

At the same time that an active BMD technology and prototyping program is pursued, the United States should seek modifications to the existing ABM Treaty as it comes up for potential renewal. These modifications, many of which may appeal to the Soviet Union itself in view of the development of China's ballistic missile force, include permitting the deployment of light area defenses (nth-country and accidental launch protection) and the defense of land-based ICBMs. Consideration should also be given to whether the existing ban on mobile components and multiple interceptors on a single launcher are not counterproductive.

In concert with the above initiatives, the United States should take the offensive in seeking *on-site inspection* for verification. The fact that the Soviet Union says it will not accept this concept seems to have caused us to forget that this is still a legitimate national security pursuit— militarily as well as politically.

Finally, we must not lose sight of the circumstance that the Soviet Union itself has shown no signs in the last two decades of reducing or even leveling off its BMD R&D activities. This being the case, a strong U.S. research and prototyping program is essential if we are to encourage arms control, perhaps actively defend ourselves, and, what is very important, avoid technological surprise ("a Sputnik of BMD"). It is useful to recall, when considering the importance of an active, relatively wide-ranging research program, that many important and profound discoveries have been made by "surprise," including the discovery of things such as penicillin, X rays, and America.

ALBERT CARNESALE

The 1972 ratification of the ABM Treaty signaled a joint decision by the United States and the Soviet Union not to have meaningful defenses against strategic ballistic missiles. The treaty is of unlimited duration, but that does not mean that it will last forever. Formal provisions for amendment and for withdrawal are incorporated in the agreement and, of course, abrogation by one or both parties could occur abruptly at any time. The existence of the ABM Treaty does not free us from having to think about ballistic missile defense.

The world is not as it was in 1972. Soviet ballistic missile forces on land and at sea have increased markedly in quantity and quality over the past decade, and the threat posed to the survivability of U.S. land-based retaliatory forces can no longer be dismissed. Nor can we ignore the potential contribution to blunting a U.S. retaliatory attack that might be made by the Soviet Union's improved (and continuously improving) network of defenses against strategic ballistic missiles, tactical ballistic missiles, aircraft, and cruise missiles. The nuclear world has changed.

What should be the role of BMD in U.S. national security now and in the foreseeable future? Would modification or termination of the ABM Treaty serve U.S. interests better than continued adherence? The purpose of this brief commentary is to elucidate some of the basic issues that must be addressed if reasoned answers to these questions are to be provided, and to demonstrate that most of these issues can be characterized as dilemmas. Despite arguments to the contrary made by advocates and by opponents of BMD, realistic resolutions of the fundamental issues involve both benefits and costs: there are no cost-free (or benefit-free) options. Difficult tradeoffs must be made.

Dilemmas are encountered along every important dimension of assessment of BMD, including the military, technological, economic, diplomatic, and political dimensions.

Military

All too often, so-called analyses of the military implications of BMD are little more than comparisons of strategic nuclear exchanges in several hypothetical worlds—worlds differing only in the amount of BMD deployed by the United States. To no one's surprise, U.S. military objectives are best met in the worlds in which we have the most BMD. On the basis of such studies, it is argued that continued adherence to the ABM Treaty is contrary to U.S. interests.

How absurd! One hardly needs stacks of computer printouts displaying the results of simulated nuclear wars to conclude that, all other things being equal, the United States is better off with more defense rather than less. In the real world, all other things are *not* equal.

The military benefits to the United States derived from the ABM Treaty are the constraints upon Soviet BMD. These constraints help to ensure the effectiveness of U.S. retaliatory forces by inhibiting Soviet deployment of defensive barriers to the penetration of our ICBMs and SLBMs. By undermining the capability of U.S. retaliatory forces, Soviet BMD would weaken deterrence and could pose a real threat to U.S. security. But modification or termination of the ABM Treaty to free the United States from some or all of the constraints on BMD also would free the Soviet Union of those constraints. To modify or terminate the treaty is to modify or terminate it for both sides, not just for the United States. A world in which the Soviet Union is constrained by the present treaty while the United States is permitted significant BMD deployment is attractive to me and to most other Americans, but it is also highly unrealistic.

What if both sides were to have meaningful levels of BMD? Would U.S. military interests be better served than they are now? It depends.

To maintain deterrence, a substantial portion of our strategic offensive forces should be able to survive an attack and subsequently penetrate to designated targets in the Soviet Union. Deployment of BMD to defend our land-based forces and our strategic command, control, and communications (C^3) facilities would enhance their survivability, but the ability of our surviving forces to penetrate to their targets would be degraded by a Soviet BMD system. This tension between survivability and penetrability is unavoidable. Its significance depends strongly upon what it is that is defended (and perceived to be defended) on each side. If a significant portion of the other side's territory (that is, its "value structure") is defended, deterrence could be jeopardized. If only strategic forces are defended, deterrence could be enhanced. Would a higher level of BMD on both sides be advantageous to the side that strikes first, or would it favor the retaliator? The former situation would undermine deterrence; the latter would strengthen it.

And what if deterrence should fail? (Thinking about the consequences of nuclear conflict is as unlikely to increase one's desire for nuclear war as thinking about cancer is to heighten one's taste for contracting the disease.) If deterrence should fail and nuclear conflict should ensue, each side would prefer to have, as part of its warfighting arsenal, survivable and enduring forces that could be used to destroy elements of the other side's strategic offensive forces, its other military capabilities (for example, theater nuclear forces and general purpose forces), its political and military leadership, its C³ facilities, and its industrial and economic base. Ideally, the ability to attack the adversary would be augmented by the ability to defend one's own forces against a first strike or against a retaliatory blow. Defenses of one's own forces and value targets contribute to one's warfighting capability, while corresponding defenses on the other side degrade one's warfighting capability. Thus, in warfighting, as in basic deterrence, the tradeoff is between the benefits of U.S. BMD and the costs (to the United States) of Soviet BMD.

Technology

The ABM Treaty restrictions on development and testing of BMD systems and components confront decisionmakers with perpetual choices. It would be difficult for any U.S. (or Soviet) leader to decide to withdraw from the treaty before he or she was confident that the United States (or the USSR) had a workable BMD system ready for relatively rapid deployment. Do we (or they) have such a system *now?* Apparently not.

Defensive systems based on the "conventional" components—fixed land-based radars and interceptor missiles—are not likely to catch up with, let alone get ahead of, the evolving offensive ballistic missile systems with which they must deal. The end result of such an offense-defense race is uncertain, but the vast majority of informed observers would bet on the offense to stay in the lead. Deployment of more promising (and less well defined) BMD components is prohibited, and their development and testing are severely constrained. For example, radars and interceptor missiles cannot be tested in mobile or deceptive basing modes. Nor is either side permitted to test exoatmospheric systems capable of operating independently of land-based radars or carrying on each interceptor missile multiple independently guided devices for killing more than one reentry vehicle at a time. And any testing of space-based BMD components of the "Star Wars" variety (which at this stage are little more than gleams in the defense scientists' eyes) certainly would violate the agreement. A technological dilemma that political leaders may soon have to face is this: whether to modify or terminate the ABM Treaty to permit testing of systems that might not work, or to continue to adhere to the treaty and possibly to forgo the acquisition of a system that might have provided meaningful defense. The choice will not be an easy one.

The long lead times characteristic of strategic weapons complicate the matter even further. A decision to deploy BMD on a wide scale probably would precede full operational capability by about a decade. In a sense, then, we face the following, somewhat loaded, question: Would our current BMD technology be able to deal with what will be the Soviet first-strike threat ten years from now? Standard projections of Soviet offensive capabilities are inadequate to answer this question. It must be assumed that the threat is a reactive one, that is, that the Soviet Union would develop tactics and deploy systems expressly designed to counter the U.S. defenses. A related question must also be asked: would U.S. offensive forces ten years from now be able, after absorbing a first strike, to penetrate a Soviet BMD that might be in place if the ABM Treaty were modified or terminated? With assumptions that are sufficiently defense conservative, it can always be shown that the BMD task for us is a hopeless one. On the other hand, outrageously offense-conservative assumptions often are employed to attribute a near-perfect level of performance to even the most Rube Goldbergian of conceivable Soviet defenses. Neither model offers policymakers much guidance. Technological realism must constrain the formulation of the problem as well as the selection of the course of action.

Economics

BMD, like all modern strategic weapons systems, is expensive. But that observation, by itself, is not a decisive argument against deployment. In addition to knowing the cost of the BMD system, the United States would want to know how that cost would compare to the cost of offensive measures (such as additional reentry vehicles or penetration aids) required to offset the defense. In other words, would the cost-exchange ratio favor the defense or the offense? How would the cost of BMD compare with the costs of other means (for example, improvements in or additions to our offensive forces) for providing the same degree of enhancement to our nation's security? How would the costs of the offensive measures required to offset an expanded Soviet BMD system compare with the benefits of a U.S. BMD system?

Questions like these call for analyses of tradeoffs among systems associated with different military services. To whom can we turn for objective and credible analyses of whether it is better to spend money for new ICBMs for the air force, or new submarine-launched ballistic missiles (SLBMs) for the navy, or a new BMD system for the army, or a real rapid deployment force for the marines? Such questions are more easily asked than addressed.

Diplomacy

The ABM Treaty is the only formally enduring accomplishment of more than a decade of U.S.-USSR strategic arms limitation talks (SALT) and strategic arms reduction talks (START). Outright termination of the treaty almost certainly would signal the end of nuclear arms control—an endeavor with a clouded future in any event. More difficult to assess are the likely effects on arms control of attempts, whether or not successful, to modify the treaty. An unsuccessful attempt to amend it might have no significant effect on superpower relations or, at the other extreme, it could lead the frustrated party to withdraw from the treaty. A "successful" amendment attempt might result in modifications far different from those originally intended—a phenomenon not unheard of in international negotiations. Any weakening of the ABM Treaty would be seen by most observers as a setback for U.S.-Soviet relations, and outright termination of the agreement would commonly be perceived as a disaster.

Allies of the United States might see deployment of a U.S. BMD system as a positive development because it could increase our willingness to risk escalation of a war that might start in Europe, the Middle East, or elsewhere. On the other hand, they could view a U.S. defense as a precursor to a return to a "fortress America" policy and U.S. isolationism.

Our allies' views of expanded BMD deployments in the Soviet Union would be unequivocally negative, though of uncertain intensity. If the Soviet Union were to deploy BMD at levels much higher than now permitted by the ABM Treaty, the deterrent value of the independent British and French missile forces could be diminished markedly. And if it were a U.S. initiative that led to modification or termination of the treaty, blame for the expansion of Soviet BMD would (with some justification) be attributed to us.

China also could be expected to be displeased with an expanded Soviet defense against ballistic missiles. Indeed, it is hard to identify any state other than the USSR that would applaud such a development. Any movement in the direction of weakening or terminating the ABM Treaty would be taken not because of the diplomatic implications, but in spite of them.

Politics

Within the United States the politics of BMD in the 1960s and 1970s was marked by unpredictability and surprise. The army worried that *every* community in the nation would want to be defended; it turned out that not one wanted to be home to an ABM site. It was the arms control bargaining chip argument that snatched the Safeguard system from the jaws of congressional defeat. The chip, or at least all but a small piece at Grand Forks, North Dakota, ultimately was bargained away in the process of negotiating the ABM Treaty. And the multibillion dollar piece at Grand Forks was constructed, operated briefly, and was ordered shut down in 1976 by a Congress that judged it not to be cost effective.

What if the ABM Treaty soon were to be modified or terminated? Would the United States then deploy a substantial BMD system? Would the Congress reverse its previous judgment of the cost-effectiveness of BMD and provide tens of billions of dollars for a new system? On these matters (as on many others), the outcome of our political machinations remains unpredictable. We might go all out for defensive systems. Or it is entirely plausible that termination of the treaty would lead to extensive BMD deployment by the Soviet Union and little or no comparable action by the United States.

Who among us does not share the hope expressed by President Ronald Reagan (on March 23, 1983) that we might some day reach a state in which "we could intercept and destroy strategic ballistic missiles before they reached our own soil or that of our allies"? Not surprisingly, Americans prefer an invulnerable homeland to a vulnerable one.

Unfortunately, invulnerability is not an available option; not now and not for the foreseeable future. Plausible defensive systems are imperfect; they have the potential to enhance deterrence and to limit the damage if deterrence should fail, but they can also undermine deterrence and provide incentives for further growth in the destructive power of strategic offensive arsenals. BMD decisions involve complex tradeoffs among military, technological, economic, diplomatic, and political factors. Hard choices have to be made. If there is one "right" choice, it is identifiable only rarely, and then only in retrospect.

What is clear is that a decision to modify substantially or to withdraw from the ABM Treaty would be a momentous one. To move from this world of little or no BMD to one in which both sides could have extensive BMD deployments would be to step into the unknown. There are many possible paths, some leading to less dangerous BMD worlds and some leading to more dangerous ones. We should strive to identify paths headed in the right direction and, within the constraints of the ABM Treaty, to develop the kinds of BMD systems that might enable us to make the journey. But, unless and until we find a path that surely can be followed to a safer BMD world, we had best not launch the expedition.

WILLIAM A. DAVIS, JR.

President Ronald Reagan's so-called Star Wars speech on March 23, 1983, has touched off an avalanche of reactions, both pro and con, that seems destined to persist for some time. The ensuing debate rivals the ABM debate of the late 1960s, both in emotional intensity and in the prevalence of misinformation. Perhaps it is a peculiar phenomenon of the American psyche that only strategic defensive proposals will arouse passions and trigger national debate. Strategic offensive systems, such as the original MIRVed ICBM concept, might be rationally viewed as more menacing, but they go by virtually unnoticed.

Herman Kahn said, during the last great ABM debate, that the coalition of opposition to ABM consisted of people who thought: (1) ABM will work; (2) ABM will not work; (3) both; or (4) neither. It seems that the same mixture of opinion marks the opposition to the current strategic defense initiative. Some of this negative opinion is sprinkled throughout the preceding chapters of this book, expressed by and large in persuasive prose. It is certainly not true that those who oppose BMD arrived at that position for want of a formal education; the opposition to BMD in the late 1960s was led by academicians. The current debate is no less blessed.

For someone who is unabashedly sold on ballistic missile defense, both technically and politically, it is difficult to decide how to present a brief contribution to this book. (The abbreviation BMD is used by true believers, and ABM is used by agnostics.) Having spent thirteen years working on the BMD program, I have undergone a pro-BMD petrification process that will not yield to specious arguments. This is an admission that serves as a warning of prejudice and a claim of some knowledge about the subject. The former is an aid to debate, and the latter is a handicap.

With these observations and caveats out of the way, I will now address the following topics: BMD and strategic stability, BMD breakthroughs, capabilities and limitations of space-based directed-energy weapons, and functions and missions of BMD systems.

BMD and Strategic Stability

The origin of the perverse theory that BMD is strategically destabilizing, and therefore should be the first item on the arms control agenda, is somewhat obscure. However, it is clear that it has always been linked to the increasingly discredited policy of mutual assured destruction (MAD). The faint temptation to describe this policy here will be resisted, but one historical anecdote says much about the intellectual strains it has induced.

When President Lyndon Johnson first broached the idea of banning ABM to Aleksei Kosygin at Glassboro, New Jersey, in 1967, the Soviet leader was appalled that anyone could seriously consider denying the protection of one's homeland. It was only after Robert McNamara's patient exposition of the concept of mutual assured destruction that the Soviet Union even grasped the bizarre rationale for such a treaty. Of course, the Soviet Union never subscribed to the MAD idea but it did eventually agree to the ABM Treaty for different reasons. It welcomed the generous offer to freeze ABM deployment while it had an opportunity to catch up in ABM technology.

Today, the MAD policy continues to defy common sense and to go against the grain of moral and ethical instincts. It is an idea that tantalizes the strategic theorists and baffles the man on the street. As Congressman Ken Kramer recently pointed out, polls show that most people in the United States *assume* they are protected from ballistic missile attack. The public would have to be massively "educated" to understand why defense is bad. The curriculum would have to include a rebuttal to

President Reagan's compelling question, "Wouldn't it be better to save lives than to avenge them?"

The current study and debate on BMD will be more constructive if the recidivistic impulse to label BMD "destabilizing" is curbed. There are enough legitimate issues on the technical feasibility, the effectiveness, and the cost of BMD systems to profitably occupy the agenda. It is patently impossible even to summarize the advocacy position on these issues that underlies this brief commentary, but it is possible to outline a positive approach to consideration of new generations of BMD systems in the context of what we have learned about BMD in the past.

BMD Breakthroughs

In the quarter century of BMD R&D in this country, there have been many technical advancements, but there have been only three fundamental breakthroughs. The first breakthrough was in the Nike-X era in the mid-1960s when phased-array radars were adopted to replace the dish antennas of Nike-Zeus and high-acceleration interceptors (Sprint, Hibex) were introduced. This combination provided the United States with the traffic-handling capability to cope with large numbers of RVs, a capability needed in the presence of MIRVed systems and essential to the credibility of BMD.

The second breakthrough is emerging now in the form of midcourse, exoatmospheric BMD capability. This brand of BMD, which is based on the use of long-wave infrared (LWIR) optical sensors, onboard data processing, and nonnuclear kill vehicles, represents a major departure from traditional, terminal defense systems. Extending the reach of BMD into the midcourse regime provides greatly increased coverage per site, deeper battlespace, and more time to perform the required functions. It also introduces the possibility of layered defense, whereby a midcourse BMD system serves as an overlay and a terminal BDM system serves as an underlay. The main virtue of layered defense is the reduction of leakage, a vitally important feature for many defense missions.

The third breakthrough on the horizon is space-based directed-energy weapons (DEW). If this class of BMD system can be perfected, then boost-phase kill can be achieved. In the boost-phase of a ballistic missile trajectory, the target (a booster tank or postboost vehicle) is softer than an RV, and the BMD system can gain the leverage associated with negating all of the RVs of a MIRV by killing the booster. Moreover, boost-phase BMD will provide another tier of defense in a layered defense system.

Capabilities and Limitations of Space-Based DEW

Although space-based directed energy weapons represent a potential BMD breakthrough, the extent of their capabilities and the severity of their limitations have become the subject of much controversy. One school of thought holds that these weapon concepts are preposterous on the surface, hopelessly vulnerable to attack, and economically unfeasible. At the other extreme are the enthusiasts who believe these weapons offer an impenetrable shield against not only ballistic missiles, but also manned bombers and cruise missiles. Neither of these views is correct.

The best BMD use of a space defense system is probably in conjunction with more conventional terminal and midcourse systems (defense-in-depth, or layered defense). Secretary of Defense Caspar Weinberger talked about defense-in-depth in his April 11, 1983, speech to the Aviation and Space Writers Convention in Washington, D.C. This elaboration on the intent of President Reagan's strategic defense initiative likened the BMD problem to the problem of defending the fleet against air attack. In this type of defense, Secretary Weinberger noted, the first line of defense is F-14 interceptors, the second tier is Aegis missiles, and the third tier is the close-in weapons on the ships being attacked.

If BMD is thought of in this way—as a series of filters that the attacker must penetrate—then the facile criticisms of each isolated type of BMD system become even more irresponsible than they appeared to be in the first place. Properly designed and coupled to the required tactical warning/attack assessment network, such a defense can become a formidable bulwark against ballistic missile attack. The whole becomes stronger than the sum of the parts. Each tier of defense will pose not only another barrier but another set of technology for the offense to worry about. Its penetration problems are compounded, and the uncertainties in attack planning are greatly multiplied.

The limitations of space-based directed-energy weapons, deployed on their own, are somewhat subtle, and they frequently escape the attention of the casual observer. One of the more fundamental factors is the availability of space vehicles at the right place at the right time to effectively enter into the BMD engagement. This problem, sometimes called the "absentee" problem, refers to the fact that of a constellation of space-weapon satellites, only a small fraction of them, perhaps as low as 10 percent, will be in position to fire at targets during the time that they must be engaged. In a sense, much of the store of "ammunition" is wasted because it cannot be brought to bear on the targets. This contrasts with the classical interceptor allocation problem in which the interceptor stockpile is deployed in the vicinity of the targets being attacked, where it can be used efficiently.

The other space-weapon limitations worthy of note have to do with survivability and preferential defense. The survivability issues are difficult to quantify, but there is legitimate concern that all space-based systems are subject to antisatellite attack. The one advantage that a DEW station has over a passive satellite is the ability to shoot back, provided that the reserve "ammunition" supply is adequate and that the keepout range is great enough. The preferential defense limitation refers to the inability of a boost-phase system to predict where the RVs are targeted, that is, the inability to carry out impact point prediction (IPP). Preferential defense, one of the basic tools used by the BMD designer to gain leverage against the offense, requires that IPP be measurable to some degree of resolution, depending on the level of preferential defense being enforced (silo level, wing level, or other area level).

Again, the limitations of space-based weapons can be partly offset by other layers in a layered defense network. Conversely, the limitations of midcourse and terminal BMD systems can be greatly alleviated by the presence of a boost-phase system. One of the great virtues of a boost-phase tier is the contribution it makes to breaking up structured attacks. Structured attacks (such as a nuclear precursor attack) in which the attacker constructs a stylized laydown to defeat a BMD system are the most burdensome that a conventional BMD system has to contend with.

In the final analysis, the utility of three or more tiers of defense, made conceivable by the projected breakthrough in space-based weapons, can only be fully appreciated by evaluating them from the attack planner's point of view. The attack planner always gives the defense more credit than the defense designer, by a wide margin. He must make "offense-conservative" assumptions, and he must make "sure" the attack will work before he is tempted to wage it. If he is looking at an array of multiple tiers of defense, with the varying characteristics summarized above, he is going to be hard pressed to build confidence in an attack mode. He is going to be deterred.

Functions and Missions of BMD Systems

Steve Weiner provides an excellent description of BMD functions in chapter 3. These generic functions have been extensively analyzed and demonstrated both for terminal and midcourse BMD systems. They may be conveniently grouped into precommit functions and postcommit functions, depending on whether they are performed before or after the decision is made to fire interceptors.

Precommit functions include acquisition, tracking, and discrimination. For terminal systems, they are performed with a radar sensor driven by a large central computer and real-time software package. For midcourse systems, the functions are performed by an LWIR optical sensor backed up by an onboard data-processing subsystem. Terminal system precommit functions must be carried out on a compressed timeline, typically of a few seconds' duration, while midcourse systems can afford the luxury of taking tens or even hundreds of seconds.

Postcommit functions include guidance and control, fusing, arming, and damage assessment. For terminal systems, postcommit functions are executed over a data link between a ground-based radar and an inflight, high-acceleration interceptor. Midcourse postcommit functions are carried out autonomously on board the interceptor.

The experience with both terminal and midcourse BMD systems clearly shows that the precommit functions (all of the things that must be done before the "trigger is pulled") are the most complex and challenging. Within the precommit category, the functions driven by responsive threat elements, such as decoys, dominate the complexity of the problem.

Although there has been less experience with boost-phase DEW systems, it is safe to assume that the precommit functions will again be the more difficult to solve and to demonstrate. This is a reasonable inference despite the widespread preoccupation with DEW devices and postcommit effects.

The primary differences between boost-phase DEW functions and those of terminal and midcourse systems derive from differences in the targets. Boost-phase systems going against boosters and postboost vehicles have to engage softer targets with different physical, signature, and kinematic characteristics. In the acquisition phase, boost-phase systems have a booming infrared signature to work with, probably defying decoy or screening types of penetration aids, and a large target area. Since many threat vehicles may be launched simultaneously, boost-phase systems share the rate saturation problem that has plagued terminal and midcourse systems.

Penetration aids for boost-phase systems will differ from terminal and midcourse systems, probably concentrating on techniques such as hardening of the booster rather than spoofing or saturation of the sensors and data processors.

With respect to BMD missions, the most cost-effective BMD system deployment (terminal, midcourse, boost-phase, or layered) depends on the nature of the target being defended. For example, deceptively based ICBM sites, such as the MPS basing mode formerly proposed for MX, can best be defended by a single terminal system such as the current Sentry system. For fixed ICBM sites, such as Minuteman and the currently proposed fixed basing mode for MX, a layered system, with terminal and midcourse tiers, is the most cost-effective solution. For most types of time-dependent targets, such as Strategic Air Command bases and submarine ports, two- or three-tiered defenses are required. For urban-industrial defense, three or more tiers of defense are required to drive the leakage of the system down (shoot-fail-shoot tactics may be employed to create a "virtual" tier of defense).

Summary

BMD is not strategically destabilizing. There have been three major breakthroughs in BMD, including the projected achievement of space-based directed-energy weapons capability. Although space-based weapons greatly extend BMD capability, they have limitations, which are best minimized by operating them in concert with terminal and midcourse systems. The functions of space-based weapons can be profitably analyzed in the light of experience and lessons learned with more traditional BMD systems. The utility of various classes of BMD systems is critically dependent on the nature of the target being defended.

JOHN S. FOSTER, JR.

The ABM Treaty has been the most important accomplishment of U.S. nuclear arms control policy. By severely limiting the deployment of

ABMs, it reinforces deterrence and reduces the chances of nuclear war. Despite the treaty's imperfections, most students of nuclear policy, regardless of their political orientation, believe, as I do, that the treaty is very important to peace and that its viability should be nurtured and protected.

The ABM Treaty was consummated because the self-interests of both sides were served by it. Its future viability depends on the continuation of this mutuality of self-interest. A threat to these self-interests and to the viability of the treaty is contained in current trends in this country and in the Soviet Union. If these trends are to be reversed, renewed efforts are needed in three areas:

—Because BMD activities have raised serious questions about Soviet compliance with both the letter and intent of the treaty, vigorous attempts should be made in the Standing Consultative Commission (SCC), established by Article VIII of the treaty, and in other appropriate forums if necessary, to obtain clarifications of Soviet activities and to gain greater confidence that these actions are in compliance with the treaty.

—The U.S. BMD technology program should be reemphasized to ensure that our demonstrated technology leads or is at least abreast of that of the Soviet Union. The pace of U.S. BMD technology is slower than that of the Soviet Union. This trend, in time, will weaken our confidence in our retaliatory forces and could eventually embolden the Soviet Union to exploit its advantages.

—Because Soviet efforts on antitactical ballistic missile (ATBM) systems, coupled with their BMD technology and other damage-limiting programs, raise the possibility of a Soviet breakout from the ABM Treaty, we should be prepared to counter such a thrust with more advanced offensive systems to maintain deterrence and with plans and programs to provide the ability to deploy quickly the best currently feasible U.S. BMD systems.

Consultation

It seems almost unnecessary to argue that we should consult vigorously with the Soviet Union to reduce the chances that the viability of the ABM Treaty will be weakened by misunderstandings. The framers of the treaty recognized the importance of such consultations by establishing the SCC. It was charged with responsibilities to "consider questions concerning compliance, . . . consider possible changes in the strategic situation" and to address other matters related to the promotion of "the objectives and implementation of the provisions of this Treaty."

Soviet activities in BMD have raised questions about compliance that, in my judgment, also threaten to change the strategic situation. These questions deserve prompt and satisfactory resolution. We, of course, have reciprocal responsibilities and should fulfill them in good faith. For example, the Soviet Union is certain to have questions about the new program called for by President Ronald Reagan in his March 23, 1983, speech. But we should have few concerns about answering such questions: the president specifically called for a program consistent with the ABM Treaty.

In summary, the ABM Treaty cannot survive in an environment of misunderstanding and mistrust on the specific subjects of the treaty itself. Every effort should be made, therefore, to ensure that the SCC is effective in reducing misunderstanding. Other forums should be used if the SCC is not effective.

BMD Research and Development

The most important reason for a vigorous BMD R&D program in the United States is to develop defensive technology against which to design and test our strategic offensive forces: their retaliatory effectiveness is essential to deterrence. But during the last ten years, our BMD program has suffered from frequent redirection and budget reductions, while the Soviet Union has pursued an aggressive BMD program on a broad front. Moreover, the closed nature of the Soviet society makes it difficult for us to know the full extent of Soviet programs or to understand the results of these programs. In contrast, a wealth of valuable information on both our offensive forces and our defensive technologies is available to the Soviet Union. Little can be done about this asymmetry, but it underscores the danger in our falling behind in a strategically important area like BMD. Given these circumstances, and the lack of a vigorous well-conceived BMD program in the United States, long-term confidence in our retaliatory forces is bound to erode. Such erosion could encourage greater boldness on the Soviet side and could lead to a greater risk of nuclear war.

Finally, we must consider the president's call for the development of a BMD system capable of damage denial. I have no illusions about the difficulties in developing and deploying such a defense against modern nuclear offensive systems deployed on the scale already extant. But the possibility cannot be ruled out that such defenses can be developed eventually. And who can deny that nuclear strategies based on defense dominance would be preferred to current ones based on offense dominance? Moreover, Soviet development of such a system ahead of similar achievements by the United States could be disastrous. We must make certain, in our own interests and in the interests of world peace, that if such a system can be developed, we are the first ones to do so.

If we are to pursue the president's objectives—and I believe we must—a number of technical and managerial steps are required:

—We must pursue "leapfrog" technologies that might eventually provide significant defensive capabilities against even very large numbers of reentry vehicles. Known technologies are all very limited in their ability to deal with large offensive threats and are applicable only to the defense of large numbers of point targets. Therefore, new concepts and innovative adaptations of breakthroughs in different technological fields will be required.

—Such concepts and technologies are now considered "exotic," but they are exotic only in the sense that they are unfamiliar. It is true that we will have very little operating experience with these weapons by the time we have to choose to rely upon them to some extent. This consideration merely suggests in what direction the most advantageous breakthroughs might be sought. Thus, for instance, systems that intercept ICBMs in boost phase (where discrimination problems are different and less severe than those during reentry) and in space (where the absence of atmosphere opens new possibilities) could offer particularly high leverage.

—Finally, we must create and maintain a climate that attracts the best people and is conducive to innovation. Such a climate is essential to long-term conduct of such an ambitious program.

Plans and Programs for Quick ABM Deployment

The Soviet Union is forging ahead with the development of ATBMs, which are not prohibited by the ABM Treaty. The Soviet Union might decide to deploy such systems, perhaps for use against U.S. Pershing intermediate-range ballistic missiles (IRBMs) in Europe. ATBMs effective against Pershing might possess inherently significant capabilities against intermediate-range strategic missiles such as our submarine-launched ballistic missiles. Moreover, strategic ABM technology is most effective against shorter-range strategic missiles such as Poseidon. By combining ATBMs, perhaps with upgrading, and strategic BMD technology, the Soviet Union could, within the next decade, have the capability to deploy widely effective defenses against the most survivable leg of our strategic triad. This might be an attractive option in conjunction with improved Soviet air defenses, hard target counterforce capabilities, and civil defense.

Whether the Soviet Union would be willing in such a situation to break out of the ABM Treaty is uncertain; nonetheless further U.S. measures to deter such a breakout are fully justified. The first such measure is obviously to maintain adequate effective retaliatory forces.[1] These are, in any event, necessary for our own security, and they promise that Soviet expenditures on defenses will be largely wasted. But such promises in regard to bombers and cruise missiles have not deterred past Soviet deployment of massive air defenses. Consequently, I believe we should have, in addition, the capability to counter a Soviet ABM deployment with one of our own. The Soviet Union would then run the risk not only of wasting vast resources (which they can ill afford) but also of suffering significant degradations in their own retaliatory capabilities.

Concluding Remarks

A much more stable nuclear balance would be possible if all R&D on ABMs could be prevented on both sides. But asymmetries in the openness of our societies, perceived Soviet needs for ATBMs and high-performance air defenses, and Soviet willingness to exploit the margins and ambiguities of international agreements make agreements prohibiting ABM R&D impractical and unsafe. We should, of course, do all that we can in our negotiations with the Soviet Union to understand its

1. Most arms control attention is now directed to reductions in offensive forces, but such reductions could increase the risk that the Soviet Union might decide to break out of the ABM Treaty. The overhanging ABM threat emphasizes the importance of relating offensive arms control measures, implicitly or explicitly, to defensive threats.

programs, to reduce the scope of such programs, and to prevent misunderstandings. But none of these measures, in my view, mitigates the need for a well-conceived, consistently exercised BMD program on our side. Without such a program we risk undermining our strategic retaliatory capabilities, and we reduce disincentives to Soviet ABM deployments. We also might unnecessarily forsake a future world in which defenses are so powerful that offensive forces are no longer useful. Although such developments now seem extremely remote, they cannot be ruled out, and every avenue should be pursued that holds the promise of lifting the threat of nuclear war from the shoulders of future generations.

RICHARD L. GARWIN

It is a relief and a pleasure to be able to write about ballistic missile defense without having first to describe the concepts, the options, the utility, and the countermeasures of BMD in general. As explained in detail in the preceding chapters, whether BMD will "work" depends very much on the strategic doctrine adopted, and the confidence required in its implementation. The Scowcroft Commission report of April 1983 contributed substantial wisdom on this score, which may soon be lost in the continuing advocacy arguments of proponents of various programs or ideologies.

Preserving Deterrence of Attack

There is a consensus that deterrence of Soviet attack on the United States by threat of retaliation is effective and must be preserved. Our strategic forces were built with this primary goal, and it is enshrined explicitly in the ABM Treaty of 1972, which states in Article I, "Each Party undertakes not to deploy ABM systems for a defense of the territory of its country and not to provide a base for such a defense, and not to deploy ABM systems for defense of an individual region except as provided for in Article III of this Treaty." To ensure this retaliatory capability against destruction before launch, and against air defense or ballistic missile defenses after launch, the United States has continually modified its strategic offensive force. The worst-case threats to the offensive force have not materialized, and we have always had a force vastly in excess of what was required to survive and penetrate and to wreak the "unacceptable damage" on the Soviet Union that we have deemed necessary to deter Soviet attack.

These excess capabilities (in number, accuracy, technical sophistication, and the like) have come to occupy more and more of the time of targeteers, philosophers, strategists, propagandists, and politicians. It is hard to argue, after all, that if deterrence fails these forces should not be *used* for whatever purpose they can serve at that time. The first such purpose would be "damage limitation" by destruction of Soviet forces before they could be launched. But improvement (or maintenance) of our capability for this entirely secondary or bonus goal has even imperiled our understanding of and commitment to the bedrock of our security— deterrence by threat of retaliation.

A similar observation can be made about our defensive capabilities. If we could eliminate the threat of Soviet attack on our civilization, society, productive capacity, and values, we would not need to *deter* Soviet attack; if the Soviet Union assessed this matter as we did, they would have no incentive to waste their weapons in such an attack. The first few dozen weapons of megaton yield launched against the United States would each kill nearly a million people, and 200 such weapons could certainly destroy U.S. society. Of course, they could not destroy the U.S. capacity to retaliate with nuclear weapons—and the will to retaliate and the capability to retaliate are adequate to deter the Soviet Union from intentional attack on the United States.

Recommendations for Silo Defense

Contrary to arguments common in the late 1970s, an "unfavorable exchange ratio" (the Soviet ability to destroy three Minuteman III warheads by the use of two of their ICBM warheads!) is *not* an "irresistible temptation" for the Soviet Union to initiate nuclear war. It never was, as evidenced by the fact that there has never been any concern that the presence at most times in a U.S. port of three Poseidon submarines, mounting 480 nuclear warheads, presented "an irresistible temptation" for the Soviet Union to initiate nuclear war. No one has doubted that in a nuclear strike on the United States these vulnerable submarines in port would be among the first and most lucrative targets, but the submarine force was built in such numbers as to accommodate their expected loss in nuclear war.

In a democracy, it is very important that the people (and the incoming administration!) not be misled about the goals or feasibility of defense prospects. Having looked at proposals for defense against nuclear weapons—civil defense, BMD, space defenses of all kinds, and the like—I judge that the Soviet Union will be able in all cases to overcome such defenses. Even more readily will we be able to overcome Soviet defenses, maintaining our capability for a retaliatory destructive strike. Ballistic missile defense is quite feasible for raising the price of attack on individual silos. But one cannot have a disarming strike against silos in any case, because of the possibility of launch under attack (LUA). Nevertheless, the deployment of silo defense is not strategically desta-bilizing (it would not be stabilizing either if the offense never attacked because it feared LUA), so if it makes *us* feel better, we can develop and deploy some silo defense. However, it would not make us feel better to have the Soviet Union deploy an area defense (nor could we count on defending our territory with area defenses).

I have recommended for years (to the Scowcroft Commission on January 27, 1983, among others) that we should perfect a "Swarmjet" defense of individual silos (the progenitor of a class of defenses dubbed "simple/novel" by the Army Ballistic Missile Defense Program Office) and also a buried-bomb ejecta-and-dust defense of individual silos. Although these do not fit the ABM Treaty's definition of an ABM system as one consisting of ABM radars and ABM interceptors, there is little doubt that 100 such defense units could be deployed under the ABM Treaty. There is no doubt that *development* could be completed and that the buried-bomb defense in particular could then be deployed extremely rapidly.

Swarmjet

The Swarmjet simple/novel defense concept was first proposed by the author and his colleagues in the JASON group, scientific consultants who sometimes study problems for the Department of Defense. The substantive work was done largely by Tracor MBA of California, and the present characterization is based on their findings.[1] Even 20 or 30 percent expected survivability of 1000 Minuteman silos would be adequate to constitute a thoroughly effective retaliatory force. In conjunction with deployment of a much larger number of small silos containing single-warhead "Midgetman" ICBMs, a yet smaller probability of Minuteman survival would still probably be adequate to deter any attack. With such a large number of targets (1000 Minuteman silos plus perhaps thousands of Midgetman silos) the Soviet Union could only attack with a few RVs per target. Swarmjet could probably charge a price of a few RVs and would furthermore have the important effect of complicating a Soviet attack and Soviet estimates of its likely success. This modest but meaningful protection would be the goal of a Swarmjet deployment.

Minuteman silo survival against a nominal Soviet RV can be achieved with a keepout distance of 500 m. We shall consider a Swarmjet system attempting to enforce a keepout distance of 500 m and also a more demanding distance of 1500 m. The system is designed to handle ICBM attack. Each silo is defended autonomously, with shotgun-type launchers that spew swarms of projectiles. The launchers are deployed in hardened silos a few tens of meters from the silo to be defended. The launchers can spew $\pm$ 42° in azimuth and $\pm$ 20° in elevation angle. Upon tactical warning of Soviet attack, covers would be removed from microsilos that protect very small radars. A cluster of such multilateration radars 5 km north of the silo, and a second cluster 8 km north of the silo, would track the RV approaching the defended silo. A typical radar range precision of 1 m and radar spacing of 2 km result in RV position uncertainties (with 2 sec of tracking) of perhaps 1-m minor axis and 3-m major axis, with a resulting along-track trajectory extrapolation uncertainty of 7 m at 500 m range and 15 m at 1500 m range.

The Swarmjet time line is compressed into 3 sec as follows: 0 sec, start track; 0.5 sec, blow doors and pressurize launcher; 1.0 sec, start pointing; 1.7 sec, launch first salvo; 1.8 sec, launch last salvo; 3.0 sec, intercept.

The projectiles kill by kinetic energy, delivering about 2 megajoules to a colliding RV. They are some 26 cm long and about 6 cm in diameter. The launchers are assumed to provide an aiming accuracy of 2 milliradians standard deviation, and the error budget allows them 4 milliradians.

1. "Swarmjet Summary Briefing" (San Ramon, Calif.: Tracor MBA, October 1981).

Projectile dispersion (the deviation of individual projectiles from their intended direction of flight) in test is less than 4 milliradians, and the error budget allows 8 milliradians. With these assumptions, a baseline design has twelve launchers, each launching 800 projectiles. At 500-m intercept range, 1000 projectiles suffice to give 85 percent probability that an RV will hit at least one projectile; at 1500-m range, about 600 rounds are required.

The system is provided with spare radars, so that destruction of the soft operating radars simply leads to the exposure of more radars from their silos—the procedure is known as Kleenex radar technology. Only as many launchers and radars are exposed from their silos as are required to destroy one warhead at a time. The rest are protected in their silos.

The primary problem with Swarmjet will arise when high winds from detonations blow projectiles off course, and thus a single precursor RV might prevent interception of follow-on RVs. Despite this deficiency, I think that the system is worth developing in view of the substantial numbers of silos that would survive a four-warhead attack (owing to the unreliability of Soviet ICBMs). Later the system could be modified with clustered interceptors to stabilize it against wind.

Buried-Bomb Defense

Burying a nuclear weapon of 100-kT yield 1 km north of each of the silos to be defended, and detonating seconds before arrival of attacking RVs, would provide 100 kT of earth in a massive plume through which no RV could penetrate. Because Soviet ICBMs can attack from either the western or eastern USSR, two bombs per Minuteman silo might be needed to cover all attack directions. A small Kleenex radar 5 km north of the silos (needing no great accuracy) would provide the firing signal after tactical warning and nuclear release from the National Command Authorities had been received.

This defense, of course, protects against any number of RVs arriving simultaneously. The lighter debris provides a long-lasting defense as it rises to high altitudes and spreads laterally, impeding access to other silos in the field. The nuclear weapons are inexpensive, since they can be very large in physical size and hence low in fissile content. By the same token, they can be relatively clean. Developments in Project Plowshare on the peaceful uses of nuclear weapons in the 1960s show that such devices can be built with fission yields below 2 kT. Appropriate choice of material for the weapon (as in many Plowshare applications) minimizes radioactivity induced by the fusion neutrons, and the weapon can be surrounded by borated water in a small room at the bottom of the burial shaft in order to minimize radioactivity induced in the earth. As a result, the radioactivity provided by the explosion of each such buried bomb would be less than 1 percent of that of a typical Soviet RV of comparable yield.

Multiple bombs could be employed to handle long drawn-out attacks. Not all silos would have to be defended with multiple bombs; instead deceptive preferential defense could be used. A large number of empty chambers could be built to house a smaller number of deceptively emplaced bombs. Each chamber and radar microsilo would have a hardened communications link to commanders.

Swarmjet can handle multiple RVs if they are *spaced* sufficiently in time so that the winds from one detonation do not substantially interfere with the flight of the small rockets. A single buried-bomb explosion will prevent access to the protected silo by any number of RVs during a brief period (which may last from tens of minutes to hours, depending upon winds, number of other underground explosives detonated, and the like). The two defenses are thus nearly *complementary*, Swarmjet discouraging drawn-out attacks and buried-bomb defense discouraging rapid-fire salvos.

Status of These Systems

On May 14, 1981, having testified the previous month before the Townes Panel on MX basing, I met with Charles Townes, Michael May, and representatives of the Army Ballistic Missile Defense Program Office (BMDPO) at the Livermore Laboratory. BMDPO presented its calculations on Swarmjet and buried-bomb defense, which agreed fairly well with the ones sketched here. The major difference was in a demand for higher kill probability for Swarmjet, resulting in a requirement for a larger number of projectiles. Asked why little had been done by the army for several years on Swarmjet and other simple/novel approaches, the BMDPO said candidly that there was just no high-level interest in a near-term limited-capability defense of Minuteman. Bureaucratically, this is not hard to understand, since a reduction in Minuteman vulnerability would hardly help advance the case for deployment of the MX missile (the same holds for improvements in Minuteman's accuracy and capability).

Judgments on City Defense

The Scowcroft Commission has validated the view that silo vulnerability by itself is insignificant in the context of a strategic force that is not vulnerable overall. The important question for strategic forces is the maintenance of confidence in our ability to deter Soviet attack by a general threat of retaliation. Whatever the reality regarding the effectiveness of defenses, this confidence would be impaired by a BMD race on the two sides—even by the acquisition of a "totally effective defense against nuclear weapons" of the type that Secretary of Defense Caspar Weinberger said he had no doubt we could achieve (and that the Soviet Union could, too).[2] Even if we had a defense that was technically "totally effective," we might still live in deadly fear that the other side could defeat *our* defense by sabotage, jamming, or deception, while keeping its defense "totally effective."

As for the feasibility of the defense of cities against ballistic missiles carrying nuclear warheads, exoatmospheric midcourse defense is extremely difficult to carry out because of the problem of discriminating each of the many thousands of RVs from the tens or hundreds of thousands of decoys that could accompany them. Since both infrared and radar sensors are readily fooled by inflated multilayer balloons, with a balloon around the RV for good measure (or to counter "good measure"!), attention has shifted to boost-phase intercept, where essentially two choices can be made: either the defensive system can be based on satellites, or it can be based on the ground in silos. (The silos might protect the defense against sabotage; by definition hardened structures are not needed if the area defense is effective!)

Satellite basing of a defensive system is extremely vulnerable to space mines—small satellites that dog the tracks of the defensive satellites at a distance of a few hundred meters, ready to explode on receipt of a radio signal relayed by a simple satellite relay net. The space mines can also be arranged to explode when a radio link is cut off, at least under certain circumstances. Space mines weighing a few kilograms should do

2. Interview on "Meet the Press," March 27, 1983.

the job, and the advance of microelectronics should help space mines at least as much as it should help defensive systems.

In testimony and interviews, Edward Teller (an advocate of defense) agrees that a defensive system based on satellites can be overcome at far less cost than would be required to deploy it: "I'm convinced that to put up a system of laser-equipped satellites to destroy incoming Soviet missiles would take much more money than the Soviets need spend to counter it."[3]

Logically, the next possibility is ground-based systems. Here the problem is intensified by the short duration of the boost phase of ICBMs. During this short period, the defensive directed-energy weapons must climb high enough from their basing area to have line-of-sight to the boosting Soviet ICBMs. The MX, for instance, burns for 155 sec and has a range of about 6000 NM, or one-quarter of the circumference of the earth. A defense based at the target must climb 300 mi. to have line-of-sight to the ICBM booster when it is at a 200-NM altitude (allowing 100-NM clearance between the line connecting the defensive vehicle and offensive booster and the earth's surface). If 35 sec are allowed for the defense to detect ICBM launch, to make the defensive vehicles reach 3000 NM in the remaining 120 sec of ICBM boost it would require an *average* climbing speed of 25 NM/sec—corresponding to a mass ratio between launch weight and payload weight of 4 million. That is, the entire defensive missile must be 4 million times heavier than the directed-energy weapon it carries! The launch weights for a 500-kg payload (assuming a specific impulse of 300 sec) are given in table 11-1. Of course, smaller defensive missiles could be used if more time was available, or if the defense could be based closer to the Soviet Union.

Thus we see that in addition to the inherent technological problems of packaging short-wave lasers or X-ray lasers and sending them up rapidly to do their job (combined with the problems of acquisition, tracking, command and control, and the like), we have an extremely difficult *performance* problem imposed by the short burn time of the offensive missiles. And the offense can more readily make that burn time *shorter* (at perhaps 20 percent weight increment to burn out within the shielding atmosphere) than the defense can improve its performance.

Finally, the problem of the "perfect defense" on both sides has to be

3. Steven J. Marcus, "Corporate Push for Space Lasers," *New York Times*, April 24, 1983.

Table 11-1. *Characteristics of Ground-Based Directed-Energy Defense Vehicles Required to Attack Soviet ICBMs in the Boost Phase*

Characteristic	Range from ICBM launchpoint to defensive launcher (NM)			
	6000	5000	4000	3000
Altitude that defensive weapon must reach in 120 sec (NM)[a]	2960	2050	1260	650
Mass of defensive missile assuming instant burn[b]	2.1 MT	19 kT	330 t	14 t
Mass of defensive missile assuming constant acceleration[b]	. . .	. . .	270 kT	450 t
Acceleration required assuming constant acceleration (g)	78	54	33	17

Source: Author.
a. Assumes that the line of sight from earth's surface has a clearance of 100 NM and that the offensive booster has reached a height of 200 NM.
b. Payload mass = 500 kg; specific impulse = 300 sec.

faced, as does the question of whether that "defense" can be used to enhance penetration against the other side's defense. Assume, for instance, that the side that strikes first launches a few short-range "escort" missiles carrying X-ray lasers at the same time that it launches its long-range ICBMs. The short-range escort missiles have a larger vertical velocity than the ICBMs, so they can see the other side's defensive missiles (as they are struggling to climb over the horizon) before the defensive missiles can themselves see the attacking ICBMs. The defensive boosters are no less vulnerable than offensive ICBMs, and the escorting X-ray lasers can make short shrift of them, allowing the ICBMs a free ride.

Recommendations

As I have argued in much testimony during the last year, as regards BMD the United States should do the following:
—Develop and deploy two competitive systems of the Swarmjet type within the ABM Treaty, initially in a few-score launchers but with the potential of providing a defense of thousands of Minuteman (and ultimately Midgetman) silos.

—Within the ABM Treaty, develop the buried-bomb silo-defense system and determine the scope of a program that would allow rapidly deployable protection of many hundreds of silos.

—Urgently negotiate with the Soviet Union a ban on antisatellite testing and on weapons in space.

—Take seriously the possibility of launch under attack and the fact that it is an effective deterrent even if all strategic systems should become totally vulnerable.

COLIN S. GRAY

On March 23, 1983, President Ronald Reagan challenged the defense-technical community to investigate the feasibility of defending the United States against ballistic missiles. Scarcely less demanding was the implicit challenge to the policy-analysis community in the president's statement: it was suggested that they consider the advantages and disadvantages of moving from an offense-dominant strategic posture to a posture wherein defensive capabilities would play major roles.

It would be difficult to exaggerate the historic significance of the president's generic endorsement of the idea of ballistic missile defense. This was the first presidential endorsement of the idea of defending the country to have been issued in more than twenty years. Whatever one may think of the technical feasibility—a subject deliberately excluded from discussion in this analysis—or the desirability of strategic defense, the importance of the policy statement in its favor is unmistakable. Furthermore, it is remarkable, if only because it is rare, to see policy guidance as far ahead of strategy and technology as it is in this instance. This is one of those historically unusual cases where a government has decided what it would like to accomplish long ahead of technical realization. There is some irony in the fact that although politicians and officials tend to be criticized for acquiescing in the face of a "technology push," when they provide a genuine measure of "policy pull" they are criticized no less forcefully. The following observation by journalist Thomas Powers illustrates the typical complaint: "Shifting to 'realistic' planning for limited war, so alarming to the general public, was not anything Carter or his advisers *chose* to do. They were pushed every step of the way by the weapons themselves."[1]

1. Thomas Powers, "Choosing a Strategy for World War III," *Atlantic* (November 1982), p. 84. Emphasis in the original.

More than ten years ago Elizabeth Young referred to this phenomenon, or alleged phenomenon, as "the ripening plum" syndrome.[2] It would seem that a president cannot win. If he approves a technology that is ready, he is charged with permitting the weapons laboratories and defense industry to occupy the driver's seat. If he approves an idea for a weapon or a family of weapons that is scarcely beyond the stage of conceptualization, he is charged with encouraging the development of weapons that cannot be designed (today), let alone made to work reliably and cost-effectively (again, today).

Without denying the validity of many of the technical questions that have been posed in criticism of the idea of defending the country against ballistic missiles, I think it is truly remarkable how confident people are that engineering problems will not lend themselves to successful assault over the course of the next twenty or thirty years. I suspect that policy views, even strategic ideology, tend to dominate and direct technical judgment. This statement carries no imputation of dishonesty. "Ripening plums" or distant weapons visions are both assessed through the prism of doctrinal preference and are endorsed or vilified accordingly.

Before turning to the case for strategic defense in general, it is necessary first to summarize what can and should be said about President Reagan's speech of March 23, 1983—given that this speech and the official studies flowing from it are the contemporary point of departure for policy argument and weapons development activity.

First, President Reagan provided a degree of political legitimacy to strategic defense that has been lacking for a generation. The absence of policy-level approval even of the concept of homeland defense has rendered research on strategic defense very much a backwater. That fact has had a major impact on the level of funding provided and, of course, on the strength of its political constituency both in Washington and in the country in general. The ABM Treaty of 1972 is the law of the land and notwithstanding the variety of interpretations that can be placed upon many of its detailed provisions, in Article I it commits the signatories unambiguously to forgo the defense of their countries against ballistic missile attack. For more than ten years the treaty has functioned both as a legal and a political-symbolic barrier to the achievement of

2. The theory of the " 'ripening plum' . . . holds that what can be done, will be done if the money is available, and that a good reason will be found when the project is ripe for deployment." Elizabeth Young, *A Farewell to Arms Control?* (Penguin, 1972), p. 195, n51.

technical progress in strategic defense. President Reagan's vision of an America defended against nuclear-armed ballistic missiles is fundamentally incompatible with the expressed major purpose of the ABM Treaty. The speech of March 23 was the first important blow that has been delivered by the United States to the integrity of the particular concept of strategic stability embodied in the text of the treaty.

Second, by implication at least, the president argued that nuclear deterrence may be an unduly weak reed on which exclusively to lean our security for the long term. As Fred Iklé has argued, it is probably unreasonable to expect any security system to function effectively at all times for decade after decade, indefinitely.[3] There is also food for thought in the following argument by Edward Luttwak:

> It must be pointed out that there is a qualitative difference between the security provided by deterrence and that provided by an active defense. The former, being the result of suasion, is subject to all the vagaries inherent in human perception and human decision; the latter, being physical, is definitive. Prudent men may well choose to pay the greater costs of an active defense for the sake of its reliability, which is independent of the decisions of other men.[4]

Many policy challenges are associated with a shift away from a nuclear deterrence system,[5] most of which are only very imperfectly understood at the present time, but there happens to be a problem with the existing theory of security. Specifically, a system of security that rests upon the premise that homelands should be assuredly vulnerable to nuclear retaliatory forces that must be assuredly invulnerable, is a system that, if it ever fails, is very likely to fail in a manner that is most deadly for our society.[6] Nuclear war is possible regardless of the quality of strategy and forces, although these presumably affect its probability. Human beings, individually and collectively in policymaking and policy-executing organizations, are liable to make mistakes.

Third, Clausewitz's argument that "defense is *the stronger form of waging war*"[7]—or, more strictly, defense-offense, since victory cannot

---

3. Fred Charles Ikle, "Can Nuclear Deterrence Last Out the Century?" *Foreign Affairs*, vol. 51 (January 1973), pp. 267–85.

4. Edward N. Luttwak, *The Grand Strategy of the Roman Empire: From the First Century A.D. to the Third* (Johns Hopkins University Press, 1976), p. 199.

5. As noted in the text below, strategic defenses may be viewed as being compatible with a policy of deterrence.

6. On the risks and attractions of rival theories of deterrence, see Keith B. Payne, *Nuclear Deterrence in U.S.-Soviet Relations* (Westview, 1982).

7. Karl von Clausewitz, *On War*, ed. Michael Howard and Peter Paret (Princeton University Press, 1976), p. 359. Emphasis in the original.

be secured by "pure defense"—appears to have no relevance in an age when countries can be devastated whether or not their armed forces are defeated. But, new technologies for active defense, married to programs of passive defense, hold out the promise of revalidating Clausewitz's thesis. A United States with a multilayered strategic defense capability for the limitation of damage to its homeland (to a low though certainly not trivial scale) should be a United States far better placed than it is today both to succeed in the prosecution of local conflict (an enemy could not escalate out of a theater war in the expectation of enforcing an improved conflict outcome) and—if need be—to expand a war in order to seek to restore deterrence through action at a higher level of violence.

The point is that technology is ever changing, and the simple, permanent fact of the existence of nuclear weapons need not mean that the historical yin-yang of shifting relative advantage as between the offense and the defense has been frozen permanently in favor of the offensive.[8] Of course, this is not to deny that the unprecedented destructiveness of individual nuclear weapons has raised the requirements for defense performance to no less unprecedented heights.

Fourth, without precluding the very distant possibility that the driving political dynamic of the superpower arms competition might cease to function eventually, the president offered a ray of hope that the long dark tunnel of nuclear fear might have an end:

> I call upon the scientific community in our country, those who gave us nuclear weapons, to turn their great talents now to the cause of mankind and world peace, to give us the means of rendering these nuclear weapons impotent and obsolete.[9]

A democracy that must deny many aspects of its fundamental character and compete steadily for decades—as opposed to surging military capability to meet a clear and immediate danger—almost certainly performs more effectively on hope than it does on fear. Sacrifice today needs to be related plausibly to the prospects for a more secure tomorrow. President Reagan was fulfilling his presidential duty when he provided unambiguous leadership on the subject of long-term trends in U.S. defense preparation. He did not *promise* an "astrodome" defense over the United States, but—quite properly and responsibly—he identified the possibility of emergence of a world wherein the United States would

8. For a useful historical perspective, see George H. Quester, *Offense and Defense in the International System* (John Wiley, 1977).

9. "President's Speech on Military Spending and a New Defense," *New York Times*, March 24, 1983.

be far less at nuclear risk than it is at present. As long as people do not expect preclusive, perfect defense, and they do not anticipate active defense capability as a panacea for complex security problems, the president's vision and direction of long-term research and development have everything to recommend it.

It must be noted that on March 23, 1983, President Reagan deliberately did not advance a deterrence or prudential damage-limitation argument for strategic defense. Instead, he spoke at the most generally appealing and comprehensible of levels: "Isn't it worth every investment necessary to free the world from the threat of nuclear war?"[10] The argument about strategic defense tends to be sidetracked too easily into deeply technical disputes about particular weapons concepts, or into near-theological disagreements over strategic desiderata that are fueled by competing doctrines of stability. What follows is an endeavor, very briefly, to summarize many of the elements of the case for strategic defenses. Although each one can be disputed, with greater or lesser plausibility, it is important that the entire array of positive arguments be appreciated.

Uncertainty for Deterrence

Any strategic defense program, be it a simple "Swarmjet" defense of missile silos or a system of space-based laser battle stations, must increase attacker uncertainty by reducing the calculability of the effectiveness of attacks that even in the absence of active defenses are fraught with imponderables. A security system with nuclear deterrence at its heart could not be other than strengthened were a prospective aggressor to be confronted with the necessity of dueling, for the first time and on a massive scale, with one or more active defense systems. In the real world of fearful human beings, as opposed to the imaginary world of dehumanized strategic logic, one should never despise the "defender's advantage." The burden of decision is on the attacker. We may harbor profound doubts as to the probable operational effectiveness of our active strategic defenses, but how does the problem appear to the potential enemy?

10. Ibid.

Offensive-Force Reduction and the Saving of Lives

States will not allocate scarce resources to the sustenance and development of forces that they believe will be ineffective. Strategic defense, in the future as in the past, will never be beyond successful challenge,[11] but the price that defense can extract for its defeat could offer profound discouragement to the planners of offensive, strategic nuclear operations. Therefore, should strategic defense technology ripen with great promise, both superpowers would have strong incentives to reconsider the strategic value of at least a large (very large, in the Soviet case)[12] fraction of their offensive striking power. Needless to say, a large-scale shift in resource allocation as between the offense and the defense could, and should, have important consequences for the scale of the potential human tragedy that would attend a war.

Reduced Self-Deterrence for the Strengthening of Deterrence

Logically at least a United States equipped with damage-limiting "layers" of active and passive defenses (back-stopping counterforce prowess of all kinds) should be more willing to take the controlled and limited strategic nuclear initiative on behalf of beleaguered overseas allies. In practice, one may be certain that serious residual doubts over the operational effectiveness of strategic defenses would serve to discourage a president from any activity that approached nuclear adventurism. Nonetheless, the deployment of strategic defenses for North America should help to recouple in the Soviet perception the security of NATO-Europe with prospective employment of U.S. "central systems," and therefore should enhance the stability of deterrence.

Insurance against Soviet Noncompliance with START

The greater the scale of force-level reductions, the more adverse could be the consequences of Soviet noncompliance. Strategic defenses

11. No defense is absolute. Its function is to require the payment of an offensive price for its defeat.
12. To date, the Soviet Union has chosen to concentrate its strategic-offensive assets very heavily in ballistic missiles, and particularly in land-based ballistic missiles.

could deter noncompliance both by holding out the promise of rendering strategically ineffective missiles deliberately concealed and by requiring—for the confident defeat of the defense—so massive a scale of secret manufacture, stockpiling, and deployment that the risks of detection would increase to an unacceptable level. A defended United States should be more willing than an undefended United States to tolerate a START regime that did not have a truly robust verification story.

Avoidance of Technological Surprise

Unless the United States pursues the research and development of strategic defense technologies, it will not know what the Soviet Union might discover from such activity. R&D in strategic defense precludes technological surprise that might render U.S. ballistic missile forces ineffective.

Deterrence of Soviet Defense Deployments

A healthy R&D program on strategic defense must serve to shorten the lead time to deployment, should the technology prove to be sufficiently attractive (in the context of predicted responsive countermeasures). A Soviet decision to withdraw from, or abruptly abrogate, the ABM Treaty of 1972 would not be unaffected by Soviet calculation of the character and likely speed of U.S. competitive responses.

A Hedge against the Failure of Deterrence

The "causes of war" are structural and have to do with the nature of man, the character of states, and the nature of the goals (and the means employed in pursuit of those goals) that states pursue—in partial competition—within a system of interstate relations.[13] But the occasions, proximate causes, or triggering events of war vary so greatly that they cannot be "modeled" very usefully. States are at least as capable of

13. The best study remains Kenneth N. Waltz, *Man, the State and War: A Theoretical Analysis* (Columbia University Press, 1954).

stumbling into war through faulty assessment, bad luck, and the like, as they are of making a conscious decision to fight.[14] No one knows how robust the contemporary system of nuclear deterrence really is. It is arguable, at least, that the system truly has never been tested: that neither superpower has ever felt a strong incentive to fight the other. That situation may not endure indefinitely. Strategic defenses hold out the possibility—all considerations of deterrence aside—of enforcing a limitation of the damage that each side *could* do to the other. It may be worth recalling that limitation of damage is the second of the classic objectives of arms control (the first, of course, being to reduce the risk that war will occur).

High Technology as the U.S. Long Suit

It is common sense to choose areas of military competition wherein strong comparative advantage lies. Strategic defense, as the highest of high technology, is just such an area for the United States. If, as seems unavoidable, the United States must sustain military competition with the Soviet Union for many decades to come—since the political fuel for the competition cannot be cut off—it is cost effective to compete most vigorously in those areas wherein the structural basis for an enduring lead is present, and with regard to which the Soviet Union, for excellent reasons, harbors the deepest of anxieties (realization of inferiority). The Soviet Union has warm production lines for today's equipment and has a substantial defense-industrial mobilization base but finds it difficult, and certainly expensive, to effect and exploit technological "breakthroughs." In short, strategic defense is a region of competition that plays to our strengths and, relatively speaking, to Soviet weaknesses.

The Armed Forces and Defense of the Country

A traditional mission of armed forces has been to provide a shield around society. It has been impossible to fulfill that mission since the early 1950s owing to the growth of Soviet nuclear strike capability. Much

14. Indeed, in the nuclear age great states are much more likely to stumble into a general conflict than they are to *choose* to fight among themselves.

of the stable-deterrent theorizing of the mid to late 1960s sought to make a virtue of what *then* was a military-technological necessity.[15] However, technological conditions change with time, and so should the theory of stability that guides defense preparation. Although it may have been necessary for the United States to recognize that it could not defend itself physically, that reality was never in any sense desirable and should not be prolonged by conscious policy choice. Popular attitudes toward the armed forces and the way in which the armed forces view themselves would be affected benignly if the vitality of the traditional mission of homeland defense were to be restored.

The Alternatives

Whatever may be said about the value of strategic defense, it should never be forgotten that the alternatives are different variants of an offense-dominant force posture—all of which either require, or at least tolerate, the vulnerability of superpower homelands. The alternative to competitive deployment of strategic defenses (admittedly of uncertain proficiency) is not a condition of "no arms race"; rather it is the continuation of the offense competition as usual.

This brief discussion has focused on the positive aspects of strategic defense. The author is fully aware of the challenges that would confront a United States seeking to deploy a strategic force balanced between offensive and defensive capabilities. For example, the United States would have to: reconsider the fundamental terms of deterrence (is strategic defense to strengthen or replace nuclear deterrence?); consider whether arms control is essential, or merely desirable, in a world with strategic defenses deployed;[16] address the meaning of strategic defense for the support of existing (or possible creation of new) foreign-policy commitments; confront Soviet realities, and take full account of prospective Soviet responses; conduct a zero-base review of the roles, size, and character of its strategic nuclear *offensive* forces in a world with

15. See Wolfgang K. H. Panofsky, "The Mutual-Hostage Relationship Between America and Russia," *Foreign Affairs*, vol. 52 (October 1973), pp. 109–18; and Jerome H. Kahan, *Security in the Nuclear Age: Developing U.S. Strategic Arms Policy* (Brookings Institution, 1975).

16. There is a school of thought that holds that strategic defenses can be effective *only* if there are massive reductions in offensive forces.

strategic defenses; and, finally, think imaginatively about the likely, and possible (if less likely), effect of deployed strategic defenses upon political behavior in times of crisis.

These problems or challenges are subjects for careful study. For the reasons cited in this discussion, I believe that they should be defined as challenges.

SPURGEON M. KEENY, JR.

For many years there has been a broadly based consensus that effective defense of urban society from nuclear attack cannot be achieved against a determined and sophisticated adversary. This extremely negative assessment of the prospects for defense in general, and ballistic missile defense in particular, reflects a general recognition of the inherent vulnerability of fragile urban society to the devastating effects of nuclear weapons. This broad consensus also includes recognition of the fact that efforts to seek a nationwide defense, regardless of its ultimate effectiveness, would probably have a dangerously destabilizing impact on the strategic relations of the superpowers. Frequent reassessments of the prospects for ballistic missile defense stimulated by rapidly evolving technology have not changed the basic conclusions but have helped bring into focus both the grim realities of the nuclear world and the limits of technology in changing these realities.

This remarkable consensus on the inherent technical limitations of a nationwide ballistic missile defense and the dangers associated with attempts to achieve such a capability was formalized at a political level between the United States and the Soviet Union in the ABM Treaty. This treaty of unlimited duration established the basic principle that neither the United States nor the Soviet Union would "deploy ABM systems for a defense of the territory of its country." Reflecting the widespread agreement on the issue, the U.S. Senate advised ratification of the ABM Treaty in 1972 by the overwhelming vote of 88 to 2. The treaty stands today as probably the most significant arms control agreement achieved to date.

The long-standing consensus was unexpectedly challenged by President Ronald Reagan in his speech to the nation on March 23, 1983. In a radical departure from previous wisdom, President Reagan set forth for the nation the "ultimate goal of eliminating the threat posed by strategic nuclear missiles'' and called upon the scientific community ''to give us the means of rendering these nuclear weapons impotent and obsolete.'' There was no hint in the speech how this amazing technological accomplishment that had eluded vast numbers of scientists for more than twenty years might be accomplished. But the message was clear that the president believed the goal could be achieved and would provide a secure shield that would ''change the course of human history.''

Any suggestion that this was simply ephemeral political hyperbole was quickly dispelled by Secretary of Defense Caspar Weinberger's explanatory statement that the administration sought a ''thoroughly reliable and total'' defensive system that would render all attacking missiles ''impotent.'' He stated that he was confident such a capability could be achieved not only against ballistic missiles but against cruise missiles as well and that ''it would guarantee that there would be no longer any danger from nuclear weapons.'' At this writing, the administration continues to proclaim its objective of changing the nuclear military posture of the United States from an offense-dominated to a defense-dominated strategy and appears confident that a technical solution to the problem can be found.

There is certainly much emotional and moral appeal in a strategy based on the defense of the population and society's economic and cultural assets. There is an instinctive receptivity to the notion of protecting family and society from the threat of extinction, and defense avoids the moral dilemma of deterrence by the threat of retaliation. The promise of an impenetrable defense provides hope of deliverance from the unthinkable horror of nuclear war. In a society obsessed with high technology that few citizens understand, a guaranteed defense provides technological reinforcement for the psychosis of denial that apparently helps many live with the constant threat of nuclear war. Yet, despite the political appeal of a defense-dominated strategy based on the defense of the population and society, no previous administration has advanced such a position as a national goal. This restraint was not for lack of interest, since the concept has been under more or less continual review for more than two decades, but because specific approaches were always found on serious examination to be fatally flawed. Some of the new approaches to ballistic missile defense that appear to be behind the administration's thinking involve very sophisticated new technology, but there is every reason to believe they are fatally flawed for the same basic reasons.

The underlying reason that ballistic missile defense is so difficult is that nuclear weapons really are fundamentally different from past advances in the technology of destruction. Today, a single nuclear warhead can destroy a major city. It is important to recognize that this is not a rhetorical overstatement; a megaton explosion would destroy multistory concrete buildings out to a distance of 3 mi. with almost complete immediate loss of life to that distance and would cause spontaneous ignition of combustibles out to 5 mi. and severe damage to frame buildings out to 9 mi. Most of the surviving structures would be destroyed, and many survivors of the immediate effects would be killed in the firestorm or outward-moving conflagration that would almost certainly follow. It is not necessary to examine the more complex, longer-term effects of nuclear explosions on the population and the environment to appreciate the fact that man and his fragile urban society are hostage to the effects of nuclear weapons.

The problem of defending urban society from nuclear weapons is compounded by the staggering numbers of nuclear weapons available to strategic offensive forces. It has been estimated that there are some 50,000 nuclear weapons in the world today, about half of which are systems with strategic missions. We are frequently reminded that the Soviet Union has some 6000 warheads on its land-based ICBMs alone. In the absence of arms control, these numbers could grow substantially.

The power and number of nuclear weapons has fundamentally changed the nature of war and the relationship of offensive and defensive forces. To be useful a nationwide defense must be extremely effective since any leakage is catastrophic to the target being defended. To render nuclear weapons "impotent" and to free mankind of the fear of these weapons, the system would have to be essentially leakproof. This requirement can be put in perspective with the familiar comparison of defense against conventional weapons and nuclear weapons. In World War II a defense that could destroy 10 percent of attacking bombers per sortie would generally be considered very successful since the offense could not accept that level of attrition given the limited effectiveness of conventional weapons. By contrast, in our nuclear world an urban defense that destroyed 90 percent of incoming weapons would be a failure since a single nuclear weapon would destroy the target and there would be no shortage of attacking warheads.

Given the stringent standards within which the defense must perform to be successful, the offense has many technical options at its disposal to defeat or complicate the operation of the defense. Moreover, in responding to these at least partly unknown technical options, the defense must be able to operate effectively as an extremely complex system the first time it is used since it can never be tested in a realistic manner. Some of the new space-based approaches to defense would appear to be particularly handicapped in this regard. In contrast, operation of the individual components of the offense can be fine-tuned in advance by extensive testing, including the development of countermeasures against the defense.

The offense always has the option of concentrating its fire power against targets of its choice while a national defense must protect all major urban areas equally well. Although systems designed to attack the boost phase of strategic missiles partly resolve this problem, any attempt to achieve a complete impenetrable defense would involve more localized defense as well. The offense can increase the size of its attack by adding more missiles to its force or increasing the fractionation of MIRVed warheads on existing missiles. The apparent size of the attack can be further increased by incorporating large numbers of decoys in the missile payload.

The offense can conceal the location of attacking warheads from radar sensors with chaff and from infrared sensors with balloons or other techniques. Alternatively, the offense can seek to blind defensive sensors with precursor nuclear explosives or a wide variety of jamming techniques. The offense can attack individual vulnerable components (such as radars or other sensors) the loss of which incapacitate the complex defense system. In the case of satellite-based defense systems, the tactic could even be carried out in advance of hostilities, possibly clandestinely.

Finally, the offense always has the option of simply circumventing the defense by introducing or emphasizing an entirely different mode of attack. A cartoon of the late 1960s captured the problem of the defense by picturing a group of generals and scientists standing in a maze of radars, computers, and missiles and looking expectantly to the right where the equipment was oriented, while unnoticed a small cruise missile was homing in on them from the left at ground level.

Today the ABM debate has been complicated by the introduction of futuristic concepts involving exotic kill mechanisms, such as high-energy chemical lasers, particle beams, and even nuclear-explosion-pumped X-ray lasers. Some systems exploit the high ground of space; others are land based for practical and defense reasons. All involve fascinating technical questions as to whether and how they would in fact perform. But whether one is considering a space-based chemical laser system that would require hundreds of satellites at the cost of hundreds of billions of dollars or ground-based nuclear-explosion-pumped X-ray laser systems that would be launched on the instant of first warning of the launch of enemy missiles, the fact remains that a sophisticated offense has a vast array of techniques to overwhelm or circumvent these systems.

The interaction of offense and defense has been analyzed in great detail for many proposed defensive systems, which have been found totally inadequate for effective defense of urban society since even the most elaborate defense could be penetrated by a sophisticated opponent at far less cost. This extremely pessimistic technical conclusion does not apply in the same fundamental way to the defense of hardened military targets such as missile silos. In the case of silos or similar redundant hardened targets, the defense has a very small volume to defend and can accept a significant leakage rate since only a fraction of the silos need survive to provide a deterrent. Nevertheless, when the technical options available to the offense are considered, even this limited application of missile defense has not proved militarily attractive. Moreover, efforts to deploy such a system might well be perceived as, or in fact be, a first step toward a nationwide defense system.

Despite the compounding of technical problems for the defense, the conclusion that a leakproof nationwide defense system cannot be achieved against a sophisticated adversary is still a technical judgment and is not demonstrable in the sense that it violates any physical law. What then is the danger of launching a major effort in the hopes that it would stimulate radical new ideas that just might lead to an impenetrable defensive system?

The danger of a major effort to achieve an effective nationwide ballistic missile defense system is that it will be an unprecedented stimulant to an arms race in both defensive and offensive systems. The Soviet Union would certainly follow our lead in efforts to achieve a sophisticated ballistic missile defense system. The Soviet research and development program in this area is comparable to our own, and it is inconceivable that the Soviet Union would take the chance of surrendering this area of development to the United States. As the programs progressed to the testing stage, each side would inevitably make a worst-case assessment of the other side's potential capabilities to negate its own deterrent retaliatory forces. To make certain that this outcome would not occur, each side would upgrade its offensive strategic force to ensure its ability to penetrate or circumvent the other side's defense. This buildup in offensive forces would involve both the quantity and quality of the offensive forces. It should be recalled that in the late 1960s worst-case Pentagon estimates had the putative Soviet ABM system of the late 1970s essentially destroying the entire force of retaliatory U.S. ballistic missiles. The decision to MIRV Minuteman III and Poseidon missiles was in large part driven by the requirement to maintain target coverage in the face of the anticipated nationwide Soviet ABM deployment of uncertain capability. More recently, the decision to develop and deploy the air-launched cruise missile reflected serious concern that existing manned bombers might not be able to penetrate the massive Soviet air defense system.

The long development cycle of any ballistic missile defense system would leave ample time for the offense to develop multiple approaches to defeat the defense either by penetration or by circumvention. Many hundreds of billions of dollars would be expended in a competition to achieve and counter an unattainable goal. Therefore, rather than create the conditions for arms control and arms reductions as has been suggested, the proposed program to achieve an effective nationwide defense appears to ensure a continuing, if not accelerated, strategic arms race that can only further destabilize relations between the United States and the Soviet Union.

The effort to achieve an effective ballistic missile defense will also increase crisis instability in the future. The coupling of an even marginally effective defense with a strong counterforce capability would be the prerequisite for a first-strike preemptive strategy. In a race to develop ballistic missile defense systems, each side would conclude that the enemy was in fact developing a first-strike preemptive strategy. Moreover, the effectiveness of a ballistic missile defense system might depend significantly on advance knowledge of the timing of the attack. In a time of crisis, this mutual suspicion as to intentions would be a major contribution to strategic instability. It is instructive to recall that when the Soviet Union undertook a relatively modest civil defense program that would not protect the bulk of urban population and would do nothing to protect the physical plant of Soviet urban society, great concern was expressed in some quarters that this indicated the Soviet intention to engage in a nuclear warfighting, war-winning strategy.

Before these longer-term consequences of attempts to achieve an effective ballistic missile defense came to pass, the most immediate casualty of such a program would probably be the ABM Treaty, the cornerstone of strategic arms control efforts to date. It will not be very long before the program called for by the president comes into conflict with various provisions of the treaty, in particular the undertaking not to develop, test, or deploy ABM systems or components that are space based. The stated goal of the program is, of course, contrary to the basic undertaking of the treaty not to deploy ABM systems "for defense of the territory of its country." If the United States, having failed to ratify the SALT II agreement, decides to withdraw from the ABM Treaty either unilaterally or by agreement, the death knell will have sounded for arms control for the foreseeable future. This will be a high price to pay for a technological will-o'-the-wisp that can only lead us into the swamp of an endless and dangerous high-technology arms race.

Perhaps the most frightening aspect of the president's proposal and its subsequent elaboration by his advisers is the strong suggestion that the authors have no conception of either the basic nature of nuclear war or the limits of technology. To deal realistically and constructively with the task of reducing the threat of nuclear war, we must first recognize that the superpowers and their allies are ultimately hostages to mutual assured destruction. It is not possible to change this reality by calling for a technical solution that does not exist. Hope for the future does not reside in technological fixes but in stabilizing arms control agreements and in serious and persistent efforts to reduce and eventually remove the underlying political tensions between the superpowers.

GLENN A. KENT

In the light of the perceived and suspected aspirations of the Soviet leaders and the awesome nuclear missile forces at their command, our most critical national security objective is to protect our population from attack by Soviet nuclear weapons and to protect the freedom of our allies around the world. Our strategy for achieving that objective rests primarily on the capability to threaten retaliatory blows against targets of high value to the would-be attacker. Our strategy is to *deter* by threat of retaliation. We do not have the capability to underwrite a strategy of *preventing* a successful Soviet attack on our population.

The strategy of deterrence by threat is sometimes presented in a most pejorative manner. But, by whatever name (including "MAD," or mutual assured destruction) it must be our strategy because we do not have the capability to prevent successful attack. If we are to change our strategy, we must possess a totally new capability.

But acquiring the capability to underwrite a "defensive" strategy and abandon the old strategy is a stern requirement. We must go from the current situation where only a few attacking weapons are needed to cause considerable fatalities to a situation where a determined and well-orchestrated attack, involving a considerable number of weapons, will cause only a very few fatalities and casualties. What is required is nothing short of a "splendid" defense. A lesser capability will provide for limiting damage in case an attack occurs; this may be a useful thing to do. But we should be clear that this is another matter and that with such lesser capabilities we must still rely heavily on a strategy of deterring by threat of retaliation. There is an important distinction between having the capability to shoot down a considerable number of Soviet missiles and RVs and any prospects for a real shift in our basic strategy. As Secretary of Defense Caspar Weinberger has pointed out, "Deterrence through a credible retaliatory capability has worked for nearly forty years, and, there is every reason to believe that this policy will continue to prevent aggression against ourselves and our allies."[1]

In addition there is another objective: to protect the U.S. population from third-country or accidental attacks. Here a strategy underwritten by the capability to *prevent* such attacks from being successful is probably quite feasible. Almost by definition the attacks will be small and, in the case of the accidental attack, not well orchestrated. Protection against such attacks would greatly reduce the coercive value of nuclear threats made by third countries and would reduce nearly to zero the effects of accidental attacks. In these cases the capability to "limit damage" is feasible and affordable; important, relevant, and worth pursuing; and a different matter from contemplating a basic change in strategy that requires a splendid defense.

To try and gain a better understanding of the future implications and risks of a massive effort to deploy a splendid defense, I will offer some projections as to the possible circumstances some many years hence. Let us examine a possible future situation that is, at least at first glance,

---

1. Caspar W. Weinberger, in a speech delivered to the Aviation and Space Writers Association, April 11, 1983, p. 4.

comforting to contemplate, in which both the United States and the USSR have deployed a splendid defense. Each side can prevent a "successful" attack by the other. Each side is impervious to attacks by third countries.

There was a critical period during the deployment stage. Each superpower became obsessed with the requirement that the other side not gain an advantage in the deployment schedule. Otherwise the side having this advantage might be in a position to deny the deployment by the other side. That critical period has passed without incident; the problem is behind us now. It turned out that our deployment cost many times as much as contemplated; that also is water under the bridge.

But there have been some disquieting effects. Both superpowers now have somewhat greater freedom to pursue a more aggressive foreign policy than before. Political analysts had repeatedly pointed out this possibility back in the early 1980s; we now see the reality. The United States has designed and deployed a multilayer defense of the U.S. homeland, with only a modest capability to defend Western Europe against nuclear attack. This came about for a variety of reasons. The multilayer approach was not as effective for the defense of Western Europe as it was for the United States. Furthermore, the large costs of the deployment that protected just the United States served to submerge the requirement to provide a splendid defense for Europe.

The Soviet Union had also focused on the defense of its homeland. While its system was more capable against long-range threats, there was still an important and relevant capability against nuclear systems launched from Western Europe and from other points around the periphery of the USSR. So the current situation is such that both superpowers can protect their respective homelands from almost any attack. Nonetheless, the Soviet Union cannot prevent the United States from launching a successful attack against Cuba, and the United States cannot prevent the Soviet Union from launching a successful attack against Western Europe. But this operational symmetry does not, of course, translate to symmetry with respect to national interests, and our allies feel less secure.

There is, in this hypothetical future situation, another more serious issue that can no longer be ignored. This has to do with the vulnerability of our defense system to a first strike by the Soviet Union. The United States has recognized this problem for some time and has engaged in numerous technology programs with the hope of developing a less vulnerable basing. However, as yet no solution has been forthcoming that could gain a consensus for going ahead with a program that could be sustained. We have invented better ways of seriously degrading the capability of the Soviet defense if we strike first. But then we have come to realize that this only worsens the situation according to Tom Schelling's law of "self-feeding instability."

Calculations by U.S. and Soviet analysts show the following results of a preemptive strike by either side:

—The Soviet neutralization of our defense system (and in particular the space components) will be so successful that a Soviet strike against U.S. command and control, ICBMs, cruise missile carriers, and bombers will ensure that any retaliatory strike by the United States with these forces and with U.S. SLBMs will be at best a "ragged" attack.

—Soviet defense will probably suffer some degradation in a brief firefight with U.S. defenses (including "antidefense" systems). Still the Soviet "defenses," by virtue of striking first, will be able to handle the ragged attack and prevent a meaningful retaliatory attack against the USSR.

Somehow or other the prospects for "assured survival" for the United States have turned into a prospect for a splendid first strike for whomever strikes first. The likelihood of war now seems to be greater. We may have invested immense resources only to have taken a great step backward in protecting our population.

In view of these circumstances, the United States is proceeding along a dual track: (1) continuing the search, which is now more urgent, for a "survivable" basing mode for our "defense"—particularly the components in space; and (2) negotiating in earnest with the Soviet Union for some sort of control on the offensive potential of each so-called defense system. There are even proposals for limiting the defensive potential of both sides to no larger than that required to handle attacks by third countries and accidental attacks.

The above depiction may be overdrawn, but its purpose was to dramatize the potential downside of deploying vulnerable defenses that work well. We should not be misled into thinking that defense is different from other types of "killers" in strategic nuclear delivery systems— such as accurate ballistic missiles used in a "counterforce" role. The purpose of both is to be killers of ICBMs that can kill populations. They differ in the circumstances under which they are operated and the environment in which the kill is accomplished. In turn the killers of

ICBMs (in whatever form) are subject to other killers that may be vulnerable to still other types of killers, and so on.

In today's world we have a serious problem: both superpowers have developed killers to operate against ICBMs that threaten populations. These ICBM killers are called accurate ICBMs. These ICBMs are, in turn, vulnerable to themselves. We should avoid repeating this situation. The problem of ICBM vulnerability is greatly alleviated by the fact that there are also SLBMs and bombers and that we are allowed to view the problem in the context of the total correlation of forces. But this alleviating feature would be lacking in the case of splendid defenses that operate against all attacking vehicles and that are at the same time vulnerable to each other.

Whatever we do we must ensure that the United States still retains the capability to threaten high-value targets in a second strike. It is a several-track approach. We must strive to have killers of the Soviet defense; we must develop countermeasures that cause modest leak-throughs of even robust defenses; we must work hard so that our killers (sometimes called defensive systems) are not vulnerable to a Soviet first strike.

This nation is now organizing a considerable effort to develop the concepts and technology to provide systems that have the purpose of killing Soviet ICBMs, SLBMs, air-launched cruise missiles (ALCMs), and bombers after they have been launched and are en route to their respective targets. The details as to what type of vehicles can be killed, how many can be handled, and what the leak rates will be are not clear.

Let such an effort proceed but not with a sense of overwhelming urgency. However, it is urgent that we ensure that any deployments we might make will not be vulnerable to a Soviet first strike. We should also strive to develop the capability to threaten the Soviet defensive systems. At the same time, the United States should try to reach agreements with the Soviet Union to stifle the never-ending hierarchy of killers.

GEORGE RATHJENS

The two most noteworthy speeches on ballistic missile defense, in my memory, have been those of Secretary of Defense Robert McNamara in September 1967 and President Ronald Reagan in March 1983.

It had been alleged that McNamara was opposed to deploying a large-scale ABM system for the defense of the population because of the cost, then estimated to be $40 billion. In reply he said,

> Let me make very clear that the $40 billion is not the issue. If we could build and deploy a genuinely impenetrable shield over the United States, we would be willing to spend not $40 billion, but any reasonable multiple of that amount that was necessary. The money in itself is not the problem: the penetrability of the proposed shield is the problem. . . . Were we to deploy a heavy ABM system throughout the United States, the Soviets would clearly be strongly motivated to so increase their offensive capability as to cancel out our defensive advantage.
>
> It is futile for each of us to spend $4 billion, $40 billion or $400 billion—and at the end of all the spending, and at the end of all the deployment, and at the end of all the effort, to be relatively at the same point of balance on the security scale that we are now.[1]

President Reagan, in contrast, has proposed that

> we embark on a program to counter the awesome Soviet missile threat with measures that are defensive . . . [claiming that] current technology has attained a level of sophistication where it's reasonable for us to begin this effort . . . to give us the means of rendering . . . nuclear weapons impotent and obsolete.[2]

What is the explanation for these seemingly contrasting views of two men who had access to the best technical expertise in the country? In fairness it must be noted that McNamara was talking of near-term *deployment,* whereas President Reagan was speaking of a long-range R&D program. Still, the differences run deeper than that.

McNamara's conclusion was based on two critical assumptions: that defensive efforts could be offset by improvements in the offense at a cost favorable—or at least not significantly unfavorable—to the offense; and that one had to expect the offense to make such efforts in response to measures undertaken by the defense. From President Reagan's remarks we must infer that he believes that one, or both, of these assumptions is not likely to hold some decades from now.

It was easy to show in 1967 that McNamara's first assumption was reasonable, especially if the objective of the defense was to ensure that the destruction of cities and populations was kept to a low level, less than, say, 25 percent. Indeed, on being polled, all of the men who had served as science advisers to Presidents Dwight D. Eisenhower, John

---

1. "Text of McNamara Speech on Anti-China Missile Defense and U.S. Nuclear Strategy," *New York Times,* September 19, 1983.
2. "Address to the Nation," *Weekly Compilation,* pp. 447–48.

F. Kennedy, and Lyndon B. Johnson and all who had served as directors of defense research and engineering agreed essentially with McNamara's assessment. Even if the defense worked perfectly and if the offense used the most conservative tactics—exhaustion of interceptors—to defeat it, the advantage would lie with the offense: it could add warheads to its forces at a cost less than that to the defense of adding interceptors plus associated radar and computer capacity. And, there were the possibilities that the defense might fail catastrophically—something not to be dismissed lightly, considering the impossibility of realistic simulation and debugging before first use—or that the offense might offset the effects of the defense's expenditures by means less costly than exhaustion (for example, by using decoys or high-altitude explosions to black out radars).

Has the balance in technology shifted to favor the defense? Is it likely to do so on the time scale President Reagan had in mind? Developments in three areas merit comment.

Fifteen years ago the problems of tracking and discrimination in the event of an attack involving many warheads and penetration aids seemed formidable, among other reasons because of problems in programming and data processing. Data-handling capability has improved so greatly that we can now expect not only to handle these problems much more easily, but to do it with equipment compact enough to be carried in aircraft or on space vehicles. Second, developments in compact infrared sensor technology raise the prospect of using sensors and processors so based for midcourse intercept. Third, there has been the work on high-powered lasers, including the X-ray laser driven by a nuclear explosion. But it should be said that although the infrared work is promising, coping with possible countermeasures is a relatively unexplored, but potentially very difficult, problem area—one not likely to be dealt with in a few years. And, although the laser work has had great press coverage, it is unlikely to be *the* key to solving the BMD problem, given that discrimination, coping with countermeasures, and system integration—not target kill—have been the most serious obstacles to BMD at high altitudes.

Thus, notwithstanding some impressive developments, it is most doubtful that a nationwide defense can be built that cannot be offset by improvements, at a lesser cost, in the adversary's offensive capabilities. This will be so especially if the objective of the defense is to "render nuclear weapons impotent and obsolete," as the president suggested. Readers will, of course, understand that this implies virtually 100 percent confidence in 100 percent effectiveness, and that a defense of such effectiveness is fundamentally different in kind from one that would be able to destroy only 99 to 99.9 percent of an attacking force. Defense at the 100 percent level is likely to be *much* more difficult and expensive. More to the point, defense that was anything less than 100 percent effective would not come close to meeting the president's objective: we would still have to live in the shadow of nuclear weapons.[3] In fact, more is required to meet the president's objective. Even if we could build a 100 percent effective BMD, there would still be the problem of interdicting delivery of nuclear weapons by other means, particularly by cruise missiles. Although Secretary of Defense Caspar Weinberger has said that we would build a system to do that too,[4] he has offered no suggestion as to how it might be done.

What of the possibility that McNamara was wrong in his second assumption—that the Soviet Union would react to a U.S. defensive effort by an offsetting upgrading of its offensive capabilities? Much that has happened since 1967 suggests that other factors in addition to the action-reaction phenomenon are important in the arms race, but there is little reason to believe that either superpower would passively accept development by its adversary of a substantial defensive capability if it could be easily offset, and there is a great deal of evidence, at least on the U.S. side, to suggest the contrary. We have developed penetration aids for aircraft and missiles in order to get through Soviet air defenses and hypothesized ballistic missile defenses, and the need to penetrate such defenses has been an important impetus to our multiple independently targetable reentry vehicle and air-launched cruise missile programs.

How, then, is President Reagan's speech to be explained? Confronted with the enormity of relying on the threat of nuclear retaliation as *the* ultimate response to Soviet "threats," in particular to Soviet nuclear capabilities, he has understandably, and rightly, recoiled, as have so many before him. But what are the alternatives? Those who truly

3. There are other implications that might be noted. With defense in the 99 to 99.9 percent effectiveness range, one would expect a vigorous defense-offense competition inasmuch as there would likely be a widespread perception that an increase (or decrease) in numbers of warheads that could be intercepted could be of great political and perhaps military significance; and civil defense would seem very worthwhile, at least at the 99.9 percent level, whereas it would not be with defenses that were 100 percent (or 50 to 90 percent) effective.

4. Interview on "Meet the Press," March 27, 1983.

understand the nature of nuclear weapons and the virtual impossibility of a truly perfect defense against a determined adversary have tended to focus their hopes on arms control and disarmament and ultimately on political solutions to U.S.-Soviet problems. But those with little understanding of technology, including those who have been poorly or inadequately advised, are more likely to see hope in "technical fixes," particularly if they see the Soviet Union as such a source of evil as virtually to preclude political accommodation. We have here the likely explanation for President Reagan's speech. It is more likely—and a more charitable explanation—than that he spoke as he did out of political expediency, fully understanding that the hope he was holding out was a false one, or at least one for which there was no foundation.

It is doubtful that there are many informed persons who fully believe in the president's, and Secretary Weinberger's, vision of an impenetrable defense. But what of less effective nationwide defenses? Might not a 50 or 90 or 99 percent effective defense be feasible and worth buying, or at least worth trying to develop? The answer is, regrettably, probably not. There are at least three points to be made.

First, it should be understood that it is, indeed, truly regrettable that such a defense is not in the cards. There have been many suggestions, perhaps most notably by Henry Kissinger, that some in the arms control community would prefer a world of mutual assured destruction to one where defense had the upper hand.[5] Such views reflect a misreading of the ABM debate of 1968–70 and of current attitudes. Nearly all of those who have opposed BMD deployment by the United States have done so not because they were happy about a mutual hostage relationship but rather because they believed, with McNamara, that technology—and the fragility of cities and industry—favored the offense, and that defensive efforts would be offset—indeed, perhaps be more than offset—by the adversary's improvement in offensive capabilities. It would be a better world if the balance were otherwise—if an improvement in offensive capabilities could be negated at a significantly lower cost by an incremental improvement in defenses—just as it would also be a better world if we could abolish poverty and injustice.

Second, defense at the high end of the range mentioned (99–99.9 percent effective, perhaps even at the 95 percent level) would be of

5. Henry Kissinger, *White House Years*, pp. 215–217; and in remarks made by him in Brussels in *Survival* (November/December 1979), p. 265.

interest if feasible. But such defense, although much less demanding than a *perfect* defense, would still be plagued with many of the same problems and is probably also beyond reach, considering that a determined adversary, such as the Soviet Union, can allocate substantial efforts to negating defenses.

Third, defense at much lower levels of effectiveness would not be very interesting even if feasible and if not offset by the adversary's improving offensive capabilities. Given the present and projected levels of offensive forces, the United States and the Soviet Union could each be destroyed as a going society even if each could intercept 50–90 percent of the adversary's offensive warheads. Indeed, defense at such levels of effectiveness might not mean any reduction in damage at all, given that each side, even if it did not upgrade its offensive weapons, would likely allocate them differently than it would if its adversary had no defense. And, if there could be no assurance that defense could reduce damage significantly, would it be politically or militarily useful? Could either side feel more secure—would either behave differently in crises—if it had such a defense than if it did not? It seems unlikely.

In sum, then, the hope and the prospects for a population defense that would be both feasible and attractive have to be regarded as poor. Worse, the attempt to acquire such defense is likely to prove pernicious; and President Reagan's Star Wars speech has not been helpful. Although we are not likely to see the development of a technology that could provide even a moderately effective nationwide defense, much less an impenetrable one, we *are* likely to see an intensification of research and development. If it goes badly, we will have simply wasted money—probably a few billions. But if it goes well, there will be additional unfortunate consequences. First, there will be an impetus to abrogate, denounce, or modify the ABM Treaty. If that happens, both the United States and the Soviet Union will almost certainly make somewhat greater efforts than they otherwise would to improve offensive capabilities as a hedge against possible ABM deployment. Second, BMD-related R&D by the United States will stimulate similar work by the Soviet Union, and the work by each may contribute to the realization of improved antisatellite capabilities. This could be to the detriment of both, particularly the United States.

Finally, there is the question of more practical defenses, particularly the defense of ICBM silos and perhaps other hardened military targets. The earlier U.S. attempt—that with Safeguard in 1968–71—suffered from two rather serious flaws: considering that Soviet counterforce capabilities were very limited at the time and for several years thereafter, the decision to deploy was at least five years premature; and the defense was poorly matched to the job, something not surprising considering that the components had been designed for a different purpose, the defense of cities. But the experience with Safeguard should not prejudice our assessment of current and future hard-site defense proposals.

Such proposals should be measured against three criteria. First, there must be some scenario(s) for use that are sufficiently plausible and worrisome to justify deploying a defense and, incidentally, modifying, abrogating, or at least jeopardizing the ABM Treaty. Second, defense should compare favorably with other means of ensuring the survival of the assets to be defended. And, third, cost-exchange considerations should be favorable: deploying a defense that could be offset by the adversary's making much smaller investments in offensive capabilities would obviously be a somewhat dubious proposition. As noted, Safeguard failed the second and the third tests (as well as the first, in the author's opinion). It proved to be possible to increase the "hardness" of many of the Minuteman missile silos, thereby increasing survivability with greater assurance and at lower cost than could have been done with Safeguard. And because the defense of each Minuteman wing was to have depended on a single expensive and relatively vulnerable fire-control radar (the missile site radar), the costs to the Soviet Union of crippling the defense would have been quite low.

But defense of hard missiles, or other hard targets, is a much easier task than defense of industry and population, particularly if relatively high levels of loss (50–90 percent) or a relatively low-confidence defense is acceptable, as may well be the case. The argument is made elsewhere in this volume. Here, I will simply assert that I do not believe it can be shown that all plausible hard-site defense systems will necessarily fail the second or third tests cited above.

There remains the question of the plausibility and seriousness of scenarios that are usually envisaged when the case for such defenses is made. The most common is the massive disarming attack against ICBMs, possibly, but not necessarily, coincident with attacks against bomber bases and in-port submarines.

There can no longer be much doubt that the accuracy/yield combinations available to the USSR are, or soon will be, good enough so that single-shot kill probabilities against the "hardest" U.S. missile silos will be very high. This, however, is a far cry from having a high-confidence disarming capability against U.S. ICBMs, given the possibilities of gross malfunction of some missiles and of failures in command and control, possibilities that cannot be lightly dismissed in executing a plan that can never have been adequately rehearsed or debugged. And, even if the Soviet Union could destroy nearly all U.S. ICBMs and some bombers and submarines as well, could it be confident that the United States would not retaliate with some of its residual force? Certainly not. The scenario has to be seen as incredible. It is hard, then, to see much of a case for defense of the ICBM force.

The ABM Treaty
and Related Documents

Treaty Between the United States of America
and the Union of Soviet Socialist Republics
on the Limitation of Anti-Ballistic Missile Systems

Signed at Moscow May 26, 1972
Ratification advised by U.S. Senate August 3, 1972
Ratified by U.S. President September 30, 1972
Proclaimed by U.S. President October 3, 1972
Instruments of ratification exchanged October 3, 1972
Entered into force October 3, 1972

The United States of America and the Union of Soviet Socialist Republics, hereinafter referred to as the Parties,

Proceeding from the premise that nuclear war would have devastating consequences for all mankind,

Considering that effective measures to limit anti-ballistic missile systems would be a substantial factor in curbing the race in strategic offensive arms and would lead to a decrease in the risk of outbreak of war involving nuclear weapons,

Proceeding from the premise that the limitation of anti-ballistic missile systems, as well as certain agreed measures with respect to the limitation of

Source: U.S. Arms Control and Disarmament Agency, *Arms Control and Disarmament Agreements: Texts and Histories of Negotiations*, 1982 ed. (Government Printing Office, 1982), pp. 139–47, 162–63.

strategic offensive arms, would contribute to the creation of more favorable conditions for further negotiations on limiting strategic arms,

Mindful of their obligations under Article VI of the Treaty on the Non-Proliferation of Nuclear Weapons,

Declaring their intention to achieve at the earliest possible date the cessation of the nuclear arms race and to take effective measures toward reductions in strategic arms, nuclear disarmament, and general and complete disarmament,

Desiring to contribute to the relaxation of international tension and the strengthening of trust between States,

Have agreed as follows:

Article I

1. Each party undertakes to limit anti-ballistic missile (ABM) systems and to adopt other measures in accordance with the provisions of this Treaty.

2. Each Party undertakes not to deploy ABM systems for a defense of the territory of its country and not to provide a base for such a defense, and not to deploy ABM systems for defense of an individual region except as provided for in Article III of this Treaty.

Article II

1. For the purpose of this Treaty an ABM system is a system to counter strategic ballistic missiles or their elements in flight trajectory, currently consisting of:

(a) ABM interceptor missiles, which are interceptor missiles constructed and deployed for an ABM role, or of a type tested in an ABM mode;

(b) ABM launchers, which are launchers constructed and deployed for launching ABM interceptor missiles; and

(c) ABM radars, which are radars constructed and deployed for an ABM role, or of a type tested in an ABM mode.

2. The ABM system components listed in paragraph 1 of this Article include those which are:

(a) operational;
(b) under construction;
(c) undergoing testing;
(d) undergoing overhaul, repair or conversion; or
(e) mothballed.

Article III

Each Party undertakes not to deploy ABM systems or their components except that:

(a) within one ABM system deployment area having a radius of one hundred and fifty kilometers and centered on the Party's national capital, a Party may deploy: (1) no more than one hundred ABM launchers and no more than one hundred ABM interceptor missiles at launch sites, and (2) ABM radars within no more than six ABM radar complexes, the area of each complex being circular and having a diameter of no more than three kilometers; and

(b) within one ABM system deployment area having a radius of one hundred and fifty kilometers and containing ICBM silo launchers, a Party may deploy; (1) no more than one hundred ABM launchers and no more than one hundred ABM interceptor missiles at launch sites, (2) two large phased-array ABM radars comparable in potential to corresponding ABM radars operational or under construction on the date of signature of the Treaty in an ABM system deployment area containing ICBM silo launchers, and (3) no more than eighteen ABM radars each having a potential less than the potential of the smaller of the above-mentioned two large phased-array ABM radars.

Article IV

The limitations provided for in Article III shall not apply to ABM systems or their components used for development or testing, and located within current or additionally agreed test ranges. Each Party may have no more than a total of fifteen ABM launchers at test ranges.

Article V

1. Each Party undertakes not to develop, test, or deploy ABM systems or components which are sea-based, air-based, space-based, or mobile land-based.

2. Each Party undertakes not to develop, test, or deploy ABM launchers for launching more than one ABM interceptor missile at a time from each launcher, not to modify deployed launchers to provide them with such a capability, not to develop, test, or deploy automatic or semi-automatic or other similar systems for rapid reload of ABM launchers.

Article VI

To enhance assurance of the effectiveness of the limitations on ABM systems and their components provided by the Treaty, each Party undertakes:

(a) not to give missiles, launchers, or radars, other than ABM interceptor missiles, ABM launchers, or ABM radars, capabilities to counter strategic ballistic missiles or their elements in flight trajectory, and not to test them in an ABM mode; and

(b) not to deploy in the future radars for early warning of strategic ballistic missile attack except at locations along the periphery of its national territory and oriented outward.

Article VII

Subject to the provisions of this Treaty, modernization and replacement of ABM systems or their components may be carried out.

Article VIII

ABM systems or their components in excess of the numbers or outside the areas specified in this Treaty, as well as ABM systems or their components prohibited by this Treaty, shall be destroyed or dismantled under agreed procedures within the shortest possible agreed period of time.

Article IX

To assure the viability and effectiveness of this Treaty, each Party undertakes not to transfer to other States, and not to deploy outside its national territory, ABM systems or their components limited by this Treaty.

Article X

Each Party undertakes not to assume any international obligations which would conflict with this Treaty.

Article XI

The Parties undertake to continue active negotiations for limitations on strategic offensive arms.

Article XII

1. For the purpose of providing assurance of compliance with the provisions of this Treaty, each Party shall use national technical means of verification at its disposal in a manner consistent with generally recognized principles of international law.

2. Each Party undertakes not to interfere with the national technical means of verification of the other Party operating in acccordance with paragraph 1 of this Article.

3. Each Party undertakes not to use deliberate concealment measures which impede verification by national technical means of compliance with the provisions of this Treaty. This obligation shall not require changes in current construction, assembly, conversion, or overhaul practices.

Article XIII

1. To promote the objectives and implementation of the provisions of this Treaty, the Parties shall establish promptly a Standing Consultative Commission, within the framework of which they will:

(a) consider questions concerning compliance with the obligations assumed and related situations which may be considered ambiguous;

(b) provide on a voluntary basis such information as either Party considers necessary to assure confidence in compliance with the obligations assumed;

(c) consider questions involving unintended interference with national technical means of verification;

(d) consider possible changes in the strategic situation which have a bearing on the provisions of this Treaty;

(e) agree upon procedures and dates for destruction or dismantling of ABM systems or their components in cases provided for by the provisions of this Treaty;

(f) consider, as appropriate, possible proposals for further increasing the viability of this Treaty; including proposals for amendments in accordance with the provisions of this Treaty;

(g) consider, as appropriate, proposals for further measures aimed at limiting strategic arms.

2. The Parties through consultation shall establish, and may amend as appropriate, Regulations for the Standing Consultative Commission governing procedures, composition and other relevant matters.

Article XIV

1. Each Party may propose amendments to this Treaty. Agreed amendments shall enter into force in accordance with the procedures governing the entry into force of this Treaty.

2. Five years after entry into force of this Treaty, and at five-year intervals thereafter, the Parties shall together conduct a review of this Treaty.

Article XV

1. This Treaty shall be of unlimited duration.

2. Each Party shall, in exercising its national sovereignty, have the right to withdraw from this Treaty if it decides that extraordinary events related to the subject matter of this Treaty have jeopardized its supreme interests. It shall give notice of its decision to the other Party six months prior to withdrawal from the Treaty. Such notice shall include a statement of the extraordinary events the notifying Party regards as having jeopardized its supreme interests.

Article XVI

1. This Treaty shall be subject to ratification in accordance with the constitutional procedures of each Party. The Treaty shall enter into force on the day of the exchange of instruments of ratification.

2. This Treaty shall be registered pursuant to Article 102 of the Charter of the United Nations.

DONE at Moscow on May 26, 1972, in two copies, each in the English and Russian languages, both texts being equally authentic.

FOR THE UNITED STATES
OF AMERICA

FOR THE UNION OF SOVIET
SOCIALIST REPUBLICS

RICHARD NIXON

L. I. BREZHNEV

*President of the United
States of America*

*General Secretary of the Central
Committee of the CPSU*

Agreed Statements, Common Understandings, and Unilateral Statements Regarding the Treaty Between the United States of America and the Union of Soviet Socialist Republics on the Limitation of Anti-Ballistic Missiles

1. Agreed Statements

The document set forth below was agreed upon and initialed by the Heads of the Delegations on May 26, 1972 (letter designations added);

AGREED STATEMENTS REGARDING THE TREATY BETWEEN THE UNITED STATES OF AMERICA AND THE UNION OF SOVIET SOCIALIST REPUBLICS ON THE LIMITATION OF ANTI-BALLISTIC MISSILE SYSTEMS

[A]

The Parties understand that, in addition to the ABM radars which may be deployed in accordance with subparagraph (a) of Article III of the Treaty, those non-phased-array ABM radars operational on the date of signature of the Treaty within the ABM system deployment area for defense of the national capital may be retained.

[B]

The Parties understand that the potential (the product of mean emitted power in watts and antenna area in square meters) of the smaller of the two large phased-array ABM radars referred to in subparagraph (b) of Article III of the Treaty is considered for purposes of the Treaty to be three million.

[C]

The Parties understand that the center of the ABM system deployment area centered on the national capital and the center of the ABM system deployment area containing ICBM silo launchers for each Party shall be separated by no less than thirteen hundred kilometers.

[D]

In order to insure fulfillment of the obligation not to deploy ABM systems and their components except as provided in Article III of the Treaty, the Parties agree that in the event ABM systems based on other physical principles and including components capable of substituting for ABM interceptor missiles, ABM launchers, or ABM radars are created in the future, specific limitations on such systems and their components would be subject to discussion in accordance with Article XIII and agreement in accordance with Article XIV of the Treaty.

[E]

The Parties understand that Article V of the Treaty includes obligations not to develop, test or deploy ABM interceptor missiles for the delivery by each ABM interceptor missile of more than one independently guided warhead.

[F]

The Parties agree not to deploy phased-array radars having a potential (the product of mean emitted power in watts and antenna area in square meters) exceeding three million, except as provided for in Articles III, IV and VI of the Treaty, or except for the purposes of tracking objects in outer space or for use as national technical means of verification.

[G]

The Parties understand that Article IX of the Treaty includes the obligation of the US and USSR not to provide to other States technical descriptions or blue prints specially worked out for the construction of ABM systems and their components limited by the Treaty.

2. Common Understandings

Common understanding of the Parties on the following matters was reached during the negotiations:

A.   Location of ICBM Defenses

The U.S. Delegation made the following statement on May 26, 1972:

Article III of the ABM Treaty provides for each side one ABM system deployment area centered on its national capital and one ABM system deployment area containing ICBM silo launchers. The two sides have registered agreement on the following statement: "The Parties understand that the center of the ABM system deployment area centered on the national capital and the center of the ABM system deployment area containing ICBM silo launchers for each Party shall be separated by no less than thirteen hundred kilometers." In this connection, the U.S. side notes that its ABM system deployment area for defense of ICBM silo launchers, located west of the Mississippi River, will be centered in the Grand Forks ICBM silo launcher deployment area. (See Agreed Statement [C].)

B.   ABM Test Ranges

The U.S. Delegation made the following statement on April 26, 1972:

Article IV of the ABM Treaty provides that "the limitations provided for in Article III shall not apply to ABM systems or their components used for development or testing, and located within current or additionally agreed test ranges." We believe it would be useful to assure that there is no misunderstanding as to current ABM test ranges. It is our understanding that ABM test ranges encompass the area within which ABM components are located for test purposes. The current U.S. ABM test ranges are at White Sands, New Mexico, and at Kwajalein Atoll, and the current Soviet ABM test range is near Sary Shagan in Kazakhstan. We consider that non-phased array radars of types used for range safety or instrumentation purposes may be located outside of ABM test ranges. We interpret the reference in Article IV to "additionally agreed test ranges" to mean that ABM components will not be located at any other test ranges without prior agreement between our Governments that there will be such additional ABM test ranges.

On May 5, 1972, the Soviet Delegation stated that there was a common understanding on what ABM test ranges were, that the use of the types of non-ABM radars for range safety or instrumentation was not limited under the Treaty, that the reference in Article IV to "additionally agreed" test ranges was sufficiently clear, and that national means permitted identifying current test ranges.

C.   Mobile ABM Systems

On January 29, 1972, the U.S. Delegation made the following statement:

Article V(1) of the Joint Draft Text of the ABM Treaty includes an undertaking not to develop, test, or deploy mobile land-based ABM systems and their components. On May 5, 1971, the U.S. side indicated that, in its view, a prohibition on deployment of mobile ABM systems and components would rule out the deployment of ABM launchers and radars which were not permanent fixed types. At that time, we asked for the Soviet view of this interpretation. Does the Soviet side agree with the U.S. side's interpretation put forward on May 5, 1971?

On April 13, 1972, the Soviet Delegation said there is a general common understanding on this matter.

D.   Standing Consultative Commission

Ambassador Smith made the following statement on May 22, 1972:

The United States proposes that the sides agree that, with regard to initial implementation of the ABM Treaty's Article XIII on the Standing Consultative Commission (SCC) and of the consultation Articles to the Interim Agreement on offensive arms and the Accidents Agreement,[1] agreement establishing the SCC will be worked out early in the follow-on SALT negotiations; until that is completed, the following arrangements will prevail: when SALT is in session, any consultation desired by either side under these Articles can be carried out by the two SALT Delegations; when SALT is not in session, *ad hoc* arrangements for any desired consultations under these Articles may be made through diplomatic channels.

Minister Semenov replied that, on an *ad referendum* basis, he could agree that the U.S. statement corresponded to the Soviet understanding.

E.   Standstill

On May 6, 1972, Minister Semenov made the following statement:

In an effort to accommodate the wishes of the U.S. side, the Soviet Delegation is prepared to proceed on the basis that the two sides will in fact observe the obligations of both the Interim Agreement and the ABM Treaty beginning from the date of signature of these two documents.

In reply, the U.S. Delegation made the following statement on May 20, 1972:

The U.S. agrees in principle with the Soviet statement made on May 6 concerning observance of obligations beginning from date of signature but we would like to make clear our understanding that this means that, pending ratification and acceptance, neither side would take any action prohibited by the agreements after they had entered into force. This understanding would

1. See Article 7 of Agreement to Reduce the Risk of Outbreak of Nuclear War Between the United States of America and the Union of Soviet Socialist Republics, signed Sept. 30, 1971.

continue to apply in the absence of notification by either signatory of its intention not to proceed with ratification or approval.

The Soviet Delegation indicated agreement with the U.S. statement.

3. Unilateral Statements

The following noteworthy unilateral statements were made during the negotiations by the United States Delegation:

A.   Withdrawal from the ABM Treaty

On May 9, 1972, Ambassador Smith made the following statement:

The U.S. Delegation has stressed the importance the U.S. Government attaches to achieving agreement on more complete limitations on strategic offensive arms, following agreement on an ABM Treaty and on an Interim Agreement on certain measures with respect to the limitation of strategic offensive arms. The U.S. Delegation believes that an objective of the follow-on negotiations should be to constrain and reduce on a long-term basis threats to the survivability of our respective strategic retaliatory forces. The USSR Delegation has also indicated that the objectives of SALT would remain unfulfilled without the achievement of an agreement providing for more complete limitations on strategic offensive arms. Both sides recognize that the initial agreements would be steps toward the achievement of more complete limitations on strategic arms. If an agreement providing for more complete strategic offensive arms limitations were not achieved within five years, U.S. supreme interests could be jeopardized. Should that occur, it would constitute a basis for withdrawal from the ABM Treaty. The U.S. does not wish to see such a situation occur, nor do we believe that the USSR does. It is because we wish to prevent such a situation that we emphasize the importance the U.S. Government attaches to achievement of more complete limitations on strategic offensive arms. The U.S. Executive will inform the Congress, in connection with Congressional consideration of the ABM Treaty and the Interim Agreement, of this statement of the U.S. position.

B.   Tested in ABM Mode

On April 7, 1972, the U.S. Delegation made the following statement:

Article II of the Joint Text Draft uses the term "tested in an ABM mode," in defining ABM components, and Article VI includes certain obligations concerning such testing. We believe that the sides should have a common understanding of this phrase. First, we would note that the testing provisions of the ABM Treaty are intended to apply to testing which occurs after the date of signature of the Treaty, and not to any testing which may have occurred in the past. Next, we would amplify the remarks we have made on this subject during the previous Helsinki phase by setting forth the objectives which govern the U.S. view on the subject, namely, while prohibiting testing of non-ABM components for ABM purposes: not to prevent testing of ABM components, and not to prevent testing of non-ABM components for non-ABM purposes. To clarify our interpretation of "tested in an ABM mode," we note that we would consider a launcher, missile or radar to be "tested in an ABM mode" if, for example, any of the following events occur: (1) a launcher is used to launch an ABM interceptor missile, (2) an interceptor missile is flight tested against a target vehicle which has a flight trajectory with characteristics of a strategic ballistic missile flight trajectory, or is flight tested in conjunction with the test of an ABM interceptor missile or an ABM radar at the same test range, or is flight tested to an altitude inconsistent with interception of targets against which air defenses are deployed, (3) a radar makes measurements on a cooperative target vehicle of the kind referred to in item (2) above during the reentry portion of its trajectory or makes measurements in conjunction with the test of an ABM interceptor missile or an ABM radar at the same test range. Radars used for purposes such as range safety or instrumentation would be exempt from application of these criteria.

C.   No-Transfer Article of ABM Treaty

On April 18, 1972, the U.S. Delegation made the following statement:

In regard to this Article [IX], I have a brief and I believe self-explanatory statement to make. The U.S. side wishes to make clear that the provisions of this Article do not set a precedent for whatever provision may be considered for a Treaty on Limiting Strategic Offensive Arms. The question of transfer of strategic offensive arms is a far more complex issue, which may require a different solution.

D.   No Increase in Defense of Early Warning Radars

On July 28, 1970, the U.S. Delegation made the following statement:

Since Hen House radars [Soviet ballistic missile early warning radars] can detect and track ballistic missile warheads at great distances, they have a significant ABM potential. Accordingly, the U.S. would regard any increase in the defenses of such radars by surface-to-air missiles as inconsistent with an agreement.

Protocol to the Treaty Between the United States of America and the Union of Soviet Socialist Republics on the Limitation of Anti-Ballistic Missile Systems

Signed at Moscow July 3, 1974
Ratification advised by U.S. Senate November 10, 1975

Ratified by U.S. President March 19, 1976
Instruments of ratification exchanged May 24, 1976
Proclaimed by U.S. President July 6, 1976
Entered into force May 24, 1976

The United States of America and the Union of Soviet Socialist Republics, hereinafter referred to as the Parties,

Proceeding from the Basic Principles of Relations between the United States of America and the Union of Soviet Socialist Republics signed on May 29, 1972,

Desiring to further the objectives of the Treaty between the United States of America and the Union of Soviet Socialist Republics on the Limitation of Anti-Ballistic Missile Systems signed on May 26, 1972, hereinafter referred to as the Treaty,

Reaffirming their conviction that the adoption of further measures for the limitation of strategic arms would contribute to strengthening international peace and security,

Proceeding from the premise that further limitation of anti-ballistic missile systems will create more favorable conditions for the completion of work on a permanent agreement on more complete measures for the limitation of strategic offensive arms,

Have agreed as follows:

Article I

1. Each Party shall be limited at any one time to a single area out of the two provided in Article III of the Treaty for deployment of anti-ballistic missile (ABM) systems or their components and accordingly shall not exercise its right to deploy an ABM system or its components in the second of the two ABM system deployment areas permitted by Article III of the Treaty, except as an exchange of one permitted area for the other in accordance with Article II of this Protocol.

2. Accordingly, except as permitted by Article II of this Protocol: the United States of America shall not deploy an ABM system or its components in the area centered on its capital, as permitted by Article III(a) of the Treaty, and the Soviet Union shall not deploy an ABM system or its components in the deployment area of intercontinental ballistic missile (ICBM) silo launchers as permitted by Article III(b) of the Treaty.

Article II

1. Each Party shall have the right to dismantle or destroy its ABM system and the components thereof in the area where they are presently deployed and to deploy an ABM system or its components in the alternative area permitted by Article III of the Treaty, provided that prior to initiation of construction,

notification is given in accord with the procedure agreed to in the Standing Consultative Commission, during the year beginning October 3, 1977 and ending October 2, 1978, or during any year which commences at five year intervals thereafter, those being the years for periodic review of the Treaty, as provided in Article XIV of the Treaty. This right may be exercised only once.

2. Accordingly, in the event of such notice, the United States would have the right to dismantle or destroy the ABM system and its components in the deployment area of ICBM silo launchers and to deploy an ABM system or its components in an area centered on its capital, as permitted by Article III(a) of the Treaty, and the Soviet Union would have the right to dismantle or destroy the ABM system and its components in the area centered on its capital and to deploy an ABM system or its components in an area containing ICBM silo launchers, as permitted by Article III(b) of the Treaty.

3. Dismantling or destruction and deployment of ABM systems or their components and the notification thereof shall be carried out in accordance with Article VIII of the ABM Treaty and procedures agreed to in the Standing Consultative Commission.

Article III

The rights and obligations established by the Treaty remain in force and shall be complied with by the Parties except to the extent modified by this Protocol. In particular, the deployment of an ABM system or its components within the area selected shall remain limited by the levels and other requirements established by the Treaty.

Article IV

This Protocol shall be subject to ratification in accordance with the constitutional procedures of each Party. It shall enter into force on the day of the exchange of instruments of ratification and shall thereafter be considered an integral part of the Treaty.

DONE at Moscow on July 3, 1974, in duplicate, in the English and Russian languages, both texts being equally authentic.

For the United States of America:

RICHARD NIXON

President of the United States of America

For the Union of Soviet Socialist Republics:

L. I. BREZHNEV

General Secretary of the Central Committee of the CPSU

Glossary of BMD Systems

U.S. Systems

BAMBI: A boost-phase system using nonnuclear homing interceptors based on satellites. This concept was studied in the early 1960s.

Global BMD: A boost-phase system using nonnuclear homing interceptors based on satellites. This concept was considered in the early 1980s.

Layered Defense: A combination of Overlay and Site Defense or Sentry. This concept was studied in the late 1970s.

Nike-X: A traditional terminal defense system oriented toward city defense. It used several phased-array radars, including the Perimeter Acquisition Radar (PAR) and the Missile Site Radar (MSR), and a high-acceleration, nuclear-armed reentry interceptor, the Sprint. This system was studied in the mid-1960s and represented a substantial advance over Nike-Zeus. Components of the system were developed and tested.

Nike-Zeus: A traditional terminal defense system oriented toward city defense. It used several mechanically steered radars and a nuclear-armed interceptor, the Zeus. This system was developed in the late 1950s and early 1960s. All major components were integrated, and intercept tests were conducted.

Overlay: An advanced exoatmospheric defense system oriented toward defense of intercontinental ballistic missiles (ICBMs), consisting of missile-borne, passive infrared sensors and nonnuclear homing interceptors. This system was studied in the late 1970s and early 1980s.

Point Defense: A simple/novel terminal defense system similar to Swarmjet, using simple radars and large numbers of unguided projectiles to defend ICBMs. This concept was considered in the early 1980s.

440

Safeguard: A system oriented toward defense of ICBMs. It was composed of traditional exoatmospheric components (the PAR phased-array radar and the Spartan long-range, nuclear-armed interceptor) and traditional terminal defense components (the MSR phased-array radar and the Sprint high-acceleration, nuclear-armed interceptor). This system was developed, extensively tested, and deployed at Grand Forks, North Dakota, in the late 1960s and early 1970s. It has subsequently been deactivated.

Sentinel: A system oriented toward area defense against a light attack by the People's Republic of China. It used the same components as Safeguard and was reoriented to become the Safeguard system in the late 1960s.

Sentry: A traditional terminal defense system oriented toward low-altitude defense of ICBMs. Both fixed and transportable versions have been considered. The system uses a phased-array radar and a high-acceleration, nuclear-armed interceptor (either Sprint or a new interceptor called Sentry). This system was studied in the late 1970s and early 1980s, and component development is under way. Essentially the same system was known as the Low-Altitude Defense System (LoADS) in the late 1970s.

Site Defense: A traditional terminal defense system oriented toward defense of ICBMs. It used phased-array radars, called Site Defense Radars, and a high-acceleration, nuclear-armed interceptor, the Sprint. The system was studied extensively in the mid-1970s, as a follow-on to Safeguard and as a hedge against Soviet breakout from the ABM Treaty. The Site Defense Radar was developed and tested.

Soviet Systems

ABM-X-3: A traditional terminal defense system using transportable phased-array radars and both long-range interceptors and short-range, high-acceleration interceptors similar to the U.S. Sprint. This system was developed and tested in the 1970s and early 1980s.

Moscow System: A traditional exoatmospheric system, using the Dog House and Cat House phased-array radars for long-range acquisition. The system might also use the Hen House early warning radars for long-range acquisition. Target and interceptor tracking is performed by mechanically steered dish antennas. The exoatmospheric interceptor, the Galosh, carries a large nuclear warhead.

Moscow Upgrades: The Moscow System is currently being upgraded with a new version of the Galosh exoatmospheric interceptor, an endoatmospheric interceptor similar to the U.S. Sprint, phased-array tracking radars, and a new, large phased-array radar for long-range acquisition and battle management to join the Dog House and Cat House radars, probably in order to employ the technology and elements of the ABM-X-3 system.

Contributors

Norman R. Augustine is president of Martin Marietta Denver Aerospace and has served the federal government as undersecretary of the army and as assistant secretary of the army for research and development. He is currently chairman of the Defense Science Board and of the Aeronautics Panel of the Air Force Scientific Advisory Board. He is president of the American Institute of Aeronautics and Astronautics and of the Association of the United States Army. During the early ballistic missile defense era he served in the Office of the Secretary of Defense in the office responsible for the antiballistic missile program. He has been involved in governmental as well as industrial capacities in U.S. ballistic and antiballistic missile programs and has led investigations of the Soviet antiballistic missile effort.

Albert Carnesale is professor of public policy and academic dean at Harvard University's John F. Kennedy School of Government. His teaching and research have focused on policies and issues associated with nuclear weapons. He participated in the negotiation of the ABM Treaty while serving as a member of the U.S. delegation to the Strategic Arms Limitation Talks (1970–72), and he headed the U.S. delegation to the International Nuclear Fuel Cycle Evaluation (1978–80).

Ashton B. Carter is a research fellow at the Center for International Studies at the Massachusetts Institute of Technology. He received his bachelor's degree in medieval history and in physics from Yale University and his doctorate in theoretical physics from Oxford University, where he was a Rhodes scholar. Dr. Carter did theoretical research at the Rockefeller University in New York, moving in 1980 to the Congressional Office of Technology Assessment, where he was an author of OTA's *MX Missile Basing*. Before coming to MIT, he was an analyst in

443

the Office of the Director, Program Analysis and Evaluation, Office of the Secretary of Defense, where his responsibilities included ballistic missile defense; MX basing; strategic command, control, communications, and intelligence; and space activities.

William A. Davis, Jr., is currently employed by Teledyne Brown Engineering as vice president for space defense. He retired from federal government service in July 1982. He spent the last thirteen years of his government career in the BMD program, where he served successively as director of the BMD Advanced Technology Center and deputy BMD program manager. Before that he worked at the army's Missile Command in Huntsville, Alabama, in a number of assignments, including the Hawk Air Defense Project and the High Energy Laser Project.

John S. Foster, Jr., is vice president for science and technology of TRW Inc. He also serves on the President's Foreign Intelligence Advisory Board. He was the director of defense research and engineering for the Department of Defense for eight years during the Johnson and Nixon administrations. From 1961 to 1965, he was the director of the Lawrence Livermore National Laboratory.

Lawrence Freedman is professor of war studies at King's College, London. He was formerly head of policy studies at the Royal Institute of International Affairs, London; research associate at the International Institute for Strategic Studies, London; and a research fellow of Nuffield College, Oxford. He is the author of numerous works on defense issues.

Raymond L. Garthoff is a senior fellow at the Brookings Institution. Before joining the Brookings staff in 1979, he served as ambassador to Bulgaria and in various positions with the U.S. Department of State. From 1969 to 1973, he was executive officer of the U.S. delegation to the Strategic Arms Limitation Talks. He has written numerous books and articles on Soviet political and military affairs, including a forthcoming major study on Soviet-American relations.

Richard L. Garwin is IBM fellow at the Thomas J. Watson Research Center, adjunct research associate at the Kennedy School of Government at Harvard University, adjunct professor of physics at Columbia University, and Andrew D. White Professor-at-Large at Cornell University. He served for eight years on the President's Science Advisory Committee (1962–65, 1969–72) and was a member of many PSAC panels concerned with strategic defense, intelligence, and other matters. He was a member of the Defense Science Board (1966–69) and has been a consultant to the U.S. government and its agencies from 1950 to the present. He has been involved in technical and programmatic aspects of many weapons systems, as well as in arms control negotiations and studies.

Colin S. Gray is president of the National Institute for Public Policy in Fairfax, Virginia, a nonprofit research organization. Previously he was director of national security studies at Hudson Institute and assistant director of the International Institute for Strategic Studies in London. He also serves on the General Advisory Committee of the U.S. Arms Control and Disarmament Agency.

Spurgeon M. Keeny, Jr., has been a scholar-in-residence at the National Academy of Sciences since 1981. From 1977 to 1981, he was deputy director of the U.S. Arms Control and Disarmament Agency, and in 1980 he headed the U.S. delegation to the U.S.-Soviet Theater Nuclear Forces Talks. He chaired the Ford/Mitre Nuclear Energy Policy Study Group in 1975–77 and was assistant director of the ACDA in 1969–73, during the negotiation of the ABM Treaty. He also served as technical assistant to the President's Science Adviser (1958–69) and senior staff member of the National Security Council (1963–69), with responsibility for military technology and arms control.

Glenn A. Kent, a retired lieutenant general, spent thirty-four years in the U.S. Air Force, primarily working on plans for the development of weapons systems. This included an assignment from 1962 to 1965 in the Office of Defense Research and Engineering in the Office of the Secretary of Defense. During that time, General Kent was involved in evaluations of the protection afforded the population by deployments of antiballistic missile systems such as Nike-Zeus and Nike-X. He was also the project leader of a study, directed by the secretary of defense and the director of defense research and engineering, of the prospects of limiting damage to the United States during nuclear war, including the contribution of civil defense, ballistic missile defense, and counterforce attacks against Soviet missiles.

George Rathjens, professor of political science at MIT, was formerly chief scientist and deputy director of the Defense Department's Advanced Research Projects Agency, special assistant to the director of the U.S. Arms Control and Disarmament Agency, and director of the Institute for Defense Analyses' Systems Evaluation Division. He was a critic of the Johnson and Nixon administrations' decisions of the late 1960s to deploy antiballistic missile defense systems.

George Schneiter joined the Center for Naval Analyses in 1981, where he has participated in studies on the application of advanced technologies to air warfare. Previously, he worked for the Aerospace Corporation evaluating and planning programs for developing reentry systems for strategic ballistic missiles. In 1973 he joined the Office of the Secretary of Defense and was an adviser to the U.S. delegation to the Strategic Arms Limitation Talks during SALT II. He became deputy director of the Department of Defense SALT Task Force in 1978. Among his responsibilities was the development of departmental policies on ABM Treaty matters. He received bachelor's, master's, and doctor's degrees in mechanical engineering from Purdue University.

David N. Schwartz is deputy director of the Office of Policy Analysis in the State Department's Bureau of Politico-Military Affairs. He was a research associate on the Foreign Policy Studies staff of the Brookings Institution from October 1982 until October 1983, during which time he co-edited this volume. He is also the author of *NATO's Nuclear Dilemmas* (Brookings, 1983), and a contributor to the recent Brookings study, *Alliance Security: NATO and the No-First-Use Question* (1983).

Leon Sloss is a consultant on national security affairs, specializing in nuclear policy. After twenty years of government service in the national security area, and several years with private research organizations, Mr. Sloss formed his own firm in 1980 to undertake policy studies. His firm has worked on studies of nuclear nonproliferation and nuclear control, as well as the political/military rationale for nuclear weapons in the Pacific theater and the international political and economic trends that will affect the aerospace market.

Sayre Stevens is currently group vice president of the System Planning Corporation and a member of the Defense Science Board. For over twenty-one years he served in the Central Intelligence Agency in a variety of positions involving technical intelligence analysis and intelligence-related research and development. He served as an adviser on the U.S. SALT I delegation. As deputy director for intelligence he was responsible for all the CIA's intelligence analysis.

Stephen Weiner has worked since 1965 at MIT Lincoln Laboratory in various areas of ballistic missile defense, including system analysis, radar and optical measurements, and interceptor guidance. Currently he is the associate leader of the Analysis and Systems Group.

Index

ABM (antiballistic missile) defense. *See* BMD (ballistic missile defense)

ABM Treaty, 20, 221–22; abandonment, 216–19; administration, 232–36, 373, 387–88; ATBM issue, 319–21; attitudes toward, 17, 254, 258–60, 273–74, 277–80, 285–87, 308–09, 311–14, 379–80; compliance, 12, 208–09, 239–43; description, 222–23; effects, 237–39; ICBM defense, 224, 249–50, 318–19; modification, 17, 219–20, 234, 244–50, 277–80, 373, 378–79; permitted deployments, 223–25; prohibitions, 207, 225–32, 247–48, 382–84; reviews under, 234–36; role, 17, 243–44; SAM upgrading, 207, 230–31. *See also* SALT I

ABM-X-3 system, 212–13

Acquisition function: defined, 55; infrared systems, 58, 79, 82–83; offensive countermeasures, 58–59; performance, 69–70; requirements, 56–58; Soviet system, 197–98, 213

Adams, Benson D., 331n, 333, 334n

Advanced Overlay midcourse intercept systems, 9, 10

Advanced Research Projects Agency (ARPA), 332, 334

Aerosols, 61

Agnew, Spiro T., 342

Ailleret, Charles, 251–52

Air-launched ballistic missiles, 75

Amery, Julian, 251

Andropov, Yuri V., 324, 326

Antinuclear movement, 34, 277

Antiradiation homing (ARH) vehicles, 108

Antisubmarine warfare (ASW), 36, 254

Arbatov, Yu., 307n, 308n, 325n, 328

Area defense, 75–78

Arms control: ABM Treaty and, 244, 245; attitudes toward, 276–77; policy options, 359–63, 372–73; Soviet policy, 286–88, 291–97, 300–08, 327–28, 338; strategy role, 34–36, 38, 40, 43, 46; U.S. policy, 280–85, 338. *See also* ABM Treaty; SALT I; SALT II; START

Arms race stability, 28–29, 178–79, 309

Arsenals, 100–01, 105, 169–70

Assurance strategies, 30–32

Assured destruction, 42. *See also* Mutual assured destruction

ATBMs (antitactical ballistic missiles), 73, 208, 215–16, 230–31, 246–47, 319–21, 389–90

Attack price: calculation, 111–13; defense strategy, 103; Densepack basing, 144; layered defense, 128, 131; mobile basing, 148, 149; multiple protective shelter basing, 137–38, 142; traditional defense, 123–24

Background radiation, 83

Ball, Desmond, 267n

Bassett, Edward W., 268n

Batitsky, Pavel F., 298–99, 313

447